Praise for *The Whole Story*

"In John Mackey's *The Whole Story*, readers may come for the business lessons but they'll stay for the stories, characters, and genuine insights into what makes for a meaningful life."

—Matthew McConaughey, Academy Award–Winning Actor and #1 *New York Times* Bestselling Author, *Greenlights*

"John Mackey is one of the most interesting and influential entrepreneurs of our time, and his memoir is filled with surprising life lessons. It's a rare founder story that manages to be both frank and fun."

—Adam Grant, #1 *New York Times* Bestselling Author, *Hidden Potential* and *Think Again*, and Host, the TED podcast *WorkLife*

"*The Whole Story* is a phenomenal read. In a league with Phil Knight's *Shoe Dog*, it takes an almost novelistic approach to the building of one of America's great brands. Here, John Mackey gives us a front-row seat as he cobbles together a small natural foods store from salvaged equipment and grows it into the $14 billion behemoth Amazon acquired. Along the way we learn the mindset necessary to build—and consciously lead—a great company. Read it for fun; come away enlightened."

—Dan Buettner, Founder, Blue Zones; *New York Times* Bestselling Author; and Host, Netflix's *How to Live to 100*

"Join John Mackey as he shares his joyful adventure of life, love, and community. His story is written the way he lives his life: raw, open, and playful. I have looked up to John my entire career as one of the great conscious capitalists of our generation. *The Whole Story* is magnificent, fun reading. Enjoy."

—Kimbal Musk, Chef, Entrepreneur, Food Activist, and Founder, The Kitchen

"John Mackey is responsible for creating a massive shift in food consciousness and *The Whole Story* reveals how—and why—he was able to do so. This inspiring book offers rare insight into what it takes to build a long, healthy, purposeful life, in all its many dimensions."

—Michael Greger, MD, *New York Times* Bestselling Author, *How Not to Die*

"It's rare to find a business leader who is as comfortable writing about his psychedelic explorations and spiritual insights as he is detailing boardroom battles and high-stakes mergers and acquisitions. Mackey moves fluidly between the many dimensions of his 'whole story,' illuminating the oft-neglected relationship between personal growth and business success.

—Rick Doblin, Founder, Multidisciplinary Association for Psychedelic Studies (MAPS)

THE WHOLE STORY

Also by John Mackey

Conscious Capitalism
Conscious Leadership
The Whole Foods Diet
The Whole Foods Cookbook

THE WHOLE STORY

Adventures in Love, Life, and Capitalism

JOHN MACKEY

Matt Holt Books
An Imprint of BenBella Books, Inc.
Dallas, TX

Unless otherwise credited, personal photos (early and current) and early historical Safer Way and Whole Foods Market photos are courtesy of John Mackey.
Photo on page 377 (bottom) by Buster Jetter.

Matt Holt is an imprint of BenBella Books, Inc.
10440 N. Central Expressway
Suite 800
Dallas, TX 75231
benbellabooks.com
Send feedback to feedback@benbellabooks.com

BenBella and *Matt Holt* are federally registered trademarks.

Printed in the United States of America
10 9 8 7 6 5 4 3 2 1

Library of Congress Control Number: 2023049237
ISBN 9781637745120 (hardcover)
ISBN 9781637745137 (electronic)

Copyediting by Scott Calamar
Proofreading by Sarah Vostok and Marissa Wold Uhrina
Text design and composition by Jordan Koluch
Cover design and illustration by Brigid Pearson
Printed by Lake Book Manufacturing

To all Whole Foods Market team members—past, present, and future.
We did this together and I will always love you.

Although this book is titled "The Whole Story," it's really *my* whole story, because every narrative is shaped by the perspective from which it is told. I've relied on my best recollection of the events described, and where possible have consulted with others to verify or enhance those memories. I've also drawn on personal journals, letters, emails, and more, as well as published sources. However, I know that others may remember things differently, from their perspectives, and I acknowledge the subjectivity of certain aspects of my story. I have not changed any names or identifying details in this book, nor have I created any composite characters, but at times, to enhance the reading experience, I've reconstructed conversations, always with the intention of preserving the essential spirit of those interactions.

Contents

PART I: WAKING LIFE

PART II: SHELF LIFE

PART III: WHOLE LIFE

PART IV: LOVE LIFE

PART I

WAKING LIFE

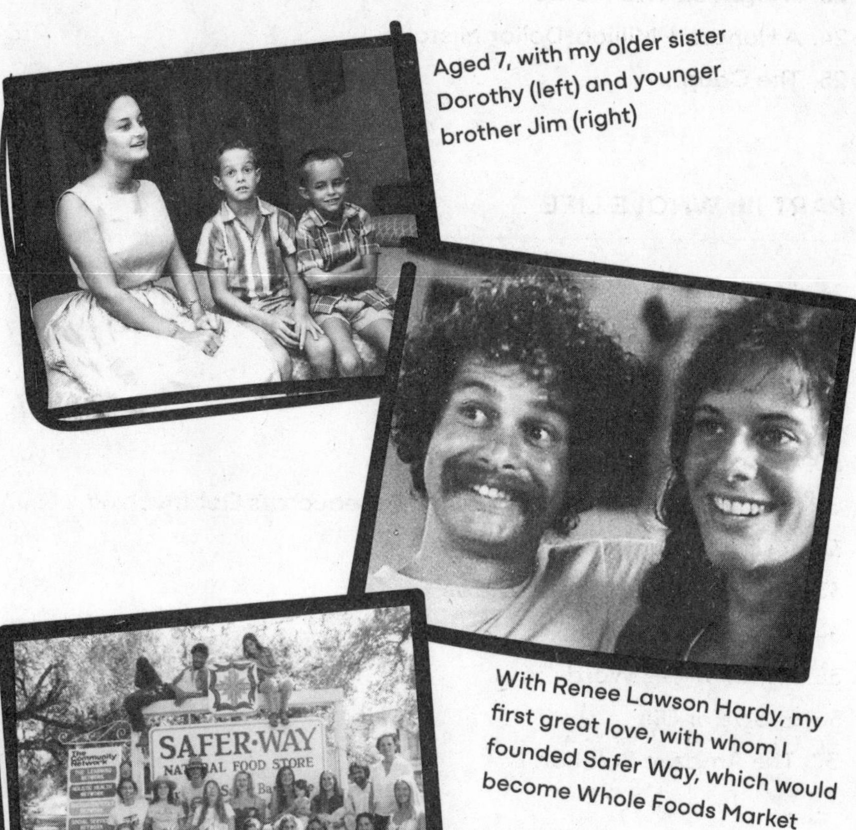

Aged 7, with my older sister Dorothy (left) and younger brother Jim (right)

With Renee Lawson Hardy, my first great love, with whom I founded Safer Way, which would become Whole Foods Market

The Safer Way team outside the Austin, Texas, store, circa 1979

Prologue

The Game of Life

Austin, Texas, August 1975

"Where do you want to go?" asked the man who'd pulled over in response to my outstretched thumb.

"I don't really care," I told him. "I'll go wherever you're going!" And I hopped into the car.

A grand adventure was calling me. I knew that much, even if my direction was unclear. I felt fearless, excited, and eager to be on the move—to wherever I might end up. So much suddenly seemed possible. At that moment, the destination didn't matter. What mattered was that I felt more alive than I had in years—perhaps ever. I think I had on a pair of shoes, but I'm not at all sure I was wearing a shirt. If I wasn't, the driver didn't seem to care. After all, this was 1975 in Austin, Texas, and there was nothing too unusual about a hitchhiking, long-haired, shirtless hippie. Besides, it was summer and hot as hell. I had just turned 22 years old.

The man behind the wheel shrugged good-naturedly. He was clean-shaven and dressed in a suit with a loosened tie, like he'd just left the office and was happy to be heading home early after a day's work.

"Well, I'm going home," he said, "so I guess I'll take you there."

As the car pulled away, I rolled down the window and closed my eyes. The warm breeze caressed my face, and I felt the powerful reverberations of the past few hours still echoing in my mind and body.

Had it really been just a few hours? It felt like a lifetime. And yet I knew that earlier that morning, I'd been pacing aimlessly in the kitchen of the small apartment where I lived, alone. I had recently dropped out of school—again. My college years had been characterized by a series of starts and stops—multiple transfers between Trinity and the University of Texas, a motley collection of elective classes punctuated by impromptu breaks to hitchhike around the country. But this time I thought I might be done for good. The academic life, with its prescribed programs and predictable outcomes, just felt too constraining to me. I loved to think, and I loved to learn, but I was no longer willing to read books someone else decided I should read. I still took classes that interested me and audited others, but I'd stopped trying to get a degree. So much for my dreams of following in the footsteps of the teachers I admired and making a career in academia. That life was not for me. Now, my only curriculum was my own curiosity. And the university library was my classroom. Piled on the kitchen counter were the books I had to show for it—Camus, Sartre, Kierkegaard, Nietzsche, Somerset Maugham, Leo Tolstoy, Hermann Hesse, Alan Watts, and many more.

It's not that I was trying to be a rebel; it's just that I couldn't conform. Not to the conventional track. Not to my parents' hopes and expectations. Not to the path my friends were taking, with all its upstanding purpose and predictability. Yes, I was getting older, and I understood, from the concerned questions of friends and family, that I was supposed to be getting serious about my future.

"John, what are you going to do with your life?"

"John, when are you going to finish school?"

"John, what kind of future do you think you'll find in the library?"

"John, when are you going to get a haircut?"

I didn't have good answers to any of those questions. I had stepped off the marked path on which everyone I knew was still marching forward. They all seemed to be disappearing into the distance, and I was left on the side of the road. One friend was becoming a lawyer. Another was going to medical school. In my mind's eye, I could see their future. Status. Security. Income. I knew the beats to that tune. I just couldn't move my feet to it.

I wanted something different, more real, more adventurous. But I didn't quite know what that was yet. And even more disturbing, I didn't have people around me who shared that feeling. I felt misplaced, somehow—caught between a life I couldn't live and a life I couldn't yet see. I thought of myself as a "seeker," but maybe I was fooling myself. Heck, maybe that unseen life didn't exist at all. Maybe I was on a quest to nowhere.

Anyone looking at my kitchen counter would probably have agreed with that assessment. Next to the pile of books stood a large collection of liquor bottles. No, I wasn't an alcoholic. But I'd been seriously considering becoming a bartender, so I'd been practicing making drinks for my friends. I liked the idea of presiding over some smoke-filled, dark-paneled establishment, dispensing drinks and wisdom in equal measure. Wasn't that the kind of thing that real-world philosophers and writers did? I imagined styling myself after the everyday heroes of some of my favorite philosophical books—Somerset Maugham's mystic taxi driver Larry from *The Razor's Edge* or Eric Hoffer, the wise, people-watching longshoreman. The only problem with those figures, as romantic as they seemed, is that they were mostly loners. I didn't want to be alone. I wanted friends, a lover, community.

Indeed, my longing for love and community had gotten so strong a few years earlier that I'd ended up joining an evangelical Christian group. It started with a girl—the most beautiful girl I'd ever known. It was just after my senior year in high school. Her name was Carol. She gave me stuff to read about Christianity, and I found it interesting. Carol and I developed a good friendship and I converted to Christianity. In my first year at Trinity, I joined a Christian group called the Navigators. Their approach was less formal than the churches of my youth, more about spiritual authenticity and personal connection with Christ. I could relate to this more countercultural Jesus, and at first, I loved being part of the community. I knew that humans had spent much of our evolutionary history in small tribes or bands, and I felt like I understood for the first time that bone-deep joy of belonging, sharing a common purpose and belief system. And I learned something about myself as well: I could evangelize with the best of them, a skill I would use later in a very different context.

Despite the upsides, my interest in a religious life didn't last. I was attached to the intimate bonds, but I soon found the dogmatism too restricting. It was my nature to ask questions, and the age-old problem of evil quickly loomed large in my rational mind. If God is good and God is omnipotent, how can evil exist? No one could give me a satisfying answer. Like many a college student before and after me, I eventually decided that traditional religion couldn't answer my questions, and I drifted slowly toward atheism. Around that time, one of my philosophy professors at UT, a powerful lecturer named Robert Solomon, introduced me to the existentialists—hence the selection of books in my countertop pile. I found their confrontation with life honest and refreshing, and Solomon became a role model for me—someone I aspired to follow in a life of deep thought and existentialism.

As I stared at the books and the bottles that August day, however, my mind darkened. Who was I kidding? I was no philosopher. I was just a 22-year-old college dropout. My old friends didn't get me anymore, and I hadn't made many new ones. In their mind I wasn't on a new path; I was on no path at all. My parents were worried about me. I didn't have a girlfriend, and I didn't know how to get one. What girl wants to date a guy who asks questions like "What do you think is the meaning of life?" before he asks her out to dinner? And besides, why would a girl like me? I didn't like myself that much. Even as I focused on that unpleasant truth, all the things I hated about myself began to flood into my awareness. It was at that moment that my gaze alighted on something sitting between the piles of books and the cluster of bottles—a small card the size of a postage stamp, inscribed with a jaunty red heart. It was a tab of LSD that I had been thinking about taking. *Why not?* I thought. Maybe it will make me feel better. Surely, I can't feel much worse.

Wrong. Turns out, if you drop a high dose of LSD by yourself while filled with self-doubt, you're setting yourself up for a bad trip. As I sat there, I could feel the drug come on. It was strong. I'd done acid several times before, but this felt much more intense. My inner turmoil began to rise like the creek in a wet Texas spring. The whispers in my head turned to shouts; the self-criticism cranked up into self-loathing. A litany of my failures and inadequacies flooded my consciousness, like waters swollen with dirt and silt and debris. As the dark and churning chaos surrounded me, I felt like I was being swept toward a waterfall, desperately clinging to a rock as the torrent roared around my ears.

My God, how much did I take? How long had I been tripping? Was it ever going to stop? Would I ever come back? I looked at my watch, but time seemed to have stopped for me. The flood kept building, and my own capacity to hold back the inner tide began to falter. Exhausted, I felt my grip loosening—like fingers slipping on wet stone—but hung on tighter. If I let go, I would be swallowed by nothingness, or so it felt. The experience of the drug was pulling apart my mind, threatening to undo the very structure of my reality. The inner workings of my consciousness were laid bare, and I realized how my mind is constantly constructing the world I see and experience from moment to moment. Now, under the influence of this powerful chemical, it all seemed to be dissolving. Was any of it real in the first place? Everything was blending together and at the same time falling apart. Any semblance of inner coherence was gone. The rushing floodwaters grew stronger, and the precipitous edge of the falls loomed closer. I was scared shitless, but also just so tired—tired of holding on, exhausted with the effort of trying to keep it together. Finally, my grip failed, and the inner tide overwhelmed me. I lost control, let go—and went tumbling into ecstasy.

I don't know how long it lasted—perhaps an instant, perhaps an eternity. Time had ceased to exist. *I* had ceased to exist, as any kind of separate self. All I was aware of was One consciousness—pure, ecstatic beingness. I had merged into that One so completely that there were no thoughts, no fears, and no emotions other than the bliss of complete release.

At some point, I began to differentiate from the One, just a little—enough that I could think and reflect on what was happening. My first thought was that I had died. It was as if I'd gone through a portal and popped out on the other side into a different dimension. In this new reality, the sense of self that I was used to—the neurosis, the problems, the fears, the yearning, the frustrations, the hopes that felt so familiar and constant in my life—was just . . . gone. Nowhere to be seen or felt. My usual self—my ego—had vanished, and somehow the bottom had fallen out of reality. And what was left was this, well, *everything*. This awesome, all-encompassing sense of oneness. I was IT. And it was me, and I was there. And it was ALL. An infinity of One. No beginning. No end. No other. God. One. Being.

I laughed out loud with joy at the wonder of it.

But as this awesome reality dawned, there was also a tremendous sadness. The realization came to me: The One is alone. There is ultimately no other, just the One, and the One can experience loneliness. It wasn't the kind of anxious loneliness I felt when I sat in my kitchen. It was a deep, pure singularity shot through with yearning. And that sense of yearning intensified and magnified until . . . *Bang!* Something like a cosmic orgasm overwhelmed me, and I was all the multiplicity of existence exploding into being.

I began to realize that existence *is* this delightful dance between nothing and everything. The One Being's experience, my experience, all of it an incredible infinity of happening. Oneness exploding and expanding out, becoming everything. The cycle of existence—from one to many and back again. Breathe in. Breathe out. Life. Death. Creation. And again! *Bang!*

Somewhere in the midst of this revelation, I knew: I didn't need to be afraid. No, it was more than that. There *was* nothing to be afraid of! Not death, not life. We're all just popping into new realities, endlessly. Another life. Another transformation. Another experience. Another adventure. This person, this "John," is experiencing the journey of life as a human being, and he's sharing it with others who are also manifestations of the One Being. I was filled with a sense of release, of joyous love, for all of it. The cosmic heartbeat pounded in my own chest, driving out any sense of being stuck or lost. *I'm completely free.* Free to be whomever I wish to be and free to create whatever I wish to create. It's just eternal play, forever and ever!

As the intensity of the experience receded just a little, and I began to become aware of my body and surroundings again, I felt an overflowing excitement. And my small apartment felt far too contained. I needed to get out into the open, under the vast sky, and explore . . . Which was how I found myself in a stranger's car, with no shirt and no direction, and no concerns about any of it.

When the man pulled up outside his home in a quiet cul-de-sac, just a few miles from my apartment, I thanked him for the ride and got out. He grabbed his briefcase from the trunk. "Have a good night, son. Take care." Standing in the middle of the driveway, watching him open the door and greet his wife, I wondered, *What next?* An idea struck me. I bounded up the walk and rang the doorbell.

"Hey, would you mind if I made a phone call?" I asked when he opened the door, a little taken aback to see me again.

"Sure," he replied, with a patient smile, motioning toward the phone in the front hallway.

I dialed my buddy Casey. "Hey man! Want to meet up at UT and play some pickup basketball?"

"Sure thing! I'll see you there."

I never showed up.

I began to walk. The intensity of the trip was starting to wane, and I realized I needed to head back to my own neighborhood, two or three miles away. As I walked, I thought about my life and about life in general. I had always been interested in trying to understand the meaning of life. It's just the way I'm wired, I guess. That's why I loved the existentialists—they went straight to the questions that mattered. Still, there was a catch. There was something that bugged me, that kept me from fully embracing their worldview. *Were they happy?* They didn't seem like they were. Yes, there was something about the philosophical confrontation with a stark and uncaring universe that appealed to me. It seemed honest and authentic, and I appreciated authenticity. Maybe we had to face life without God. And yet, I couldn't escape the gnawing sense that there had to be more to life—much more. I wanted to live a life of depth and intellectual courage.

But I didn't want to be depressed all the time! I also wanted to live a life of adventure, joy, and love. Maybe there really was more meaning in the universe than could be found in the minds of Sartre and Camus, or my philosophy professor, Robert Solomon.

These thoughts tumbled around my head as I walked the streets of Austin, heading home. As the sun sank toward the western hills, they took on even more urgency. After all, I'd just experienced the beauty of existence directly, or so it seemed. That sense of love and ecstasy was still vivid in my awareness. My atheist-existentialist self, and all the angst and self-loathing that was connected to it, seemed distant, an afterthought, another person's problems, another life entirely.

Up ahead on the sidewalk, a man appeared, walking toward me. He had blond hair with sideburns and an impressive mustache. I quickly recognized him—Professor Solomon! He'd often told the class that he loved to walk the streets of Austin—and here he was! I quickly moved to intercept him.

"Professor Solomon," I called out. He didn't immediately recognize me—hardly surprising, I guess, since he'd only ever seen me fully clothed. But I pressed on. "I'm a student of yours," I explained. He nodded politely.

"Professor, I want to ask you," I continued, very earnestly. "Do you believe that your life has any objective meaning or purpose besides the subjective meaning you give to it in your own mind?"

He smiled, somewhat wistfully, beneath his mustache, and was silent for a moment. And then, simply and plainly, he said, "No, I don't believe life has any meaning besides the meaning we give to it in our own minds."

"But if you think life is objectively meaningless, I don't see how you could be very happy." My bluntness has always been both a virtue and a curse, but in this moment, I think it was a blessing that I found the courage to give voice to the one concern that mattered most to me, without beating about the bush.

"You're right," he responded, looking me in the eye. "I'm not very happy."

I nodded. He nodded. And we continued walking in our respective directions. It was a short encounter. A brief, uncluttered, but profound exchange. And to this day, I am not totally certain whether the conversation actually happened or not.

Whether it was a literal event or merely an LSD-induced hallucination—whether I actually met the great philosopher on an Austin sidewalk and confronted him about his life and state of mind or was simply talking to myself—I'll never know. It felt real, but I suppose it could well have just been part of the trip. Solomon died suddenly many years later, while changing planes in the Zurich airport, on the very day that we had agreed to have dinner together. I had not seen him since my student days and was looking forward to telling him this story to see if he had any memory of it. But in the end, I don't think it matters. Real or not, the encounter was hugely impactful for me.

Solomon was a role model, a man who represented a path forward that I was considering for my own life. And suddenly, I found it wanting. Missing something essential. *That seals it,* I thought, as I nodded my farewell to the professor on the sidewalk and continued on my way home. *I'm not an existentialist.* Happiness. Adventure. Love. Joy. Purpose. Creativity. Play. Community. These were the things I wanted in my life.

Even as the intensity of the LSD receded in my awareness, I could still feel the buoyant echo of the experience, speaking to me, communicating tacit messages from some deeper or higher place in my own consciousness. Messages that spoke of love. *Love! Love is the most important thing in the world.* That simple, glorious truth was wonderful to contemplate. And there was more. Another word jumped to mind—*possibility. Yes, that's it! So much possibility. I'm free to create a life, my life, a wonderful life.* My earlier sense of emptiness at having no clear path forward had been replaced with a feeling of openness and potential. There was so much I could do! And it felt close at hand. I had no idea *what* I would do or *where* I would go, but I was more confident than ever that the adventure of a lifetime was waiting. Somewhere. Nearby.

As the last rays of the afternoon sun shone down on my bare skin, I felt ready for the next chapter. I was 22. Unsure about pretty much everything. Shy. Socially awkward. Single. Still filled with questions and doubts. But the world was breaking open. It was time to get moving. The cosmic game of life was inviting me to play. I could feel the yearning building, and I couldn't wait to discover what I wanted to become . . .

Chapter 1

The Threshold of an Adventure

Vegetarian. In 1976, in Texas, that word held a certain exoticism. I rolled the syllables around my mouth, as if testing how palatable it might be. A friend had just told me about a great place called Prana House—a co-op where young men and women lived communally, sharing space, chores, meals, and a whole lot of fun.

"You should check it out!" he'd encouraged me. And I loved the idea. There was just one problem—I'd have to become a vegetarian. The co-op was all about natural foods, and it didn't allow any meat. *Could I do that?* I wondered. I barely knew what a natural food was. I'd been raised during the heyday of TV dinners and fast-food restaurants, and my favorite meals included fried chicken, bacon and eggs, and hamburgers (without any green stuff). I rarely ate a vegetable unless it was a potato, although I did like fruit. But the idea of the co-op appealed to me. It sounded cool and different. I was looking for a new direction in life and new people to meet (and by people, I confess, I mostly meant interesting women). Maybe I could fit in over at Prana House, and I wouldn't miss the burgers too much.

When I moved into Prana House, there were 18 residents, mostly University of Texas students. It was a very large and beautiful old Victorian home, probably built in the late 19th century. It had 10 bedrooms with double occupancy, a very large kitchen, and great common and dining rooms.

As it turned out, I did fit in well at Prana House. There was no one telling me to get a haircut, or a degree, or a career. And between the members and a rotating cast of vegetarians who paid to eat with us, there was always someone interesting and fun to hang out with. I became a committed vegetarian and surprised myself with how much I enjoyed eating foods like beans, buckwheat, and broccoli. I began to learn about natural foods and why they were better for our health and for the planet. We would sometimes go and work on the farms where our food was grown. I even learned how to cook, since every resident was expected to take their turn preparing our shared meals as well as doing kitchen cleanup and other chores. And while we were cooking and eating together, we'd share passionate conversations about the social issues of the day, the promise of Eastern religions, the music we loved, and all the ways our generation was going to change the world for the better. I had left the conventional culture of my upbringing behind, and I wasn't just dreaming about new adventures. I was starting to live them. My new friends taught me to meditate, and I learned the Transcendental Meditation (TM) technique made famous by the Beatles.

My hopes of meeting interesting women at the co-op were soon fulfilled as well, in the form of an exotically beautiful girl named Debbie. I fell hard for her, and soon we were spending our days and nights together. Unfortunately, however, our fledgling relationship began with an expiration date. Debbie had plans to move to San Francisco to join a utopian commune called Kerista, a free-love experimental community that practiced "polyfidelity." This meant living in committed "pods" where members rotated sleeping partners according to a schedule. She suggested I visit her there. I hated the thought of losing Debbie, but I wasn't sure I wanted to share her, either. Nevertheless, I decided to check Kerista out.

Community had always attracted me, ever since my evangelical Christian phase. Prana House had reawakened that appreciation for close-knit connection, and I wondered if Kerista could do the same. In the end, however, although I enjoyed my visit, I didn't want to leave Austin. I headed back to Prana House, single but resolved. Debbie stayed on the

West Coast and would end up living in that community for the next couple of decades until it disbanded in the early nineties.

Soon after my return, a meeting occurred that made me forget all about the loss of Debbie. I looked across the dinner table one night and saw a young woman I didn't recognize, with long brown hair and a warm, generous smile. Her name was Renee Lawson, and she'd just moved into Prana House. She was 19; I was now 23. Renee had a personality that seemed permanently plugged into some hidden source of life-positive energy. In her presence, my own self-doubt and hesitations melted away. All of the little cracks and crevices of self-consciousness in my soul seemed to smooth over with ease. I reveled in her *joie de vivre*, and soon we were deeply in love.

Around this time, I took on the role of food buyer for Prana House. I also got a job at the Good Food Company, a chain of five small vegetarian natural foods stores scattered around central Austin. One afternoon, as I was coming to the end of my shift, I looked around the store. Baskets of fresh organic produce were laid out on one side. Shelves were neatly stacked with cans and boxes of food and bottles of vitamins. Customers were measuring and weighing beans or grains or nuts from the bulk-foods bins into brown paper bags. The bulletin board by the door advertised community events and services. And it occurred to me: "I could do this. I could run a natural foods store. It's not that difficult. It would be fun!"

When I got home to Prana House, I sought out Renee. I had to share my idea with someone. Taking a deep breath, I grasped both her hands in mine and said, "Renee, I think we should start our own natural foods store. I really think we could do this together. What do you think?"

Renee didn't laugh or turn away. She listened carefully, a sparkle in her eyes, as I described my vision. Then, she broke into a smile.

"That sounds fantastic. Let's do it, Macko Man!"

Let's do it. I often look back at those three words as marking one of the most important moments in my life. I'm grateful to Renee for many things—for being a loving partner for many years and for birthing and growing the company with me in its infancy. But as much as anything,

I'm forever in her debt for the way she responded when I first gave voice to my dream. I was inspired and excited—but also full of hesitation and self-doubt. If she'd been cautious, dismissive, or amused, I might never have entertained the idea again. A negative or even indifferent response might have put a stopper on my bubbling ambition. But that wasn't Renee.

Renee was an adventurer, a lover of life, and it was her enthusiasm that buoyed me through my own doubts. Creating our own natural foods store may have been my idea, but it was her infectious energy for the venture that made it possible for me to cross that threshold of hesitation and embark on the entrepreneurial journey that would come to define so much of my life.

Let's do it! she said. And so, we did.

Chapter 2

Safer Way

We weren't aiming for subtlety when it came to naming our new natural foods store. Our goal was to offer customers a better, healthier option than the conventional grocery retailers, and we made sure that this was unambiguously stated in our name: Safer Way. Some people laughed when they heard it—which was fine with me. I thought it was clever, but I also took it seriously. I really did believe that the foods and supplements we'd be selling would offer our customers a better chance of staying safe and healthy. A name that communicated this, while taking a not-so-subtle dig at one of America's biggest supermarket chains, seemed perfect.

Once we had a name, our idea quickly gained momentum, bursting out of our shared imagination and into the real world, along with a growing list of things to do. And that reality began to clash with our lives at Prana House. There were co-op meetings, often lasting late into the evenings. We each had chores—cleaning and cooking and laundry. And there were housemates who wanted to hang out, make music, drink a beer, and muse on the meaning of life and how to dismantle capitalism—all the things one naturally wanted to do when one lived in a co-op in the late seventies. But now Renee and I had time for less and less of it.

While Prana House had truly been a blessing in my life and opened so many doors, I began to wonder if my time, our time, in that community was coming to an end. Another passion was calling us, and it was demanding every bit of energy that we had to give. There simply did not seem to be enough time in the day for both.

High on our list of priorities was finding a place for the store itself. We got on our bicycles and rode around central Austin, trying to imagine where we'd like our store to be. It didn't occur to us to look for an actual retail storefront; in fact, we thought it would be kind of fun to use a house. In those days, Austin still had a lot of big old homes, like the one where Prana House was located. We knew about zoning, so we looked for a house that was zoned for commercial use. When we found a charming, vacant, three-story Victorian house at 8th Street and Rio Grande, it seemed perfect. Well, almost. Some renovations would be necessary to get it ready to open.

First, however, we'd need to raise some money. My evangelical skills would come in handy in a whole new context as I turned to friends and family for funding. Renee had a few thousand dollars saved, and I put in $10,000, loaned to me by my father at 5% annual interest. Other friends and family members chipped in too, including Jim Sud, a friend from Houston with whom I had played high school basketball. We'd stayed connected when we both came to school in Austin, but Jim had dropped out of his MBA program when his father had passed away unexpectedly a couple of years earlier, and he'd gone home to take over the family business in the oil and gas industry. Jim introduced me to a friend of his, Don Schaffer, a pediatrician with a gift for comedy, who sometimes did stand-up routines in Houston clubs after he finished his shifts. Don invested too.

All told, we raised $45,000—$5,000 shy of my $50,000 goal, but I hoped it was enough. One way or the other it would have to do.

My father, Bill, contributed $10,000 of his own and was supportive of the idea. Or perhaps it's more accurate to say that he was supportive of my passion for the idea. I'm not sure what he thought about the actual idea—he wasn't a tofu-and-granola kind of guy—but he could see how committed I was, and I'm sure that mattered to him. In fact, since I started telling him about my business idea, it seemed like we had a lot more in common.

Growing up, our connection had centered on sports. Bill Mackey *loved* sports, especially baseball and football. He nurtured my athleticism and often took me to games. He was also highly competitive, a trait that extended beyond sports. We would regularly play board games and card games as a family. My victories were few and far between, and that fueled my own strong competitive streak. My father's competitive drive was relentless, but it had a positive side as well. If I ever beat him, I knew beyond any doubt that I had earned it.

The first time I won a game of Ping-Pong as a teenager, I looked across the table at him, suddenly suspicious.

"Did you let me win?" I demanded.

"Hell no," he said, putting down his paddle. "I never just let you win at anything. Congratulations, son."

I believed him. In fact, I don't remember one time when he let his children win.

While I'd idolized my father as a boy, the distance between us had grown as I got older. He simply did not share my passion for asking big questions about meaning and purpose and God and life and death. As I brought up these topics more frequently during my teens and college years, he and I seemed to have less and less to talk about. He'd attended church when my brother, Jim, and I were young but couldn't relate to my insatiable spiritual curiosity. Maybe that's why he would fall asleep in his pew every week, as my mother nudged him to try to stop him from snoring. For him, church was a duty, not a spiritual experience.

When I was about 20, and not long out of my evangelical phase, I'd asked him, "Dad, what do you think about God? Do you think there is life after death? Do you think there is any meaning to all of this?"

"John," he said, "I remember, when I was about your age, I sat down and I thought really hard about that for a day." He paused, and I waited in anticipation of the conclusion he was about to share from those deep reflections many years ago. And then he continued, "But I couldn't figure it out. So I really haven't thought about it since."

That was my father. No time to waste worrying about things that he couldn't get his head around. He was practical, responsible, dependable, and his considerable intelligence had been put to great use in the service of those values. The more questions I posed to him about life, the universe, and our place in it, the shorter our conversations seemed to get.

In my youth, I'd chafed against what I saw as his conventional and unimaginative mindset. But as I learned more about history and culture, I'd come to empathize with what made him that way. Like most of his peers, my father had grown up during the Great Depression in the 1930s. When Pearl Harbor was bombed by the Japanese in 1941, he was just 20 years old. He wasted no time joining the military and marrying my mother, Margaret. His generation had to grow up fast. They had no time to indulge youthful dreams or ponder the meaning of life; they had to rebuild a country devastated by the Depression and war.

Dad was dedicated to his family and became a caring, dutiful provider, but he had not followed his own passions in life. That simply wasn't what people did in that era. My own idealistic and somewhat circuitous approach to finding my life's path bemused him, but I like to think that perhaps some part of him admired it as well. Perhaps he glimpsed, in my seeking and questing, a life he'd not lived but could grudgingly accept, even if he didn't truly understand it.

It was much harder for my mother to get on board with my life choices. She still couldn't get over the fact that I'd dropped out of college. A former teacher, and one of a proud lineage of college-educated women, she saw education as the key to a successful life. She never gave up hope that I'd wake up from my strange, impractical obsession with being a grocer, go back to school, and become something respectable like a doctor or lawyer. Her father had been a doctor, and she'd named me after him: John Powell. That's who I should have been in her eyes.

In my father's eyes, however, I'd shifted from being an aimless, hippie dropout to a youthful entrepreneur with conviction and energy. I'm sure that he saw that as a huge upgrade, regardless of what he thought about the specific business prospects of Safer Way. In fact, I suspect he began to see in me a son who was much more like him than he'd ever realized. For the first time in my adult life, my father's life skills and my own passions seem to come into alignment. He was an astute businessman with immense financial acumen. He'd taught accounting at Rice University and then became the very successful CEO of a healthcare company named Lifemark. We finally had something besides sports to talk about! I shared my plans and ideas for the store, and he offered advice and mentorship. Mostly, it was very good advice.

Renee and I got to work right away, refashioning the old, three-story Victorian house to fit our needs. We couldn't afford to hire a big firm or a general contractor, so we just asked some friends to help, on the cheap. One friend did a bit of carpentry; another was a good electrician; another was a painter. We bought some used commercial refrigerators; started procuring dry goods; spent hours and hours working on the building; and little by little, Safer Way began to take shape.

One afternoon in May 1978, I looked around our site from the vantage point of a stepladder, proud of how far we'd come. Our motley crew of friends were hard at work painting the main room on the first floor, assembling shelves, and hanging light fixtures. And then a guy walked in through the open door, not even bothering to knock. Clearly, he wasn't one of us, or a friend of ours. Our crew wore shorts and colorful T-shirts. This guy was all buttoned up in an official-looking uniform, red-faced on the already warm spring day.

"What are y'all doing here?" he asked, taking in the piles of construction materials, the dangling wires, and the paint-stained faces.

I wiped off my hands on my shorts, climbed down from my ladder, and walked over, offering my hand. He didn't shake it. Undeterred, I said, "We're getting ready to open a natural foods store."

His face turned a darker shade as he looked around the room again and then back at me.

"Can I see your building permit, please?"

Ignorance seemed like the best strategy. Besides, it was true—I had no idea what the rules were around construction. "What's a building permit and why do we need one?"

The red-faced man looked incredulous. "A building permit is the approval you need from the city before you are allowed to construct or remodel anything. You need one so the city can be sure that you are following city codes and regulations." He shook his head, as though my innocent question had confirmed all the worst things he already thought about my generation. "You kids can't just do this on your own. You need permits. You need to get architectural drawings and engineering plans and get them approved by the city. You need to obtain the proper licenses and clearances. You can't just build a store without authorization."

He pulled out a handkerchief and mopped his brow. "I need you to stop all construction here immediately until you have the proper city permits. I'll be back to make sure you aren't continuing to work without permission."

Permits. Plans. Clearances. Licenses. My heart sank. It all sounded slow and potentially costly. I just wanted to build a great store with the small amount of capital that we had. We needed to buy equipment, stock up on inventory, and pay wages. But I now understood that I would have to deal with the city officials if I wanted to continue to pursue my dream.

The next day I headed down to the city planning office to ask the powers that be exactly what we needed to complete our project. The message was more or less the same as we'd gotten from our unwelcome visitor. As they explained the process, I felt like time was simultaneously expanding and slipping away from me, as if I was staring into some infinite regulatory continuum that had no beginning and seemingly no end. It reminded me of the nightmarish bureaucracy described in Franz Kafka's novel *The Castle,* with its copious and meaningless paperwork. I tried to push down a rising sense of panic.

"How long will it take to get these things finalized and approved?"

The city bureaucrat stared back at me for a brief moment, disapprovingly, as if the question itself was a violation of code. Then he gave a casual shrug.

"I don't know; a few months, maybe more."

The sense of panic was increasing. "Sir, I understand. But there's no way we can wait that long. We simply don't have the funds to delay our opening for months." I tried to infuse my words with a firm, unquestionable sense of urgency, but somewhere between leaving my mouth and arriving across the desk, that sentiment seemed to lose all its momentum and dissipate into nothing.

"I'm sorry, son; that's just how it is."

Just how it is. Four little words written in red tape that can dash even the most beautiful entrepreneurial dreams. I couldn't believe it. Our business was doomed to fail before it had really gotten off the ground. There was simply no way we could hire a professional architect and a design firm and then sit around and wait months for city approvals. We'd be unable to pay rent. Our inventory would be out of date. The store would never open. Regulations like these seemed designed to keep upstarts like me and Renee from even trying.

I stumbled out of the planning office and headed back to our once-promising store. How was I going to break the news to Renee? How was I going to tell our friends that all their hard work had been for nothing? What was I going to say to my father and our other investors? And what was I going to do with my life if I didn't have a store to build?

When I arrived back at the site, our landlord's car was parked outside. He greeted me at the door. Mr. Eddie Joseph was a Lebanese immigrant, much older than me. I imagine he was in his early seventies, but in the eyes of my 24-year-old self, he seemed more like 100. He was a warm and encouraging landlord who seemed to get a kick out of the idea that his building was being taken over by hippie health nuts.

"What's wrong, young man?" he asked in his accented English. My emotions were apparently written all over my face. He sat down on the front step and motioned for me to take a seat beside him. After I finished pouring out our sad tale of impending death by bureaucracy, he nodded calmly and put an arm around my shoulders.

"Don't worry," he said.

"What?"

"Look, John, I know you want to build this store. But if you wait for the city and listen to the people in those city departments, you will never get it done."

"But Mr. Joseph, what are we supposed to do? They'll just shut us down."

"Here's what you do," he replied, his sympathetic, wizened face taking on a slightly mischievous expression. "City inspectors leave work no later than 5 PM and they sleep at night." He pointed his finger directly at my chest. "*You* build the store at night."

We took his advice. As the afternoon drew to a close and buttoned-up people in official uniforms were heading home for dinner, a small team of dedicated workers would arrive at the store and get busy. We worked late into the evening, safe from the prying eyes of city officials. If they happened to come by the store in the middle of the day, it looked deserted. There were no workers to question, no one to fine or rebuke or censure or correct. But while those officials were safely on their couches with loosened ties and full bellies, we built Safer Way.

Of course, we weren't going to be able to avoid dealing with the city forever. There was no getting around the fact that businesses need permits and licenses, nor did we intend to. But we managed to work it out over time and not let it delay our opening. After we were open, every so often a bureaucrat from one city department or another would wander into the store. They were easy to spot; none of our customers had that air of officialdom.

"Where is your health department certificate?" the official would demand.

I'd ask politely, "Which certificate is that, sir?" and we'd have a conversation about it. Then a city health department official would come inspect our store and tell us what we needed to fix, and we would receive our certificate. Some weeks later, another official would arrive at the store to check out our weights and measures, and after we passed the inspection, we would receive that certificate too. Little by little, we eventually obtained every last permit and license we needed to operate a natural foods store in the city of Austin, all while we were already operating a natural foods store in the city of Austin.

That was my first lesson, courtesy of Mr. Joseph and the Austin city bureaucrats, in dealing with regulations. I'm not saying this approach is always advisable. But as any entrepreneur knows, regulatory structures often do not always match the on-the-ground realities, and they tend to favor well-capitalized, established institutions over innovators and newcomers. Certainly, there is an important place for good regulations, the smarter the better. In most cases, regulations should be cordially respected and followed. Occasionally, they need to be politely resisted. And every once in a blue moon, they need to be strategically subverted. Without the wisdom of Mr. Joseph, Safer Way might have died a slow death by red tape before it was even born.

As we prepared for the grand opening, my life narrowed down to few simple activities. Most of the time, I worked, but when I wasn't working I was reading, running, playing basketball, or spending time with Renee. That felt like all I needed to be happy in life. At 25, the angst about my future and my purpose that had dogged me for so many years was gone. I loved what I was doing, and I was in love. Life had become simple, beautiful, joyful, and purposeful. Renee and I were on a wonderful adventure with an inspiring mission, serving people and serving a larger vision of a healthier world. We were still living at Prana House, but it felt like we existed in a parallel universe. We worked while they slept. We slept while they lived the co-op life.

In September 1978, Safer Way opened its doors. The old Victorian house looked very beautiful and welcoming—with a big sign on the lawn outside that proclaimed "Safer Way Natural Food Store." The first floor was the grocery store, and the second floor was a vegetarian café and bookstore. The small space under the eaves on the third floor would be our office.

Inside, near the front door, we had two old mechanical used cash registers and a little bulk-food area where we sold flour, whole grains, beans, nuts, and seeds out of large bins and herbs and spices out of glass jars. In an adjacent room we sold fresh produce, and in another there was a little dairy cooler and a freezer. The remaining space was lined with shelving for vitamins and canned goods and so forth. Every product we sold had been carefully chosen from catalogs and order sheets that our suppliers provided us with. Just as much care had gone into what was *not* on the shelves: there was no meat, poultry, or seafood. We were proud of our commitment to being vegetarian. The store represented the world as we felt it *ought* to be—a world where animals didn't have to suffer to feed people and where food came from farms, not factories. It was the world we wanted to live in, and we hoped our customers felt the same.

After the grand opening, our lives went from busy to flat-out crazy. We rarely even made it back to Prana House for dinner, and those shared meals were the heart of the community's culture. Living in Prana House just wasn't going to work for us any longer. We needed a new home. Safer Way's fast-growing inventory also needed a home, so we found a duplex near the store and rented it, with the idea that we'd live in one room and use the living room as our first warehouse.

That worked great for a month or so. Then, one evening, Renee and I were organizing the bags and boxes when we heard a knock at the door. I opened it to see our landlord. This guy was much less friendly than Mr. Joseph, but I welcomed him in. He looked around, taking in the crates of canned goods, sacks of beans, and boxes of vitamins. It was obvious this wasn't for personal use! Renee and I looked at each other, helplessly, as he marched around lecturing us on why we couldn't run our business out of a residential rental property.

Our explanations fell on deaf ears, and he basically evicted us on the spot. We were homeless, and so was all the inventory. We rented a tiny warehouse space on the east side of town, not the safest neighborhood by a long shot. I didn't like to go over there, especially at night, and I certainly didn't want to live there. But we couldn't afford to rent an apartment as well. There was only one other option—we could live above the store. Perhaps that was appropriate. The store had taken over our lives anyway, so we might as well sleep there too.

Chapter 3

My Father, My Mentor

Two flights of slightly creaky stairs—that was my daily commute. Every morning, Renee and I would wake up early in the little office under the eaves that now doubled as our apartment. We'd roll up our futon and I would head out for a long morning run, usually stopping off at Barton Springs for a cold swim before running back to Safer Way. There was no shower at the store, but we did have an old industrial-strength Hobart dishwasher for the café, so we used the hose as a makeshift shower. It was simple living, but it worked for us. We'd eat our breakfast at the second-floor café, and then Renee would get the café ready to open, while I'd go down to the first floor to open the store. As I bounded down those stairs two at a time, I'd often smile at the thought of all those folks who had to get in their cars and sit in traffic, or squeeze into a crowded bus or train, to get to work.

Renee and I had agreed that this was how we'd divide our focus and energy—me running the store and her running the café. I had some experience in retail, from my time working at the Good Food Company and also being the buyer for Prana House. Neither of us had any experience running a restaurant, but Renee had worked for Domino's as a delivery person, so we concluded she was marginally more qualified than I was to manage the café.

Safer Way was far from an overnight success, but little by little we began to grow a steady flow of customers. Most of them were young, countercultural types like us, but at some point, I began to notice that our clientele was expanding. People who lived in the neighborhood would wander in, curious about what the hippies were eating. Men in suits would stop by the café to get lunch. We even had the occasional celebrity grace the store. One morning, I'd barely unlocked the door when a heavily bearded man walked in, wearing flowing white robes and mala beads around his neck. I recognized him immediately: spiritual icon and psychedelic pioneer Ram Dass (a.k.a. Richard Alpert). I'd read his book *Be Here Now* several times and been intrigued by the spiritual odyssey he'd taken. We engaged in a nice conversation—such a nice conversation, in fact, that I got the distinct impression that he was flirting with me.

On another occasion, one of our servers came hurrying down the stairs and pulled me aside. Allen Ginsberg, Beat poet and countercultural hero, was in the café, she told me, in a dramatic whisper.

"That's great!" I replied.

"Yes," she said, "but there's a problem. He's smoking."

We had a beautiful deck just outside the café, where people could enjoy their lunch alfresco. In those days, smoking in restaurants was still common, but it was against our healthy ethos, and we had a strict no-smoking policy. A debate ensued—were we really going to tell Allen Ginsberg he couldn't smoke in our place? And if so, who would deliver the news? Or should we just let it go? As I recall, no one could quite summon up the courage to rebuke the legendary poet, or at least by the time we did, the need had passed.

In general, however, I was not overawed by celebrity. When a beautiful, Oscar-nominated actress showed up in the store, you can bet there was a lot of gawking. But when she began to eat trail mix out of one of our bulk bins, that was a step too far. "Excuse me, ma'am," I said, "you'll need to buy that before you eat it." She looked a bit taken aback, but she removed her hands from the trail mix.

One evening, about six months after our opening, I was on the third floor, examining the financial statements of Safer Way and the restaurant. Renee was out with friends. The summer was long gone, but evenings in Austin were still relatively mild, even in the winter, and I'd opened the windows to let in some fresh air. As I carefully reviewed the numbers, I heard a familiar noise from the street outside. *Putt, putt, putt.* Renee and I had both purchased these tiny little mopeds that barely went 25 mph and sounded kind of like a hair dryer. Usually, that auditory signal of my love returning home would have made me happy, but today I was gearing myself up for a difficult conversation.

It was clear from the financial statements I was looking at that Safer Way was barely getting by, paying our employees, and keeping the shelves stocked. And that was with Renee and me taking essentially no salaries, living above the store, eating in the café, and working 80 hours a week. A few times, we'd taken $100 just to pay for gas and essentials. But we lived on next to nothing. In many respects, our entrepreneurial adventure was everything I'd hoped it would be, but unless there was a bit more money in our future, it was also going to be short-lived. The store was making a small profit but the café was not; in fact, it was eating up what little profit the store generated.

Outside, I heard the creaking stairs, and a few moments later, Renee's bright face appeared in the doorway, her long hair windblown from the ride.

"What's up, Macko Man?" she asked, smiling. Renee's unflagging enthusiasm for life was usually a spark to my own—like a pilot light that never stops burning, always ready to ignite new creativity and fun. Tonight, however, I was unmoved by her upbeat tone.

"I'm looking at our financial statements," I replied.

Her face fell, like I'd doused the pilot light with a bucket of cold water. "And how do they look?"

"The store isn't doing great, honestly, but it is profitable. The café is . . . well, it's not."

"Look, it's hard to run a café," she protested. "I'm learning on the job."

"So am I," I replied, "and the store is making money. But all our extra cash is going directly into the café. I'm doing my job here. You need to do yours."

Anger and hurt flashed across her face, and I immediately regretted my words. It wasn't the first time we'd covered this territory. The discrepancy in the fortunes of the store and café had been apparent for a while, and now it was becoming a source of tension between us. What didn't help was that I was being unfair. It was much harder to run a café than a small store. My job was nowhere near as multilayered and intricate as Renee's.

The café was inherently a much more dynamic system—with so many variables to anticipate. And Renee was right—she had no experience to draw upon. Neither did I. In fact, the more I learned about both businesses, the more I realized how much there was to learn. I could sense how much better I would be able to do my job as I gained experience. Our failings weighed on me, but that sense of potential growth pulled me forward. I knew I could do better, and I wanted to do better. Up to this point, we had built our business on a dream, fueled by ambition, desire, enthusiasm, a sense of adventure, hard work, and a lot of help from our friends. But to be truly successful, it was going to take something more—business experience and intelligence.

I apologized to Renee that night for blaming her unfairly for the café's struggles, and she accepted my apology. Renee was not one to hold a grudge, but I knew we couldn't keep having this fight. If we were going to be both lovers and business partners, we were going to need to improve our business acumen. Otherwise, our entrepreneurial dreams would fail, and I worried our love might get damaged in the fallout. Luckily, when it came to business intelligence, I knew where to turn.

Every month or two, I would make a trip to Houston to visit my parents. My little hair-dryer moped wasn't up for the journey, and our only other vehicle was the "truck"—an old mail truck we'd purchased at auction and painted with the Safer Way logo. I often worried that the truck wouldn't even make it from the warehouse to the store; driving it a couple hundred miles was out of the question. So I'd throw my backpack on my shoulders and set off on foot, sticking out my thumb once I reached the highway. Hitchhiking worked well in those days, and it never took long to find a ride on the well-traveled roads between the two cities. In the spring of 1979, I made the trip with a clear intention. As I made polite conversation with the chatty couple who had picked me up, my mind was occupied with a dozen questions that I wanted to ask my father. It was time, I'd decided, to take more advantage of his extensive business experience. If anyone could help me learn how to make Safer Way more profitable, it was him.

It was just past dinnertime when I arrived at my parents' familiar door, having walked the last few miles from the highway. My mother had saved me a plate with some potatoes and some rather gray-looking green beans. "I know you don't want the pot roast," she said, her tone making it clear that she was somewhat offended by my dietary choices—as if I thought I was too good for her food. "I just saved you the sides. I hope it's enough." My vegetarianism was baffling to my family, who couldn't quite fathom what I would eat if hamburgers and fried chicken were off the menu. This was understandable, since my mother had borne witness to my childhood disdain for vegetables. She'd probably never heard of half the things we sold at Safer Way, and though I'd tried to describe the wonderful meals we cooked at Prana House and later at the café, I could tell they just didn't fit into the categories she considered food.

"Thanks, Mom, this looks great," I assured her. Luckily, I've always loved potatoes. I took my plate and sat down beside my dad, who was absorbed in an Astros baseball game on television. For the next couple of hours, we enjoyed our first shared love: sports. And then I turned to our new common ground: business.

I had lots of specific, highly practical questions, but I wasn't here to ask my father to weigh in on all these issues. There were just too many, and there would be new ones tomorrow—and the next day. I needed to learn enough to be able to answer the day-to-day questions of running the business myself.

"Dad, I'm here because I need to learn more about business. I feel like I'm barely scratching the surface. I appreciate all the advice you've given me, but I need to learn how to think better for myself. Where should I start? What should I read?"

That got his attention. He turned off the television, stood up, and motioned for me to follow him into his office. The far wall was lined with bookcases. "Son," he said, pointing toward the shelves, "here's where you start."

He pulled out a thick book with a black-and-red dust jacket with bold yellow type—*Management: Tasks, Responsibilities, Practices.* The author was Peter Drucker. It didn't look like the kind of book I tended to read, but I took it, weighing the heavy volume in my hand. My dad also gave me Alfred Sloan's memoir about his years with General Motors. Could a car manufacturer really teach me anything about running a natural foods store? I was skeptical. But hey—I didn't know what I didn't know, so I might as well read it. I filled my backpack until it could carry no more and took the whole collection back to Austin, where I added more titles from the local library and bookstores. If it looked like it had something important to say about business, I read it. In fact, I devoured it.

And I learned. By night, I read about business. By day, I worked in the store. Every few days, I'd call up my father and talk to him about what I was reading. Slowly but surely, I began to see the challenges our small business was facing from a more holistic perspective. And it became clear to me why Safer Way seemed to have a ceiling on its success. It wasn't just that Renee and I didn't know what we were doing (although we didn't). It wasn't just that we needed to attract more customers or sell more products (although we did). What I now understood was that there were important competitive disadvantages in the marketplace that were working against us and giving our rivals a better chance of success.

Take my former employer, for example, the Good Food Company. They had five stores compared to our one little store, and as a result, they were able to negotiate better prices than we were from the wholesalers and therefore price their products more competitively while still making a profit. We were also supplied by Yellow Rose, a co-op distribution center that was owned by the various food and housing co-ops in Austin. Here too we were at a disadvantage, this time because we were a for-profit business. The folks at Yellow Rose were anti-capitalist, so they wouldn't give us the same prices they gave the food and housing co-ops. To compete more effectively in the local economic ecosystem, Safer Way would need to think strategically about these challenges.

As I broadened my thinking beyond the balance sheet of our store, I came up with a new idea. Clearly, order volume mattered when it came to getting better prices. But we couldn't order more until we were bigger, and we weren't going to get bigger unless we could get better prices now and become more competitive. It was a catch-22. Unless—what if we teamed up with other small stores and pooled our buying? Soon, I'd convinced two other small, independent natural food stores to join us in creating a buying club, Texas Health Distributors. We set up a small warehouse and placed our orders together, getting products at far better prices.

One of those stores was Clarksville Natural Grocery, a beloved neighborhood store run by two guys named Craig Weller and Mark Skiles. Mark was about my age; Craig was eight years older. Technically, Clarksville was a competitor, being just a couple of miles away, but once we created the distribution company, we became allies. The orders would be delivered to the warehouse, and I would load them onto our former mail truck, still puttering along, and head off to deliver the goods to our partners. The first time I arrived at Clarksville, I unloaded their order and turned around to leave, but Craig stopped me. He was a striking figure—tall and broad shouldered. I thought he looked like Robert Redford in a grocer's apron, waving a clipboard.

"Wait, I need to count it. Make sure everything's in order."

I spun around, affronted. "What, you don't trust me?"

He frowned. "No offense, John. We do this with all our orders."

I was offended, and I'm sure it showed. I would later come to learn that it really wasn't personal. Craig was just that kind of retailer—thorough, detail oriented, and hard working. His no-nonsense, straight-shooter quality was a sign of his deep integrity and work ethic. But I didn't know that when I delivered that first order, and so I stood there, irritated, while he slowly counted each of the items, checking them off his list.

The next week, I pulled up again, and Craig and his clipboard were waiting to meet me. This time, however, as he went through the order, we got to talking and my irritation quickly faded. In the weeks and months to come, I began to look forward to the time it took for Craig to check off his list. We had long conversations about our stores, about the products we were selling, about retailing, and about business in general. I got to know Craig and eventually Mark too. And I came to deeply appreciate the quality of their store and the care that went into it.

Clarksville had been bootstrapped to an even greater extent than Safer Way. We'd had just enough capital to buy used equipment; they got much of theirs from the dump and refurbished it. Their refrigeration consisted of old coolers that had been abandoned in the store they rented, a former 7-Eleven, and another they found in a junkyard. Craig, who was talented with his hands, had made each of the large wooden bulk-food bins himself. Little by little, they had become successful, and they were continuing to grow.

I kept hearing stories about Craig and Mark's above-and-beyond commitment to customer service. Mark was known for having a stack of records ready and switching them out depending on who walked through the door. Jamaican customers were welcomed with reggae. If some older folks came in, he'd switch to classical. And of course, he had plenty of sixties and seventies rock music to make their typical hippie clientele feel at home.

Their deep service ethos was exemplified in an encounter that probably happened right around the time I was getting to know them (although I wouldn't hear about it until some years later). A young girl—no more than four years old—walked into the store alone one afternoon. Craig recognized her—her mother, Mary Kay, was a regular customer. The little girl had a very unusual and pretty name: Evening.

"Can I help you?" Craig asked, squatting down so he was the same height as the girl. She told him that she would like a cookie, and that her mother had an account at the store. (Clarksville was also well known for its generous credit system.)

"Did you walk over here all by yourself?" Craig asked.

When she nodded, Craig stood up, found her a cookie, and then he said, "How about I walk you home?" And he locked up the store and did just that.

When I heard this story many years later from Mary Kay—who would end up being an important person in my life, along with that little girl named Evening—it didn't surprise me at all. That's just the kind of guy Craig was. He and Mark were also committed, resourceful, and innovative. What they'd achieved was impressive, and their success was tangible in the growing volume of the orders that I continued to deliver, week after week.

Safer Way was also growing, and we were beginning to break even as our first year ended. Overall, however, we'd lost $23,000—half of the capital we'd started with. I was learning so much; I could feel the possibilities ahead. But could I learn fast enough to keep the business afloat?

Chapter 4

The Fellowship

As Safer Way passed its first birthday, Renee and I were in need of a break. It had been a long, uninterrupted push since we'd first come up with the idea for the store. And while building and running Safer Way was an adventure, we were still young, and we yearned for other kinds of adventure as well. In the fall of 1979, Renee came up with an idea for a trip: traveling and hitchhiking around New Zealand. She had a friend who lived there. Admittedly, it wasn't the most responsible decision for the cofounders of a fledgling business that was still barely profitable. But luckily, by this point, we had team members we could trust.

One of these was David Matthis. David had shown up one day back when we were still building out the store and getting ready to open. He introduced himself and asked if we were hiring. We got to chatting, and I found out we knew many of the same people. Austin was a much smaller city in those days, and we ran in similar circles. As we talked, it became clear that he had some knowledge about the natural foods business. He and his wife, Karen Saadeh, had previously owned a much smaller natural foods store in Austin called The Balanced Way. I liked him immediately, and his knowledge and experience were considerably greater than that of most of our would-be team members. I asked him if he could start by getting our vitamins in order.

"Sure," David replied. "When do you want me to start?"

"As soon as possible," I replied. "But let's start with a trial period of two weeks, and then we'll talk." Two weeks later, we agreed on another two weeks. And two weeks later, we extended his employment again.

Somewhere between our opening in September 1978 and the end of the year, David became a full-time employee. He would end up working with Safer Way, and then Whole Foods Market, for most of the next four decades.

By the time Renee and I were ready to take off for New Zealand, David was our most trusted team member, along with our accountant, Tom Calzone, so we left them with most of the responsibility for making sure the business was running smoothly.

Our trip lifted us out of the day-to-day grind, but we didn't really leave the business behind. Indeed, once I settled in for the long flight, I passed the time by reading an industry trade journal that had recently begun showing up in my mailbox: a large-format, colorful magazine called the *Natural Foods Merchandiser.* The inaugural issue, in February 1979, had captivated my attention with its cover story about a Los Angeles–based natural foods store named Mrs. Gooch's. I'd read it so many times that the pages were smudged and tattered.

The cofounder and namesake, a former kindergarten teacher named Sandy Gooch, was a larger-than-life figure, famous for her high standards when it came to food quality. The article described the store as a "one-stop shop" because, unlike most natural foods stores at the time, it sold meat, poultry, and seafood alongside the kinds of products we sold at Safer Way. I'd never heard of a store that did all this under one roof. The idealist in me was proud of our strictly vegetarian ethos, but the entrepreneur in me saw a massive opportunity. Imagine if customers were able to do their entire grocery shopping for the week without having to set foot in a conventional supermarket! According to the article, Mrs. Gooch's was doing a staggering $100,000 a week in sales at their best store (in contrast to Safer Way's $8,000–$10,000 a week).

Other issues of the *Natural Foods Merchandiser* profiled stores like Bread & Circus in Boston and Frazier Farms in San Diego. The magazine's publisher, Doug Greene, seemed to be on a mission to tell the story of how the natural foods industry was changing, and it was a story I intended to be part of. As I gazed out the window at the clouds on that seemingly endless flight, I thought about Safer Way and how it might grow into something that could be featured on the front page of *Natural Foods Merchandiser.* One thing was for sure: It would need to become much larger.

In an era when health food stores were generally small and focused mostly on selling vitamins and supplements, these new-format natural foods stores were larger, brighter, fresher, and—well, *new.* They were also very different from the nonprofit food co-ops of the era (I'd been a member of several). The photos in *Natural Foods Merchandiser* had an upscale vibe, with handwritten signage and educational information as well as beautifully displayed food. According to the article, Mrs. Gooch's managed to achieve a cross section of clientele as well, attracting West Coast hippies in search of a more natural lifestyle but also Hollywood royalty.

Over the next few weeks, as Renee and I enjoyed the vast spaces and beautiful vistas of New Zealand, I felt elevated into a broader perspective on our company's future. Perhaps the distance helped. We spent a lot of time talking about how we might grow. Texas Health Distributors had helped us get better wholesale prices, but I still worried about our competitive position. One conclusion just seemed inescapable: Size mattered in the retail business. Our store was just too small to gain the kind of market share necessary to be very successful over the long term. We were in a great and growing niche, as those stories I'd been reading confirmed. We had both learned a great deal and we were making smarter decisions. But no matter how savvy we became at running the store and café, it wasn't going to change the square footage of that old Victorian house that Safer Way occupied.

By the time we returned to Austin, the seventies had given way to the eighties. I headed to the store to say hello to the team with only one thing on my mind—expansion. David, Tom, and I sat together on the deck of the café. They updated me on the business, which was doing better thanks to a big sale they had put on ahead of the holidays. I thanked them for their hard work and for holding down the fort while Renee and I were away. And then I got straight to the point.

"Guys, I want to expand. We need a bigger store—something like Mrs. Gooch's or Bread & Circus. Or bigger! I know we can be successful if we have more space." I explained my thinking around our position in the Austin natural foods market.

They both looked a bit surprised. "A bigger store would be great, John. But won't that take more capital? We're just barely starting to make *this* store profitable. Is it the right time? Have you spoken to your father? What does he think?"

What did my father think? I had grown a bit frustrated by that question. Every time Renee or David or Tom had serious questions about one of my new schemes or ideas, this was the way they tried to back me down: bring up my father. The business expert. The grown-up in the room. The one who could keep John in line. It frustrated me, in part, because it was more than just a little bit true.

"Look, I know that I need to talk to my father, and the other investors. And yes, we'll need more capital. But imagine the store we could build. This one is already starting to grow. It's even starting to be profitable. We're making money, guys! And a larger store would be so much more attractive. I mean, the time is right."

It was true; we were beginning to be profitable, although I may have been overstating my case. Our meager profit came with a list of caveats. Renee and I were only taking about $200 per month in salaries. We weren't exactly paying high wages or giving team members luxurious benefits. Still, we were learning, and my confidence and knowledge of the market was improving. And along with that increase in knowledge came the realization that despite our name, we couldn't afford to play it safe and wait until we had larger profit margins. As tempting as it might seem to stay small, it wouldn't be the "safer way" at all, because we'd keep falling further behind. I understood that reality now. This wasn't the time to wait and consolidate our gains; it was time to push forward.

I had no idea how we were going to fund our expansion, and I was putting off the inevitable talk with my father. In the meantime, I started looking for locations. I soon found one that seemed very promising—just half a mile from Safer Way, on Lamar Boulevard at 10th Street, a busy thoroughfare. The building had previously been a nightclub (not the most obvious precursor to a natural foods store), and it had burned down. (Not the best omen, if you were superstitious. Luckily, I was not.) On the plus side, the name of the club had been Mother Earth (which sounded like a natural foods store already). And it was *huge* by our standards: 10,500 square feet, about three times the size of our current store. It would take a lot of work to rebuild, but we weren't afraid of hard work. Now I just had to sell the idea to the Board.

That's right, Safer Way had a Board of Directors, though calling it that might conjure up a misleading image in a reader's mind. This wasn't a dozen men in suits who met downtown in a penthouse conference room. It was basically my father, Jim Sud, Don Schaffer, Renee, and me. And while Jim and Don were good friends, and Don's great sense of humor brought a welcome levity to our meetings, both of them naturally deferred to the greater experience of my father. Convincing the Board to invest in a new store meant convincing Bill Mackey that it made good business sense.

David, Tom, and I planned another trip to Houston. I hoped that having some of my team with me might communicate that this wasn't just my wild idea; it was something we all believed in. The Safer Way truck was in even worse shape by this point, and hitchhiking didn't work so well in numbers, so we took David's car, a used Volvo that seemed reliable. The three of us planned to use our time on the road to hone our pitch, so we asked Karen to drive. Renee stayed in Austin to mind the store.

"You got this, Macko Man," she'd told me as we said goodbye. "Just be yourself and believe in your vision. Show your father how much you've thought this through. It's such a great idea. He can't say no."

As we drove from Austin to Houston, and I rehearsed what I'd say to my father, I felt the confidence she'd ignited coming through my voice. *Just be yourself.* That's right. This was who I was—it was my passion and my purpose and it really was a great idea. But it wasn't just the business idea that had me energized. It was also the sense of camaraderie I felt in that car as David, Tom, and I hashed out our plans and discussed the market. Maybe it was because they'd run the business while Renee and I were in New Zealand, but David and Tom were highly engaged and invested in Safer Way's success. They felt like partners, not just employees. There was a spirit of collaboration between us, a friendship, or, as I began to think of it, a fellowship. It was a term I took from one of the favorite books of my youth, J.R.R. Tolkien's *The Lord of the Rings.* Like Frodo and his little band of hobbits, we were bonded by our shared journey. It was no longer just Renee and me and our harebrained idea. More people were getting on board and traveling with us on this entrepreneurial adventure. I loved that! We were doing something meaningful together, and everyone was excited about it. Now I just needed to enroll my father in that same level of enthusiasm.

His initial response when I laid out our plans wasn't exactly encouraging.

"What the hell is this, John?"

I shrank inwardly at his tone, feeling like the teenager who'd dropped out of school—again. "This makes no sense," he continued. "The point of business expansion is not to take a failing business and replicate it!"

"We're not failing!" I protested.

He softened his tone a little. "Okay, okay. But you're still figuring this out. It's not time to expand yet. You're learning. Stay where you are for a few years, and if you make this little business a real success, then we can look at options for expansion. It's too soon. You're still too new at this."

My father was not one for soft-pedaling his message. He was opinionated, strong-minded, and confident, almost daring anyone to disagree with him. How many times had I sat at our dinner table as a child and witnessed this side of him? He liked to debate and argue, was very good at it, and had little patience for what he felt was muddled thinking. Debating, in our house, was as much a competitive sport as baseball, cards, or Ping-Pong. And it was just as hard for any of his children to win. I had watched my younger brother, Jim, wilt under the barrage of his will. I was keenly attuned to the tacit disapproval that was leveled at those who were unable to meet strength with strength. Even now, as an adult, I could still feel self-doubt, insecurities, and the need for his approval rising up. After all, he had decades of business experience. What the hell *did* I know? I'd been running Safer Way for just over a year and was barely turning a profit. But I pushed those feelings aside for the moment and focused on my own strategic convictions. *Be yourself. Believe in your vision. He can't say no.*

Mentally, I picked up my Ping-Pong paddle and found my stroke.

"Listen, Dad, I understand. Of course we need to get better at running the business, and we are working hard to do that. But we also need to seize the moment. The natural foods market is growing. If we don't expand now, we'll miss our shot. In two years, it may be too late. Right now, we are at a competitive disadvantage because of our small size. The business environment is tilted against us, and we need to change that. We *have* to change that. Location and size matter a lot."

His counterargument came slamming back across the net. I parried. Back and forth we went. David and Tom looked a little dizzy as they watched. I could tell Dad didn't agree with me, but I think he respected how passionate I was about the issue. After years of debating with him on countless topics, I had become pretty skilled at the art of argument myself. I knew he wasn't going to just let me win. Slowly, however, he seemed to concede that I had a legitimate business case. For all his strong opinions and his forceful manner of sharing them, my father could be convinced by a good argument. Finally, he seemed to temporarily relent. He didn't miss a shot, but he served me a gentle volley:

"Okay, son, here's what I'll agree to. If you can find another major investor, then I'll put some more money in too, and we'll expand. But you have to find someone else to share the risk."

On the drive home to Austin, I was thrilled. I understood that my father probably believed he had won the argument. No doubt he thought that in all likelihood, I'd come back to him in a few weeks or months acknowledging that there was no other investor dumb enough to put lots of money into this crazy, unproven venture that wanted to grow before it was ready. But he had given a conditional yes. And I could see the new store already taking shape in my mind. As David, Tom, and I discussed our ideas, I felt a growing confidence that I could find someone who would share this vision and be willing to put their money behind it.

It was energizing to imagine the store we could create—but more than that, it was *fun*! Who knew business could be so much fun? I'd always loved science fiction and fantasy literature, entering imaginary worlds and living vicariously through the characters inside them. But this was even better. It was a new world, but it wasn't just fantasy. We could and would build this store—this beautiful edifice of food, health, teamwork, and business—out of nothing more than dreams, hard work, and some investors' capital. I felt, momentarily, like some ancient alchemist dabbling in the act of creation. What a joy it was, in that moment, to be an entrepreneur. I was beginning to love this thing called "business."

Why don't more people know what fun this is? I wondered. My accountant father had always given me the impression that business was about money, finance, math. My university professors and friends at Prana House had given me the impression that business was about greed and profiteering. It had always seemed so serious, so hard, so unemotional. But this was quite the opposite. This wasn't work; it was more like playing a game. And I loved to play! Give me clear rules, fair and intense competition, and problems to solve, and I thrive. Could this really be what business was all about? Well, I couldn't speak for anyone else, but here I was—an actual businessman—and I'd never had so much fun in my life.

As the miles ticked by, David, Tom, and I got carried away envisioning the various departments we'd have space for in the new store. More organic produce, more natural foods, a bigger selection of vitamins. It would be like a real supermarket where people could do all their shopping, not just a fraction. And we could educate people about a better way to eat. In fact, I envisioned a dedicated information center, where people could ask questions about the products we carried and how to prepare them. Natural foods were still new to most Americans, and I had seen many new customers in our store looking a bit disoriented. Growing the business also meant growing and educating our customer base.

At some point, I noticed that Karen kept turning her head while keeping her eyes on the road. Clearly, she was listening very attentively as she drove. But it was only when I mentioned the information center that she finally piped up.

"I could do that."

"Do what?" I responded, surprised by her tone of conviction.

"I could be the information person. I'd love to do it."

I had the distinct feeling that Karen was inspired as much by the sense of connection she felt between David, Tom, and me as she was about the store itself. She wanted to be part of the fellowship! And why not? Except . . . was she qualified? As David's wife and our willing chauffeur for this important trip, I already considered her an honorary member, but how much did she really know about vitamins and natural foods?

"I know quite a lot," she declared. "I have a Bachelor of Science in nutrition!"

I was surprised—and intrigued. Karen continued, "Growing up, we ate natural foods, whole grains, very little sugar, and raw milk when available. We took supplements." Her mother, she added, had read many nutrition writers, including Adelle Davis, an unconventional nutritionist in the middle of the 20th century.

"Okay, okay," I told her. "That's great. But there is going to be a test. There is a lot to know—about vitamins, cooking, nutrition, supplements, all kinds of stuff. How about this—I'll give you a list of books to read, then I'll test your knowledge. If you pass, you get the job."

My mandate was clear: find another large investor. But before I set about the search in earnest, I had another trip to take. I wanted to see for myself some of the new natural foods stores I'd been reading about in *Natural Foods Merchandiser* and meet the folks behind them. I planned a pilgrimage-come-market-research-trip to both coasts.

The store that made the strongest impression on me during that trip was Boston's Bread & Circus, a three-store natural foods chain owned by Tony Harnett (who had bought the original store from the founders, a husband-and-wife team who sold food and wooden toys, hence the name). The 10,000-square-foot store that I visited was in many respects the closest to what I imagined our new store could become. When I stepped off the dusty Cambridge street and into their produce department, I looked around me in awe, like a pilgrim entering a place of worship. Taking in the profusion of fresh, colorful produce stacked high on table after table, I was filled with a mix of reverence and envy. How were they able to offer such a selection, such quality? If there was one thing I'd learned in my short tenure as a grocer, it was that perishables are incredibly hard to do well. But Bread & Circus had cracked the code.

On that visit, I also met Harnett himself—an Irishman about a decade older than me, whose preppy attire and pristine store signaled a different mentality from the hippies who were often synonymous with the natural foods movement. Tony was charismatic and engaging, good-naturedly showing me around his store and answering dozens of questions before taking me out to lunch. I liked him immediately and came to think of him as a kind of big-brother figure.

After leaving Boston, my head full of shiny apples, crisp lettuce, and colorful carrots, I traveled to Southern California to get a look at Mrs. Gooch's in Los Angeles (hoping I might run into Jane Fonda or Dustin Hoffman in the aisles) and Frazier Farms in San Diego. Each visit gave me new ideas when it came to store layouts, displays, creative signage, product mix, and more. I wasn't sure I wanted to—or could—emulate Sandy Gooch's whimsical approach to store décor. Her window displays, built out of quirky antiques, plants, stuffed animals, and objects she found on the street, were like nothing seen before or since in retail food stores. But I liked how her stores featured educational signage to help customers learn about the products. I was also impressed by how they had achieved a broad product mix while maintaining their founder's legendary quality standards.

By the end of my whirlwind tour, I was overflowing with exciting ideas. But more than any specific insight, what I gained from those visits was confidence. My vision of a larger format natural foods store was not crazy. It was timely! Clearly, there was a tremendous untapped potential in the market. I was ready to seek out new investors, knowing that I'd be speaking with a passion born of much more than my personal vision. This wasn't just my great idea; I had seen evidence with my own eyes that this was the next wave of the healthy eating movement.

I thought long and hard about how to meet my father's challenge. For a small business, the most natural place to look for investors is among friends and family. But I'd already done that for our seed round, so I needed to broaden my search. Still, I knew a total stranger was unlikely to take a chance on me. I needed someone who knew me a little or at least had sympathy for our mission. Maybe a customer? Or someone who was already passionate about natural foods?

As I mulled over the issue, I took some time to clear my head by playing basketball. One afternoon, following a hard pickup game, I walked out to the parking lot with another player, a guy named Jay Templeton. "Great game, John!" he said, and then to my surprise, he slung his gym bag into the back of a shiny brand-new truck and drove off. I stood there, stunned. It was rare to see young people in the late seventies driving cars like that. *Is Jay rich?*

I asked some mutual friends and learned that Jay had inherited some money and owned a construction company. This was no time to be shy. I immediately gave him a call and explained that Safer Way was relocating to a new, larger store, and I'd like to pitch him on the idea. As it turned out, Jay was receptive because he was a customer! His offices were only a couple of blocks away and he frequented the café.

A few days later, I pitched him on the concept. He listened carefully and expressed genuine enthusiasm for the idea. The amount I asked for was $50,000, and to my great delight, he agreed. And just like that, I had done it. The new site, the plans for the new store—it could all really happen. I was so excited that I immediately called my father. Bill Mackey wasn't quite ready to concede the game, however.

"That's good to hear, son, but I'm not sure this is truly the right time. I really think we should wait for a better moment."

"But Dad, we had a deal!" I reminded him of the terms he'd set. Reluctantly, he conceded. He invested more of his money, and he also loaned me more money for my own shares, further incentivizing me to make it a success. When all was said and done, we raised about $100,000 in new funds. Now we just had to convince the owner of the Lamar site to lease it to a bunch of twentysomethings with more energy and enthusiasm than experience or expertise.

Chapter 5

A One-Stop Shop

"A what?"

The man looked me up and down from beneath his stylish Stetson hat, taking in my long hair, mustache, and faded blue jeans. The quizzical expression on his face matched the tone of his voice.

It was early 1980, and armed with my new infusion of capital, I'd sought out the owner of the burned-out nightclub on North Lamar. His name was Ben Powell. Ben was an attorney, living in Houston, who had attended Harvard Law School and once worked for President Lyndon Johnson. His family was from Austin, and they owned a lot of property in the area. He was a classic Texas good ole boy—hardworking, no nonsense. At this first meeting, I explained our intentions for the site. *A natural foods supermarket.*

Clearly, that combination of words didn't register in his vocabulary. Earnestly, I tried again.

"We're opening a natural foods supermarket," I repeated, launching into my best evangelical pitch for the store. Finally, Ben stopped me.

"Son, you're going to build some kind of hippie food store?"

"No, sir," I responded again. "It's a natural foods supermarket."

"That's what I said," he retorted. "A hippie food store."

"Sir, we're selling natural foods," I said in the most patient voice I could muster.

He looked even more confused. "Natural foods? What's a natural food?"

"It means food that's not highly processed. Like whole grains, beans, fresh fruits and vegetables, nuts, and seeds." I kept listing all the bounty we would sell.

"Son," he interrupted me, "people don't eat like that anymore. There are not enough hippies in the whole damn world, let alone in Austin, for you to sell enough groceries to make that kind of store a success."

"But sir, some people *do* eat like that," I explained eagerly. I told him that more and more young people were eating like this. Yes, hippies—but not just hippies. People across the country were realizing that it was a healthier way to eat. Our store was going to be the best natural foods store in all of Texas. As I made my speech, his stern expression began to soften into a smile. Finally, I ran out of words, and he let out a booming laugh.

"John," he said in his slow Texas drawl, "I like you. You remind me of myself when I was young. So damn idealistic and optimistic! You think you can take on the world. Life's gonna teach you a few things before it's done with you. That I can say for sure." He paused, running his leather bolo tie slowly through his fingers. And then he looked me right in the eye and said, "What the hell, son—let's do your damn hippie food store."

We had money, and now we had a site: 10,500 square feet! And with each person who put their faith in us—Jay, my father, and now Ben Powell—I was more determined than ever to make the business a success. There was one more piece of the puzzle that I knew would make an enormous difference: my friends at Clarksville Natural Grocery. I didn't want to just become a bigger competitor down the street. I wanted Craig and Mark to join our fellowship! I respected their vision, their expertise, and their work ethic, and I was convinced that if Safer Way merged with Clarksville, we could create a natural foods supermarket that would leave all our other Austin rivals in the rearview mirror.

For some weeks now, as I came and went with deliveries, I'd been telling Craig and Mark about the plans for the new store. Eventually, I pitched them on the idea of a merger. They listened but were hesitant.

Between their customer base and ours, the new store would immediately break even, I explained. And with such a splashy new location, we would gain many new customers as well. Mark seemed pretty interested; Craig was less sure. He was older, perhaps a bit more conservative. It can be hard to let go of something when you've worked so hard to make it successful. They'd literally built out that store with their own hands, and they each owned half of their business. Merging would mean giving up control and owning a smaller piece of a bigger pie.

Clarksville had been planning on expanding too, but just to a second store in the same small-natural-foods-store mold. Their new location wasn't as good or as large as ours. Our vision was something quite different. It was significantly larger than any natural foods store in Austin, giving us room to add new product lines and feature them in the right way. And it would feel like a supermarket—a wide-open space, with aisle after aisle, not separated into rooms like Safer Way's Victorian house. We would be able to pull customers away from the Good Food Company, the co-ops, and even the conventional supermarkets. I explained all of this to Craig and Mark again and again as I unloaded boxes and waited for Craig to go through his list. And while they thought about my proposal, we started building out the Lamar site.

Ben Powell had agreed to finance the rebuilding and had brought in Bill Houston, a builder friend, who would help us turn the burned-out nightclub into a fresh new store. Another salt-of-the-earth Texan, Bill worked incredibly hard—doing the work of several men. We put our money into inventory and equipment, and we even managed to save some cash for working capital. And Ben rented the site to us cheap: $3,750 a month. On the long list of people who made Whole Foods Market possible, Ben Powell and Bill Houston each have a special place.

Occasionally, Craig and Mark would drop by the new site after work, and I'd show them around. Like a tour guide leading people through the ruins of an ancient city (only in reverse), I'd paint a picture of the different departments in the store and where they were going to be. One of my superpowers is my evangelical enthusiasm. When I become excited about a vision of the future, I can often persuade others to believe in it too. I began to recognize this strength as I worked to sell Mark and Craig on the merger and saw their attitudes slowly shifting. I also realized that I'm good at envisioning mutually beneficial outcomes. I genuinely saw a future in which we would be stronger together. I wasn't trying to make a deal that gave Safer Way the advantage, and I think they could feel that. By uniting, we could create a much more successful company than we could by competing against each other.

Finally, Craig and Mark agreed to the merger, but not until we were almost done with construction. With just a couple of weeks to go until the grand opening, we had to get the merger agreement signed, close down their store, and transfer all the inventory from both Safer Way and Clarksville to the new location. It was a chaotic time, but I was still having so much fun.

We also needed a name for our new, joint business. Craig and Mark didn't like Safer Way. They thought it was too clever and didn't say enough about who we were. We couldn't keep the name Clarksville Natural Grocery at the new location, because, well, we weren't in Clarksville. We needed a completely new brand. And there was no way we were going to spend money on some expensive marketing agency to come up with a name.

We gathered one afternoon in the back office at the new store to discuss the issue—Craig, Mark, Renee, and me, as well as David and Tom. We spent hours going over possibilities—envisioning names that would hang on our storefront in just a few days.

"What's wrong again with Safer Way?" Renee asked. The name still made her smile, and it was like someone was trying to rename our baby.

"I don't like Safer Way." Craig restated his position. "It's your store. Plus, it's derivative. It's kind of a joke. We need something new and fresh, that tells customers who we are." He had a point. It wasn't just our baby anymore. It was growing up and had two new additional parents.

"What about Safest Way?" I joked.

"Maybe we can share some store names we all like, from other stores, just to get a sense of direction," Renee suggested helpfully.

I jumped in. "I love the word 'market,' like Common Market." There was a Common Market retail store nearby.

"But that's not a food store," Mark said.

"True, but I still love that word. And I think it fits us. Market sounds like farmers and fresh produce and community. We are a market."

"Okay, let's build on that," Craig said. "What kind of market are we?"

"Well, we're a food market," Mark said.

"A natural foods market," David added.

"An organic foods market?" I suggested. But I could tell from the looks on my cofounders' faces that they thought that term was too obscure. And it was, back then. The term "organic" was more commonly associated with "chemistry" than with anything you'd expect to find in a grocery store.

"A health foods market?" Mark suggested.

"Well, I guess that's what we are," I conceded. "It just sounds a bit . . . boring."

Stumped, we sat in silence for a minute. I looked around the makeshift office—piled high with boxes and files and all the detritus of a store under construction. And then Renee reached out into the chaos and picked up a magazine.

"Hey, look at this." She held it up. The cover was emblazoned with three words: *Whole Foods Magazine.*

"*Whole Foods Magazine* . . . Whole Foods . . . Market!" I don't remember who said it first, but it rang true. That's who we were. The name issue was solved.

Now we just needed a logo—and a very large sign for our very large store. And we needed both fast.

The store was taking shape just as we'd envisioned. There was a large produce department, a big bulk-foods area, plenty of shelving for dry goods, refrigerators, freezers. And it wasn't just Safer Way writ large—there were whole departments in this new store that hadn't existed in our previous incarnation.

Safer Way had been strictly vegetarian, reflecting the way Renee and I liked to eat. It sold no meat, no poultry, and no seafood. But as I'd matured and learned about the realities of running a business, I'd been forced to confront the fact that my high ideals inevitably restricted our market, keeping Safer Way in a smaller niche. When you're trying to create a new world, how much should you compromise your ideals in order to bring people along with you? As I thought about expansion, I realized that I wanted the new store to serve more people. It would still contain all of the healthy foods we loved—and many, many more—but it would also welcome people who were curious about natural foods and different diets but not fully committed. I didn't want those people to have to go to a big, sterile, corporate supermarket just because their tastes were more traditional. We decided that alongside the bulk foods and vitamins and fresh produce, we'd have a dedicated meat and seafood department, beer and wine, coffee and tea, and a broader selection of products. The new store would be less purity focused and more service oriented. It would be less restrictive and more educational.

When it came to that last point—education—I hadn't forgotten what we'd discussed that car ride: the information center. In fact, I'd sent Karen Saadeh a list of books to study before we conducted a test of her knowledge. Renee and I now considered David and Karen good friends, so we'd hang out a lot, and every so often Karen would tell me about her study progress. Finally, one Sunday afternoon, we met on the third floor of Safer Way. We sat on the floor, surrounded by books, and I started asking her questions—the kind of questions that customers had been asking since Safer Way opened. *How long do I cook brown rice? What kind of vitamins should I take when I'm pregnant? Should I be worried about getting enough protein if I'm vegetarian? What the hell is in tofu?*

Karen's answers were confident and knowledgeable. She had been doing her homework! I was learning new things about one of my favorite topics from her. In fact, she knew more than I did about many aspects of health, vitamins, USDA standards, cooking, natural foods, and disease prevention. I hardly noticed that several hours had passed while we were absorbed in conversation. It was dark out. When I paused for breath after a rather impassioned response to one of her answers about organic produce, Karen asked, hesitantly,

"So—when will you let me know if I got the job or not?"

"Oh, sorry! You had the job hours ago. I'm just enjoying the conversation."

She looked relieved as I smiled apologetically and extended my hand. "Welcome to the team."

Once Craig and Mark and their team joined the preparations for the new store, I began to realize that this merger had a value-added component—another big win—that I hadn't fully appreciated: the people. Indeed, it became clear that the "who" might end up being much more important than the "what." Craig and Mark brought so much talent and experience to the table.

I soon learned that Mark's people-centric approach to business didn't just apply to customers, it extended to team members as well. With a store so much bigger than either of our previous ones, we needed a lot of new people to staff it. Mark took over hiring and did a great job. I was curious about the secret of his success, so one day, not long before opening, I shadowed him as he went through a few interviews. A young man showed up at the store with an application, and Mark went over and introduced himself. They exchanged a few words out front, then Mark asked the guy to follow him around while they talked. Mark proceeded to walk briskly through the aisles, still under construction, turning and asking the young man questions, and pointing out where the various store departments would go.

After the candidate left, I approached Mark. "What did you think? He seemed enthusiastic."

"Yeah, nice guy," Mark replied, "but we aren't hiring him."

"What? Why not? He looked good. And we need more people."

"Nope. He couldn't even keep up with me, walking through the aisles. There is no way he is fit for this grocery store. You've got to be able to keep up the pace. That's a minimum requirement for this job." The "walk with me" interview format was his particular brand of test. If you couldn't keep up with Mark, you didn't belong at Whole Foods Market.

Craig too was an invaluable addition to our team. I already looked up to him as a kind of quintessential grocer—someone who knows every inch of his store, every detail of the business, and the name of every customer. But once we became partners, I saw that my initial impression, as positive as it was, didn't do him justice. He also had a work ethic that was remarkable. We all worked very hard in those days, but Craig took it to another level. He'd once told me he'd worked at Clarksville for 18 months without a day off, and now I believed him. His quality of work and attention to detail stood out, even among a team that truly cared about building a great store. And it wasn't just the hard work; it was the spirit in which he did it. It wasn't any sort of drudgery to him; he really seemed to be enjoying himself. I once heard him say that he was "born to work," and I saw evidence for that every day as we prepared to open. As the many night shifts and long hours took their toll on most of us, he seemed to thrive, exuding a buoyant positivity.

By the time construction was complete, we were running low on money. We simply weren't going to be able to meet payroll unless we opened right away. But we weren't ready. We didn't yet have our beer and wine license. (When I called the city, I got that death-by-red-tape answer: "This is just how it is.") We didn't have a butcher, so the meat department was empty. The list of unresolved issues was long, the most obvious being a significant lack of inventory. That's where the last-minute merger with Clarksville was a godsend. They brought inventory with them. But the new store was so big that even our combined inventory and everything we could find in the warehouse was still easily swallowed. With just a few days left before opening, the shelves felt half-empty. I paced the aisles, trying to think of a way to fill the gaps.

The solution we found was juice. Apple juice. It was a popular product in those days, and we were able to get a hell of a deal on a full tractor-trailer load of Knudsen apple juice at a good wholesale price. We would fill up the empty shelves with gallon jugs of apple juice! The truck pulled up outside the store one day, and the driver rolled down his window.

"Hey, man, where's your loading dock?"

Loading dock? We didn't have one. Nor did we have a pallet jack. All we had were a couple of dollies and a lot of people. So we got everyone out and made a long line, passing the cases of juice into the store. We featured it on every open shelf and sold it at a special opening week price of $0.99 per gallon. I think we lost some money on that apple juice, but it played a critical role. Customers felt like they were getting a really good deal, and it created a convincing illusion that the store was filled to the brim.

On the eve of the opening, there was so much left to do. The team stayed late, cleaning and stacking shelves, organizing the back room, and creating signage. Around 2 AM I had finally had enough. I called it a night, and Renee and I left to get a few hours of sleep before the morning preparations. Craig was still there when I left.

Around dawn, I showed up, sleepy and still exhausted but excited about the day ahead. The store was quiet. I walked through the produce section, marveling at all the tropical fruits, fresh sprouts, vibrant greens, and mushrooms with exotic names. I straightened a few bottles of vitamins and checked that we had enough change in the cash registers. The sun came up, its warm light filtering through the windows of the store, illuminating the crates of apples and oranges and bananas. Suddenly, I became aware of a subtle, consistent noise. What was that? It was coming from outside the store. As I made my way to the front door, I finally recognized the sound—*whistling*. And there, with a broom in his hand, was

Craig, whistling quietly as he swept the front steps. I was quite sure he hadn't gone home that night.

Craig and I would share quite an adventure in the years to come as we built a great natural foods company—most of it wonderful, some of it challenging. His contributions to Whole Foods Market are as numerous as they are significant. But among all the great memories I have of our time together, perhaps my favorite is that impression of him from the first morning of the first day of the first Whole Foods Market, whistling happily as he prepared for the first customer to walk up those freshly swept steps and through the door.

With just a few minutes to go before opening, I took a final walk through the store. I don't know where Renee was—probably putting the finishing touches on some signage or rearranging a display. But as I walked, I saw her everywhere, and my heart was filled with appreciation for her particular talents. Renee was many things, but one of her greatest gifts was that she was a consummate creator of beauty. Natural foods stores of the sixties and seventies had a reputation for being a bit, well, too natural. Slightly grungy, even dirty. Safer Way had been spotlessly clean, but there's only so much you can do to brighten up the small dark rooms of an old Victorian house. Renee and I wanted this new store to be different, and perhaps more important, to feel different to our customers. That didn't mean we wanted it to feel like a conventional grocery store—which in the seventies had an air of sterile, institutional, functional cleanliness, kind of like a hospital. We wanted our store to be warm, colorful, showcasing the beauty of the foods we sold. In our minds, natural food and healthy eating were beautiful and our stores should highlight that truth. There was only one problem—while I consider myself to be a lover of beauty in many forms, I'm not so good at creating it. Thankfully, Renee was. She had that knack for placing beautiful elements throughout the store—engaging signage, artful displays, thoughtful touches. As I made my final tour of the first Whole Foods Market that morning, I appreciated every detail, soaking up that signature aesthetic quality that would come to define the experience of shopping our stores. To this day, when I talk to people about why they like Whole Foods, I almost always get some version of "I just feel good when I'm in the stores." For me, that feeling always reminds me of Renee.

On September 20, 1980, at 9 AM, we opened. And somehow, by some miracle, the gods of business smiled. Or that's how it felt. The store filled up. There were more customers than we expected. In fact, there were many, many more than could be explained by the combined total of Safer Way's and Clarksville's customer bases. We couldn't believe how crowded the store was! Apparently, there had been a buzz about this large natural foods supermarket taking over the old nightclub on Lamar, a busy Austin thoroughfare. We hadn't done any advertising, but the word got out anyway. And customers seemed to love it. I did, however, overhear one person exclaim, "This is a great store. But I've never seen so much apple juice in all my life!"

In retail, profit margins can often be quite thin, and it had taken Safer Way more than a year to stop losing money. But when people would ask me, "How long did it take until Whole Foods Market first became profitable?" I would answer, only half-joking: until about two o'clock in the afternoon on the first day.

Our sales far exceeded expectations. And they never slowed down. We quickly sold all that apple juice and just about everything else in the store as well. Whole Foods Market was an instant success. Within about six months, we became the highest volume natural foods store in the US, doing over $200,000 per week. It was the right place, the right timing, and the right type of store. Customers were ready for a one-stop natural foods supermarket. Austin was a great city for it. And the location, as I had hoped, was perfect. The *Austin American-Statesman* called us "the Cadillac of natural foods stores." And while I'm not sure I ever saw a Caddy in our parking lot, there were plenty of luxury cars parked right alongside the Volkswagens and mopeds that our friends drove—a testament to the breadth of the customer base we were attracting. Before our first year was up, we were already actively envisioning a second store—this time, even bigger. I wanted a 20,000-square-foot natural foods supermarket that could better compete with the big boys.

Everything came together, and suddenly—unexpectedly—we were riding a wonderful wave of growth. For the first time in my short entrepreneurial career, I tasted real success. I found the experience completely exhilarating. It seemed like nothing could stop us—nothing, that is, short of an act of God.

Chapter 6

The Hundred-Year Flood

A rainy spring in Austin is nothing out of the ordinary. But as Memorial Day weekend approached in 1981, the thunderstorms were particularly intense, and the creeks were swollen. Whole Foods Market had been open about nine months and was still going strong. Sunday was my day off from working at the store, but Renee was covering the closing shift, so I'd gone over to David and Karen's home for dinner. We were playing cards when the phone rang. It was Renee.

"Hey, John," she said, "the creek's rising pretty fast. Should we be worried?"

My mind flashed back to the summer before, when we'd been building out the store. We'd developed a close relationship with Bill, our builder. We liked him, and for whatever reason, the feeling was mutual. After the work was done for the day, we'd often linger at the site with some beers, and he'd regale us with stories about his life, the military, his marriage, and his children. It was during one of these conversations, on a hot summer night, early in the construction process, that he happened to mention the fact that our store was built in a hundred-year flood zone.

"What does that actually mean?" I asked him, taking a swig of my beer and looking around the construction site.

"It means that every once in a while, Shoal Creek just overflows its banks, and that water comes right down Lamar Boulevard and it all fills it up. I think last time it happened was before I was born, but it could happen again—about once every hundred years."

Once in a hundred years? I'd take those odds. And I told him so.

"Well, John," he said in his thick Texas drawl, "I think just to be on the safe side, let's put down a two-foot concrete slab, and we'll build the store two feet higher. How's that sound? Then, if the creek gets high, it'll have to get over that slab."

So that's what he did. And I didn't think much about it again, at least not until that rainy Memorial Day Weekend in 1981, when I received that call from Renee.

"I'm sure it will be okay," I told her. "This is why we built the extra slab."

I went back to my game, but it wasn't long before the phone rang again. This time I could hear the note of fear in Renee's voice although she was trying to be upbeat.

"The creek burst its banks. The street is full of water and it's getting close to the top of the slab. What should I do?"

I didn't know what to say. I couldn't believe this. A hundred-year flood? In our first year?!

How do people keep out floodwaters? Sandbags. In my mind's eye, I saw our bulk-foods department, full of sacks of flours, grains, and beans. It was the closest thing we had to sandbags, so I told Renee to get the team to carry those sacks up front and pile them against the door.

Twenty minutes later, the phone rang again. Now the panic in Renee's voice was loud and clear. The waters were still rising, and they were starting to leak through the bulk-food sack barricade.

"Hold on," I told her. "We're coming over. Call Craig and Mark and everyone else and tell them to come too." David, Karen, and I ran out into the torrential rain, jumped in our cars, and raced to the store. The streets were dark—the power was out in many neighborhoods. The noise of the creek was overwhelming. We couldn't drive to the store—there was just too much water flowing down Lamar, so we parked up the hill and walked. As we approached the store, the first thing I saw was Renee, standing outside the darkened store, dripping wet and shaking.

It turns out that stacking the bulk-food bags was a good strategy—to a point. It worked until the weight of the water was so great that it just broke through the windows like a tidal wave, deluging the store, knocking over produce cases and shelving. Renee and Jeff Martin, one of the brothers who operated a café in the store, had been trapped in the back office. They climbed the shelving and Jeff popped out a ceiling tile so they could climb over the wall and swim out of the store. She was still in shock when we arrived. We held each other, speechless, as the rain poured down around us, staring at our ravaged store.

Suddenly, a thought penetrated my state of drenched disbelief. *The money!*

In those days, all our sales were in cash or checks. We didn't take credit cards, and few people used them anyway. Most days, Mark would take the cash to the bank at the close of business, but on Saturdays and Sundays we'd stash all of it in our little floor safe in the back office.

Breaking away from Renee, I scrambled over the sodden sacks of beans and grains and sloshed and waded my way back through the store. Canned goods and bananas bobbed past me. The murky water was slick with oil from broken bottles that had fallen with the shelves, and the strange musk of sodden herbs and spices mingled with the sharp tang of spilled wine.

Thankfully, there was less water in the back, but there was no getting the safe open. We just had to pray it was still dry. But the cash from the day's sales was in a locked file cabinet. Karen appeared with several three-pound cans of protein powder, which she proceeded to dump into the floodwaters, and we filled the cans with change. Grabbing a brown paper bag from the shelf, I began throwing bundles of bills inside. Holding the bag up high so it wouldn't get wet, I started sloshing my way back to the front of the store. As I neared the front door, the shape of a man appeared out of the darkness.

"Hey, buddy," he said, in a conspiratorial whisper. I didn't recognize his voice. "Did you find anything in the back room?"

A looter! And there I was, holding about $100,000 in a brown grocery bag in my arms.

“You know, man, I think it’s just a bunch of dirty food,” I said, trying to sound nonchalant. “But you should go check for yourself.”

He looked at me, expressionless in the dark, nodded, and moved on. I clutched the bag a little closer to my chest. It might be all that was left of our dream.

PART II

SHELF LIFE

The Whole Foods Market team, after devastating floods almost destroyed the store, May 1981. I think Craig Weller was the only person over the age of 30

With Craig Weller (center) and Mark Skiles (right), cofounders of Whole Foods Market

The Whole Foods Market Board, 1987, left to right: Anthony Harnett, Jack Bixby, John Mackey, Bill Mackey, Jim Sud, Jay Templeton, Craig Weller

Chapter 7

After the Flood

A hundred-year flood? In our first year? I could still hardly believe it, though I'd witnessed it with my own eyes. Could our dream have drowned so quickly? As the first light of dawn began to creep across the sky, I leaned back against the front wall of the store and closed my eyes, letting my exhaustion take hold. Maybe if I allowed myself to sleep for a moment, I would wake up and discover that it had all just been a nightmare. Maybe I'd dreamed the raging, stinking waters and the deluged store. But then I felt a hand on my arm and opened my eyes to see Renee's mud-streaked face, framed by still-damp hair.

"Hey," she said, "the early-shift folks are about to arrive for work. We should go talk to them."

I sat up and looked around. A dozen or so people were sitting on the steps—Mark and Craig, David and Karen, a few more of our close friends and team members—looking pretty much how I felt. Dirty, damp, despairing. And a bit hung over. The collection of empty beer and wine bottles told the story of how we'd gotten through the last few hours, after salvaging what we could from the ruined store. It looked like the aftermath of a great party, but this had been more like a funeral. The adrenaline had receded from our systems as the waters had receded from the street in front of us, and we'd sunk into a morose silence as we sat there drinking and looking out over the darkened city. Now, the daylight began to reveal the devastation that remained: piles of mud and silt, vehicles wedged against buildings, trash strewn through front yards and parking lots and caught in fences. Cars were literally wrapped around metal pipes that crossed the creek, flung there by the waters as they hurtled through. It was the worst flood that Austin had seen in seven decades. Later, I would learn that 13 people had died (one body was found in a tree), and damage was widespread throughout the city, amounting to tens of millions of dollars lost for businesses and families.

Team members began arriving for their shift, shocked at the scene that greeted them. Several people burst into tears. Whole Foods Market wasn't just a workplace for them—they loved the store almost as much as we did. Jerry, the bread vendor, arrived with our delivery. We looked at each other helplessly. Where were we supposed to put bread? There wasn't a dry place in the store, and we weren't going to be open for business again anytime soon. We had to turn him away. Together, we trooped inside to survey the damage.

It was bad. At the height of the storm, the store had been eight feet underwater. Everything inside was destroyed or rendered useless. All our equipment and inventory would need to be replaced. We estimated that the inventory alone was worth about $400,000, and virtually all of it was financed by our suppliers. We milled around in the front of the store, not sure quite what to do or where to begin, until eventually someone brought a few chairs and most of us sat down again, looking at each other in stunned disbelief. No one mentioned the word "insurance," and I didn't have a copy of our policy on hand, but I was more or less certain that it did not contain the word "flood."

As I stared at the soggy remains of Whole Foods Market, I felt much older than my 27 years. I wondered what it all meant about the future—and about my future. It wasn't immediately clear that we could recover from this. Maybe God or the Universe had passed judgment upon this particular dream. Maybe John Mackey wasn't meant to be a grocer after all? At the very least, I thought wryly, that would please my mother. But then I thought about my father, who had been so supportive, investing his time and his money in the business. How would he feel if we failed? I didn't want to let him down, or our other investors.

I thought about my partners—Renee, Craig, and Mark. I thought about all our wonderful, quirky, passionate team members. I had loved every moment of building the business with all of them. I'd really felt as if this was what I was here to do. But maybe not? Maybe this adventure had run its course? Maybe it was time to pursue other passions? Idly, I imagined Renee and myself hitting the road and hitchhiking around Europe. We didn't have to think of the store as a failure. After all, we had all done our very best to make it a success, and it had been—temporarily. Not everything was in our control. Sometimes things just don't work out.

"Oh man, this shit stinks." Mark's exclamation broke into my reverie.

He was right—and not just metaphorically. There was a pungent odor in the air. It was summer in Central Texas, after all, and temperatures would be close to 100 degrees later that day. Inside the store, the contents of the broken jars and bottles, now exposed to the quickly warming air, were beginning to smell bad. Really bad. Everything in the refrigerators and freezers was getting warm, and many of them had fallen over, spilling their contents into the floodwaters. The entire meat cooler had overturned, and we couldn't get it open. Part of me was glad not to confront its disgusting contents, but I knew that the longer we left it, the worse it would be. And no small part of the smell was due to the fact that the sewers had overflowed and mixed with the floodwaters. Later, every person who had waded through the store would need a tetanus shot.

We couldn't just sit there in the foul-smelling store forever, so we got to work. We filled grocery carts with everything we could grab and wheeled it all outside to the dumpster, which was soon full to the brim. There seemed to be oranges everywhere—I guess they were particularly buoyant, and their waterborne migration had taken them to every corner of the store. The noxious soup I'd waded through last night had turned to a thick sludge, slick with oil and treacherous with broken glass. At first, we'd hoped some of the unbroken packaged goods might be salvageable, but the City of Austin would soon make it clear that nothing that had been touched by the floodwaters could be washed and resold, no matter how well it was sealed. Basically, the entire contents of the store were a loss.

Once we'd pulled out enough of the mess that we could see the floor,

I grabbed a bucket and started mopping. I noticed another guy doing the same thing—but weirdly, I didn't recognize him. We had several dozen team members in those days, and I thought I at least knew everyone's faces, even if I occasionally forgot a few names. I wiped my bleary eyes. Was it just the lack of sleep that was making this guy look like a stranger to me in the unlit store? I went over and introduced myself.

"I'm sorry, I don't remember your name. I'm John."

"I'm Larry. I live just down the street. I'm off work today for the holiday, so I thought I'd come by and help clean up. That's what neighbors do for each other."

I was taken aback. "Are you a customer?"

He broke into a big smile. "Are you kidding? I love this store. I shop here all the time. I want to make sure you guys come through this. I'd hate to lose you."

My spirits were immediately lifted. This guy was giving up his Memorial Day to sweep sludge off our floors! I thanked Larry and went back to mopping with a renewed vigor.

Reaching the end of my aisle, I turned to see Craig's tall, angular figure, mopping with the same singular focus and dedication he brought to every task. He'd already cleared several more aisles than me. I went over and told him about Larry.

Craig nodded. "Yes, I saw him. And he's not the only one. There are several locals who have joined the cleanup crew. It's amazing! And we sure can use the help!"

As the day wore on, more and more volunteers showed up. They came, uninvited and unpaid, for no reason other than that they loved the store and didn't want to see it fail. Despite the fact that I'd been awake for almost two full days and nights, I felt buoyed by this incredible team spirit. Heck, maybe we *could* recover. Maybe Whole Foods Market *did* have a future beyond this flood. People cared about us. People wanted us to succeed.

The outpouring of support continued in the days that followed. Before the flood, I'd liked to think that Whole Foods Market was more than just a grocery store; now I had no doubt. Our customers didn't just come in to shop twice a month when they needed groceries; they liked to drop in several times a week, knowing they'd run into someone they knew in the checkout line, chat with the guy who ran the produce department, or stop to ask Karen's expert opinion about a particular supplement. We were a hub of their community, and they showed up to help us because they didn't want to lose all of that. I started to feel like we had no choice but to survive—just to reward these incredible customers! Although it would be some years before I'd have the words for it, I was getting my first taste of the power of having not just shareholders but *stakeholders*—people who feel like they have a stake in your company, whether it be financial, practical, or emotional, and to whom you feel accountable.

Surviving, however, was going to take more than volunteers. It was going to take a lot more money. We still had a great business, with loyal customers, but without insurance, there was no capital to get us back on our feet. Our cash reserves pretty much amounted to what we'd pulled out of the filing cabinet that terrible night, and what we'd retrieved from the safe the next day. Our old Prana House friend Karl Martin, who, along with his brother Jeff, operated the Martin Brothers Café, hid this cash behind the washing machine at the co-op, where he still lived. That turned out to not only be a safe place but a fitting one, since that money was filthy. We were so broke that we took all the small change from the tills and deposited it in our bank account to help cover expenses—after washing it to get rid of the floodwater stench.

We're literally laundering money, I thought. Unfortunately, no amount of laundering would make some of the smudged, dampened checks acceptable to the bank, so we had to track down the customers and get them to write new ones. Our team members weren't asking about payroll yet, but we knew they couldn't work for nothing for too long.

That first morning, it fell to me to break the news of the disaster to our Board members. The thought of calling my father was too painful. He would read about the flood soon enough in the paper and call. In the meantime, I started with Jim Sud, who also lived in Houston. His wife, Lecia, picked up, and told me Jim was out for a run, so I asked if he could call me back. And then I waited, happy to postpone the hard conversation a little longer. Putting my feet up on the desk, I leaned back and closed my eyes. At first, my consciousness was filled with scenes and sounds from the night before—cars floating by on the street, the roaring of the creek, mud and tears on Renee's face. Oranges swam before my eyes. But then it all began to blur together, and I let myself sink, gratefully, into sleep. It felt like hours, but it must have been about 20 minutes later when I was awakened by the shrill ring of the phone.

"Good morning, John." Jim sounded a bit out of breath but cheerful. Clearly, he hadn't yet read the paper or turned on the news.

Tired and raw from everything that had just happened, I didn't have any small talk in me. I just came right out with it.

"Jim, the store is gone."

"Gone? What do you mean, gone?"

Jim listened to my description of the night's events until I ran out of words. Then he said, "Listen, John, I'm really sorry. But we can get through this. I'm sure our insurance will cover it. We can rebuild. It will work out."

I was silent for a moment, and then quietly, I told him. "Jim, we don't have flood insurance."

Now it was his turn to be silent. I explained the situation—the flood zone, the extra slab, the prohibitive cost of coverage. Jim was clearly taken aback, but he's one of those people who is steady in a crisis. And he was more than just an investor and board member—he was a good personal friend. He knew that the last thing I needed that moment was someone telling me I'd screwed up. Instead, we talked about options for raising money. He encouraged me to try asking the bank for a loan—after all, the business had a track record of great success, even if it had been brief. When I hung up the phone, I felt a little more hopeful—and a little more ready to talk to my father.

The flood was big news in Texas and even got national attention. Every day, as we worked to clean up the store, newspaper reporters and television crews would come by looking for flood stories. I guess we made a good headline, and our team members were photogenic. I even did a few interviews. The media attention was extensive enough that when I called up one of our suppliers to explain our situation and ask if he could front us some inventory, he already knew all about our predicament.

"John, I'm sorry this happened to y'all, and I'm going to let you have the new inventory," he said. "I'll give you a suggestion too, son. Maybe next time you do an interview, you could mention your suppliers and the fact that we're helping you out. Oh, and maybe you could at least put a shirt on, you know, for the camera."

The media coverage helped. We had products to put on the shelves. But we still needed cash. Remembering Jim's advice about asking for a loan, I put on not just a shirt but a tie as well and went down to our bank, City National. Nervously, I explained the situation to Mark Monroe, the local banker who had worked with Safer Way. To my surprise, he was receptive and friendly, and after a couple of meetings he told me the bank had agreed to a $100,000 loan. I was thrilled. I could hardly believe they'd asked for nothing more than my signature, based only on our brief track record of success. What a helpful bank!

Years later, when the loan was long paid off, I'd learn quite by chance that there was a reason the application process had been so easy. A stranger approached me at a conference and shook my hand. "John, you won't remember me, but I used to work for City National Bank. That was quite a thing that Mark Monroe did for you, after that big flood."

"Yes, it sure was," I replied enthusiastically. "He was a great guy, and a great banker. I have to say that I was a little surprised they approved that loan for us. But it made an enormous difference."

He looked puzzled. "Oh, you don't know what happened?"

"I guess not," I said, confused.

"The bank didn't approve that loan," he went on. "The bank turned it down. Mark Monroe personally guaranteed that loan for you. That's the only reason you got the money."

I was stunned. Mark had never said a word. I asked the man why he would have done such a thing.

"I remember that he said, 'I know John Mackey has integrity and will pay this back no matter what it takes.' So he just did it. I guess he liked you."

I immediately inquired as to where Mark was living, so I could reach out and express my gratitude. But the man shook his head. "Sorry, but it's too late to thank him. Mark died a few years ago."

So many acts of generosity and good faith have helped Whole Foods Market survive and grow over the years. But amid the pantheon of contributors to our success, I reserve a special place for Mark Monroe, an unsung guardian angel who quietly tipped the scales in our favor and helped us get through what was perhaps our darkest moment. Without that loan, we might have had to call it quits, no matter how much goodwill and hard work our team members and customers brought to the cleanup process.

Between the loan money, the cash we had rescued, some extra capital that our investors kicked in, and several hundred thousand dollars of fronted inventory from our suppliers, I started to feel like we might make it after all. Whole Foods Market was going to rise from the sludge, like a soggy phoenix! My overwhelming experience, however, wasn't one of triumph over difficult odds; it was a new sense of humility.

Death had brushed up against us. It had been a close call. We had enjoyed so much success and grown so quickly since opening the new store, and I could see in hindsight how that had led to a certain arrogance. It's so easy to get cocky, and the flood was a heck of a slap down. Whole Foods Market would not have survived had it not been for so many people who loved the business and believed in us—from our customers to our suppliers to our banker to our investors to our team members. A local band even did a fundraiser to help us get back on our feet. Our success, I now realized, depended on much more than the vision and hard work of our small team. It depended on the entire community around us. That's what makes a business successful and resilient over the long term, and it should never be taken for granted.

Only four weeks after the flood, we reopened. It was truly wonderful to be back in business. The store was not just restored; it was improved. We took advantage of the rebuilding to fix some flaws in the original design. Quickly, we picked up where we'd left off and continued along our amazing growth trajectory. Still, there was a new sense of urgency among the partners, and not just about the success of this one store. We began discussions about expansion. We didn't want to have all of our eggs in one basket, especially given that we had just watched all of our eggs *and* baskets float away down the river! When the next "hundred-year flood" came in a few years, we wanted to be more diversified. Clearly, the potential in the business was remarkable, and we were determined that it would be built to last.

Chapter 8

All Work and All Play

With the flood in our rearview mirror and plans for a second store already taking shape in our near future, Whole Foods Market barreled toward its first anniversary, although we were all too busy to stop and celebrate. We were still a relatively small team, and every one of us worked hard to keep up with customer demand. Initially, that meant each person basically did everything—we just showed up to work and plugged whatever hole needed plugging. If cheese needed to be cut, someone scrambled to the cheese counter. If produce needed to be stacked, someone stacked produce. If the store was busy and we needed more people on the registers, people would drop other tasks and go check out customers. Everyone pitched in and moved around in response to the daily and hourly demands of the store—like a living system. That's the way most small retail stores operate. It was dynamic, ever changing, sometimes chaotic, but always fun.

Some days, I'd look up from the boxes I was unloading and catch Renee's eye as she served a line of customers, and we'd break into smiles of disbelief that our little dream had turned into this. I'd think back to that day at Prana House when she'd said, "Let's do it, Macko Man!" We'd done it—and then some! Other times I'd run into Mark in the aisles, always moving at high speed, or stop to watch David carefully stacking produce, or notice Craig hard at work building something in the back room, or listen in as Karen patiently answered customers' questions at the information desk. I'd see in their faces the same pride that I felt in the store we'd created together. We worked incredibly hard, but it didn't feel like work. It was more like play—a deeply satisfying and purposeful form of play. And yet, we were actually getting paid to do it!

Now that the store was back up and running, and sales were very strong, we began taking more of a salary. I remember how it felt when my paycheck reached $800 a month. I'd never imagined such riches! I bought myself an actual motorcycle to replace my hair-dryer moped. It was time for something with a little more power. I loved that bike, although it always scared me a bit when I rode it fast. I'd never been someone who dreamed of getting rich, but the feeling of financial success was intoxicating—not just for me personally but for the company. Our investors were going to be well rewarded. My father would be so proud. Our business was working. In fact, it was working very well. And it was so much fun!

The Whole Foods team members were an eclectic bunch—artists, lawyers, musicians, geologists, college dropouts, Vietnam War veterans, grad students, and more. And they all felt like family. Many of them were overqualified for the job, but they didn't seem to mind. I doubt many other grocery stores had so many advanced degrees on their payroll. Our team members seemed to appreciate how rare it was to have a steady job where no one cared how long your hair was or what you wore (at least to a point). Dress code was one of those things we tried to be relaxed about, but of course there were a few rules, even at the very beginning. Shirts were mandatory—you could choose whatever shirt you liked but you had to wear one. We also wanted people to wear aprons so that customers could tell who the team members were. Besides that, we pretty much let people be themselves, whether that meant rainbow hair or full punk makeup. The sense of being a bit "edgy" was part of our appeal. The closest we ever got to a uniform (besides the aprons) was one summer when all the management team took to wearing macramé headbands with healing gemstones attached, in an attempt to stimulate our third eyes.

Little by little, our small leadership team began to specialize, focusing on our natural strengths. Renee had an unquestionable flair for store design. Craig took over the master schedule, a logistical challenge to which he was well suited. Mark continued to oversee hiring and training. He cared deeply about the interface between team members and customers, and he and Craig deserve a great deal of credit for instilling a service ethic in Whole Foods Market from the very beginning, just as they'd done at Clarksville.

There were some features of the Clarksville store that we didn't import to Whole Foods Market. One was their very lenient customer credit system. It was like something from a general store in a 19th-century Western frontier town, complete with some bad debts that would never be paid. Luckily, Craig felt more strongly than I did that this had no place in our new store. When the subject came up in an early store leader meeting, he announced an end to it, declaring, "This is the perfect time to stop that nonsense." Mark and I wholeheartedly agreed.

At Whole Foods Market, Mark no longer acted as DJ for our customers, but he still liked to crank up the music for the team members on the early shift, until Craig turned down the volume for opening. Austin has always had a thriving music scene, and many of our team members played in local bands. At the end of the day, they'd throw their personal cassette tapes in the sound system and everyone would dance in the aisles as we cleaned up for the night.

I began to specialize too. As much as I liked working in the store, I wasn't really a grocer the same way Craig was. To be honest, I was happy to leave the details of the day-to-day operations to others, and I didn't feel the need to look over their shoulders. We hired good people and I trusted them to do their jobs. What I loved was the creative aspect of the business—thinking through how we might grow, what new product offerings might excite our customers, or how I could energize our team members. As Craig observed once, "John, you're really good at thinking about the future; I'm good at taking care of the present."

I also liked to be out and about, rather than spending every day in the store. I was happy to focus a good deal of my time on our wholesale company, Texas Health Distributors (THD), working with suppliers to get better prices and more products and looking for more customers. We let go of our mouse-infested 5,000-square-foot warehouse and rented a "giant" 35,000-square-foot warehouse to replace it.

I also spent time thinking about expansion and scouting potential new store sites. I could look at an old warehouse or even an empty lot and envision a big, spacious natural foods supermarket, with customers flowing in and out, carts piled high. And those visions all had one thing in common: the new store was even bigger than the first. The 10,500-square-foot Lamar site had seemed enormous in comparison with Safer Way, Clarksville, and the little hole-in-the-wall natural foods stores of the previous era. But the first Whole Foods Market was quickly beginning to feel too small.

Another thing that didn't fit so well as we grew was our free-form approach to roles. Pretty soon, it was clear that the "everyone does everything" method was reaching its natural limit. It was just too hard to manage. One evening, after closing, we finally sat down to discuss it. There must be a better way. Someone suggested that we divide into teams. That sounded like a good option, so we made a list of departments: produce, meat and seafood, grocery, cheese, front end, information, and so on. But when it came time to assign team members, I hesitated. Wouldn't people get bored doing the same thing every day? I knew I would. And would we run into the problem of people being overspecialized and only knowing how to work in one part of the store, so we couldn't be flexible when needed? In the end, we came up with a compromise. We'd have teams, but people would be able to change teams frequently.

This seemed to work better. But another problem quickly arose. We needed more sustained expertise in the various departments. The only way to accomplish that was to have at least one person stay permanently in each respective team. To solve this, we assigned "Team Leaders." These folks would naturally develop more of an expertise in their area of the store, ensuring that the quality of our service and offerings stayed high.

That worked even better! And as we saw that certain people had a natural feel for one area or another, we'd encourage them to stay there. We were proud of our "breakthrough," feeling like we'd discovered an important retail secret. Someone suggested we should write about it—maybe such hard-won wisdom deserved a book? Other businesses would want to know about this novel and creative management method.

Thankfully, we didn't write a book declaring that, in effect, a bunch of granola-selling hippies had rediscovered the power of one of the most fundamental concepts in economics—division of labor and specialization. If we had, we might have found out that our breakthrough had, in fact, been part of human civilization for millennia and a well-established business practice for many, many centuries. But sometimes, in life and business, one has to independently reinvent the wheel to fully appreciate its significance!

Our leadership team continued to feel like a tight fellowship. We'd hold meetings at our various homes, sitting around on the floor, taking breaks to play volleyball in the yard. Our meetings usually began with a meditation or a minute of quiet, and they always ended with what we came to call "appreciations," where we'd go around and share things we appreciated about each person. This might have been inspired by something I'd read—maybe Ken Blanchard's book *The One Minute Manager,* with its simple but brilliant advice to "catch people doing something right." It might have been one of the many Japanese management books that I read. This was the early 1980s, when Japan was close to its peak of worldwide economic success and influence. To this day, appreciations are a pillar of my approach to every relationship, whether in business or in my personal life, and I continue to be amazed at their power to open peoples' hearts and raise morale.

Those early meetings weren't all love and light. We had intense, sometimes heated debates. We all cared deeply about Whole Foods Market—it was much more than a job to every one of us. We showed up at work every day to create the kind of world we wanted to be living in. Mostly, we agreed on what that world should look like, but not always. Whether we were appreciating or arguing, however, we did it with passion. To this day, when I talk to my partners from that era, they'll tell me those were some of the best days of their lives.

Keeping the shelves stocked was a challenge, especially in those early days when natural foods producers tended to be fairly small companies. Sometimes we'd fill a whole shelf with one product to make up for the gaps left by items that were out of stock. Five-gallon jugs of spring water were particularly useful space fillers.

We tried to get organic produce as much as possible, but it was hard back in those days. There were very few certification organizations to ensure that what you were getting was truly organic, and those that existed were not often used. We sought out farmers we could trust, visiting their farms ourselves so that we could give our customers confidence in what they were buying. Prices were high, but we encouraged customers to keep choosing organic so that more farmers would see that it was a worthwhile business and eventually it would become more affordable.

Not long after we opened, we started to get locals coming to our store to ask if we'd sell their homemade products—things like tofu, yogurt, honey, granola, or baked goods. We welcomed them, giving them shelf space they couldn't get at the larger supermarket chains, and many of their products became customer favorites and went on to become very successful brands. Soon, I began to realize that we were more than just a natural foods store; we were a platform for an entire ecosystem of new products and businesses. And featuring them in our store benefited us, our customers, the producers, and the growing influence of the entire natural foods movement. It was a mutually beneficial growth cycle.

At least, most of the time it was. One popular local supplier was a woman named Barbara who baked muffins and cookies and bread. Each item was carefully wrapped in Saran wrap and hand labeled. Customers would wait in line on Tuesdays and Thursdays when her deliveries came. We felt like she was the best-kept secret in Austin. Then, one day, Mary, a new team member who'd previously worked in hotel food service, took a bite of one of Barbara's blueberry muffins.

"This is a Sara Lee muffin!" she declared.

"Oh no," said the folks in the bakery department. "Barbara baked these herself."

Mary was unconvinced and went out and bought a box of Sara Lee muffins. We all gathered round for a taste test, and she was right: they were identical. The next day, we paid an unannounced visit to Barbara's bakery, where, sure enough, we found a pile of empty Sara Lee boxes. We still had a lot to learn about vetting our vendors. Luckily, Barbara's fraud was busted pretty early and didn't reflect too poorly on the natural foods industry. I'd read about far worse examples of fraud, which made me shudder. Natural foods were still fighting to be taken seriously, and these incidents fed into people's preconceptions that it was all just a scam. Thankfully, we knew many of our suppliers personally and trusted their integrity. When we took on a new one, I often went out of my way to visit their facilities and ensure that we were only offering the highest quality products to our customers.

Like many of my early "fellowship" comrades, I look back on those days as some of the happiest of my life. I was in love with our store. Many nights, after the store was closed, the sound system shut off, and our team members had headed home to bed, I'd linger. Walking through the darkened aisles, I'd smile at what we'd created—like a doting father who likes to sit and watch his child sleeping. And I couldn't wait for our baby to wake up the next morning and bring joy to so many people all over again.

There was a palpable sense that we were doing something new, something important, something that could help change the world for the better. Our personal lives and our work lives blended together into one stream of work-play, tumbling from day to day as we learned on the job, tried new things, celebrated our wins, and took our mistakes as learning opportunities. The folks building Whole Foods Market weren't just my colleagues—they were among my best friends. I could spend all day working alongside David, and then head over to his place to have dinner with him and Karen. Mark and I could engage in a friendly competition to see who could stock the shelves faster, and then head to the tennis courts after work to compete some more. And of course, there was Renee. Her sunny energy made me smile every time our paths crossed at work. At the end of each long day, we'd collapse into bed, and each morning we'd wake up ready to do it all over again. What more could I want?

And yet, late in the summer of 1981, a nagging feeling crept up on me. I loved Renee. I loved our life. I loved the business we'd created together. But was this forever? I had just turned 28 years old. Were there other things—other relationships—that I still needed to experience?

"I was just thinking . . ."

I hesitated, wondering how Renee would take the proposal I was about to make. We were sitting at our kitchen table, having just arrived home from the store. "Maybe . . . we should try seeing other people?"

The surprised and hurt expression on her face made me regret my words almost immediately. It wasn't like there was anyone else I wanted to date at that moment. After being with Renee for over four years, I just felt like I wanted the possibility. But as Renee's eyes filled with tears, I realized I hadn't really thought this conversation through. The last thing I'd intended to do was hurt her. I grabbed her hands in mine.

"I don't want to break up," I assured her. "I love you so much. It's just—well, we've been together a long time. And we're both still young. I thought maybe it would be good for us to have some other experiences."

She cried some more. I told her again that this didn't mean I loved her any less. She still wasn't very keen on the idea, but eventually, she agreed to give it a try. Things remained tense, however, and I wasn't sure this was really going to work.

A few days later, dating was suddenly the furthest thing from my mind. I was riding my motorcycle through an intersection when a car turned, right in front of me, without warning. I was going to hit it, head on! There was nothing to do but brake hard, and the next thing I knew I was flying over the handlebars, in an awful kind of slow motion. Weirdly, my mind was very clear, and something came to me that I'd learned in practicing aikido. *You need to relax. You need to flow with this.* And I did—landing quite softly in the street and sliding. I might even have walked away mostly unscathed, if it hadn't been for the bike, which clearly hadn't been practicing aikido and fell on my ankle very heavily indeed. The car that had caused the accident just drove away.

With a broken ankle in a cast, I hobbled around on crutches, wishing things weren't so tense between Renee and me. I should never have mentioned the idea of seeing other people. I just hoped we could get back to the way we were. In the meantime, I did my best to keep working. My bike was in the shop, so I got out my old moped, strapped my crutches across the handlebars, and rode over to the store and the warehouse. Looking back, it doesn't seem like such a great idea, but I had no other way to get around. There was no Uber back in 1981, and taxis were expensive and difficult to find.

One night, I was working late at the warehouse on my own. Riding all the way across town in the dark at 25 miles per hour didn't sound like fun. I called Renee and told her I was going to crash on the cot for the night. "Okay," she said, "I'll see you at the store tomorrow."

I settled down with a blanket and a book, but I couldn't get comfortable. My ankle ached. The cot was narrow and hard. I was all too aware that East Austin wasn't a safe neighborhood, and every noise outside put me on edge. At one point, some drunk guy started banging on the door. I ignored him, and eventually he stumbled off down the street, but I knew I wasn't going to get any sleep. This had been a bad idea. I'd rather be at home, with Renee. I strapped my crutches onto the moped and puttered off across town. When I reached the duplex, I let myself in quietly and hopped down the hallway as lightly as I could, not wanting to wake

Renee. But when I opened the bedroom door, Renee wasn't asleep. And she wasn't alone.

"Well, this is kind of awkward," Renee said, sitting up abruptly and pulling the sheets over her.

I glared at the good-looking young man sitting beside her in our bed. "Who the hell are you?"

"You know David," Renee said quickly. "He works for the Martin Brothers." Oh yeah. That guy from the in-store café! He'd had a crush on her ever since the store had opened. Now I recognized him. I'd only ever seen him before with his clothes on.

Of course, this seeing-other-people thing had been my suggestion. But that didn't make it feel any better! Maybe it was because I was just young and foolish, but I hadn't expected Renee to act on it quite so quickly. She hadn't even liked the idea! But she sure seemed to have warmed up to it fast.

"What's he doing here?" I asked.

"What does it look like?" she retorted. "You're the one who said we should see other people."

"Well, yeah, but that was just a few days ago. We might have talked about it first!"

She looked a little embarrassed but didn't back down.

"I invited him to spend the night since you said you weren't going to be here," she said, glancing over at her companion, who looked ready to make a run for it. "So would you mind sleeping on the couch?"

Would I mind? I minded very much. This was our home, after all! But I wasn't sure what I could do about it. I couldn't exactly fight the guy, on my crutches. And besides, it *had* been my idea. Now it was looking like the worst idea I'd ever had!

As the days turned into weeks, Renee kept seeing David the café guy, and it was pretty obvious to me that she had fallen in love with him. And then one day she came and told me she wanted to quit Whole Foods.

"Quit? Why would you do that? I know we've been having some difficulties, but we can work them out. I was stupid. I love you, and Whole Foods is our baby. You shouldn't leave."

"Come on, Macko Man," she said softly. "Whole Foods is your trip. You're the one who really wanted to do this. It's been fun, and I'm proud of what we've built. But I'm tired of doing the same things, day after day. I want to do other things. I want to see the world."

I could hear it in her voice—that authentic longing for a new adventure. Renee had always been a free spirit—that was what had drawn me to her in the first place—and although she'd thrown herself into the creative challenge of the business, I knew it didn't satisfy her soul in quite the same way it did mine. She was restless.

Shortly after that conversation, Renee and David left Austin to go and live in Belize. I was heartbroken—and mad at myself. What kind of idiot tells the woman he loves to start seeing other people? Renee had been my best friend, my creative muse, my business partner, and my lover. Everywhere I looked in the store, I saw her touch. But now she was gone, and I had no one to blame but myself.

Chapter 9

To Grow or Not to Grow?

There may not be a quick cure for a broken heart, but a fast-growing business is a good distraction. As the reality set in that Renee was not coming back anytime soon, I threw myself into Whole Foods Market with even more fervor than usual. Top of my priority list was the search for a site for our second store. Surely our success could be replicated elsewhere. I just needed to find a good location and persuade yet another landlord to take a chance on us. I also needed to persuade my partners and the Board that this really was the right time for us to expand.

In Renee's absence, executive decisions were made collectively by Craig, Mark, and me. Admittedly, this made me a little apprehensive, because my partners' relationship with each other went back further than my relationship with either one. I worried that if it came to a disagreement, I'd find myself outvoted without Renee to back me up. I was technically the CEO, but I needed their buy-in for something as big as a new store. So I worked hard to convince them both that now was the time to expand. I made the eggs-and-baskets argument, especially resonant after the flood. I pointed to our explosive success as evidence of Austin's appetite for natural foods. And I talked about what was happening around the country—the stores I'd read about in *Natural Foods Merchandiser* and visited on my travels. Many of these were small chains with several stores within a city or region. This was the way the movement was growing, and if we didn't stake our claim in the Lone Star State, then someone else certainly would.

I didn't want to cede the market in which we had been first movers.

Now wasn't the time to sit back and simply enjoy our success; it was the time to press our advantage. After some discussion, our small executive team agreed to back my plan, and the Board agreed, provided we found a good site. My search for a location took on a new urgency.

I didn't know much about real estate back then, but what I could say with confidence, based on my very limited experience, was that we needed to be on a busy road in a convenient location. In other words, somewhere a lot of people would be driving by on their way to somewhere else. And the site needed to be significantly larger than the Lamar store.

One bright fall morning in 1981, I had a promising lead. I drove up to North Austin to check out a new shopping center that was being built at the intersection of Highway 183 and Burnet Road, known as Crossroads. Since recovering from my broken ankle, I'd gone out and bought a car—a used silver Mazda RX-7. The old Victorian houses of the neighborhoods I knew well slowly gave way to small homes in working-class neighborhoods and then bigger, newer family homes sitting on spacious lots. The streets widened, taking on a more suburban feel. I noted the new cars parked in driveways, kids playing on sweeping green lawns, the occasional glimpse of a sparkling pool behind a house. Would these people shop at a Whole Foods Market? They could certainly afford to—but would they want to? There weren't many hippies in North Austin in those days, and mainstream suburban America still hadn't really caught on to natural foods. But it was all changing fast. I'd noticed more customers in the store recently who looked like they'd come from the office or the country club—the kind of folks who probably lived in these homes.

The site, though still under construction, was impressive. It checked almost every box. It was about eight miles from the Lamar store and located on a busy road, with natural exposure to passing traffic. It was conveniently close to a fast-growing neighborhood. The store would be 18,767 square feet—almost double the size of our original store. While we knew we were perhaps a bit ahead of Austin's migration northward, I felt sure we could eventually win over these well-off suburban folks with the quality of our merchandise and the warm community atmosphere of our store. Jim Ross, the leasing agent, was about my age, and I liked him right away. We signed a lease and got to work on the second Whole Foods Market.

The more I thought about the new store, the more excited I felt. My mood was also lifted by a new relationship. The pain of breaking up with Renee was beginning to fade, and I had found a new lover, Cheryl. She worked for Whole Foods Market, which irked Craig, who frowned on relationships within the company. He was always lecturing Mark and me about this, like a stern older brother. But where else were we supposed to meet women? Whole Foods Market was where we spent all our time. Cheryl and I began to date, and soon we decided to live together.

Cheryl was Store Team Leader at the new Crossroads store and wanted to live closer to work, so we moved to one of those suburban-style North Austin neighborhoods, not far from the new store. The house was on a circular block called Trone Circle, but privately I called it Clone Circle. Every house looked exactly the same. I was used to the charm and character of Austin's historic homes and felt out of place in this cookie-cutter neighborhood. The upside was that I got to spend a lot of time at the new store, helping to design the space, using what we'd learned at Lamar to make this store bigger and better. More products. More beautiful signage and enticing displays. More checkouts to serve more customers. More of everything that had made our first store a grand success. And some new things too—like our first scratch German-style bakery created and operated by my friend George Ekrich, who had apprenticed as a baker in Germany. We hoped that when the Crossroads store opened that fall, it would all translate into more sales.

"C'mon, let's make it double or nothing." I set the Ping-Pong paddle down for a moment and stared challengingly at Mark across the table.

"Okay, John, but you're a glutton for punishment. Go ahead, serve."

Perhaps my competitive instincts were getting the best of me and setting me up for another painful defeat. But I had to try. My cofounder was very talented at Ping-Pong, which is why I liked to play with him. He presented a challenge, and I badly wanted to beat him. But he had crazy fast reflexes. Sometimes, I felt like I was a boy playing my father all over again, giving every bit of effort to try to eke out a victory, but over-matched, nonetheless.

I served, a bit too high and short and promptly watched him bury the ball in the back corner of the table beyond the reach of my paddle. *Damn it, John, focus!* I told myself. At least I needed to put up a good fight. And besides, I had another reason for prolonging the game: it would help to postpone the uncomfortable conversation that I was pretty sure would follow.

Mark had come over, I suspected, because he wanted to talk about the business. In recent executive meetings, I'd sensed a new tension in his questions and concerns. And with good reason. The Crossroads store, which had opened a few months earlier in September 1982, was under-performing expectations, and everyone was a bit shaken by that. Unlike Lamar, it hadn't been an overnight success. It wasn't just that sales were lower than we had hoped for; it was losing money. As Craig commented wryly, we'd picked the site because 83,000 cars went through that intersection every day, but we hadn't realized that the key word was "through." And the people who lived in the nearby neighborhoods hadn't been so quick to embrace an alternative to the conventional supermarkets. They'd stop in for a few specialty items that they couldn't get elsewhere, but they weren't yet filling their carts like customers who embraced the natural foods lifestyle of central Austin. And worse, sales were down slightly at Lamar as well, which some of the team thought was due to the new store taking customers away from the original one. Had we picked a location that was too close? Were we just cannibalizing ourselves?

I still had faith in Crossroads and believed that we just needed to give it time. After all, nobody up there knew us yet. We hadn't built a reputation in this community. I was confident that once word got around about how great our products were, how beautiful our store was, how friendly our staff was, it would pick up. But I understood that the Board and my partners were concerned—Mark, in particular. In fact, I suspected it was causing Mark to doubt the wisdom of ever expanding at all beyond the first store.

I hoped this wouldn't interfere with our friendship and working relationship. I was never going to be satisfied to stay small, and even if this store didn't work out, I'd want to try others. If Mark and I were at odds about every expansion, it would be hard to get Craig to vote with me. Plus, I genuinely valued Mark's friendship. Craig was like an older, wiser brother, but Mark and I were the same age and had many shared interests. Besides our ongoing Ping-Pong rivalry, we played various other sports, and we'd even gone scuba diving together in the Caribbean a couple of times. We often went to dinner together after work.

That spirit of friendship was still alive when I grudgingly conceded defeat at the Ping-Pong table and we moved out to the porch with a couple of beers. I sensed that Mark, like me, was a bit reluctant to get to the real point of his visit, and he passed some time updating me on his always-colorful love life. Finally, he took a swig of his beer and came out with it.

"John, what are we going to do about Crossroads? I saw the most recent numbers. Ugly. I'm worried."

I launched into the response I'd been practicing in my head. "We need to be patient. We shouldn't overreact to this slow start. It's a new market for us and it's going to take some time. It's still a good location and it will come around."

Mark frowned. "Okay, but let's compare it to Lamar. It was profitable from day one. And it's still growing two years later. Can you believe that? It's a fucking gold mine! Why do you want to dilute that with new stores that may or may not be as successful, and that cost us money to build and operate? We could live happily off just the Lamar store for years and years. Heck, we could even expand that store."

His voice grew quiet as he took on a more persuasive tone. "Look, John, we've done it. We've made it. We're lucky. We could retire rich. Let's not snatch defeat from the jaws of victory. Whole Foods Market is an incredible gift. Let's not screw it up."

I sipped on my beer, trying to tamp down my frustration with his lack of vision. "Mark, I don't want to screw it up either. But I want to build a company; not just own one great store. Whole Foods Market could be massive. We could have stores all over Texas, the way Mrs. Gooch's does in Southern California and Bread & Circus in Boston. We could change the way people eat in Texas. Maybe in America."

I could tell from Mark's expression he was unenthused. "John, you're such an idealist. Just don't let your grand visions run us off a cliff."

As I watched the taillights of Mark's car disappearing around Clone Circle, I wondered if he was truly committed to the natural foods mission. I knew he personally believed in eating healthily. But was he interested in trying to change how other people ate? For me, it was becoming a calling—something I felt I *had* to do. My evangelical streak was lit up by the sense that what we were doing was more than a business. I knew it could be successful. It *had* to be. We just needed to get through this slow start with Crossroads. And start working on the next store as well.

This one would be an even bigger step for us. It wasn't just outside our neighborhood; it was in a different city. Whole Foods Market was coming to my hometown: Houston.

I was excited, and more than a little nervous, about opening a store in the city where I'd grown up, and where my parents, many of my friends, and several Board members lived. Houston was the natural next step for us. It was a big city. It was also a bastion of the establishment. Austin, even then, had a reputation for being quirky, but Houston was wealthy, conservative, and traditional in its values. It had been hard enough breaking into the Austin suburbs; this would be a whole new challenge.

I found what I thought was a great spot, at the intersection of Shepherd Drive and Alabama, which back then was one of the hippest areas in Houston. As I put on my only suit and tie and got ready for a meeting with the owners, I thought back to that first conversation with Ben Powell, who owned the Lamar site. It seemed like a lifetime ago, but I could still hear him exclaim, "What the hell, son, let's do your damn hippie food store." Back then, I'd only had the modest success of Safer Way to lean on, and my conviction owed much more to youthful enthusiasm than to market insight. Now, I could point to our thriving Lamar store, and even Crossroads was starting to turn a profit. And I could speak confidently about the natural foods movement and the successful stores in other states. Still, when I walked into that Houston conference room and looked at the men sitting across the table, for a moment I still felt like that naïve hippie kid with little more than a dream to his name.

The man who stood up and shook my hand introduced himself as Stanford Alexander, CEO of the Weingarten real estate investment trust. I grasped his hand firmly and said, "John Mackey, CEO and cofounder of Whole Foods Market, Texas's first natural foods supermarket." Just saying the words out loud, I felt my confidence grow. I shook hands with Alexander's partners and launched into my pitch. By the time I'd finished describing our plans for the new store, I was so excited I didn't see how they could possibly say no. "I have no doubt the store will be successful," I concluded, and I meant it. My momentary doubts had been banished—but when I looked at the men listening, I still saw those doubts written all over their faces. It had been easy to convince myself; it wasn't going to be so easy to convince the Weingarten REIT.

These guys weren't strangers to the grocery business. In fact, they'd started out as a chain of conventional supermarkets all over Houston. They'd soon realized, however, as Houston grew, that their real estate was more valuable than their stores, so they'd switched tracks and become landlords. They could appreciate that Whole Foods Market was a successful business—in Austin. But they just couldn't imagine why anyone in Houston would want to buy the things we were selling, because they themselves wouldn't.

Alexander summed it up. "John, your success is impressive. You deserve credit. But this isn't Austin." His partners laughed—they all knew exactly what he meant. This wasn't hippieville. "Folks here are busy and they want convenient food," he continued, "you know, TV dinners, frozen food, things they can stick in the microwave." I understood why he'd say that—he was describing my parents perfectly. But I also knew that things were changing—and maybe they were changing faster than Stanford Alexander and his partners realized. Natural foods were breaking out of the counterculture.

In the end, I was persuasive enough that the Weingarten partners agreed to take a chance on us. And not just us—we brought along a couple of other Austin companies to set up shop in the same location, including the Whole Earth Provision Co., an outdoor gear store inspired by Stewart Brand's countercultural magazine *Whole Earth Catalog*, and a large bookstore named Bookstop, founded by a guy named Gary Hoover, with whom I'd become good friends after they opened a store near ours in the Crossroads shopping center. We were all excited about creating our own little countercultural outpost in the big city. And I was thrilled that Whole Foods Market was moving beyond Austin. So much had changed in just a few short years. Who knew where we'd find ourselves next?

In my personal life, things were changing as well. Renee had recently returned to Austin, having broken up with David, who was still in Belize. I was still with Cheryl when I heard that Renee was back in town, but my heart leaped. I'd never been able to fully let go of my regrets about losing her. Even as I'd moved on in some ways, throwing myself into a new relationship and the new stores, I'd missed the bright light and warmth she'd brought into my life.

Am I still in love with Renee? I'd often wondered. I kind of knew the answer. I heard she'd moved into a little apartment above Grok Books, the spiritual bookstore owned by our mutual friend Philip Sansone. A few days later, she came around to the Lamar store. It was so good to see her. I tried not to think too much about my personal feelings toward her but instead asked her if she was planning to come back and work. She looked hesitant.

"I don't know," she said. "Maybe part time?"

Clearly, her feeling that Whole Foods Market wasn't really her thing hadn't changed much during her year in the Caribbean sun. She was hesitant to throw herself back into the business, although she was still a part owner. But as she and I spent more time together, my question was answered: I *was* still in love with her. And it turned out she felt the same.

I broke things off with Cheryl, moved out of the suburban house, and in no time at all, Renee and I were back together.

Chapter 10

The Network

"Welcome to Whole Foods Market," I said, holding open the door with one hand and gesturing with the other toward the bustling produce department of our brand-new Shepherd store in Houston. It was 1984, and I'd given hundreds of store tours by this point, but I'd never felt quite this nervous before. A dozen or so people filed through the door, and I studied each of their faces as they passed, trying to read their first impressions. I cared more about what these folks thought than anyone else in the world, with perhaps the exception of my parents. These were my fellow entrepreneurs and my inspiration—the owners and leaders of the country's best natural foods stores. These people had shown me that it was possible to sell natural foods in supermarket-sized one-stop shops. And now, here they were, visiting *our* store!

Tony Harnett from Bread & Circus; John Moorman and Dan Volland from Mrs. Gooch's; Peter Roy from Whole Food Company in New Orleans; Stan Amy from Nature's Northwest in Portland, Oregon; Terry Dalton from Unicorn Village in Miami; Lex Alexander from Wellspring in Raleigh-Durham; Mark Retzloff and Hass Hassan from Alfalfa's in Boulder, and a few others filed through our doors. By the mid-eighties, I knew them all quite well, because we were connected through an organization known as the Natural Foods Network—or, as we called it, the Network.

The first seeds of this association of natural foods retailers had been sown a few years earlier, in the spring of 1981, when Doug Greene, prophet of the movement and publisher of *Natural Foods Merchandiser*, decided to hold a trade show in Anaheim, California. It was the perfect moment to do so. There was still no national chain, so we all tended to operate in our own geographic regions, while reading about each other in the pages of Doug's trade magazine. The trade show was an opportunity for us all to meet in person. Whole Foods Market had been open for less than a year at that point, and we were working round the clock to keep the busy store up and running, but Renee, Craig, and I made time to fly to California and attend the inaugural Natural Products Expo. Mark stayed in Austin to mind the store.

When we stepped into the conference center, we were overwhelmed at the scale of the event. I remember feeling like a farm boy who'd suddenly arrived in the big city. Over 3,000 owners, producers, vendors, and companies attended, with several hundred booths. New brands, some local and some national, were coming into existence almost overnight, many of which we featured on our shelves. Indeed, all our vendors were represented—industry pioneers like Erewhon, Celestial Seasonings, Knudsen, Westbrae, Arrowhead Mills, Lundberg, and Nature's Path. It was fun to meet them in person. I was wearing my favorite Knudsen T-shirt, with the slogan "Get Juiced Naturally," and their sales rep got a kick out of hearing how we filled our shelves with their apple juice in order to look like we were well stocked for opening day.

One evening, Craig and I were invited to attend a cocktail reception hosted by a leather-suited man named Warren Ehring, founder of Consumer's Cattle. He was one of the only people in the industry selling what he claimed was natural beef (a claim that was later called into question). After welcoming us, Warren announced grandly, "There's someone I want you to meet. John Mackey, Craig Weller, this is Peter Roy." He ushered forward a young man with sandy hair and a boyish smile. "Peter owns the Whole Food Company in New Orleans. John and Craig own Whole Foods Market in Austin." Warren paused, as though the similarity in our company names was an original joke he'd just come up with, deserving of laughter or applause. "You three should have a lot to talk about," he concluded with a self-satisfied chuckle. And we did—we had much more in common than just the names of our stores.

I knew about Peter because his store had been featured in the most recent *Natural Foods Merchandiser.* It was a little smaller than ours, but similarly thriving. Peter told me he had once visited Safer Way but had not yet made it to the new store. He wasn't shy about asking questions, but his warm Southern manner made it seem quite natural to skip from small talk to sales numbers in a matter of minutes. He wanted to know everything about how we were running the store—our product mix, our strategies, our bestsellers. And Craig and I answered his questions directly; there seemed little reason to hide anything.

After all, we weren't competitors; in fact, we were essentially trying to accomplish common goals, just in different markets. That's why we'd never thought it a problem that our store names were so similar—there was no danger of confusion when we were hundreds of miles apart. It seemed to me that being transparent about what was working and what was not might help each of us achieve our common goals and better compete with the large mainstream supermarkets in our respective cities.

Later, Peter would tell me that our willingness to share so much information pleasantly surprised him and encouraged him to think further about the benefits of associating with fellow natural foods retailers. A conversation that had begun with Warren promising to introduce him to "the guys who ripped off your name" ended with a sense of camaraderie. As we shook hands and said good night, I told Peter that the next time he was in Austin, he must visit our store. I made a mental note to keep this connection alive.

I needn't have worried about staying in touch. As I would soon discover, one of Peter's superpowers is networking and building relationships. He's a born politician—in the best sense of the term—with a natural ability to connect with people, to read a room, and to tell stories. It wasn't long before he showed up in Austin, and I had a chance to show him around our store. It was helpful and encouraging to talk to someone who was walking such a similar path in another market. I was glad to have made a friend in the business. I also had an idea about how we might collaborate more closely—and solve a little problem I was having with Texas Health Distributors.

Since the merger between Safer Way and Clarksville, things had become considerably more complicated for THD. Back when we'd been two independent stores, we'd convinced several important vendors to work with us. But once we'd become one company, it was increasingly difficult to claim that THD wasn't just another name for Whole Foods Market, since the overwhelming number of orders went straight onto our shelves. I was concerned that unless I could bring in more partners, I was going to lose the discount that THD received from our suppliers as a legitimate wholesaler. My proposal to Peter, a few weeks after his visit, was that he start to buy products for his store through THD.

It took about five seconds to convince Peter. After all, on products he received from THD, he would lower his costs by almost 20% overnight! All we had to do was send over a truck once a week from Austin to New Orleans. With that new deal in place, THD stayed in business and quickly became the primary supplier to Peter's New Orleans store. It was an arrangement that had a side benefit as well: Peter and I stayed more closely in touch and established a cooperative relationship between our two businesses. It wouldn't be long before Peter, the consummate networker, decided to take that cooperation a step further and start the Natural Foods Network.

It was early 1983 when Peter first called to tell me about his plan.

"John, I've been talking to Doug about this idea, and I wanted to run it by you. I think we need a new industry association, an exclusive one, with all the big natural foods store owners and executives. A kind of club where we can get together, discuss our businesses, talk shop, support each other, explore best practices—that kind of thing. It will be fun. Plus, it will help to distinguish us from the pill shops."

The "pill shops" Peter mentioned, with a slight note of disparagement, were the traditional health food stores, many of which had built their businesses on selling vitamins and supplements. Those stores sold other products, like packaged foods, herbs, spices, and so on, but their profits came primarily from vitamins and supplements. We sold vitamins and supplements as well—they were a healthy revenue stream for Whole Foods Market from day one—but our approach was to emphasize the positive benefits of natural foods and a healthy lifestyle, rather than stoke fears of deficiency. Plus, we were all a little suspicious of the vitamin industry—and with good reason, as Peter pointed out during that call with a story about how Sandy Gooch had decided to test one of the brands of evening primrose oil sold in her store and discovered it was 100% peanut oil.

"You know there's probably more of that kind of thing going on than we realize," Peter concluded. "Who's to say what's really in some of those pills?"

The point of all this was that we—the real natural foods retailers—needed our own association. The pill shops already had one, the National Nutritional Foods Association, but none of us who really cared about food felt at home in that community. And the pill shop guys didn't like us anyway—they saw us, with our much bigger, one-stop stores, as a threat to their businesses. I loved the idea of our own club. And I knew Peter well enough by this point to know that there was no one better suited than him to creating it.

"Sounds like a plan," I told him. "Count us in!" And so, the Natural Foods Network was born. The first meeting, which Craig and I attended as representatives of Whole Foods Market, was held that fall at a hotel in New Orleans. Peter played host, inviting everyone to tour his store and offer critiques and suggestions. Some of the members were folks I knew from my own travels and visits to various stores; others I knew by name and reputation but had never met in person.

One guy who immediately caught my attention was a striking man with a British accent, piercing blue eyes, and a head of unruly black curls. We hit it off right away. S.M. "Hass" Hassan was cofounder, along with Mark Retzloff, of Boulder's Alfalfa's Market. Born in Kashmir, he'd been raised in London but had moved to Colorado in his early twenties. Like me, he'd worked in food co-ops and small health food stores before Alfalfa's was born. We quickly discovered a shared passion for the entrepreneurial life, and for building community. Hass's brilliant mind made for interesting conversations, and I soon would learn that he has a deep and unusual integrity.

The non-competitive spirit of my first conversation with Peter carried over into the Network. We openly shared our strategies, our best practices, and even our numbers. I recall members handing out copies of their financial statements without any reservation. Whoever was hosting the meeting (we had about three a year) would invite everyone to tour and critique their stores, as well as ask questions and get ideas. It never even occurred to us to protect our individual business models from each other. Each regional store, or small chain of stores, saw itself as an outpost of the same movement. Our competition wasn't each other; it was the big national supermarket chains like Safeway and Kroger.

I learned so much from those visits, coming home to Austin brimming with ideas for new product lines, marketing strategies, management approaches, store design, and more. And the Network quickly felt like more than a business association. These were friends—fellow travelers who were walking the same road that I was on. The Network was an extension of the fellowship that I'd experienced with my cofounders and early team members—a fellowship that had sadly become strained in the past few years. With Renee still reluctant to get back into Whole Foods, tensions rising between me and Mark, and Craig feeling torn in his loyalty, I yearned for a return to our earlier sense of shared purpose. The Network couldn't entirely make up for the fraying of those bonds at home, but it helped.

When our turn came to host, in 1984, I chose Houston as the venue because our new store was the most impressive. Plus, several of the members had already visited Austin, and I wanted to show them something different. I was quite nervous—as one of the younger members of the group, I still sometimes felt a need to prove I belonged. Also, I was a bit worried about the cost of the event. It was customary for whoever was hosting to treat the others to dinners and entertainment. Over the course of our last few meetings, I'd noticed that several of my fellow members enjoyed the good life, so to speak. They'd done well in their respective businesses, and their lifestyles reflected success and affluence. When they'd hosted, we'd been given the VIP treatment. I was happy to see that natural foods could make people rich, but I also didn't feel like I was in that category. Sure, Whole Foods was successful, but Mark, Craig, and I were frugal. We kept our costs down and reinvested our profits. We ran leaner and hungrier than most of the other natural foods retailers.

Partly, this was driven by my own desire to keep growing. I didn't just want to live off the gravy from a few profitable stores; I wanted a bigger footprint in our market. Partly, it was inspired by my father, who was always telling me, "John, if you want to grow the business, the best way to grow it is to keep costs down, be as profitable as possible, and plow the profits back into the business." I took his advice to heart, and most of the time I never really thought about my personal wealth—except when I spent too much time with my fellow natural food retailers. I didn't judge them for their lifestyles, but I did worry about entertaining them in the style to which they were accustomed. Craig and Mark were worried too. I think they felt the free-spending ways of the Network were a bad influence on me.

Those fears were not unfounded. On the last night of the Houston gathering, we all went out to eat—about 10 of us, as I recall. The food was great, though a bit rich for my taste, and the wine was flowing freely. And not just any wine—very good wine, chosen by Lex and Peter, both connoisseurs. When the last toast was raised and the last plate was cleared, I was handed a bill for more than $1,000. In the early eighties that was a lot of money to pay for dinner! I stared at it, trying to hide my horror. I'd never spent even $100 on a dinner before. How could I bill this to Whole Foods Market? What would my partners say? I couldn't bring myself to do it, so I pulled out my personal credit card instead.

The next day, I told Craig about the dinner. "What should I do?" I asked him.

Craig looked stern. "Yeah, Whole Foods shouldn't spend that kind of money," he said. The dinner stayed on my credit card. It was worth it for me to stay connected with those guys, even if I sometimes couldn't relate to their lifestyles. I was learning so much from every gathering, and I had no doubt it was all making me a better leader for Whole Foods Market. What I could not possibly have known back then was that over the course of the coming two decades, Whole Foods Market—the lean, hungry upstart of the bunch that once wouldn't buy them dinner—would not only surpass each of those other businesses but would end up buying pretty much all of them, one by one. The era of regional stores would soon come to an end, and we would begin our journey to becoming a national brand.

Chapter 11

Wacky Mackey

Hey, John, Orwell didn't see THIS coming, did he?"

"What? Oh, right—*1984*." I laughed at my friend Philip Sansone, owner of Grok Books and Pied Piper of all things mystical, who I had happily followed into many a new and mind-altering experience. He winked at me and then moved on to another part of the room and a new conversation. He looked just like I felt—happy, joyful, brimming with love. It was in fact 1984, and the world around me bore little resemblance to Orwell's dystopian vision. Indeed, I wasn't sure the world had ever looked more beautiful. I was spending the weekend with a small group of friends at the Austin home of a woman named Jacquie Small, and we were all being introduced to a new psychoactive substance that had recently become popular in therapeutic circles. Its technical name was MDMA, but its more descriptive street name was Ecstasy (also known today as Molly). Within a year or so, it would be illegal, but for now, it was still under the radar, though growing in popularity, and completely legal.

The guest of honor at this weekend gathering was a physicist named Paul Taylor who had spent time at the Esalen Institute, that West Coast mecca for human-potential pioneers, and was in town for a few days. Jacquie, a local maven of the New Age, was hosting. I hadn't met her before, but I liked her energy. She was older than me—perhaps 50—with flowing dark curls, strangely magnetic eyes, and swirling clothes. She moved with ease through the assembled guests, as if gathering up the energy and love we were all experiencing and spreading it around the room.

MDMA, properly used, is truly a love drug, a prosocial empathogen that opens your heart and temporarily dislodges the normal, everyday ego concerns. Back in 1984, I didn't have any of those words to describe it. I just knew that it felt amazing. Hanging out with new and old friends in a blissful state of love and appreciation was just the tonic I needed. At one point I caught a glimpse of myself in a mirror, and the big, loving smile on my face made me laugh out loud. People around me joined in, and we all laughed together.

Maybe it was because I'd been working hard for what felt like years, without much of a break. Whole Foods was a labor of love, for sure, but it was so consuming that my other interests had taken a back seat, especially my explorations of consciousness. I never stopped reading voraciously, but the spiritual pursuits, psychedelic experimentation, and personal growth focus of my earlier life had been neglected.

Now, I felt powerfully reminded of the importance of this inward journey. "I mustn't forget this," I thought to myself, "even when the MDMA wears off." I looked around for Philip, to tell him to remind me, but he was sitting on the couch gazing deeply into the eyes of a woman I didn't know, and I didn't want to interrupt. I felt a deep love for him, for the stranger beside him, and for everyone in the room. Each of them seemed lit up with their own unique light. Connecting, sharing, smiling, laughing—love was finding a hundred sparkling ways to express itself in these faces. I felt energy moving through my body and began to dance, letting the love move through and around me.

This feeling of love partly reminded me of my experience on LSD—that sense of cosmic, all-embracing energy. But it felt safer, softer, without the wild and sometimes frightening edge that went along with every acid trip. And I wasn't alone—everyone in the room was sharing this experience. If I closed my eyes, I felt all the people I loved who were not there that weekend—especially Renee and my Whole Foods Market comrades. Love was an enormous part of what got us started on the journey together. Love fueled our creation of the store and turned it into something we could never have imagined. And love had kept it alive even through the most difficult moments. I felt a deep reaffirmation that the spirit of love was foundational to my own purpose. Without judging myself harshly, I could see how it had been too easy, in the day-to-day bustle of business, to lose touch with this wonderful truth and get stuck in my head. I resolved to live more from my heart, to let this innocence and playfulness inform more of my decisions. When the weekend was over, I felt deeply refreshed.

Whole Foods Market was now almost four years old (plus a few more if you count its prior incarnations as Safer Way and Clarksville Natural Grocery). We had three stores and more on the way. The heady days of the sixties and seventies had given way to the 1980s—and while it wasn't an Orwellian dystopia, by any means, neither was it the Summer of Love. Reagan was president, and my friends and I were moving into our thirties. We owned businesses, and many had families. We weren't living in co-ops and communes anymore. Instead, our countercultural interests were channeled into what was broadly called the "New Age." A fresh sense of experimentalism was in vogue—transformation modalities had come out of the spiritual subcultures and were being codified as radical new kinds of therapy. As psychedelics became harder to come by, these therapies and practices promised similar insights and states of consciousness without the drugs. I was curious—and of course, Philip Sansone knew everyone in that world and was happy to make introductions. It was Philip who introduced me to Jacquie, and it was Jacquie who introduced me to the practice of breathwork.

Breathwork, in broad terms, is a technique involving a facilitated session of guided breathing that puts one in an altered state of consciousness, allowing deeper spiritual insight and opening up a pathway toward clearing mental and emotional baggage. There were two popular forms of breathwork in that era, one created by Leonard Orr and Sondra Ray that became known as "rebirthing" and another known as Holotropic Breathwork, developed by Stanislov and Christina Grof. Grof was a pioneering psychiatrist who did research on LSD in Prague in the 1960s before he was invited to come to the US, and he eventually ended up as a scholar-in-residence at Esalen. Jacquie, a transpersonal psychologist, had trained with Grof for six years before creating her own variation on the practice.

Soon after meeting Jacquie, I began doing breathwork sessions with her at her Austin center. Previously locked doorways in my own psyche and consciousness opened up to me. For the first time in years, I felt like I was making real progress on my spiritual path. It never failed to amaze me how powerful the simple act of breathing could be, and how much it could reveal about the deeper layers of the self and its history. In fact, the reason that one school of breathwork was called "rebirthing" was due to the tendency of participants to reexperience some aspects of their actual birth. In the very first breathwork session I ever did, I had a vivid experience of being stuck and trapped in the birth canal, fearful and in pain, and then lifted out into the light. I later discovered that I had been a Cesarean baby, and my birth had been long and difficult.

During this period, Jacquie and I developed a close relationship. I respected her a lot and wanted to help make her work more widely accessible. When I get excited about something, I'm not one to keep it to myself! Could we create a business around these new transformational modalities, one that would expose more people to Jacquie's powerful techniques? We eventually came up with a business plan for a transformational center called LifeWorks. It would feature holotropic breathing, various forms of meditation, yoga, new therapeutic techniques, and generally cater to many of the consciousness-raising practices that were booming in the New Age. Philip was excited about it too and agreed to invest. LifeWorks would be to meditation, consciousness, and spirituality what Whole Foods was to natural foods—at least that was our vision for it.

I told Renee about all of this, and she was enthusiastic, as always, though she didn't share my love for breathwork. She was pursuing her own explorations of consciousness through psychedelics and other modalities. Indeed, although we lived together again, I often felt like our lives were moving on diverging tracks. She wasn't very involved with Whole

Foods, though she was still an owner of the company and supportive of my passion for it. And after the initial excitement at being back together faded, another concern arose. There just didn't seem to be much of a spark between us any longer. To my frustration, our physical connection had dwindled, and she seemed just fine with that. I was not.

Maybe we needed a love booster? After my experience taking MDMA, I wondered if taking it together might revitalize our relationship and supercharge our love for each other. I hoped that if she could see me the way I'd seen everyone while under the influence of that drug, she might just fall back in love with me.

That's not what happened. Under the heart-centered intensity of the MDMA, we didn't fall back in love. Yes, we certainly recognized our deep and abiding love for each other, but with an unexpected twist. MDMA is not merely a love drug—it can also act like a truth serum, revealing the way things really are rather than the way we would like them to be. The truth that Renee and I discovered was that we were deeply connected, but not as lovers. We were more like brother and sister. I became clear about something else as well—the purpose of our relationship. We hadn't come together for ourselves; we'd come together to give birth to Whole Foods Market. It probably would not have happened without her—her encouragement, her unquenchable enthusiasm, her optimism. "Let's do it, Macko Man!" Now, our baby was born; it was crawling, maybe even walking. That purpose was served. It was time to move on. Life was calling us to follow different paths, and while our love for each other was real, our time as lovers was finished.

In addition to the breathwork and MDMA, there was one other important influence on my personal growth that began in 1984. My friend Curtis, who had attended that MDMA gathering at Jacquie's house, handed me a book one day, with a dark-blue leather cover and gold lettering. *A Course in Miracles,* it was called. It seemed vaguely Christian but also New

Age—a blend that felt slightly uncomfortable to me. Christianity was my past. I didn't really have any desire to go back to a more traditional religious path. Then again, when I looked at the book, it didn't seem too traditional. In fact, it seemed pretty far out, even by the standards of the eighties, claiming to be "channeled" from Jesus. But I wanted to be nice, so I took the book and promised Curtis I would read it.

A few days later, I picked it up, not expecting much from the content. But after 50 pages or so, I stumbled upon a passage addressing the problem of evil—the question that had bothered me so much as a young Christian. In short: How could an omnipotent, omniscient, and loving God create a world that includes so much pain, suffering, and death? The only conclusions I had come to were that either there is no God, or he or she isn't all-powerful, all-knowing, or very loving. I'd opted to believe God didn't exist and became an atheist. *A Course in Miracles* had a different answer—one that got me so excited that I jumped up and began to run around my home.

The book offered a dream metaphor: We are currently asleep and having very bad dreams full of pain, suffering, aging, and death. These dreams aren't real or true in any absolute sense, but we certainly experience them as real while we are dreaming them. The course promised a spiritual path to help us gently wake up from our bad dreams to who we really are—beings of pure love, peace, and joy. This explanation rang deeply true to me. After completing several joyful laps of my home, I grabbed the book again and kept reading. I couldn't wait to find out what it would tell me about how to wake up from the dream.

I learned that the key was to remove the blocks to love's presence through practicing forgiveness instead of fear, judgment, and attacks on others. The dreams we experience here are actually reflections of all of our thoughts and emotions. We are always unconsciously creating the world that we are experiencing. Our task here is to become more conscious and begin to transform our waking dreams to happy dreams of love and then to share that love with everyone we encounter. This message spoke directly to my heart. I felt like I was reading a truth I already knew and had experienced but hadn't yet learned to live and express. Forgiveness became a very important part of my own path in the aftermath of my encounter with *A Course in Miracles*. And I was determined that these new insights wouldn't remain closeted off in my personal life. I wanted them to inform the business as well.

"You know what I think we should aim for? Let's build the happiest workplace in America—a workplace based on love. We can do it."

Mark and Craig looked at me like I was speaking in tongues. We were in a management meeting, talking about various aspects of the business. The subject had turned to our employees, when I'd come out with this declaration.

"John, don't you think our employees are already happy? We pay them a decent wage. It's a great workplace." Craig couldn't relate to some of my more idealistic visions, but he was gentle in his rebukes. I always felt he respected me, even if he sometimes thought I was a bit misguided. Mark, on the other hand, was blunt, and at times even exasperated.

"Based on love? What the hell does that mean?"

He had grown much less forgiving of such talk over the years we'd been working together. "What book have you been reading now? Or are you confusing this with your other New Age business? John, you need to get your priorities straight. We've barely made it through these difficult new store openings. Let's get the numbers adding up before we start spouting happy talk about love and forgiveness."

I smarted under his sharp tone. I knew that he privately referred to me as "Wacky Mackey" and thought that my spiritual pursuits were not just crazy but detrimental to the business. He believed that the time I was spending on LifeWorks was time taken away from Whole Foods. He didn't see how the businesses would feed each other. I wasn't stupid and I didn't have my head in the clouds. Or maybe I did. But what was wrong with that? Heck, there wouldn't be a Whole Foods Market if there hadn't been a Wacky Mackey first. I was determined to show him and everyone else that love was good business.

The year 1985 brought another new store to the Whole Foods family. Lamar was still going strong; Crossroads was improving and starting to make a little bit of money. Shepherd was doing okay and rapidly growing. I had enough experience to reset my expectations. I stopped anticipating anything resembling the explosive opening sales numbers at Lamar. That had been a unique situation and set an unnecessarily high bar for other stores to meet. I had confidence that stores would become successful and highly profitable if given time. I could see the growth rates and they were very favorable. Patience was key.

Our fourth store was slated for a new shopping center in South Austin named Brodie Oaks. This one was even closer to the original Lamar location, just under four miles. At the same time, we decided to open a natural foods restaurant in the same location, called Wildflower Café, under the capable leadership of Peter Steinhart, a mutual friend of Craig's and mine, who had some experience in the restaurant business. After the challenges of the Safer Way Café, I knew better than to think we could do it ourselves. But the opportunity beckoned nonetheless. Someone was going to find great success creating a large-scale natural foods restaurant in Austin. Why shouldn't it be us? We just needed an operator like Peter who knew what he was doing.

Jacquie, Philip, and I also decided that Brodie Oaks would be the location of our first LifeWorks. Philip's store, now renamed BookPeople, was also moving into Brodie Oaks. My friends and I looked to have a stake in almost every spot in the shopping center. It was an exhilarating thought—a little retail empire of love and transformation.

Sadly, our aspirations never materialized. Wildflower Café was unsuccessful. A restaurant of that scale is not an easy endeavor, and we never found traction, eventually losing our entire investment—to the tune of some $88,000. The new Whole Foods Market at Brodie Oaks opened and while moderately successful, it had an unfortunate side effect—it immediately cannibalized Lamar, which lost 20% of its sales almost overnight, a serious blow to our profitability. For the first time since the flood, we were losing money. We were still learning how close we could place new stores without damaging existing sites, and Brodie Oaks was a bracing lesson in that regard.

As for LifeWorks, it never even made it out of the starting blocks. Jacquie decided she didn't want to put her own money into the business, after all, and without her financial commitment, I reluctantly decided to back out of the lease. I was deeply disappointed. I still believed there was a place for this confluence of healing and personal growth modalities. But perhaps the time just wasn't right.

Chapter 12

A Declaration of Interdependence

Currently, I'm greatly puzzled by the concept of competition as the driving force in this reality, which it of course is. Is war the logical conclusion of competition or is it just some sort of aberration? Why do some people become more creative when competition is removed from their personal reality, and others become decadent and degenerate? Is competition something to transcend or embrace? I do not yet know."

These musings were penned in a letter to my old girlfriend Debbie, still living in the Kerista commune in San Francisco. In the mid-eighties, my thoughts seemed to bounce back and forth between two dramatically different worlds: on one hand, the burgeoning world of spiritual and esoteric exploration that captivated me, and on the other, my ongoing readings about business, economics, and capitalism. As I wrote to Debbie that day, I reflected at length on both.

In particular, I struggled to reconcile my direct experience of the unity or oneness of all reality—which I also felt in the playful, cooperative spirit of the business—with the focus on competition that I found in my readings of free market economists like Milton Friedman and Friedrich Hayek. Both felt like essential elements of life. Both felt positive to me. Competition could be generative. And yet competition, taken too far, also had a dark side, like war.

Cooperation could be generative too. Some days, the camaraderie among the team at Whole Foods Market felt intoxicating—everyone playing a choreographed role, moving through the stores like dancers in a chaotic but beautiful ballet of form and function. If ever there was an experience that made me believe in the power of cooperation, that was it. I loved the community and creative energy that we generated together. And yet, I was also acutely aware of how being an entrepreneur had channeled my own competitive instincts. I thrived on competition, loved to excel in sports and in business. I was driven to outdo our competitors, to win in the marketplace. The competitive drive was critical to our success, and my readings convinced me that it was essential to the entire capitalist enterprise.

I found it fascinating to read about economics and capitalism writ large, and then to reflect on how those processes were playing out in our still-young company. I was amazed at how a good idea could become a store, and a successful store could become several, turning into a real business, and a real business could grow to become a large company. And that chain of success could potentially change an entire industry. Of course, none of this would have been possible without a large degree of political and economic freedom—as Friedman pointed out again and again in his books. Safer Way could never have gotten started if Renee and I had not lived in a place where we had the freedom to start a new business. Thankfully, the barriers to entry were pretty minimal. "Wherever you have freedom, you have capitalism," Friedman wrote, and I could see the truth in his words.

Capitalism, I began to understand, was not so much a top-down imposed system but, rather, an evolutionary result of letting people choose their own economic paths. And if economic freedom was the foundation of capitalism, then both cooperation and competition seemed to be the essential engines that made it run.

These thoughts, while compelling to me, were near heretical among many of my friends. While Texas was a conservative state with a proud business tradition, the countercultural types who made up my social circles and much of the Whole Foods Market team and customer base were politically progressive. Probably more than a few were closet socialists.

Competition, to them, was about selfishness and greed and should be transcended in favor of love and cooperation.

Love and cooperation are beautiful qualities—of that I had no doubt. My most profound glimpses into the nature of the universe had shown me a dance of love and unity. I wanted the world I lived in, and the business I worked in, to reflect those ultimate spiritual truths. And I knew that unrestrained competition—without any rules or ethics constraining lying, cheating, and violence—could be highly destructive and would undermine the foundation of capitalism and our collective prosperity, as I wrote in my letter to Debbie. But I also saw the positive power of competition. And I saw the downsides to cooperation. Taken too far, it could lead to a kind of stultifying bureaucratic collectivism that made it hard to get anything done and would stifle creativity and innovation. I thought of my experience at Prana House—I had loved the community, but discussing all community decisions exhaustively as a group was very time consuming. I didn't ever want to imagine a larger society based around such impractical ideals. And so, around and around I went in my mind. Competition, cooperation—both seemed necessary; both were powerfully creative; both had dangers if pushed too far. Of course, a synthesis of both in healthy forms was the answer to my puzzle, but I did not realize it back then.

My musings about cooperation and competition were not merely philosophical or focused on big-picture social and cultural ideals. In the mid-eighties, I had a much more personal example to grapple with. Indeed, the force of competition had taken an unpleasant turn at the heart of Whole Foods Market, as Mark's growing frustration became an all-out war for control over the direction of the company—the first real challenge to my leadership.

Mark was livid about the failure of Wildflower Café and the damage that he believed my overenthusiasm for growth had done to the business. He was convinced that "Wacky Mackey" had taken a gold mine and turned it into a money pit. When he, Craig, and I met to go over the financial statements for the Brodie Oaks store in South Austin and its impact on Lamar, his long-simmering frustration boiled over. The degree to which he had lost confidence in my leadership was as clear as the numbers on the financial statement. And just like those numbers, our relationship no longer had a net positive result.

"This is a disaster. We should have never opened these new stores. You got us into this, John. This is on you."

I was taken aback by the intensity of his tone.

"Look, Mark," I said, "I get it. I'm not happy about the recent financial results either. But we're in this for the long haul. I think it's really important that we—"

He broke in before I could finish.

"You're a terrible CEO, John. Look at what you've done! We built this beautiful store into an incredible success, survived the flood, and then you had to go and completely screw it up. All this talk about creating the happiest workplace in the world—we won't have a workplace at all if we keep going like this. And for what? So that you can have fun starting new things rather than focusing on the good things we already have. You're going to run this company into the ground."

The rest of the conversation didn't go much better. There was no point trying to argue with him—at least not at this moment. And his grievances were at least partially true. We had stumbled. Our growth had come at a cost. My plans had not always come to quick, positive fruition, and some had failed outright. Of that, I was guilty as charged. But the new stores weren't a mistake; I was still sure. We just needed to give them time to grow into successful stores. Mark clearly didn't have that patience. He wanted to stay small and enjoy our profits. To me, our mission was much larger than one store. And in building a bigger company, mistakes and setbacks are inevitable. What was missing in Mark's snapshot condemnation of the state of the business in 1985 was another truth—that beneath the sluggish sales numbers, our new stores were growing.

Was Mark right about the future? Or would my growth ambitions prove to be not so wacky after all? Only time would tell. I was learning how to lead. We were learning how to grow. America was learning how to appreciate natural foods. We didn't yet know it, but we were riding a massive cultural shift in attitudes and learning how to do it skillfully. The trend lines were encouraging, even if the momentary picture was frustrating. But while I saw the former, Mark saw only the latter. And if time was what we needed, I wasn't sure we had enough, at least as far as our friendship was concerned.

That was the most painful part of this conflict: we really had been good friends. We had been brothers in building Whole Foods. We'd shared those special formative years, with their triumphs and near disasters, and that was something I treasured. We'd also had so many fun times outside of the business. Ironically, the healthier form of competition had been the lifeblood of our friendship. But Mark's latest outburst had made his business frustrations personal. He was pointing the finger at me—at my leadership. Our friendship wouldn't survive if our business partnership didn't. There was no way that we could continue to work together unless something changed.

To be clear, it wasn't the fact that Mark and I disagreed that bothered me. I welcomed disagreement and strong opinions. I believe debates lead to better decisions, and I always encouraged my team to voice their perspectives. But what I don't believe is acceptable is for someone to be openly hostile and divide the company into factions.

That was perhaps the most concerning element of Mark's rebellion. Little by little, I could see that there was a John camp and a Mark camp forming. We had prided ourselves on having a healthy culture, and I felt this division in the company was quickly undermining that spirit.

I knew Craig felt pulled in two directions. He was naturally loyal to his longtime partner, and he seemed sympathetic to some of Mark's concerns about my leadership, though he never would have put them in such stark, angry terms. But most of all, Craig loved Whole Foods Market. That was his priority. He and I might disagree at times, but I felt confident that we would always be able to reasonably work through whatever issues came up. If it came down to a choice between me and Mark, though, which way would he go? I wasn't sure.

I spent several days thinking about how to respond to Mark. It felt like he'd escalated things to a breaking point. I wasn't sure he'd be able to find a way to walk it back and accept my leadership after such open hostility. And yet I was hesitant to force the issue at that moment. Things might look so different in six months as the new stores were given more time, and the situation might resolve itself. But Mark wasn't willing to give it time. Maybe the best course of action was to insist that we all allow some time for the emotions to settle down and the sales and profits to improve. The only way I could see doing that, however, was if Mark wasn't around inciting conflict—at least for a while. I sought advice from my father and other Board members and discussed the situation at length with Craig. They all agreed that my idea made sense: ask Mark to take a six-month sabbatical, with full pay, and then revisit his role.

When I put the proposal to Mark, I made sure to be clear: "After six months, if you want to come back, I'd be more than happy to welcome you. But you must find a way to accept my leadership of the company. I'm not stepping down. And Whole Foods can't be pulled in two different directions. If you don't want to come back, I promise to do my best to find someone to buy you out if that's what you want. But take some time before you make a final decision." Mark reluctantly agreed.

While one friendship was breaking down, a new one was beginning. The previous year, while attending an industry event put on by Bill Thompson, one of our vitamin suppliers, I met a young man named Chris Hitt, who worked with Bill on something called the American Farm Foundation, a nonprofit that was trying to raise the profile of organic farming. I liked his energy right away. He was a few years older than me and had a similar passion for the food business, although he'd come to it by a very different route. Chris had previously worked in Washington, DC, as a staff member for George McGovern—a job that included, among other things, co-authoring the 1977 edition of the *Dietary Goals for the United States*, which raised the alarm about American eating habits and recommended that people eat more fruits and vegetables. When McGovern was pushed out with the Reagan landslide in 1980, Chris landed in a Missouri nonprofit, working on organic farming with Bill and a man named Alan York, who would go on to become one of the more celebrated regenerative farming experts in the country.

Chris and I had a good deal in common. He was both smart and idealistic, and he'd clearly thought deeply about what mattered to him and what kind of impact he wanted to make in the world. We fell into a deep discussion about a whole range of subjects, from food and farming to personal growth and spirituality. Like me, he'd experimented with various transformational practices, and he didn't seem to think it at all strange to talk about reincarnation or meditation in the same breath as marketing strategies and customer experience. It was a relief to meet someone who liked both Wacky Mackey and CEO Mackey and understood how they could be the same person. We stayed in touch, and it wasn't long before he asked me to join the advisory board of the American Farm Foundation, which I agreed to do. I invited him to Texas for a visit, eager to show him around our stores.

Mark left on his sabbatical, but I could feel the lingering effects of the conflict. Our team members seemed a little wary, unsure about what it all meant. I wanted to do something to unify us, to strengthen the culture. I'd also been feeling the need to define Whole Foods Market's mission and values and start building our culture more consciously.

It wasn't just Mark's rebellion that had sparked this. It was also our growth. When we'd been just one store, with everyone working together and pitching in wherever they were needed, it had been easier to feel like we were all on a shared journey. Our values had always been implicit, and they naturally informed our culture. We'd never needed a plaque on the wall. Many of us had been together since the beginning, and we'd been bonded together by trials like the flood and triumphs like our reopening. But now, our fast-growing team was spread across multiple stores, and we kept bringing in new people. It was time to codify our values and bring the team together more formally in a shared commitment to those values.

And I had an idea who might help us with this task: my new friend Chris Hitt.

Chris was thoughtful and had a way with words. In his political and nonprofit work, he'd learned how to facilitate diverse groups and bring them together in shared visions. When Chris visited Austin sometime in early 1985, I pitched him on the idea. How would he feel about leading a Values Clarification workshop for Whole Foods Market? We'd invite all the executives and Store Team Leaders and anyone else who wanted to participate. Chris loved the idea, and a date was set.

That weekend turned out to be one of the most important gatherings in the history of Whole Foods Market, setting the stage for our emergence as a values-driven company. More than 60 team members volunteered their time to participate—a fact that boosted my confidence in our shared mission before we'd even begun the process of trying to put it into words. These people cared. They felt invested enough in the company that they'd give up their weekend to talk about what we were trying to achieve together.

By the end of the gathering, we had developed, with Chris's help and impressive writing talents, a "Declaration of Interdependence"—built around a commitment to our core values. Its title, besides being a nod to the Founding Fathers, was an acknowledgment of what I'd realized on the morning after the flood, when our customers showed up to help us salvage the store. Our company was the hub of an interdependent ecosystem, and our success relied on the health of multiple key constituencies—investors, customers, suppliers, team members, communities, and even our environment.

I was thrilled with the result of our weekend: Whole Foods Market's first Vision, Mission, and Values statements. I was also excited that many of my own nascent thoughts about the nature of business were being put in writing for the first time. But truly, they weren't just my thoughts—they were the spirit of the company and our collective learning.

During the six months that Mark was absent, our fortunes improved. Little by little, the new stores were finding their feet, and we were no longer losing money. The panic about Brodie Oaks cannibalizing Lamar was slowly subsiding as the local community discovered that store and it grew its own customer base. Our decisions to expand looked more strategically sound, and Mark's frustrations seemed less relevant by the day, though I doubted he saw it that way.

As the end of the agreed-upon period drew closer, I was preoccupied by the need for a resolution. Would Mark be able to put aside his criticisms and find a way to return to the company he had helped build? Would he be able to see all the positive change that had happened in his absence and let go of his anger toward me? Could we find a way to work together again without clashing? Surely, he would want to be a part of Whole Foods Market's bright future. But would the past get in the way?

When I reached out to him and broached these questions, he was less enthusiastic than I'd hoped.

"I told you, John," he declared, "I don't want to sit by and watch you run this company into the ground. That hasn't changed."

The bitter edge in his voice was still there. Whatever the six months had done for him, it hadn't appeased his resentment. I tried not to take the bait. Clearly, I wasn't going to convince him that we were on a better track.

"Okay," I told him. "As I promised, I will do what I can to find someone to buy you out."

But Mark had other ideas. He didn't just want to take cash for his shares and walk away. He wanted a piece of the company for himself. In fact, he wanted what he'd always wanted: the Lamar store. He proposed that he and Craig should take that store, and the other owners could take Crossroads, Shepherd, and Brodie Oaks. To me, the idea was ridiculous!

"I'm not going to give you the Lamar store! That's still our best store and giving it away would be a terrible business decision. I would be willing to trade either Crossroads or Brodie Oaks to you, but not Lamar or Shepherd."

The reality was that Mark had very little leverage. Together, he and Craig owned about 20% of the business. I also owned about 20%, and my father and the other Board members, who owned the rest, were aligned with me. When I talked to Craig, he made it clear he wasn't interested in dividing the business.

With the situation at an impasse, I didn't really have another option than to force Mark out, but I wanted to make one last attempt to come to a mutually agreed-upon solution. Hoping to break up the now dysfunctional relationship dynamic, I turned to Chris for help. Would he be willing to facilitate a meeting between the partners—Craig, Mark, and myself?

"I'm thinking of a kind of 'vision quest,'" I explained. "Something that gets us out of our usual arguments and helps us look at the future, see a bigger picture of where the company is going and what each of our roles might be in that future." Chris agreed, and my parents said I could use their beach house on Crystal Beach, just north of Galveston—a place we'd sometimes spent weekends during happier times as an executive team.

On Friday afternoon, Craig and I picked up Chris from the Houston airport, and we drove down to the coast together. Mark said he'd meet us there. As we crawled along the freeway with all the families headed out of the city for the weekend, I felt my spirits lighten a little. This would be good for us. Mark had agreed to come, so maybe he was ready to have a more constructive conversation. And perhaps we could even revive a little of our friendship as we hung out on the beach and played some volleyball or cards. I missed that.

We arrived in the late afternoon, and Mark pulled in soon after us. He and Craig embraced warmly; our greeting was awkward. He didn't know Chris, having missed the Values Clarification workshop, so I took a few moments to introduce them. After we'd unloaded our bags, I suggested a brief walk before sunset. I wanted to share my hopes for the weekend and get us all on the same page. It wasn't high season, so the beach was almost empty. We strolled across the sand, the sun at our backs, with the Gulf stretching to one side of us and a row of raised, stilted beach houses on the other.

"I appreciate you all being here this weekend," I began. "I know there's a lot of tension right now about how the three of us should go forward with the company, and I thought it would be good to hash it out between us. We probably haven't spent enough time, as owners of the business, really envisioning how we see its future. I invited Chris to lead us on this 'vision quest' because he knows the company well and helped us clarify our values. I trust him to help the three of us get everything on the table. Tonight, I thought we could—"

Mark stopped dead. "Tonight? I can't do anything tonight. I have a date, in Houston."

"A date? Mark, we're supposed to be spending the weekend together."

"Look, John, I didn't agree to this vision quest crap. I agreed to come out here for a meeting. This is your fantasy, not mine. I don't want to be part of it. I'm not going to stand up my date so Chris can hypnotize me with some wacky voodoo stuff."

And with that, Mark turned on his heel and headed back to the house. From a distance, I watched him grab a bag, throw it in the back of his Karmann Ghia sports car, and drive off. I turned to Chris and Craig and shook my head. "Well, I guess Mark's made his position clear. But I still think we should go ahead with the weekend. Craig, are you good with it? Chris, are you in?"

"Sure," Chris replied. Craig nodded. He had seemed genuinely interested in the exploration of our future, but I knew it was hard for him to witness the fracturing of my and Mark's relationship. I imagined he probably agreed with at least some of Mark's criticisms, although I trusted his loyalty to the company and our own friendship. All of this made me more determined to go ahead with our plans for the weekend. If Mark and I couldn't repair our relationship, at least maybe Craig and I could figure out a way to move forward that could help us both, and the company, be more unified.

"I'm getting this very strong image in my head. I'm on this platform; I guess it's like an elevator. I'm going up and up. Floors are passing by. I'm going higher and higher. But I can see that at some point I'm going to get off. I'm going to stop. And I see that other people are staying on the elevator and headed up to higher floors."

Craig's voice was quiet and focused, and his eyes were closed. It was Saturday afternoon, and Chris had been walking Craig and me through a series of visualization exercises and conversations about Whole Foods, its future, and our roles in it. My hope that Chris would prove adept at leading this sort of workshop had been borne out. He was skilled at guiding us toward the questions that really mattered and helping us use our intuition rather than just our rational minds to peer into our future. Craig's elevator vision made clear to him that he was with Whole Foods Market for the ride—but not forever. At some point, he intended to step out of the company, even as it ascended higher.

He felt a peace of mind with that realization. Craig was 40 years old at this point, whereas I was only 32. Our ambitions were different. A few years earlier, I'd thought that the business was just a temporary adventure for me; now it had become so consuming that I couldn't even imagine getting off the elevator. But Craig could. I was reassured that it wouldn't be anytime soon, but I think he was reassured to know that he wouldn't be doing this forever. We both affirmed our commitment to the company and its mission.

As we packed up on Sunday to head back to Austin, I was happy about the weekend, but the still-unresolved situation with Mark weighed heavily on me. He had come and gone during the weekend, but he mostly ignored the three of us and our activities. It felt like we were already moving forward as a leadership team, and he was being left behind. I just didn't see how it made sense for him to stay. But what was I to do? Mark was still a part owner of the company.

As we merged onto the freeway, Mark's sports car sped past us, but when we pulled over outside of Houston to get gas, I saw that he'd done the same. I didn't want us to go home with things still unresolved, so I got out and went over to talk to him. We stood on the roadside, the weight of all those months of disagreement still heavy between us.

"Mark, this isn't working," I said. "Surely, that's obvious."

"Sure is," he replied sarcastically. A lot of what Mark said these days, to me at least, was delivered with a heavy dose of sarcasm.

"Okay, so let's accept that," I said. "I've already made it clear that I'm not giving you Lamar, and the Board backs me. Craig wants to stay with the company."

"Well, I don't," he said. "And just so you know, every company I've ever left has ended up bankrupt. I'm sure this one will be no different."

He got back in his car and drove away. Eventually, I was able to get Jim Sud and Don Schaffer to buy his shares. As I recall, he walked away with about $300,000 for his 10% of the business. In 1985, that seemed like a lot of money, and it was a fair price. But history would prove that to be a very poor financial decision indeed on his part.

Mark and I permanently went our separate ways. A once-promising partnership and a valued friendship had failed. It saddened me, but I accepted that there was no other way. And I knew it really wasn't personal, even though it had often felt that way. We simply had fundamentally different visions of the company's future. Beneath the acrimony, the sarcasm, the bitterness, and the power struggles, that was what drove us apart. Nevertheless, I remained the villain in Mark's narrative. He was the first to really challenge my leadership. He wouldn't be the last.

As much as I might want to build cooperative relationships with all my partners, it wasn't always possible to do successfully. Human beings are also wired to compete. We envy those we perceive as having more success, attractiveness, wealth, fame, power, and so on, and we have a tendency to insist on the fundamental rightness of our own versions of reality even when it comes at great personal cost. I was learning all of these lessons, even as I was trying to become more skilled at balancing the inevitable authority of my leadership position with my desire to collaborate and share.

I too was often convinced I was right, even when it brought me into conflict with people I cared about. I also had a tendency to sometimes override others when I perceived them as barriers to my own creative ideas, or to be overconfident that eventually others would come to see the world as I saw it. Mark never did. And in the end, we saw the future so differently that we simply couldn't continue to walk the same path together.

Chapter 13

Texas State Champions

Sometimes in business you have to build things from the ground up. Other times, you can take legitimate shortcuts. In early 1986, having opened four Whole Foods Markets that were now doing well, I was excited to have found an opportunity for a shortcut to store number five. I showed up at a Board meeting at the Shepherd store in Houston ready to propose an acquisition—our first since merging with Clarksville Natural Grocery back in 1980.

The Board, by this point, had expanded. In addition to myself and Craig, my father, Don Schaffer, Jim Sud, and Jay Templeton, fellow travelers, and mentors from the beginning, we now had three new directors: Anthony Harnett, founder of Bread & Circus; Gary Hoover, founder of Bookstop; and Jack Bixby, a friend of my father's, who had been CFO of an oil and gas company. My father was still the most influential member of the Board, and his advice continued to be invaluable to me as the company grew. But little by little, the Board was becoming more formal and corporate. This was no longer the small "band of brothers" of Safer Way and Whole Foods Market's startup years.

My proposal that day was that we move into the Dallas market by acquiring a business named Bluebonnet Natural Foods. "They're a copycat store," I explained to the Board. "They tried to replicate our success but they're not doing very well. They leased a large space and basically copied our format, but while they have pretty good sales, they're losing money." To me, this was good news. It meant they didn't know how to run the business. It was one thing to copy our format but another thing altogether to re-create everything we were doing behind the scenes to make the business successful and profitable—our culture, our business model, our supplier relationships, and more. Because we had those things established already, it stood to reason that we could make their store a success even if they couldn't. And we could benefit from the fact that they'd already put so much in place. I'd talked to the owners, and they seemed keen to sell.

I looked around at the Board. "I think it's a great opportunity for us. It might not be long before they go bankrupt."

Several Board members scanned the proposal Craig and I had put together. It outlined the basic terms of the deal we envisioned, including a purchase price: $1 million.

Jim spoke up. "John, I like the idea of expanding to Dallas. But let me ask you something: a million dollars seems like a lot to pay for a struggling business. Is this a situation where we could buy it for pennies on the dollar in six months or a year? Is it really a fair price?"

I'd anticipated this question. A million dollars was a lot of money. But I was confident we could recoup it quite quickly. After all, our Houston store was beginning to perform very well, and Dallas wasn't such a different market. Bluebonnet was also located in an ideal spot. But there was another reason I had come up with that number. I was reasonably certain it could get the deal done.

"It's a great question," I replied. "And you're right. Maybe we could wait and pick up the business for cheap in bankruptcy. But here's my thinking: What would we be getting then? A broken carcass, with debtors attached, and frustrated customers who are already finding other places to shop. Team members who have quit or feel angry. Whereas, if we buy them now, at a decent price, we'll own a business that still has a lot of value and will be easier to turn around. We could buy them in a year when they're almost dead; I want to buy them now while they're still alive."

I could see that the Board members were receptive to my argument. And I felt confident in the logic behind it. In that moment, it struck me how far I'd come personally from the idealistic but naïve young man who'd first attended a Board meeting with his father and a couple of sympathetic friends. I'd grown into my role as CEO. I wasn't looking to the Board to tell me how to lead the company, although I still valued their advice. I was telling them what I'd concluded about our best next step.

"I think the way to look at this is not just about what *they're* getting. It's what *we're* getting." We'd eliminate a potential competitor and gain an established store with decent sales in a large, new market. This would help to cement our position as the leading natural foods retailer in Texas. Yes, we would have to work hard to make the store profitable—shortcuts only go so far—but I was confident we knew how to accomplish that. By writing that million-dollar check, we'd expand the footprint of the company overnight by 20%, without having to do the work of finding a location, negotiating a lease, and building out a store.

Confident that my case was being heard, I brought the pitch to a close: "In a couple of years, a million dollars will look like nothing for this fantastic location and established customer base. I like to think of it as a win-win deal. It's a win for us, and it's definitely a win for them."

My brief speech had been the product of a great deal of thinking and talking about this acquisition—and about acquisitions in general. Somewhere I had come across this notion of a "win-win solution," which really appealed to me. It was already shaping the way I thought about all kinds of business deals. Of course, there was a school of thought that said, "Negotiate to the final dollar. Drive the hardest bargain you can." Sometimes that works; sometimes it blows up in your face. I was interested in a different approach. Instead of asking "What is a fair price?" or "What is the least I can pay?" I thought it was more productive to ask two questions. First, "What price will get the deal done?" Second, "Am I willing to pay it?" Find a number that can work for both sides, and that represents a win-win outcome. Later, I would learn that this is Warren Buffett's approach to dealmaking as well and I carefully studied his thoughts on the matter.

Another important aspect of acquiring a business, and one that was brought home to me in the Bluebonnet deal, is the simple truth that we all are irrational when it comes to valuing our own businesses. There is no point spending precious time trying to convince a business owner that their business is not worth what they think it is. That's a perfect recipe for conflict and frustration. Again, the better option is to ask oneself, "What price is enough to convince them to sell, even though it might not be as much as they think they should get? And am I willing to pay that price—or something close to it?" It simplifies negotiations. The price we were willing to pay for Bluebonnet was a million dollars. I was pretty sure they would accept it, even though I knew they'd still think it was too low. Of course they would! That store was their baby. Every entrepreneur, like every parent, has overly optimistic assessments of the quality and future potential of their offspring. I received approval from the Board to make a million-dollar offer to the Bluebonnet folks. I hoped they'd see that it was a great deal for both of us.

I planned to head back to Austin that evening, but before I left, I dropped by my parents' house. Pulling up outside, I recognized my sister's car. Dorothy was spending more time at the house these days, since she and her second husband, Jean-Claude Lurie, had moved to Houston a couple of years earlier. I was glad they were here—it was good to have Dorothy close, especially since my mother's recent stroke had confined her to a wheelchair. And Jean-Claude, who now worked at Whole Foods leading the Shepherd store, had become a dear friend and mentor—like an older brother to me. A wise and charming man, he had endured the Nazi occupation of Paris as a teenager, forced to drop out before starting high school to avoid using his mother's Jewish name and risking arrest. He won first prize in violin at the Paris Conservatory but had no formal education. He was one of the most brilliant men I ever met, as well as a wonderful father to my nephew Andy. I loved staying in their garage apartment every time I visited Houston and watching sports with Jean-Claude or shooting hoops in the driveway after work.

Stepping inside, I went straight to my mother. "Mom, it's great to see you! How are you feeling?" I kissed her on the cheek, nodding to my sister and Jean-Claude, who were both standing nearby. Even after hearing about her recent struggles, I was surprised to see how gaunt she was, and how much older she looked.

She smiled weakly. "Hi, John, how did your meeting go? Your father hasn't come home yet."

"It went well. The Board approved my plan. We're expanding again, this time to Dallas."

"Well, that's good to hear. Dallas is a big city for sure." Her voice lacked enthusiasm. She turned to Jean-Claude, gesturing toward me with a hand that held a lighted cigarette. "This one has such a good mind. I tell you; he could do anything with it. Law. Medicine. Finance. Politics." She took a drag and shook her head. My mother still couldn't accept my chosen profession.

I was long past arguing this point with her, but Jean-Claude was having none of it. He threw up his hands in an exaggerated Gallic gesture of dismay. "John is doing amazing things! Whole Foods Market is becoming a large, impressive business."

I appreciated the support from my brother-in-law. But for all the impression it made on my mother, Jean-Claude might as well have been speaking French instead of heavily accented English. I decided to change the subject.

"Mom, you must be enjoying having Dorothy living nearby again. Andy is getting bigger by the day."

The mention of her grandson's name immediately softened my mother's face, and the conversation moved back onto less contentious ground. My father soon returned, and as we sat down to dinner, he put a hand on my shoulder.

"You did well today, son. I like the way you're thinking."

The boardroom wasn't the only place I was feeling more like a grown-up and less of a naïve young man. Back in Austin, my personal life had changed quite dramatically as well. Over the past year or two, I'd embraced a period of exploration and experimentation—emotionally and spiritually. Breathwork, meditation, MDMA, *A Course in Miracles.* I'd ended my relationship with Renee with a great deal of gratitude and no lingering regrets. In so doing, I opened myself up to the possibility of new love. It wasn't long before I found it. Mary Kay was someone I had been attracted to for many years, but I hadn't acted on that attraction while things were still in flux with Renee. We had been acquaintances even before the days of Safer Way, moving in similar circles. By 1984, she was working for Whole Foods, managing the Crossroads store, and that summer we began dating and quickly fell in love.

Once again, I had gotten involved with someone who worked for the company. Craig probably disapproved, but a funny thing had happened to him after years of frowning upon Mark's and my intra-company love lives. He too fell in love—with someone who worked for the company! Renee Hanlon had been with Whole Foods Market since the early days and had recently become Renee Weller. She and Craig were a wonderful couple, and I was happy for him. But that didn't stop me from enjoying a little payback. When I started dating Mary Kay, Craig wisely kept his thoughts to himself.

Mary Kay was beautiful, smart, vibrant, and intense—all qualities I loved and valued deeply. She would end up being the second great love of my life. I often worked with her at the Crossroads store, and in the evenings we would sometimes lock up the store, put on our favorite music, and dance playfully and passionately through the aisles. I immediately sensed that life with Mary Kay would be an exciting adventure, and I was more than happy to sign up for the ride.

There was another side to Mary Kay as well. She was a mother to three daughters. The middle one of those daughters, Evening, then aged nine, was that same little girl who once upon a time showed up at Clarksville Natural Grocery unaccompanied. When Craig shut down the store to walk her home, he had no idea that one day she'd become his business partner's stepdaughter. Evening's sister Chica was 13, and her baby sister, Allison, was just two. I loved kids and had always thought I'd have my own family someday. When Mary Kay and I decided to move in together in late 1984, I got a ready-made family overnight.

Another milestone in this accelerated maturing was the purchase of my first home, a four-bedroom house. At 2,500 square feet, it felt grand, and when Mary Kay moved in, each of the girls got their own bedroom. I embraced my new role wholeheartedly. I helped with homework, I did my best to befriend each of the girls, and I loved their mother as best I knew how. By and large, I was happy, and my life narrowed down once again into a few primary activities—work, family, and my daily exercise, which in those days was usually basketball or running.

Family life suited me, but being a surrogate father had its own challenges. The children were naturally a bit suspicious of me, especially in the first year or two. As a teenager, Chica was too old to really care about my presence in her life, and Allison was too young to have a strong opinion. Evening, however, was wary around me. A quiet, self-contained child, she remained guarded even as we spent more time together. No matter what I said or did, I didn't seem to be able to get past this nine-year-old girl's relative indifference. I had to conclude that she just didn't like me. Still, I was determined to win her trust, so as I tucked her into bed one night, I decided to ask her outright. Sometimes children appreciate directness.

"Evening, why don't you like me?"

She looked up at me, her blue eyes serious, and then slowly replied, "It's not that I don't like you. It's just that there's no point. I know you'll eventually leave just like all the other men my mother gets together with."

Evening was, as it turned out, both right and wrong. She was right, as perhaps only a child can be, about the patterns of her mother's relationships with men. Eventually, Mary Kay and I would indeed have a difficult, fiery breakup. But she was also wrong, because by the time we finally did split, I had been with the family for almost six years, watched all three daughters grow up, and had truly come to love them as my own. The bonds I developed with the girls—especially Evening and Allison, with whom I spent much more time—are still going strong, far transcending my temporary relationship with their mother.

"No, I'm sending you a check right now. I need you to reinstate our account. Yes, that's right. Bluebonnet Natural Foods. The company has been sold, and Whole Foods Market is the new owner. We will settle the outstanding bill of the previous owner. I'm sorry you've had to wait for your money, and I look forward to doing business with you."

How many calls like this did I make during those first weeks after acquiring the Bluebonnet store? In many ways, Bluebonnet was in worse shape than we'd expected. Their supply chain infrastructure was beginning to break down, and I quickly realized I needed to be on-site to oversee these rather fragile relationships with the store's suppliers, many of whom had been left hanging with bills unpaid. Mary Kay and I temporarily moved to Dallas for six months, and she became the Store Team Leader while I worked closely with her on turning around the newly acquired business. This was only Whole Foods Market's second acquisition, so it was a steep learning curve. While it was true that buying a ready-made store had saved us a lot of time, we definitely underestimated what it would take to get it on its feet.

Working to fix the many problems that troubled Bluebonnet was an important experience for me. I knew that Whole Foods Market ran a lean operation. We didn't have a lot of overhead because we resisted building in too much centralization and the bureaucracy that entails. Instead, we relied on good management at the store level. We took our profits and reinvested them in the business. Craig and my father had each in their own way been essential in helping us embrace this spirit of frugality. What I learned in Dallas showed me the power of our business model. We were well positioned to perform a quick turnaround. In only about six months of hard work and restructuring, we streamlined their operations, paid their outstanding debts, reorganized the store, and built a thriving, profitable natural foods business where there had once been a failing company. When Mary Kay and I were ready to move back to Austin, I asked David Matthis and Karen Saadeh to move to Dallas and run the store.

As I witnessed the Bluebonnet team members slowly transform into a successful Whole Foods team, guided by some of our best leaders, I realized that we had crossed a knowledge threshold. We were starting to get good at this! We didn't have all the answers, but we knew how to build and run a solid, successful natural foods store—not just once or twice, but five times and in three different cities. We were no longer a startup; we weren't reinventing ourselves with each new store. And that truth made me even more excited about our future and all the opportunities that lay ahead. We were now, indisputably, the reigning natural foods retailer in Texas. And I began to get the itch to look to new horizons.

Chapter 14

California Dreaming

The pressure in my ears was growing uncomfortable. Frustrated, I tried the various tricks that scuba divers use to clear them, but it wasn't working. The rest of the diving group was descending below me, and I soon lost sight of them in the deep blue that appeared to go on forever. Eventually, I succeeded in releasing the pressure in my ears and began my own descent. The South Pacific waters grew cooler and quieter as I gently floated down, enjoying the sensation of the world and all its concerns receding above me. I slowed my breathing, exhaling fully and releasing the momentary irritation I'd felt, allowing my body to become heavier and drift downward. I felt my energy shift too, becoming calmer and more focused. Diving is a little like meditation in this way—it never ceases to amaze me how the subtle modulation of breath helps me to navigate the soft currents of the ocean and also changes my inner experience in the process.

As my eyes adjusted to the depths, I looked around for Mary Kay and my dive group, and I noticed something strange in the water below me—a shapeless bulky object. It definitely wasn't another diver. In my struggle to clear my ears, I realized, I must have drifted a little away from the rest of the group. The next moment, I had no doubt what the object was—and no doubt that I needed to get away from it as fast as possible. It was a bait ball—a mass of dead fish that the dive master had flung out of the boat to attract sharks. And it was doing its job. As I watched in horror, a couple of dozen sharks ranging from 6 to 12 feet in length swam into view, attacking the ball in a feeding frenzy, tails thrashing through the water, cold beady eyes fixated on the bait. I was almost on top of them.

Fortunately, the sharks decided the bait ball was more enticing than I was, and I was able to quickly swim away, my sudden rapid breathing aiding my upward progress. I soon caught sight of the group, watching the sharks from a safe distance, and made my way over to join them.

After we'd resurfaced, the dive master was understandably upset. I was effectively put in the penalty box for all future dives I did with him. The heart-stopping incident didn't blunt my enthusiasm for the sport, although it did give me a new respect for the predators that roamed the ocean.

It was late summer 1986, and after an intensive six months in Dallas getting Bluebonnet back on its feet, Mary Kay and I were taking a much-needed break. We had decided to combine a vacation with some market research, so this dive trip to Tahiti was sandwiched between two road trips, the first of which had taken us from Austin to Los Angeles. We drove all day and all night, stopping only to refuel our car and our bodies, in the way you can only do when you're young and less beholden to sleep. Other tourists might have headed for Hollywood Boulevard hoping to see the stars; we went straight to the nearest natural foods store.

It had been a few years since I'd visited Mrs. Gooch's, and I was curious to see how our West Coast comrades had developed their iconic stores. I was also eager to show Mary Kay a few of the places that had inspired me when first creating Whole Foods Market, and to look for ideas we might apply in our new locations. Besides Mrs. Gooch's, we checked out some Trader Joe's stores and paid a visit to the great stores that Frazier Farms had created in San Diego. Touring grocery stores might not sound like that much fun, but it's something I never tired of doing. Mrs. Gooch's window displays were as quirky as ever, and the California produce was enviably fresh and bountiful. Trader Joe's was intriguing—not exactly a natural foods store, but definitely not a conventional grocery store either. I'd visited their stores years earlier when I'd been out there for a Natural Foods Network meeting and had been confused about their appeal. They seemed to focus on deep-discount wine and a hodgepodge of other items distinguished only by their low prices. No produce. No fresh meat or seafood counter. I'd hoped they would stay that way and not pose much direct competition to natural foods supermarkets like ours. Now, I took note of some changes. The stores seemed to be developing more personality, with quirky signage and product branding. And their private-label offerings, of which there had been only a handful last time I visited, now dominated the shelves. Whole Foods Market had yet to venture into private-label territory, so this was very interesting to me. One thing was clear: Californians loved Trader Joe's, and I already knew that California was a reliable innovation bellwether for what might eventually be a national trend. I made a mental note to pay more attention to their development going forward.

On this trip, I noticed a difference in the way I was seeing the stores I visited. I was no longer the upstart kid from Texas who'd gazed with wide-eyed amazement at the size and bounty of the new natural foods supermarkets in California. Whole Foods Market was now a profitable multi-store chain, with a presence in three of Texas's largest cities. I was its CEO, and at 33, that title felt more comfortable to me every day. The instincts and ideals that I'd followed in our growth had proven to be sound business practices. We'd weathered some rough moments, like the slow starts of each new store and the departure of two of our four founders. But with five stores now up and running, I was beginning to have a sense of knowing how to do this—and do it well. And when I walked the aisles of our West Coast counterparts, I was pleasantly surprised to see that in many ways our own stores equaled or surpassed what we saw. Of course, there were always things we could improve, and Mary Kay and I studied every detail, but I felt a growing confidence that Whole Foods Market had come of age and could now stand side by side with the stores that had once inspired me.

Buoyed with this new sense of confidence, we left our car in LA and flew to Tahiti for two magical weeks. We spent our time lying on the beach reading, playing a lot of backgammon, eating some great food, and doing a lot of what healthy young couples always do. And of course, scuba diving in the island's famously shark-rich waters. As the vacation came to an end, I felt refreshed and energized. I'd dived deeply into another side of myself, immersed myself in ideas and stories and play and adventure and love, and now I was bobbing back up to the surface, ready to reengage with the world of business and growth and strategy.

Back in California, we hit the road again, driving up the coast on the legendary Route 1 through Big Sur. As we passed the Esalen Institute, perched on the cliffs above the Pacific, I peered through the trees, trying to catch a glimpse of the place where so many of my spiritual heroes had come to meditate, teach, and explore the inner universe. I wished we could have stopped for a few days to soak in the famous hot tubs and talk about consciousness and altered states. But we had a lot of places to get to before our road trip led us back into America's heartland and home to Texas. Next stop, Northern California.

Arriving in San Francisco, we went to the Kerista commune to visit my old girlfriend Debbie (who now called herself MIK, short for Mighty Is Kindness). She was still thriving in that unconventional culture. Sitting around a fire that evening with MIK and her friends, I wondered again about the road not taken. Could I have been happy here? Some part of me was still drawn to the closeness of this community, although I'd chosen a very different life path. I was happy in my current life as a family man and entrepreneur. I couldn't imagine what my life would have looked like if I'd followed MIK into this experimental lifestyle. I caught Mary Kay's eye across the room and smiled at the expression on her face as she listened to the conversation—half intrigued and half bemused.

During the week we spent in the Bay Area, I was struck afresh by how different it felt from the southern part of the state. Los Angeles was high-octane, brash, and sun drenched. San Francisco, and the surrounding area, felt softer and more introspective, like the persistent fog that shrouded the hillsides and clung to the towering redwoods. I felt an immediate kinship with folks I met there—like me, they'd embraced the countercultural lifestyle so deeply that it had become an identity. And whereas in Austin hippies still felt a little like outsiders, here we felt like a critical mass. In the Bay Area in the late eighties, the counterculture was steadily becoming the establishment. At least, it was in many regards. But one strange truth slowly dawned on me as we drove around, visiting natural foods stores. Mary Kay and I were eating lunch at a little store in Mill Valley, Marin County, when it suddenly came into focus.

"Oh my God," I exclaimed, "you know what's crazy? Northern California has no natural foods supermarkets!"

As unlikely as it seemed, it was true. Sure, there were plenty of wonderful small local stores, and the conventional stores in California carried a better selection of organic produce and natural foods, but there was no equivalent to Whole Foods Market, Mrs. Gooch's, or Bread & Circus. Perhaps the closest was the Berkeley Co-op, which in its heyday had had locations across the Bay Area. When this became clear, I was astounded. Of all the places in the country, how could the Bay Area—the birthplace of the counterculture—have missed out on the natural foods supermarket revolution? Mrs. Gooch's had been around for a decade by now, and yet they'd had no inclination to venture north. And no new player had emerged in this obviously ready market. I could hardly believe it. Mary Kay looked at me, knowing what I was thinking before I said it. "You're not going to suggest that—"

"—Whole Foods Market should expand to Northern California!" I finished the sentence for her, laughing out loud at the obviousness—and the ridiculousness—of the idea. Could a bunch of Texans really show up in the San Francisco Bay Area and be successful selling natural foods? Would it just be like selling ice to Eskimos? They might laugh us out of town. But then again, *someone* needed to do it. And for all their rich countercultural history, the Northern Californians hadn't gotten around to it yet. Whole Foods Market might be just what they'd been waiting for.

I couldn't wait to get back to Austin and tell the rest of the team my idea. But our road trip wasn't nearly over yet. We headed north again, camping in various state and national parks, making our way through Oregon, Washington, Idaho, Montana, Wyoming, and into Colorado, where we stopped for a few days with Alfalfa's cofounder Mark Retzloff and his wife, Terri, at their beautiful farm outside Boulder. We ate delicious fresh food and I admired his bustling downtown store. Boulder was another city where the counterculture had taken root, and I felt immediately at home there.

Leaving Boulder, we drove through New Mexico and then back to Texas. All in all, the trip was a wonderful six weeks, and it felt invaluable, not just personally but from a business perspective as well. Sometimes you need to get out of your familiar environment to see your next move. We were the market leader in Texas. But I wasn't satisfied with that. I was ready to test our concept outside of our state, and to find out whether Whole Foods Market had the potential to be a national company.

Back in Austin, we gathered the leadership team to talk about expansion. Where would Whole Foods Market go next? By this point, I was set on Northern California. The enormous opportunity there just seemed obvious to me. Chris Hitt, who had joined the company not long after Mark's departure a couple of years earlier, loved the idea right away. Craig was enthusiastic too, but with one hesitation.

"What about Mrs. Gooch's? Won't they see that as their territory?"

Craig had attended many of the Natural Foods Network meetings with me, so he knew our fellow store owners well. We all shared an unspoken agreement not to open stores in each other's cities. But this was different.

"They've had 10 years!" I retorted. "Besides, Northern California and Southern California are almost like different states. They're hundreds of miles apart. If they considered it their territory, they'd have gone there by now."

Craig shook his head. "I don't know. How would you feel if they decided to open up a store in another part of Texas—like San Antonio?"

Eventually, he conceded, though I could see he was still worried. And if I was honest, I didn't really know how Sandy Gooch or John Moorman would feel about us showing up anywhere in California. But I wasn't exactly going to pick up the phone and ask them for permission! As far as I was concerned, they'd left themselves open to this by not taking the opportunity sooner. Nor had they ever indicated to anyone in the Network that they had any interest in expanding into the Bay Area. If they'd had such ambitions, it was a closely kept secret.

Before we made a final decision, we wanted to involve our team members. After all, they each had a stake in the future of Whole Foods Market, and some of them would be called on to move to the new state and help get the store open. We polled everyone in the company with the question: Where should we open our first store outside of Texas? I guess we shouldn't have been too surprised when the poll had a clear winner: Hawaii.

While sun, sand, and surf certainly sounded appealing, 2,000-plus miles across the Pacific Ocean was a step too far for our still-young company at that point. Luckily, the second-place location matched my own ambitions: California. The decision was made.

And so it was that about a year later, on a happily fog-free Northern California morning, I found myself in the office of Palo Alto real estate developer Charles "Chop" Keenan. We'd initially wanted to open our first California store in San Francisco, but we just couldn't find an acceptable location. Going into a new market was particularly tough in those days because no one knew who we were. Our brand had no cachet outside of the markets in which we were already operating. It was hard to persuade landlords to rent their premium retail locations to a bunch of young people running a grocery store they'd never heard of. When we struck out in San Francisco, we turned our attention to the South Bay.

Silicon Valley was already beginning to transform the area into an economic powerhouse and would eventually became the epicenter of a tech revolution that would change the world. There were multiple semiconductor factories in the region and Stanford University was growing in influence. Plus, the limited geographical footprint of San Francisco made spillover inevitable, and all the surrounding cities were growing fast. One person taking advantage of this trend was Chop, a power player in Bay Area real estate. He owned a parcel of land in Palo Alto that we'd earmarked as a good site for our new store, and I'd flown out to Palo Alto to negotiate the lease with him personally.

Chop's style was brash and abrupt, given to declarative statements. As I took a seat across from him, I scanned the bookshelf on the wall, half expecting to see a dog-eared copy of the popular eighties business bestseller *Winning Through Intimidation*. That sure seemed to be his approach.

"Mackey, the lease has to be 20 years," he told me emphatically.

We had never signed a lease that long. In 20 years I would be incredibly old—54! I couldn't even think that far ahead.

"That's a long time," I hedged. "We're not really looking for a 20-year lease."

Chop leaned back in his big leather chair, looking me straight in the eye. "I only do 20-year deals, Mackey. If we're not going to sign a lease for 20 years, we might as well stop this conversation right now. Just tell me and I'll find somebody else. There are plenty of other guys who'd happily sign this deal if you don't want to." I wasn't sure if that was true—it seemed likely that it was another bullying tactic. But after months of location hunting, I was impatient to get to the next phase and actually start building our first Bay Area store.

At this point, I became aware of something a little off in the room. I'm a reasonably tall guy, but as I sat there across from Chop, he seemed to tower over me. Eventually, I figured out that he was sitting on an elevated platform—another lesson in the fine art of intimidation, I supposed. Adding to my disadvantaged position was the fact that my chair was situated so that the bright sunlight streaming through the window hit me square in the eyes. Chop had me right where he wanted me, I mused. And I wasn't sure how to rebalance the power dynamic. Indeed, I had the uncomfortable feeling that in this particular negotiation, I was like that ball of shark bait, and the man sitting across from me was just as relentless as those Tahitian ocean hunters.

Squinting up at him, I reluctantly agreed to his terms, and I walked out of his office thinking I'd lost out for Whole Foods. Little did I know at the time that I had just made what would turn out to be an incredible deal! Locking in the lease for 20 years was wonderful for Whole Foods, given how rents would rise in Palo Alto over the coming decades. But on that day, the only thing that mattered to me was that we had our site. We were finally going to get the opportunity to test our business model in the backyard of the counterculture.

Chapter 15

Not Just a Grocer

I pulled into my parents' familiar driveway, cut the engine, and sat there for a moment in the darkened car. It was September 1987, and I was spending the week in Houston, working at the Shepherd store and staying with Dorothy and Jean-Claude, which also gave me a chance to spend time with my parents. Through the kitchen window, light spilled into the front yard. I could see my father pouring himself a drink at the counter. He looked tired.

In his mid-sixties, my father was still vital, but my mother's long-drawn-out illness was weighing on him. I'd been visiting more frequently that year, knowing that my mother probably didn't have much longer to live. Her stroke a couple of years earlier had left her partially paralyzed and bedridden, and she'd undergone multiple heart bypass surgeries.

My father looked up and saw my car, raising his hand in greeting. I got out and went inside. He was eager to hear what was happening with the business, so I let him get me a beer, and I told him more about my recent trip to Palo Alto and our plans for the new store. He brightened as we talked. I also told him how well the former Bluebonnet store was doing—so well, in fact, that we were thinking about opening a second Dallas store.

"Listen, John, this all sounds great. But we need to find a new source of capital if we want to expand more rapidly. I'm not putting any more money in. And I don't think any of our other investors are ready to put up that kind of cash."

I nodded. I knew he was right. The Palo Alto store, at 20,000 square feet plus a 10,000-square-foot basement, was our largest yet, with a lease cost that was much higher than our Texas stores. And I didn't want to stop at one store in the Bay Area. I had my eye on other cities too. This wasn't a moment when we could continue to get by on bank loans and small new investments from our current investors. We'd need millions to finance the plans I had in mind. Which meant one thing: venture capital. That's where Dad was going with this conversation. He told me he had a friend at an investment banking firm and would talk to him about setting up some meetings. The implications scared me a bit, but I didn't see another option.

"Thanks, Dad," I said. "I'll call you tomorrow when I'm back in the office to discuss this further. For now—" I hesitated, reluctant to change the subject and bring his mind back to the difficult situation at home, but I wasn't really here to talk business.

"How's Mom?" I asked.

"Not good." He shook his head, looking tired and resigned. "The nurse says she may not have long. I'm trying to make sure she gets the best possible care."

"I know you are, Dad." I felt the burden he'd carried for many years. I loved my mother, but I knew it wasn't easy taking care of her. I appreciated that my father had been able to provide her with home care during her final months.

"I should go and see her," I told him, putting down my beer.

Walking into the bedroom, I was hit by the smell of stale cigarette smoke mixed with disinfectant. For a moment, time collapsed, and I was a small boy again. The woman on the bed was not my mother but my grandmother, who had lived with us for a few years when I was a young boy. She too had been bedridden, smoking her way through her final years, but I'd loved coming to see her. Her face would light up whenever I came through the door.

"Come sit here beside me, John," she'd say in her raspy voice, and then she'd turn on the radio and we'd listen to baseball games together, back when the Houston Major League team was still called the Colt .45s and later when they changed their name to the Astros. If I closed my eyes, standing in the bedroom doorway, I could still hear the announcer's voice in my head, the roar of the crowd, and my grandmother pounding her frail fist on the pillow when our team scored a run.

But now, when I opened my eyes, the old woman in the bed was my mother.

"Hi, Mom," I said, sitting down in the chair beside her and taking her hand. I knew she was glad to see me too, though she didn't show it like my grandmother had. I never had any doubt that she loved me, but I'd always been closer to my father, drawn to his confidence and more positive outlook. My mother had always been prone to worrying about everything. As she aged and lost her health, her anxiety had turned bitter, and her resentments swirled around her like the ever-present cigarette smoke.

Like her mother before her, Mom stubbornly clung to her cigarettes. She was only 64, but she looked much older—literally wasting away before our eyes. She lit another, closing her eyes as she inhaled.

"Mom, those damn cigarettes, they're killing you. They've destroyed your health. Don't you know that? That's a big reason why you're so sick now."

She looked at me sadly. "John, I know, these things are terrible. I'm so glad you don't smoke. But at this point in my life, they're the only thing I have left that gives me any pleasure." And she took another drag.

We were silent for a moment, and then she said, "You know, I'm dying."

"Yes, I know," I told her, "but hopefully not for a long time yet." I wasn't sure if she knew what the nurse had told Dad.

"Well, who knows?" She broke into a hacking cough, and I passed her a glass of water. "I could have another stroke at any time."

I couldn't really argue with that. It was true. But I hoped she still had some time. She stubbed out her cigarette and turned to look at me, a serious expression coming over her face.

"John," she said, "I want you to make me a promise. I want you to promise me that you will go back to school and finally get your degree.

Your father and I, we gave you a very good mind. You're very intelligent. I saw all your IQ and aptitude tests when you were younger. You could be so much more in life if you would just apply yourself to it. I hate to see you wasting your life."

I sighed. I'd heard this so many times before—ever since I was in high school and began to long for something more than the ordinary life my mother envisioned for me. Even after visiting our Houston store, she still didn't understand that I'd found a career that both fulfilled my soul and was bringing financial rewards as well.

"Mom, I'm never going to go back to school," I told her. "I'm doing what I love to do. And Whole Foods Market is going to be a great company. I'm more than just a grocer—I'm a successful entrepreneur. We have five stores now in Texas, and soon we'll have stores in California too."

But she just shook her head. She didn't say the words outright, but I knew that to her, my chosen path had no real future. It pained her to see me wasting my potential on what she felt was a lesser class of job.

I hated seeing the disappointment in her face. "You know what," I added, struck by a sudden idea, "maybe I will get a degree someday, but it will be one of those honorary degrees that some university will give me because I've become a wealthy businessman and I'll make a large donation!" I laughed at the thought, but my mother clearly didn't think it was funny at all. I didn't know what more to say after that.

A wistful look came over her face, and she said, "You were such a cute baby, John. You know, when you were born, you had a full head of curly hair. And just look at you now." She cast a disparaging glance at my bushy mane. "You were such a sweet boy." I felt her love and her sadness, and I wished I could give her what she wanted. But young and idealistic as I was, I couldn't lie to her.

Looking back, some part of me wishes I had. What would it have cost me to just make the promise she asked for, to let her believe that her son would find his way to the life she dreamed he would have? Back then, it would have felt like an affront to my integrity. But my more mature self might have handled things differently.

I didn't know then that this conversation would be the last one I would ever have with my mother, and that when I said goodbye that night, turned around, and walked out of her room, it would be for the last time. She died a few days later from a stroke. Perhaps, if I'd reassured her and made that promise, it would have given her some comfort at the end. I'll never know. But I'll always regret that her last moment with me was one of disappointment. I like to think that if she'd lived a longer life, she would eventually have come to see how ennobling and purposeful my business venture was, and she would have been proud of me. Perhaps, wherever she is, she feels that way now.

Chapter 16

The Hitchhiker's Guide to Capital

"Are they really all on the same road?" I asked Bill Ashbaugh, our banker, after looking over the itinerary of meetings he'd just handed me.

He laughed. "That's right! Sand Hill Road, Menlo Park, otherwise known as the Wall Street of the West Coast. At least it makes it easy to do multiple meetings in one day."

"I guess it does," I agreed. "California, here we come!"

It was time to take the plunge and seek venture capital. But I did so with considerable reservations—many of them reinforced by my father. Indeed, although he'd been the first to conclude that we needed to take this step, he'd also been the voice of caution.

"Make no mistake, John," he'd said when we'd revisited the subject a couple of months after my mother's death. "You can't trust VCs. You may need them, but you can't trust them. So you've got to be smart. The moment you take them into your company, they're going to be looking out for themselves and their investors. Which means: How do they get their money back? They'll need an exit strategy."

I knew what that meant: either an IPO (initial public offering) or a sale of Whole Foods Market to a competitor. Once you start down the venture capital road, that's the next logical step. I honestly hadn't given it a lot of thought beyond the fact that we needed more capital to grow. My father was right, however—if we were going to raise money from the VCs, we needed to start thinking today about preparing the company for the inevitable consequences.

What would it mean for me, as the CEO, to have VCs and eventually public shareholders to answer to? I liked running the company the way I did, with my supportive Board and a small group of patient investors whom I knew personally and trusted. I wanted those investors to be richly rewarded, which an eventual IPO might well achieve. But I didn't know how I felt about bringing in outside investors with their own interests and agendas.

My dad must have been reading my mind. "John, I know you love running this company. But any new money is going to want a seat on the Board. And they'll start looking to replace you. VCs seldom think that the people who start businesses are the best people to manage and grow them. They'll want some MBA professional manager type to come in and take over. They won't have the power to make that kind of change right away, but you must understand who and what you're dealing with. The politics of the Board will become increasingly tricky."

His words inflamed my fears. And yet, there were no other viable options if we really wanted to expand faster.

"Okay, thanks, Dad." I really meant it—I appreciated his advice and wisdom more than ever in moments like this. "I understand the risks, but I still think we need to go forward. Please reach out to your friend and get him to start setting up some meetings."

Dad promised that he would. "Have a good day, son."

"Wait—" I said, then hesitated, not sure how much to throw at my father in one sitting.

"What is it?"

"Well, there's one more thing I wanted to run by you before I speak to the full Board. You remember Peter Roy, in New Orleans? He wants to sell his business to us and join our team."

By this point, although the Network had just about run its course, I'd become quite close to Peter. Merging his Whole Food Company with Whole Foods Market would give us a total of seven stores and wouldn't cost us much cash, as Peter was willing to be paid mostly in stock. I thought the deal was a no-brainer. Everything lined up. Peter's two stores weren't doing too well financially, but I knew we could quickly change their fortunes and make them profitable. Plus, this deal had one enormous benefit: It added an experienced natural foods executive to our team. With his gift for relationships, I knew Peter would be a real asset, especially as we moved into California and went out looking for investors. Peter was ambitious and entrepreneurial, and this was a much bigger platform on which to exercise his unusual talents. My father agreed that it was a good move, and soon after our conversation, the Board signed off on the acquisition.

Peter wouldn't be the only new face on the Whole Foods E-Team (as we now called our executive team) in 1988. As we considered venture capital, significant expansion, and an eventual IPO, that meant we needed to up our game at the executive level, especially when it came to financial matters. The next phase of our growth would require a great CFO, and while Nancy Wimberly, our existing chief accountant, had done a good job up to that point, she was not looking to take on more responsibility. So I asked her if she knew anyone who would be a good fit, and she gave me a name: Glenda Flanagan.

Glenda, a University of Texas–educated accountant with a background in public accounting at Ernst & Young, had been living in a rural town 40 miles west of Austin, running a small office supplies company that was a family business. The company had failed, and she'd moved back to the city, so the timing was perfect.

The first time I interviewed Glenda, I was sold. She was exceptionally bright, knowledgeable, and easy to talk to, with a keen sense of business. We hit it off immediately. It wasn't long before she was working down the hall from me. And very quickly, I found myself walking the few steps to her office multiple times a day. "Glenda, what do you think about . . ." or "Glenda, can I get your advice about . . ." She was a crackerjack accountant, a hard worker, and a clear thinker. Sooner than I expected, I began to value her counsel as much as that of any of my longtime partners.

This expansion of the E-Team couldn't have come at a better time, with so many growth opportunities on the table. We just needed capital. And with Peter joining the Whole Foods Market team, I thought there was no one better suited to winning over prospective VCs than the master natural foods networker himself. We'd hired Rauscher Pierce, a regional investment banking firm based in Dallas, and they'd set up meetings with a couple of VC firms in Houston and one in Dallas, but first Peter and I were headed west to the iconic Sand Hill Road, where many of the largest VC firms were based.

As our plane banked over San Francisco and descended for landing, I looked down, fascinated, at the Presidio, the former military base at the northern end of the city that also was the fictional home of the Federation of Planets in my new favorite TV show, *Star Trek: The Next Generation*. It looked pretty futuristic to me! But my mind soon drifted to a nearer future, as I scanned the tightly meshed street grid of the city and wondered how many Whole Foods Markets we might eventually build on those busy intersections. Surely, large natural foods supermarkets were meant to be thriving in this place.

As we drove south out of the city, I told Peter how my family had spent a year here, when I was nine, my father taking a short-lived job in Redwood City. I marveled at how much things had changed in the intervening decades—what had once been a series of small towns south of San Francisco was now an unbroken urban sprawl, punctuated with high-rises and connected by sweeping freeways.

The next morning, we drove our rental car up Sand Hill Road, just north of Stanford University in the heart of Silicon Valley. It was a perfect day, 70 degrees and sunny. The last wisps of morning fog were slowly receding over the western hills, and every building, tree, and stretch of manicured lawn seemed to be lightly touched with a golden glow. *I could get used to this,* I thought. We straightened our ties and went into our first meeting in high spirits, enthusiastically launching into our presentation.

It fell flat. The inviting warmth of the morning perfectly contrasted to the downright chilly reception we received indoors at that meeting. And the next. And the next. Most of them turned us down before they'd even heard our complete pitch. This was the Bay Area, home of high-tech innovation and countercultural ideas—and yet they didn't show much interest in us. Where was the spirit that had given rise to the Free Speech movement, Haight-Ashbury, the Summer of Love, Lotus 1-2-3, and Apple's personal-computing revolution? The VCs we met just saw two guys with a passion for our business but not a college degree between us. It wasn't enough.

By the end of the second day, I was exhausted and beaten down. I swore that if I heard the words "hippie" or "granola" one more time, I was going to throw someone in the bay.

There was, however, one exception to our generally chilly reception on Sand Hill Road. Oak Investment Partners listened all the way through our pitch with genuine interest, gave us some positive feedback, and recommended we meet with Jerry Gallagher, the head of their newly launched retail branch in Minneapolis. We agreed to do so. After a couple of days, we were more than happy to see the back of the Golden State—at least for now.

Back in Texas, we met with Phillips & Smith, a Dallas VC firm largely focused on retail investments. They too were uninterested, but I wasn't surprised. Like many of the VCs in California, these were older guys who didn't really understand the turn the world had taken as my generation had come of age. I thanked them for their time, and Peter and I got up to leave, when Don Phillips, one of the partners, stopped us.

"Wait a minute," he said. "Sit down. I want to be sure you understood why we're not investing."

I wasn't sure I wanted to know. It felt like asking a girl out on a date, getting rejected, and then having her turn around and spell out all the ways she finds you unattractive. Did I really need to listen politely while this guy added insult to injury? But Peter had taken a seat, so I reluctantly joined him.

"It looks like you've got a nice little business here. But you're just in a few markets. And your stores are just hippie stores, selling hippie food to people who look just like you."

I gritted my teeth. Where was the San Francisco Bay when I needed it? Peter, sensing my frustration, kicked my foot under the table, as if to say, "Hear him out, John. Let him say his piece."

Phillips continued with his description of our customers. "They're all young. They've all got long hair and not much money and that isn't going to change anytime soon. That's just never going to be a very large market. I'm looking to invest in companies that can grow and go public someday. I just don't see how that's going to be you. And even if I'm wrong and this 'natural food' thing really catches on, how are you going to compete with Safeway? Those guys will eat you for breakfast—you and all that crunchy granola you sell."

A dozen retorts sprang up in my mind, but I wasn't going to waste my time arguing with this guy. I'd heard it all before. He was stuck in the past and would never see the future that was calling us forward. But inwardly I was pumped up. His conviction fueled my natural competitive drive. When someone dismisses me like that, it just makes me determined to prove them wrong. Back in high school, I got cut from the basketball team after my junior year because the coach didn't believe I had what it took. But I didn't quit. Instead, I switched high schools, started at point guard on my new team, and in my senior year we had a very successful 25–13 record, in which I played a key role. I would do the same in business, I vowed, and I hoped that one day this misguided VC would realize that he had just made a terrible mistake.

"Thank you, sir," I said, "I appreciate your feedback. Have a good day."

Peter and I shook hands with the partners and walked quietly down the hallway to the elevator. The moment the doors slid closed, I loosened my tie and let out my pent-up feelings. "He's full of shit," I told Peter, "and we're going to prove it. He's going to look back and regret the day he didn't invest in Whole Foods Market."

In our next meeting, we finally got a positive response. Richard Smith at Ventex in Houston was willing to invest. They eventually put in $2 million, which I was thrilled about. And we received $1 million from Criterion Ventures, another Houston firm, represented by David Hull. After striking out on the West Coast, it was a relief to have firms closer to home who believed in our future. And it was no mystery why it was a different experience. Houston VCs just had to walk down the street to see what the future of their investment looked like. Shepherd had surpassed Lamar and become our highest sales-volume store. All you had to do was spend a few minutes walking around that store to understand that something extraordinary was happening, and that Whole Foods Market had tapped into a rich cultural vein. I later learned that the wife of one of the partners at Criterion was a loyal customer. Maybe that had something to do with it too.

Finally, we met with Oak Investment Partners' Jerry Gallagher. Jerry was the former CEO of Mervyn's, a clothing company that would go on to be bought by the parent company of Target. In other words, unlike most VCs, he really knew retail. And like any good retailer, he didn't want to sit and talk numbers in an office; he wanted to see the stores. He flew to Texas, visited all of our locations, and was clearly impressed. He wanted to invest, but at a lower pre-money valuation than Ventex was offering.

"Listen, Jerry," I said. "I'd love for Oak to be the lead investor. But the valuation you're offering just isn't as high as the other guys."

Jerry leaned back in his chair, smiling patiently. He was younger than most of the VCs I'd met, though still older than me. I genuinely liked him, and I think he liked me too.

"John," he said, "we're a top-tier VC firm. Just having us on board is going to raise the valuation of the company when you want to go public. Because here's the thing: all money is not the same color."

It would be some time before I understood the truth in Jerry's words. At that moment, all money looked exactly the same to me, and I was still getting over my disbelief that not one but two venture capital firms were already willing to invest some in our company. I wanted Oak on board as well, but I wasn't going to compromise on our valuation.

For a couple of weeks, we didn't hear from Oak, and I assumed they were out. I was disappointed—I'd liked Jerry and felt he understood our business better than any of the other VCs. But then he called and told me Oak was in for $1.5 million. Later, I'd understand how being funded by a prestige VC firm acts like a magnet to other VC firms the next time you need to raise money, and I'd appreciate that we'd been lucky not to lose Oak.

Ventex took the lead in the $4.5 million investment round when it closed in September 1988. Whole Foods Market, by that time, was doing about $50 million a year in sales. That $4.5 million garnered the venture capital firms a total of 34% of the business, putting the post-dollar valuation of the company at around $13.5 million. Partners from all three firms joined the Board: Richard Smith, David Hull, and Jerry Gallagher. Don Schaffer and Jay Templeton both stepped down. I knew that we had entered a different phase of our business life. The new directors wanted to see the company succeed, but their incentives were different. Now we were on the clock.

As time went on, I began to think of our VC partners as hitchhikers with credit cards—they were along for the ride and benefiting from our forward progress, and as long as they felt we were going where they wanted to go, they'd help pay for gas. But they did not have the same level of commitment to stay in the car for the entire journey. If we got lost or diverted from the road we'd promised to take, they might try to grab the wheel. I knew we couldn't afford to let them drive. Nor did I put it past them to hijack the car, hire a new driver with an MBA from Harvard, and leave me standing on the side of the road. Eventually, they themselves would need to exit—and I needed to ensure that they didn't push me out first.

With the influx of precious capital, we moved ahead as fast as we could on the Palo Alto build-out, as well as a new location—the Richardson store—in the Dallas metro area. Craig and Peter moved out to California with their families to take on their new roles as President and Vice President of the Northern California region, which also meant they would be Store Team Leader and Associate Store Team Leader of our single store in the region. They went to work on building the 20,000-square-foot store (with a 10,000-square-foot basement) into our best Whole Foods Market yet. We were excited and confident that it would work. Texas was coming to Silicon Valley! Even when the general contractor went bankrupt in the middle of the build-out and didn't pay their subcontractors, precipitating an unexpected expense and mini cash-flow crisis, we weren't too worried. We had a good team in Palo Alto and we had capital. The wind was at our back—or so it felt.

Opening day finally came in early February 1989. I flew out there, taking the now familiar three-hop trip on Southwest from Austin to El Paso to Phoenix to San Francisco. Our "company jet," as we jokingly called the airline, didn't fly direct from Austin back then, but it was cheap, and at least they served free peanuts.

Arriving in California, I felt less like a tourist. I was now the leader of a new business in Palo Alto. I walked through the aisles of the new store, thrilled at what we'd created. It was a truly beautiful store—perhaps the most beautiful one yet, although I had to admit I thought that about every new store we opened.

I spent some extra time checking out our new deli. The struggles of the Safer Way Café and the failure of the Wildflower Café had made food service a thorny topic in the company. Our only success in that arena—the café at the Lamar store—had been fully outsourced to the Martin Brothers. But when Peter Roy joined the company, he had pushed for us to branch out into prepared foods. He was convinced this could be a great market for us and a boon to the stores. I'd agreed to let him use the new Palo Alto store as a test run for a new attempt.

Peter hired a seasoned Austin restaurateur, Alan Lazarus—who had taken to calling himself the "Deli Lama"—to create and operate the Palo Alto deli. And it sure looked good! Of course, we had no sales data yet, but the opening day crowd was enthusiastic. I was impressed with the job Alan had done. It fit the store nicely, and I could see how it might attract a dedicated lunchtime crowd. Maybe we would finally crack this code!

As I was standing there breathing in the aroma of hot food and enjoying the sight of customers lining up for lunch, a stranger approached me. He was tall and good looking—well over six feet, with the kind of smile that belonged in a dentist's advertisement.

"John?" he asked. "I've been wanting to meet you for a long time. Walter Robb. I'm a friend of Peter's."

He shook my hand and told me he was in the natural foods business himself—selling rice, as I recall—and had once owned his own small store in Weaverville, California. He complimented me on the store and launched into a series of rapid-fire questions. I'd never met anyone with such a focused curiosity about our business. I liked him right away, although I could barely get out an answer before the next question came. After doing my best to satisfy his keen interest, I had to move on, but I had a feeling this wouldn't be the last time I connected with Walter Robb.

Palo Alto—like every store we'd opened since Lamar—started slowly. But I thought about Crossroads, Brodie Oaks, and Shepherd, which were all now thriving after their sluggish beginnings, and felt optimistic that eventually we'd see the same in Palo Alto. Clearly, Californians loved the kind of food we sold; sooner or later they'd love us too.

The late eighties were a time of new beginnings for Whole Foods Market, but they were a time of endings in my personal life. As 1989 drew to a close, I was coming to terms with the hard truth that my relationship with Mary Kay had run its course. The excitement, intensity, and passion that had made our love so great had a downside, and it came in the form of drama, jealousy, and mistrust. The writing had been on the wall for a while, but I loved her daughters and hadn't wanted to disrupt our family. Eventually, however, I had to admit that I needed something different in my personal life. My work came with plenty of intensity and conflict already; I didn't need that at home too.

Mary Kay and the girls moved out, but she still worked for Whole Foods Market, so it was awkward. I vowed that this was going to be the last time I ever dated someone within the company. It was just too complicated when things didn't work out. Plus, I felt so guilty about the breakup that I gave her a bunch of my stock, something I'd previously done with Cheryl as well. When my dad heard about this, he was furious.

"John, either you need to stop giving your shares to your ex-girlfriends or you need to stop dating!" he told me in the sternest voice he could muster.

I didn't really have a good answer for that, but I resolved that next time I fell in love, it would be with a woman who was outside of my business world, someone who brought more balance to my life. I just wasn't sure how I'd ever find the time to meet such a woman, when almost every waking hour was spent at work.

Chapter 17

The People's Republic of Berkeley

Even before the Palo Alto store was open, we'd already begun thinking about our next outpost in Northern California. My vision had always been to open several stores in the region, establishing our presence as the first movers in that market. We were still striking out in San Francisco, so for our next store, we looked across the bay.

The city of Berkeley had famously been home to a large co-op that specialized in natural foods, with several locations in the area—probably the closest thing the region had seen to a natural foods supermarket, at least in scale if not in style. Indeed, the dominant presence of the co-op may have explained why no other player had moved into Northern California before we did. Founded during the Great Depression, the Berkeley Co-op, at its height, had been the largest in the country, with over 100,000 members and 12 stores. In the sixties, however, the co-op, like many aspects of life in Berkeley, became a repository of political activism complete with dramatic internal power struggles. By the eighties, the organization had fallen upon hard times, lost influence, and it finally collapsed in 1988, shortly before Whole Foods Market opened in Palo Alto.

It was a sign of the times. Even the "People's Republic of Berkeley" had limited patience for the endless infighting, disagreements over boycotts, poor service, management turnover, and fraught employee relations. Like many progressive organizations that reached their ascendance in the heady days of the sixties and early seventies, the co-op found that its ideals of harmony and equality ran into rough waters when it came to the everyday challenges of running a successful business. This was something I could relate to from my personal experience of the much smaller food co-ops I'd belonged to in Austin—Wheatsville, Woody Hills—and housing co-ops like Prana House where Renee and I had lived. In fact, one of the reasons Renee and I had moved out of Prana House had been our frustration with co-op politics! We just got tired of the interminable meetings, which were often spent debating relatively trivial things such as whose turn it was to clean the bathroom and which companies we should boycott.

After the collapse of the Berkeley Co-op, the locations went up for sale. And the person who stepped in to purchase three of the now-available sites was none other than Chop Keenan, our Palo Alto landlord. He had arranged to let a local grocery chain, Andronico's, take two of the sites. But the last one he reserved for Whole Foods Market. He called me up and asked if we wanted to expand into Berkeley.

"I've got a site for you at Telegraph and Ashby," he declared, in his usual done-deal manner.

I was familiar with the site, and with the other former co-op locations, one of which was on Shattuck Avenue in North Berkeley, near the university and just down the road from Alice Waters' iconic restaurant Chez Panisse. To my mind, that one seemed like a better fit for Whole Foods.

"We would love to bring Whole Foods to Berkeley," I told Chop, "but how about the Shattuck location? I think we'd prefer to be up there."

"I'm not offering you that location," he replied. Chop had a plan, and once again, it was his way or the highway. I could just picture him staring me down from his big leather chair on his raised platform. I knew, by now, that it was pointless to argue, and I wanted a site in Berkeley. So we settled for the one a bit farther south at the busy junction of Telegraph and Ashby.

The takeover of the sites was a complicated deal since the Berkeley co-ops were in bankruptcy, and it had to be finalized in court. Both Chop and I appeared before the judge. I put on a suit and tie and took my place in the courtroom to listen as Chop made his case. Among the issues on the table was the community's concern about losing three grocery stores to a developer who might turn them into who knew what. But Chop was prepared to reassure them that every one of those sites would remain a grocery store.

"Your Honor, I've got three grocery tenants already. I've got all three leases signed. Andronico's is taking two stores and Whole Foods Market is taking the other store. In fact, Mr. John Mackey, the CEO of Whole Foods Market, is right here in this room." He gesticulated grandly in my direction. What was I supposed to do? Stand up? Wave? Take a bow? Eventually, I inclined my head toward the judge in what I hoped was a respectful manner.

"Your Honor," Chop continued, "I'm ready to buy these properties right now. In fact, I have a check! I have a cashier's check for seven and a half million dollars right here today."

The judge looked at Chop with a skeptical eye, not in the least bit intimidated by the force of his personality. "Could I see that check, Mr. Keenan?"

Without hesitation, Chop reached into his pocket and, with a flourish, pulled out a slightly crumpled check and handed it to the judge.

There was a moment or two of silence. Then the judge started laughing. He looked up and announced to the courtroom, "Well, this looks like a genuine check."

And that was it. He approved the sale and we had our first East Bay store.

When I visited the site a few months later to check in on progress, it was fascinating to see the transformation. This store was under the leadership of Peter Roy, who I'd asked to come over from Palo Alto. Peter was still relatively new to the company, but as a former CEO who had run his own successful natural foods business for years, I'd thought he might benefit from having a store to manage. He was enthusiastic about the opportunity in Berkeley, and he soon began to develop a vision for its unique personality.

Each new Whole Foods location had its own original design—and this was even more true in those early days. We had decided there would be no cookie-cutter stores in our company. Too many companies have essentially one or two templates that get rolled out in every location. Maybe that's less expensive and more efficient, but we were after something different. We wanted every store to reflect the local community—its values, its culture, its aesthetic, and its local products. Every store would have the opportunity to innovate and add new, original elements.

This approach fit my management style as well. The last thing I wanted was to micromanage a fleet of copycat stores from my office in Austin. I wanted people to innovate, take risks, create great stores, manage them locally, and surprise and inspire all of us with their success. Peter was happy to do just that.

As soon I walked into the almost-finished Berkeley store, I noticed how different it was from its sibling across the bay. The upscale, European finishes of the Palo Alto store were gone, replaced with stained concrete floors, natural wood shelving, and clean, functional design. Peter described it as more of a "proletariat" look—a style designed to fit the Berkeley culture. "There was no way we could just transplant a Palo Alto store to Berkeley," Peter explained to me. And he was right. The two cities may have been less than 50 miles apart, but they were different worlds, requiring different stores.

Unfortunately, the Berkeley store came with a great challenge that had nothing to do with the location or the design or the leadership. It was something as native to Berkeley as those concrete floors and wooden shelves: union activism. Right out front, from the day we opened, were protesters, holding placards, shouting into bullhorns, and accosting customers as they approached our doors.

"Who are these people?" I asked Peter. "They don't work for us! So why are they picketing us?"

Peter explained that the local labor union had sent these protesters to do what they call an "informational picket." The information they were intent on conveying, forcefully, to everyone who showed up to check out our store, was that Whole Foods wasn't unionized. And they were determined that it would be, just as our predecessor, the Berkeley Co-op, had been. Several local politicians shared this feeling.

There was little logic to their demand, given that the co-op had failed, and its disproportionately high wages, mandated by the union, were part of what had made it unsustainable (one customer had been quoted in the *New York Times* a few years earlier saying that the co-op was "the best argument there is for capitalism in Berkeley"). Besides, our people didn't seem to want a union. They were happy working at Whole Foods Market and felt well compensated. Nevertheless, the union was determined to have its way.

Peter had already been visited by a union representative, a man who looked like he could have come straight from the "gangster" division of central casting. Peter invited him into his office and tried to explain Whole Foods' position. He took pains to be respectful and courteous, and for a while, this visitor listened attentively. But only to a point. Abruptly, he got out of his chair, slammed his palm down on the table, and exclaimed, "Let's cut the bullshit! This store has always been a union store and it will be a union store again!" Then he stormed out without another word.

The store was doing okay, but the union activity was certainly depressing sales. Some folks wouldn't cross a picket line to shop, especially in Berkeley. This might have been the eighties, but Berkeley was not exactly a hotbed of capitalism. We needed to get these protesters out of our parking lot.

On my next trip to California, I set up a meeting with the mayor of Berkeley, who gave me a more politely worded but no less definitive version of the same message Peter had gotten from the union guy. After I'd carefully explained to her my concerns about unionization and assured her that our team members didn't want it, she declared, "I haven't heard such nonsense since the 1950s! You need to get a union in there."

I was out of patience.

"Well, I haven't heard such nonsense since the 1960s," I retorted.

These interactions only compounded my frustration with the approach of unions, at least as they generally operate in a contemporary American business context. The adversarial "us vs. them" attitude was the antithesis of what we were working so hard to create. Whole Foods Market fostered a positive relationship with our growing number of team members. Indeed, the morale of our labor force was very high. Many of the people who worked in the company did so because they shared the company's mission of selling healthy, natural foods that nourished people. Yes, we generally paid higher than other comparable jobs in the local area, but, as I had discovered early on, pay was only part of what motivated our people. Our higher purpose wasn't a marketing slogan, or an afterthought: It was authentically felt by the people who worked in our stores, to some degree or another. People often told me they didn't just feel like they had a job; they were a valued community member at Whole Foods. And we didn't operate as a traditional top-down management hierarchy. Our people were organized into teams, and much of the day-to-day decision-making was decentralized, as the individual personalities of our stores attested. The idea of inserting an unnecessary dividing line between management and the rest of the team ran counter to our core values and, I worried, could destroy our company culture.

During my many visits to Berkeley in that era, I thought deeply about these issues, read about the history of the labor movement, and pondered the nature of the relationships human beings create when we do business together. I was also engrossed in a powerful book by my former philosophy professor Robert Solomon entitled *Ethics and Excellence*. He captured my feelings about the union precisely: "[T]he single most important point in both good business and business ethics [is] that a sense of cooperation that does not presuppose an antagonistic sense of 'individual versus the corporation' is essential." Through Solomon, I discovered the work of Ed Freeman, author of *Strategic Management: A Stakeholder Approach*. Finally, I had a term for the various members of the interdependent business ecosystem: stakeholders! Freeman elegantly translated some of the philosophical ideas that inspired me into concrete business strategy and management practice, especially when it came to creating mutually beneficial win-win relationships.

Mutual benefit—*that's* what I saw business as being about. Perhaps an antagonistic struggle between labor and management was appropriate in another time and place. To me, it seemed like a relic of a world I was trying to leave behind. There is no intrinsic reason why employers and employees must be enemies. In fact, management and labor can and should work together as partners, fellow stakeholders—with openness, trust, community, shared purpose, joy, and love—to fulfill their common goal of serving the customer's needs. As I watched the protesters pacing our small Berkeley parking lot, I became more deeply aware that we weren't just in the business of selling natural foods. We were also in the business of trying to do business differently. If only the locals would let us.

Some of our Berkeley team members decided to try explaining to the protesters that they didn't want a union. That was when we figured out that these so-called activists weren't actually union folks at all. Most of them were in fact a bunch of people the union had hired (and was paying very poorly with no benefits) just to picket us. The irony of this situation was not lost on our better-paid nonunion team members. They even felt kind of sorry for the protesters, despite their irritating presence. Soon, our people had befriended some of them, and the protesters would come into the store for free coffee. One hot summer day when the union held a rally outside the store, Peter wheeled out a cart full of Ben & Jerry's Peace Pops and started handing them out. Peter had style! A few of the hired picketers eventually came over to work for us when they found out we paid much better than the union and offered benefits as well. But the protest dragged on for the first 18 months of our Berkeley store's existence.

The silver lining of the story is that this threat to our culture and values had the effect of pulling us together. It was the first time in our 12-year journey as a company that our internal philosophy was challenged by an outside force, and it had the effect—for me and for many of the team—of bringing greater clarity and commitment to that philosophy. I captured my thoughts in a pamphlet I shared with the company, entitled "Beyond Unions."

I was a capitalist—of that I had no doubt. But I would not be boxed in by history's definitions of that term, with all the attendant greed, power-hungriness, and antagonism that is too often associated with it. My everyday experience of business was one of innovation, teamwork, cooperation, solving problems, and creating value for our customers. But that experience was at odds with the generally negative public perception of corporate life. The gap rankled me and pushed me to think more about what business is—and what it could be. Indeed, a new way to think about capitalism was beginning to take shape in my mind, and at least in some small way it was inspired by my early adventures in the People's Republic of Berkeley.

Chapter 18

The Woman in the Dream

Do you mind if I, um, look in your refrigerator?"

The most beautiful woman I'd ever met seemed a little taken aback. But she graciously said, "Sure," as if it wasn't a completely weird request from a guy who'd come to pick her up on a blind date. As she went to finish getting ready, I opened her refrigerator and took stock of the contents. Okay, I know it's a bit strange, and in hindsight it probably wasn't the best way to make a good first impression. But I'm in the natural foods business, and you can learn a lot about a person by what's in their refrigerator. I wasn't going to get involved with someone who ate a lot of junk food! Besides, I was utterly floored by my date's astonishing beauty, and I just said the first thing that popped into my head.

Her name was Debbie, and she'd been introduced to me by my buddy Tom Robinson. Knowing that I needed to try something different if I was serious about not dating women I met at work, I'd asked my married guy friends to introduce me to single women they knew. Tom got a certain look in his eyes right away.

"Oh man. I know just the woman . . . the timing might be great. She just ended a relationship."

When I called her, however, Debbie didn't think the timing was great at all. When she heard I'd just gotten out of a long-term relationship, she was hesitant to go out with me.

"I don't want to be your rebound relationship," she said. "We should wait."

"I don't want to be your rebound relationship either!" I said. "But I'd still like to meet you." I persuaded her to give me a chance, and we'd been trying to set up a date for a couple of weeks, but our busy schedules were not cooperating. It was looking like it would be six weeks before we both had an open evening, but then I had an idea. "Would you be interested in going with me to my friend's wedding on Saturday night?"

Having only recently gotten out of my long-term relationship with Mary Kay, my dating skills were rusty and my social graces were, well, not so graceful. But Debbie said yes, which was how I came to be poking around in her fridge that evening.

The appliance in question only added to my positive impression of its owner. It was packed with fresh fruits and vegetables, natural foods, and even several items that had clearly been purchased at Whole Foods Market. Satisfied, I moved on to her bookshelf—a more socially acceptable way to investigate a potential partner—and was encouraged to see books about spirituality and philosophy.

When Debbie came out of the bedroom, probably relieved to see that I was no longer perusing her perishables, we talked about our shared love of reading and discussed a few favorite books. She was smart, funny, and easy to talk to, and I began to relax. I felt almost like I knew her already, though this was the first time we'd actually met. And then I heard a little voice whisper inside my head: *This woman is more awake and conscious than you are.*

The whisper was quickly drowned out by a flurry of protests from my wounded ego. *No way! You don't even know her!* What I did know was that she was seven and a half years younger than me (I was now 36), she worked as a software consultant, and we had some mutual friends. Why would I assume she was somehow more advanced on the inner journey than I was? I'd built a business and traveled the world and explored my own consciousness through spiritual work and psychedelics. And yet the whisper persisted. *This woman is more awake and conscious than you are.*

By the time we got to the old Victorian house, Green Pastures, that my friend had rented out for the wedding, I was regretting my plan. There were only a few dozen people there, but I knew almost everyone. Lots of friends were greeting me and hoping to catch up. I didn't want to sit through a bunch of endless speeches and make polite conversation with other guests. I just wanted to talk to this amazing woman and get to know her better. This was going to be my only chance for six weeks. And as crazy as it seemed after only a couple of hours in her company, I was already falling in love.

The ceremony seemed to drag on forever. Finally, it was done, and everyone milled around while the photographer took the official pictures. A woman I knew had cornered me and was chatting away. I couldn't even keep track of what she was saying. My mind was filled with the overriding need to be alone with Debbie. Soon, they'd be serving a formal dinner, and we'd be trapped here for hours making small talk, listening to toasts, and clapping politely. A bell was ringing, signaling that we were to take our seats. The woman was still talking. She didn't even pause for breath. There was no opening for me to gracefully end the conversation, and my window for escape was quickly closing. Finally, I just interrupted her mid-sentence and turned to Debbie.

"Do you want to get out of here and go eat somewhere else?"

I couldn't quite read the look on her face, but I sensed I'd said something wrong. After a moment, however, she slowly said, "Okay, if that's what you want to do." We grabbed our coats and left before the dinner started.

I took her to a little Thai restaurant I knew, and the awkward moment seemed to be behind us. Soon, we were deep in conversation and it became clear to me that the little voice in my head had been right. She was probably the most conscious person I'd ever talked to. She had deep emotional intelligence; a sparkling, mischievous sense of humor; and a kind of relaxed confidence I found incredibly appealing. As the dinner came to an end, I knew two things. One, I was probably in love with this woman. And two, somehow, I'd already blown it. I didn't quite know how, but I was pretty sure I'd upset her and she didn't really like me. I'd begun the evening feeling like I was testing her with my stupid refrigerator review, but somewhere along the way the tables had turned. She'd been testing me, and I had clearly failed the test.

Still, when I drove her home, she invited me in and suggested a game of Ping-Pong. I'd never seen anyone play quite like she did—it was as if she was dancing around the table, hypnotizing me. I probably missed a few shots as a result, but I still won (although to this day, she claims that she did). Suddenly she put down her paddle and said, "Let's jump!"

Jump? I was about to ask what she meant, but she was already demonstrating, leaping up and down, her face lit up and her dark hair flying.

"Now you do it," she said, "and I'll take photos of you."

"But why?" I asked.

"Because people's true personality comes out when they're jumping!" she replied.

And so, I jumped. I was happy to jump for her, because I knew I was already a darn good jumper. I could jump high enough to dunk a basketball with two hands when I was in my early twenties. One time, I'd taken some kind of modern dance class at the University of Texas, and the dance instructor had been so impressed with my aerial abilities that she'd stopped the whole class and said, "Watch this man jump!" Whatever else I'd done to make a poor impression on Debbie that night, I could at least get this part right. And so, I jumped and she laughed and snapped photos. Later, when I saw the pictures, I did indeed look joyful and free.

As the night wore on, I could sense it was time to go. And something told me that despite our deep conversation and the fun we'd had, Debbie had already made a decision that I wasn't going to get another date. I tried to kiss her as I was leaving, but she wouldn't let me. She just said good night in a very formal tone and closed the door.

Back at my place I couldn't sleep. How could I have screwed this up? I was so furious with myself. I replayed the evening over and over, trying to figure out where I'd gone wrong. Why had I asked to look in her refrigerator? Who does that? Was that what upset her? Or was it something else? Finally, at a loss to explain it, I sat down and wrote her a letter. I poured out my heart, telling her how much I liked her, and that I realized

I'd done something wrong. I admitted that I didn't know what it was, but whatever it was, I apologized for it anyway. I told her a little bit about myself, who I really was, and who I thought she was. And then I closed by saying that I was sorry we wouldn't be seeing each other again, but I'd enjoyed meeting her and I hoped she would have a happy life. At 5 AM, I drove to her house and slipped the envelope under her door.

Later that day, she called me.

"I read your letter," she said, "and it was a great letter. You're absolutely right. I wasn't going to go on a second date with you because what you did to that woman is pretty much inexcusable."

"What woman?" I asked.

"The woman at the wedding!" she said. "Remember, she was talking to you and you just cut her off. You were so rude!"

"But she was never going to shut up!" I protested. "I needed to get us out of there."

"Well, you could have done so in a more tactful and gentle way," she insisted.

I wasn't going to argue with her. "I'm sorry," I said. "You're right."

"Anyway," she paused, "I decided that anyone who could write that good of a letter deserves a second date. Let's try one more time."

Our second date went much better. We met in Pease Park and we both brought our dogs. My yellow lab, Nikki, fell instantly in love with her golden retriever, Milo, and the two of them played joyfully together while we talked and strolled on a warm spring day.

I learned more about her childhood, growing up in San Antonio. Her life had been marked by tragedy when her younger sister, Lisa, died of bone cancer at the age of 16. Debbie was only 19 at the time, a sophomore at the University of Texas. She watched her sister endure an agonizing death and saw her parents nearly bankrupted by medical bills and her father became deeply embittered. It was a harsh entry to adulthood. Her parents worked hard and recovered financially, but her father was never the same.

"It's been 10 years," she told me. "And I still miss Lisa every day."

The dogs came barreling by, in hot pursuit of a squirrel. Nikki loved to chase small animals and had occasionally been known to actually catch and kill one.

"What are they doing?" Debbie asked, horrified. "Milo is the sweetest dog! He's never chased another animal in his life."

"Well, he looks like he's enjoying himself!" I said as the two dogs circled a nearby tree, barking loudly and looking longingly up at the disappearing squirrel.

"Your dog is corrupting mine," she said sternly, but I could detect a hint of mischief behind her overly serious tone.

As we strolled on, calling the dogs who reluctantly abandoned their chase, she asked me more about my childhood. I told her about my love for sports, about dropping out of school and disappointing my mother, and about the sense of purpose I'd found in Whole Foods Market.

I believe it was sometime that day that I said to her, "You know, you don't really seem like a Debbie." I'm not sure why, but the familiar girl-next-door nickname just didn't seem to fit the depth and intelligence of this extraordinary woman.

She looked surprised, but then she nodded.

"My family and friends always called me Debbie."

"You seem more like a Deborah to me. It suits you."

She smiled and said, "I like it too," and from that day on I called her Deborah.

After our third date, I later learned, she knew she was going to marry me. I wasn't quite there yet, but I was deeply in love. That night, when I got home, I fell asleep and found myself in a powerful lucid dream. I was aware that I was dreaming, and as soon as I looked around I knew I'd had this dream before.

I'm in Pease Park in Austin, the site of our second date. It's a beautiful day; the colors are vivid and the air is fresh. Standing in the park is a stunningly beautiful naked young woman. This time, I recognize her as Deborah. But I go up to her and ask, "Who are you?"

She smiles. "You know who I am."

"Well, what are you doing then?" I ask.

And she says, "I've been waiting."

"Waiting for what?"

"For you. I've been waiting for you to catch up."

"Why?"

She grabs my hand. "So that we can run together." And we begin to run through the park, holding hands and laughing joyfully.

And then I wake up.

Upon waking, I was in shock. I knew I'd had this dream many times before, but I'd forgotten it until now. And all this time, the woman in the dream had been Deborah. No wonder I felt, on some level, like I already knew her. And then another recognition struck me. I flashed back to my LSD trips, to two particularly intense journeys when I'd felt myself merging with the One. Both times, it had felt like a feminine presence—like I merged into that opposite polarity and then the polarity itself dissolved. That was her too! Her essence had been there in those experiences, waiting for me. Until that day, I'd never particularly believed in the notion of soulmates, but if there were such a thing, I decided, then she must be mine.

Who the hell gets lost on the way to their own wedding?

That was the panicked thought that raced through my mind on the early afternoon of November 16, 1991, as I made my way through the crowds on the River Walk in San Antonio. The wedding party was staying at various hotels on the waterfront, and my father, who was my best man, had agreed to take me to the venue. His hotel was just a brief walk down the road, but after taking a "shortcut" down to the river, I realized I must have gone too far. I doubled back, looking for an exit, but nothing seemed familiar. A mass of people seemed to close in around me, many of them tourists enjoying a stroll along San Antonio's iconic attraction, in no hurry to get anywhere.

Don't panic, John. Focus.

I tried to clear my mind and retrace my steps. Finally, I was able to determine my location, but I still arrived 30 minutes late to the rendezvous.

"John, where in the hell have you been? I thought for moment you were a runner."

"Well, you were half right. I did panic—but not about the wedding!" I briefly explained what happened and motioned for my father to move faster. "C'mon, let's go." The last thing I wanted was for Deborah to think I'd left her at the altar. I might not have been the most punctual bridegroom, but I certainly didn't have any doubts about the commitment we were about to make.

I'd proposed, completely unconventionally, over the phone, about 15 months after we'd first met. Who proposes over the phone? Well, I guess the same guy who asks to look in his date's refrigerator right after he first meets her. I confess, it was not every girl's dream of a guy on one knee with a beautiful engagement ring promising her lifelong love and devotion. I was home recovering from the flu, watching the old Richard Dreyfuss romance movie *Always.* As the credits rolled, I was laughing and crying and overwhelmed with the beauty of love. Before I knew what I was doing, I'd picked up the phone and called Deborah and asked her to marry me. And although she laughed at my clumsy and impulsive way of popping the question, her answer was, "Yes, of course we're getting married."

Marrying Deborah, I soon learned, would mean marrying into a very large Catholic family, emphasis on the "large" and the "Catholic." The former meant the wedding itself would be a grand affair, held in her family's church in San Antonio. The latter meant that I had to go through some very awkward rituals associated with her family's faith. For consecutive weekends, Deborah and I had to attend weekend mini retreats called, rather intimidatingly, Engaged Encounter. These involved listening to older Catholic couples counsel us about long-term marriage in the context of the faith. There were two primary messages that they were intent on imparting to us—one about divorce (don't do it) and one about sex (don't do it with birth control).

The message we received about marital longevity was simple, and probably relevant for any couple embarking on a marriage, though perhaps less so for an older, experienced couple like Deborah and me. They essentially told us that hard times will inevitably come to any long-term relationship, and couples should expect that. "God has joined you together and you should shoulder the burden of those difficult times together as well," was the gist of it.

The sex part was a lot more uncomfortable. If you've never had to sit through extended meetings where Catholic elders explain the rhythm method while insisting it's not the rhythm method, let me tell you, it's a strange and awkward experience. I had to suppress the desire to laugh on numerous occasions—and sometimes failed. Deborah and I had not yet come to a decision about having a family, but we soldiered through these meetings to get to the ceremony. I admit, I was a little surprised by the seriousness and rigidity of it all. We were given homework assignments, but Deborah and I spent that time writing love letters to each other.

Finally, the day arrived and I was thrilled, though my tardiness might have led people to believe otherwise. My father and I made it to the venue without further incident. But before I could walk down the aisle, there was one more unexpected hoop to jump through. The priest who was there to perform the ceremony pulled me aside in a separate room.

I looked at the paper he handed me, surprised. It was a formal agreement between me and the church stating that I would raise any children that might come from the marriage as Catholics. The priest explained that he couldn't perform the ceremony unless I signed.

Really?

"Wait a minute," I said suspiciously, pen hovering. "You're telling me that you won't perform the ceremony, even with all of these hundreds of people that have come here today, many from far away, unless I sign this agreement that you just showed me for the first time?"

The priest nodded, a beatifically innocent look on his face. I fumed. This was outrageous! I'd never let someone spring a contract on me at the last minute in a business negotiation. But I tried not to express my frustrations too strongly. This was Deborah's family's faith, after all, and while she wasn't a practicing Catholic, I knew the tradition meant everything to her family, and her family meant a lot to her. After thinking the situation through for a few minutes, I signed my name. Privately, I had no intention of considering it binding. As far as I was concerned, this was coercion and not enforceable.

Finally, the moment came. I stepped up to the altar, smiling at my assembled groomsmen—my brother Jim, Jean-Claude, Peter, Chris, Jim Sud, Philip Sansone, and my old high school friend Casey Wren. Deborah looked absolutely stunning in her wedding dress. She was radiant with love, and under the influence of that mesmerizing spell the worries of the day faded and my heart expanded. As the priest began to speak, a storm erupted outside, complete with a resounding clap of thunder.

"A good omen!" the priest exclaimed. "The groom is going to be wealthy!"

I raised my arms to the heavens, and everyone laughed.

Later, at the reception, we feasted on natural foods prepared by the "Deli Lama" himself, Alan Lazarus. My father stole everyone's hearts with a rendition of the Frank Sinatra song "Young at Heart," and my nine-year-old stepdaughter, Allison, belted out Peter Cetera's "Glory of Love." The applause was even louder than the thunder in the church. Perhaps all of it was, as the priest had said, a sign of riches to come. But the truth was, I already felt like the richest man alive.

Chapter 19

The Second Happiest Day of My Life

The two happiest days of my life (so far) happened in quick succession. Deborah and I were married on November 16, 1991, and on January 23, 1992, Whole Foods Market did its initial public offering (IPO) on the Nasdaq stock exchange.

For any entrepreneur, going through a first-time IPO is one of those formative moments that you only get to experience once, and you never forget. It's a threshold into a new maturity as a company leader—for better and for worse. It's exciting, it's heady, and can be deeply satisfying; it can also be dizzying and overwhelming. For me, it was all of these things. On the happiness scale, I can honestly say it was second only to my wedding day, because it gave me the opportunity to reward all the believers who had faith in me for so many years. The IPO would pay them back—and then some!

The IPO would also give us access to much-needed capital. Whole Foods Market was gradually becoming a national company. We were now 12 stores in four states, and I had my sights on continued expansion. Unfortunately, we lacked the cash for further new stores or acquisitions. An IPO would unlock significant new possibilities.

Of course, we could have stayed private and sought more capital from our VC partners, but that would have meant giving them control of the business. I was looking to do the opposite—to move beyond the influence of the VCs. When the morning of the IPO dawned, I felt almost giddy with relief at the thought that the hitchhikers would soon be exiting the Whole Foods Market car.

Over the past few years, I'd come to understand all too well why my father had cautioned me about VCs. Their investment had been essential and much appreciated, but it had come at a high price—in fact, it almost cost me everything I'd built. I'd learned the hard way that VCs have strong opinions about where the car should be going and how quickly it should get there. And if you start falling behind—as you almost inevitably will—on the often overly optimistic projections you gave them when you were trying to convince them to invest, you're in trouble.

As we fell behind on some of our projections, and our Palo Alto store took longer than anticipated to get going, our hitchhikers had started to exert some pressure. They kept reminding me that none of our team had "actual supermarket experience." Never mind that we'd been running Whole Foods Market for more than a decade by this point—they felt we needed people who'd worked in the "real world." They believed we needed "professional management."

I wanted to keep the VCs happy, so we hired an executive search firm, and we spent many months looking for someone who fit the bill. Eventually, we found a guy named Win Smith, who'd been the CEO of Smitty's, a Phoenix-based company that had been bought by Smiths, a bigger chain. Win loved Whole Foods Market and was excited to join our team as President and COO. *Maybe this won't be so bad after all,* I thought. On the day he was due to start work I got a phone call from his son. "Mr. Mackey, I'm very sorry to have to inform you that my father had a heart attack and died this morning."

I was in shock! We all were. We'd liked Win and looked forward to having him work with us. It was only later that I realized that, in all likelihood, the VCs had envisioned him as my successor. I'd unwittingly hired the guy who was going to take my driver's seat in the Whole Foods car. Had it not been for his tragic demise, perhaps my story would have had a very different next chapter.

As it happened, during the year we'd been conducting the executive search and hiring process, things had begun to look quite different at Whole Foods. Sales at the Palo Alto store were beginning to grow quite strongly and it had become profitable. Shepherd was doing fantastic, and our new Richardson store was starting to grow as well. So when the VCs wanted us to start the executive search process all over again, I felt a new confidence to push back. We'd already wasted too much time and money trying to hire someone I wasn't sure we really needed. It wasn't professional management that would make the difference, it was just time. Time was our friend, and time was proving us right. The other E-Team and Board members were ready to back me—especially my father.

He'd seen the writing on the wall before I had. "Of course, they were planning to try to replace you, John," he said. "Just because Win was a nice guy doesn't mean he wasn't there to take your job. We need to get these VCs out before they push you out."

When I raised the prospect of an IPO in the next Board meeting, the hitchhikers weren't very enthusiastic. "It's too soon," they said, pulling out their metaphorical credit cards and pointing toward the gas pump. "You're not ready to go public. Let's do another round of venture financing and grow the company another few years before you IPO."

Afterward, my father followed me into my office, fuming. The moment the door closed, he let rip. "We've got to get those fuckers out of the company before they take over!"

Since the VCs only owned 34% of the company, they weren't able to block our collective decision to go forward with an IPO, and we began the process of hiring investment bankers. In the meantime, I began to move on another acquisition. Wellspring Grocery, founded by Lex and Ann Alexander, constituted two stores located in Durham and Chapel Hill, North Carolina. Peter, who knew Lex well, leveraged that relationship to help the deal go smoothly. We were able to negotiate a purchase price that was mostly in stock, with the promise that the forthcoming IPO would quickly make our stock a more lucrative commodity.

With the addition of Wellspring, the story we could tell Wall Street ahead of the IPO improved significantly. Wellspring was a modest company, but now our business could truly be said to have national reach, from coast to coast, rather than just being a regional success story. Our team was proving to be effective at acquisitions. Of course, we were still quite small by Wall Street standards. But we had a narrative that we thought would play well on the Street.

Robertson Stephens and Rauscher Pierce were the two investment banking firms that took us public, as many of the bigger names thought we were too small to tap the public markets. They organized our IPO road show, which was a whirlwind, as these things usually are. Peter, Glenda, and I traveled around the country selling our company to investors. We made stops in San Francisco, Chicago, Los Angeles, and finally, New York. Being chauffeured around Wall Street in a limousine, taken to Broadway shows, and wined and dined with would-be investors at fancy restaurants in Manhattan—we knew we were a small fish in a huge pond, but for a brief moment, we were treated like royalty. We extolled the future potential of the business to investors, and the promise of organic and natural foods got some national attention as well.

Beyond the glamorous moments, it was exhausting—back-to-back-to-back meetings, day after day, for two weeks. In the end, we met with more than 40 different investment groups, many including multiple firms. Early on, I realized that I had to limit the wining part of the wining and dining if I were to be on top of my game for meetings the next morning, so I made a decision not to drink any alcohol until it was all over. Even completely sober, I thoroughly enjoyed it all and I could tell that Peter and Glenda did too. Peter was a natural at this—more media savvy than me. I had the authority and conviction that comes with being a founder and having nurtured a company through every minute of its growth. We found an easy rhythm in the meetings, taking turns speaking while the other one caught his breath. Peter's storytelling skills and extroverted personality helped carry us through meeting after meeting, and Glenda was always ready to jump in with a clear and incisive summary of our finances.

At the end of the road show, Glenda and I returned to Austin for the IPO, and Peter went back to Berkeley. We weren't a big enough deal to ring the bell or have a confetti drop at the Nasdaq center in Times Square. But the IPO, small though it may have been in the scheme of things, was an enormous milestone for our team. The offering was significantly oversubscribed. We were planning to raise over $20 million and looked forward eagerly to seeing the stock start trading on the Nasdaq.

On that cool winter morning, I was in the Whole Foods Market headquarters at Timberline Office Park in Austin when Glenda came rushing into my office.

"John!" she announced breathlessly. "They started the stock at 17!"

My brain froze for a second. "But our asking price was only 12." Initially, it had been set at 10, but the demand had been so high it was raised to 12.

"I know, I know. They raised it!"

I stared at her, disbelieving. Watching investors bid up our IPO by a significant percentage was just one more amazing addendum to the excitement of the day. By the end of the first trading afternoon, the stock closed at $28 and Whole Foods Market was valued at $100 million. Even though my shares had been diluted over the years (and siphoned off in guilty breakup gifts to ex-girlfriends), my own net worth was now over $7 million. I was rich! How did that happen? It seemed to me like a crazy amount. It was exciting, even shocking, to suddenly be worth so much after so many years of having almost no money.

That evening, after the markets closed, I slowly drove home, still in something of an altered state. I opened my first beer in several weeks and sipped it slowly on the porch, breathing in a sense of gratitude and wonder for how far we'd come.

I thought back to the little Victorian house where Safer Way had begun, and the modest dreams of success that Renee and I had shared as we woke up each morning on the top floor, took our showers in the dishwasher, and converted our bedroom to its daytime form as the store's office. I thought about Craig and Mark taking the leap of faith to merge with us and build an entirely new store, bigger than any natural foods store in the state. I thought about the hundred-year flood, and our near-death experience.

I called my father, just to hear the pride in his voice and to share our mutual excitement at the success of the company he'd so wisely helped me build. I thought about my mother, wherever she was, and wondered if she might finally be proud of her "grocer" son. I thought about the many people who were celebrating tonight, enjoying their well-deserved reward for their belief in those crazy hippies and their strange new notions about how to eat. I even thought about the VC hitchhikers, appreciating that they'd taken the risk to invest millions in a CEO and an executive team with barely a degree among us and no "actual supermarket experience." We'd been able to successfully drive the car to where they ultimately wanted it to go, and they all made a very nice profit in a very short period of time.

All of those expectations, all of that collective hope for our future, I had carried for 14 years. Now, I felt it lifting from my shoulders. I knew there would be new burdens to shoulder as we began our life as a public company. But just for a moment, I set down my beer, closed my eyes, and let the joy and relief overwhelm me.

Chapter 20

Territory and Talent

The papers on the conference room table were laid out carefully, as if for an important business meeting. It was a spring day, a few months after the IPO, and I was in Durham, North Carolina, on my first trip to see the Wellspring stores since we completed the acquisition. I was looking forward to getting a better sense of what we'd bought—sizing up Whole Foods Market's latest assets. That day, however, was about to take a surprising turn. Lex Alexander, cofounder of Wellspring and now an executive at Whole Foods, stood beside the table, waiting to begin his presentation. But this was no business meeting. He wasn't about to lay out our sales, or revenue, or profit. He was there to share his passion for olive oil.

"Today, I want to talk about flavor," Lex began as the group of executives fell quiet. "And flavor has everything to do with quality." He proceeded to expound on the virtues of olive oil, taking us into a world I knew very little about. As I listened, I began to see our acquisition in a new light. Wellspring was a simple business and didn't yet add a great deal to Whole Foods Market's bottom line, besides giving us a presence in a new state. But Wellspring came with people—people like Lex. The man pouring samples of golden olive oil for us to taste was now part of our team. And he brought something to the table that I recognized that day to be unique and valuable—perhaps one of the most unexpected benefits of the deal.

Lex came from a different branch of the natural foods movement than I did. Back in the days of the Natural Foods Network, he'd been one of the "foodies" of the group. Their focus was less on the health benefits, social values, and environmental standards associated with the products we sold and more on the pleasure, beauty, quality, and artistry of these foods. Their stores proudly showcased curated cheeses, handcrafted pastas, estate olive oils, artisan balsamic vinegars, specialty coffees, and more. I readily admitted back then—as I still do today—that I'm not really a foodie. Sure, I've eaten and enjoyed some of the best plant-based cuisine in the world, but I am much happier and healthier living on whole grains, beans, nuts, seeds, fruits, and vegetables.

"Food as health" and "food as pleasure" were distinct though overlapping parts of the natural foods movement. There was tension, at times, between the two, and they both generated passionate, committed subcultures. Until this point, Whole Foods had primarily focused on food as health—a sensibility no doubt imparted by its founders. Some of my fellow natural foods pioneers had placed more emphasis on food as pleasure, and their stores reflected that sensibility. As I listened to Lex describe the variations in taste and quality between the different oils he poured for us to sample, and the reasons that he loved each of them, I felt a new appreciation dawning for that other perspective.

Lex, I realized, was a kind of epicurean genius. His sheer knowledge, care, and attention to detail when it came to food and how it was made was remarkable. I wasn't honestly sure I had the taste buds to tease apart the subtleties that Lex was describing, but I did have the business intelligence to recognize an important trend when I saw it so clearly displayed in front of me. The foodie community was going to be a huge part of the natural foods movement. And I wanted Whole Foods to be the place those people shopped. I felt excited about how our newly acquired talent might help us to reach customers with more discerning, sophisticated palates.

We had already taken baby steps in that direction, but I credit Lex's influence and also Peter Roy for understanding this trend, and for helping bring it alive at Whole Foods Market. Several other Wellspring team members, in addition to Lex, ended up excelling in our company, and all of them added to this new cultural infusion. In that sense, the Wellspring stores and the talent that came with them added much more to our overall philosophy and the trajectory of our future than they did to our physical footprint.

On that same trip to North Carolina, I did some PR for the acquisition. The Raleigh-Durham area had an alternative print weekly called *Indy Week* covering arts, music, and culture. I agreed to do an interview, thinking this would be a perfect outlet to reach the local countercultural types who shopped for natural foods. I enjoyed the conversation and thought I'd represented Whole Foods well.

A couple of weeks later, I got a copy of the paper, and was shocked at the picture of myself and the company through the journalist's eyes. We were presented as a bunch of rapacious Texas moguls swooping in to take over and forever alter a beloved local chain. This was the era of the soap opera *Dallas,* and I might as well have been J. R. Ewing, riding in on a horse with a ten-gallon hat and a pistol. Of course, I immediately regretted doing the interview and feared it would suppress our sales. It was a timely reminder that the way we were perceived back home was not the way we were perceived in more progressive enclaves like Durham, Berkeley, and Palo Alto. To them, we weren't kindred spirits in the counterculture; we were outsiders, capitalists, and perhaps worst of all, Texans.

Despite this momentary bad press, 1992 got off to a great start. We'd now successfully made four acquisitions—Clarksville Natural Grocery, Bluebonnet, Whole Food Company, and Wellspring—and we had the capital to match our ambitions. Not only did we have cash; we had a new currency—our stock. Companies that had been out of our price range suddenly seemed within reach when we considered the possibility of paying in stock, which was now highly liquid. And with each possible acquisition, I looked forward to both expected and unexpected gifts in the form of territory and talent.

When it came to territory, Northern California was still a high priority. Our stores in Palo Alto and Berkeley were thriving. San Francisco was still challenging, from a real estate standpoint, so we looked farther north—to Marin County, land of redwood trees and golden hills, where rock stars rubbed shoulders with the original hippies in a series of charming small but affluent towns. It was here that my journey, and the journey of Whole Foods Market, would intersect with the journey of another pioneer and change both of our futures for the better.

That other journey had also begun in 1978, around the time Renee and I were opening Safer Way. That year, a Stanford graduate named Walter Robb, who had tried his hand at law school and farming and liked neither, decided to head north in search of love, nature, and a life of purpose. He found it in an unlikely place: the small mountain town of Weaverville, in Trinity County, California.

After arriving in Weaverville with his new wife, Walter borrowed $10,000 from his stepfather and started a small natural foods store in this tucked-away gold-rush town. Toiling away in this store for the next 10 years didn't exactly produce a gold rush for Walter, but it was still quite a retail education. He'd drive all the way to San Francisco before dawn to buy produce at the Ferry Plaza Farmers Market, haggling over a case of tomatoes or broccoli. Finally, due to changes in his personal life, he sold the store and moved back to the Bay Area, where he and I would first meet at the opening of our Palo Alto store, when he peppered me with questions.

Walter settled in one of Marin County's most popular towns, San Rafael, just a dozen miles north of the Golden Gate Bridge. He bounced around the industry for a while, before deciding that it was time to take a leap and open his own natural foods supermarket. He found a 15,000-square-foot space in a great location in Mill Valley on Miller Avenue, signed a lease, and was about to get to work, when fate—in the form of Whole Foods Market—intervened.

Of course, Peter Roy, who was running the Berkeley store at the time, knew Walter. Peter knew everyone. He had even put out some feelers to try to hire Walter as we were building our Bay Area stores, but nothing ever came of it. By 1991, when we set our sights on Marin County, Walter's name came up again. Since he was already planning a store in Mill Valley, and we liked the location he'd secured, we figured it was worth another try at hiring him—and acquiring his as-yet-unopened store in the process.

Like any entrepreneur at heart, Walter was hesitant to give up control of his business. But the truth was he had little to show but a lease and a passion for the project. He'd been planning to bootstrap the store with minimal capital. Partnering with Whole Foods would change the game for him completely. He did his due diligence, speaking at length with Peter, me, Lex, and other leaders at Whole Foods. He specifically wanted to know how entrepreneurs had been treated once they were inside our company. Little by little he became more open to selling his prospective store and coming on board.

When it came to the final negotiations, I met Walter at a popular coffee shop in downtown Mill Valley called The Depot. As we waited for our drinks, he told me about the local celebs who frequented the spot, although none of them made an appearance during our meeting. Eventually, we got down to the numbers, and I took note of the difference between our respective styles of dealmaking. My approach in negotiations was still to show up with what I hoped would be close to the final number—one that I considered both fair and a win-win deal for both parties. Walter was detail oriented, as I would later learn he is in all things. He wanted to get the best deal, and he wanted time to think through every element of it. But in the end, we managed to come to terms. Walter would still open the Mill Valley store, and run it, but he would do it under the Whole Foods Market banner, and he'd be supported by all the necessary investment and resources that our larger company could offer.

"Walter, I'm so happy to have you as part of the team," I told my new partner.

"John, I love Whole Foods' culture," he replied. "Every time I go to one of your stores, I can see that the team members are happy. They're enthusiastic about the store. You can feel it. It's no small achievement."

"What do you think we can do better?" I asked.

His answer surprised me. "That's easy. Retailing."

"Retailing?" I wasn't even sure exactly what he meant. Weren't we already doing a pretty good job at retailing?

"Just the Xs and Os of retailing. I think there is a lot of room for improvement." Seeing the confusion on my face, he went on: "You may not know this, but the word 'retail' comes from the French, '*retailer*.' It means the cutting of the cloth—cutting something into small units to sell and share. But it also implies that retailing is a process of constantly shaping the offering. It's not about building one thing and being done. It's about constantly sharing, offering, marketing, and creating a space for people to shop. It's a true art. I think the store is a canvas, and we paint our own type of beauty on that canvas. I really believe that."

Listening to Walter wax poetic about retailing, I felt the same way I'd felt when listening to Lex talk about olive oil. I couldn't fully relate to the content, but I connected to the passion. I sensed that some of this man's particular genius was revealing itself.

"I see some sloppiness in the stores," he continued. "I always think about retailing as being an hour-by-hour job. How does the store look at opening? At noon? At closing? How does each department look? What about the parking lot? What consistent high standards can you maintain through the day? And then you wake up and do it again. That's what makes a great store. I think we can do better. That's what I intend to do here in Mill Valley, and I hope we can up our retail game in the other stores as well."

Walter was true to his word. On July 1, 1992, the Mill Valley store opened, and his attention to detail was evident throughout the space and throughout the day. It quickly became one of the highest grossing stores in the company, and before long, it was our number-one store. The whole company took note. Northern California was growing rapidly, becoming a significant part of the business. And even more notably, in Walter Robb we had gained a retailing force to be reckoned with.

Chapter 21

Coast to Coast

There are many reasons to acquire another company—you get territory and talent; you eliminate a potential future competitor; you get a shortcut into a new market. And sometimes, there's just something that company does so well that attempting to copy them is not enough. So it was with Bread & Circus. The very first time I'd stepped through their doors back in 1979, I'd been struck by the quality of their fresh produce—lush, colorful, dewy mountains of perfectly hand-stacked fruits and vegetables. We'd tried, with limited success, to replicate it, but by the early nineties, I knew we still hadn't matched the remarkable job Bread & Circus had done with what our industry calls "perishables."

For non-grocers, perishables might seem like an abstract concept, just one more product category in the overall store mix. But those in the business understand just how critical this category can be to success—and how hard it is to do well. The name says it all. Perishables—meaning fruits, vegetables, meat, seafood, bakery, dairy products, and prepared foods—are, well, perishable. They have a short shelf life, so it takes careful management to keep them fresh and appealing, maintain quality, and minimize waste. For all these reasons, perishables play an enormous part in differentiating one store from another.

Once the Network got going, I became good friends with Bread & Circus's CEO Anthony Harnett, who went by Tony in those days, and took every opportunity to learn from him. He joined the Whole Foods Market Board in the late eighties. Beyond our love of natural foods and our entrepreneurial outlook, we also shared a deep interest in personal growth and spirituality. We attended spiritual talks and workshops together, including one by an Austin teacher named Blair who "channeled" a spiritual being named Father André.

One time, when we were listening to Father André, he unexpectedly declared that Tony had been a Roman centurion in a past life, and I had been his slave. This was an era when past lives were all the rage, but I didn't have any particular beliefs on the topic myself. However, as Father André made his unusual pronouncement, I felt a searing pain in my body and I screamed out loud. Whether through the power of suggestion, strange recall, or an overactive imagination, I felt like I was indeed being tortured! And when I looked at Tony, I could have sworn I saw a shadow of cruelty pass over his face that was entirely absent from the personality of the man I knew. It was at the suggestion of this same channeled spirit that Tony decided to go by his full first name, and from that day onward he asked all his friends to call him Anthony.

As our friendship deepened and the natural foods market expanded, I couldn't help but occasionally broach the subject of a merger or acquisition. Our conversations usually went something like this:

"Anthony, would you ever consider selling Bread & Circus?"

"I would if I could get my number."

"Okay . . . what's your number?"

"$30 million dollars."

"That's a lot of money."

"Yes, it is. But that's my number."

It really was a lot of money for a company with only six stores. While their overall sales were quite impressive, the company wasn't profitable—as was the case with many natural foods stores of the era. I suspected it was because their administrative expenses were far too high. Anyway, in the early Network years we didn't have $30 million, but after our 1992 IPO, I started to think seriously about whether Anthony and I could finally do a deal. Perhaps we could bring all that talent and expertise and real estate into Whole Foods Market—not to mention those perfect perishables and the secrets behind them.

One of those secrets, I would learn, was not a process but a person. A.C. Gallo's story, like mine, began with dropping out of college in the early seventies. A.C. had studied chemical engineering at Northeastern University in Boston for several years until he decided that the subject, and maybe even college itself, wasn't really his cup of tea. He decided to take a job at a nearby store where he liked to shop—Erewhon, a small, macrobiotic natural foods store. Perhaps it shouldn't have been surprising that A.C. would take to the grocery business like a fish to water; his grandparents had owned an Italian grocery store in New York, out of which his grandfather ran a wholesale produce business. His father also worked there, and at the age of 10, A.C. would accompany him on Saturday morning delivery runs. Later, his father owned an Italian restaurant, where A.C. worked during high school. He thrived at Erewhon and found the experience of retailing highly fulfilling. One day, a guy named Tony Harnett showed up looking for a job. Tony ended up at the wholesale warehouse, working his way up to shipping manager, and he paid his team so well that A.C. eventually joined him there, where the two became friends.

A few months later, in the summer of 1975, Tony left Erewhon to purchase the original Bread & Circus, a natural foods store and toy shop in Brookline, Massachusetts. A.C. continued to work at Erewhon until the following summer, when he took a break to drive across the country and to pursue his interest in self-exploration. In 1977, back in Boston and in need of a job, it occurred to him that maybe he should call his old buddy Tony. And that's how, a year before Renee and I opened Safer Way, A.C. joined Bread & Circus, then a single 3,000-square-foot store with 10 employees, stocking shelves and running the register. Four months later, the produce manager left. Someone in the store pulled A.C. aside and said, "You're Italian; you should be great at produce." Whether it was due to A.C.'s genetic or cultural heritage, his natural talents, or other factors we will never fully divine, truer words have rarely been spoken. A.C. took over the management of produce at Bread & Circus and never looked back. In those days, he used to head down to the Boston Market Terminal at 4 AM to buy produce off the trucks. And when in 1979 Bread & Circus expanded to become one of the country's first natural foods supermarkets with a 10,000-square-foot store in Cambridge, A.C.'s produce was front and center. It was that store that I first visited. I don't remember meeting A.C. that day, but no doubt he was there, his apron neatly tied over a button-down shirt, unobtrusively straightening a pyramid of potatoes or polishing an apple until it was as shiny as his shoes.

In the summer of 1992, feeling flush from the IPO, I broached the topic of an acquisition with Anthony yet again. He still wanted $30 million. But this time, we signed a non-disclosure agreement, and I was able to look at their financial statements. As I'd suspected, Bread & Circus was losing money or breaking even at best. Their stores were performing very well—producing 9% profits on their high sales—but their G&A (general and administrative expenses) were at 10% of their sales, and that was killing their profit margin. For some perspective on that number, Whole Foods Market's G&A at the time was closer to 2% of sales. I'd seen this situation before, and it only made me want to do the deal more. I had confidence that we could fix this problem and do so quickly, and on the other side we'd have highly profitable stores.

To be fair, in this case it wasn't just useless bureaucracy. Bread & Circus had a strong store-support network that was, in part, why they had top-notch stores and the best perishables in the business. We'd need to be skillful as we cut back their overhead to avoid sacrificing what made them special. After looking at the books, I returned to the negotiating table to try to get Anthony to a more reasonable price.

It wasn't just my friend (and past-life torturer) I had to negotiate with. I also faced opposition to the deal from an unexpected source: my father. Bill Mackey had always had strong opinions, but it felt like we were coming into conflict more often these days. Was he just getting more conservative with age? Was it because his net worth had increased so much after the IPO, and he was worried about losing it? I wasn't sure, but it was frustrating and confusing. We'd fought before, but I'd always felt he had my back. Even when we didn't agree, I'd been able to appreciate where he was coming from. Now, it just seemed irrational.

"We're doing fine, John," he growled. "Why do we need to buy this damn company and take on all their problems? Why do we want to go to Boston anyway? And Anthony is asking too much. Hell, his company is actually losing money!"

I tried to be patient, explaining how this merger would give us a whole new platform in a whole new region. I talked him through the numbers, and eventually, I was able to convince him. But he remained reluctant, and I grew tired of arguing with him at every Board meeting.

Anthony and I kept negotiating. He loved Bread & Circus, and it wasn't easy for him to cash out. For a true entrepreneur, it rarely is. They often love their company as if it was their own child, and in one important sense, it is, because they birthed it. Anthony wasn't just worried about losing control of his company; he also wasn't convinced our company was worthy of adopting his baby.

"John, Whole Foods is a hippie company. That's who works there and that's who shops there. I know you're doing decent sales and making some money. But look at your culture. It isn't professional. It isn't efficient. Your stores are successful, but they're not great. Our stores are great."

To say I was tired of the "just a bunch of hippies" refrain would be putting it mildly. But after I'd gotten over my irritation, I had to admit that some of Anthony's observations were right. It was true that we were less conventional than Bread & Circus, which was a more buttoned-up company. Their team members were clean cut and uniformed. I had grown up as a middle-class American kid who had enthusiastically joined the counterculture; Anthony had grown up as a poor Irish kid who was upwardly mobile. For all his spiritual interests, Anthony didn't like hippies. He wasn't interested in dropping out; he was interested in moving up the ladder of wealth and status. Also, he was right—they did have great stores. That's why I wanted to buy them! I didn't want to lose what was unique and great about our culture, but I did want to import some of Bread & Circus's secret sauce into Whole Foods. I loved their stores, and I wanted ours to get better and better.

I also had an ace up my sleeve that Anthony didn't know about.

"Anthony, if you don't think our stores are good enough for Bread & Circus, I want you to do something for me. Fly out to San Francisco and visit our new store in Mill Valley." The store had only been open a few months then, but secretly, I believed it to be as good if not better than any of the Bread & Circus stores. "I think you'll be surprised," I told him.

After that conversation, it was me who was surprised. Anthony flew out to San Francisco the very next day! He spent the weekend in Mill Valley, checking out the new store and talking to Walter. On his return, I could hear in his voice that something had changed. He was suitably impressed. "That's a great store, John," he said. And he seemed much more serious about making this deal happen. I arranged to fly up to Boston to come to terms on our biggest acquisition to date.

One of the final sticking points of the negotiation centered around a non-compete clause. We'd already agreed that Anthony wasn't going to stay with the company. But now he insisted that he be free to open up one other store in the Boston area. Naturally, I resisted.

"I just want permission to do one store," he protested. "Nothing that would compete with you."

This concerned me. It certainly didn't sound like the words of someone who was retiring from the business.

"Anthony, you need to sign a non-compete clause. I'm not going to go head-to-head with you in New England. What kind of stupid company would we be to buy a chain of stores in this region and then let the former owner immediately compete with us, flush with fresh capital that we provided?"

"John, you don't get it. I don't want to build a company. I just want one store to play around with. And I agree to not build it near any Bread & Circus or Whole Foods Market stores. I'll give you a 10-mile non-compete zone."

I still didn't like the idea, but I finally agreed to those terms. Anthony insisted on one final unconventional element in the contract as well. He wanted a right of first refusal on the Bread & Circus stores, if—or when, as he put it—Whole Foods Market failed and/or ended up selling or closing them. "I worry you're going to run this business into the ground, John," he told me bluntly. Anthony and I were friends, but that didn't stop him from feeling superior about how he ran his business. I couldn't help but remember Mark Skiles telling me the exact same thing when he left Whole Foods back in 1985.

We agreed on a price of $28 million—$8 million in cash and $20 million in stock. We also agreed to do a secondary public offering immediately after we closed on the deal in order to sell all of his remaining stock quickly and cash him out. Whole Foods stock traded up on the announcement of the acquisition, and Anthony ended up getting his number—$30 million—after all.

The natural foods prize of the East Coast was finally ours! I flew up to Boston with a group of our best people to begin the process of integrating the new company and making it profitable.

The first order of business was to cut back their bloated support staff. Bread & Circus had been run in a very top-down style. That's not necessarily a bad way to run a business, and from everything I heard, it sounded like Anthony treated his people well. But our culture was different. We were all about decentralization and bottom-up empowerment. We didn't micromanage. We wanted to distribute more authority to the stores and Team Leaders. Along with our informal dress code and the proliferation of long hair, beards, and mustaches among our male executives, it was quite a culture shock.

Some of the staff found the new management approach disconcerting. And the round of administrative layoffs didn't help morale, at least initially. We wanted to get their G&A overhead down from 10% to maybe 3–4% of sales, while still preserving the many strengths of Bread & Circus as we went about making these changes. I was particularly sensitive to the perishables team—I wanted to know what they were doing right before I tried making cuts. When the subject came up in our meetings, I advised caution.

"Let's take it easy on perishables. We need to protect those. Also, I want to keep A.C.—the guy in charge—and his people." I barely knew A.C. in those days, but his work spoke for itself.

"Okay, makes sense," our team agreed.

"But what about this flower coordinator?" someone asked.

"The perishables team has an independent flower coordinator?" I'd never heard of such a thing, but I learned that it was a full-time role.

"That seems a bit excessive!" I laughed. "There are only six stores. Surely, the produce coordinator can also do the flowers."

Even that small cut, however, was a step too far for A.C. Despite my efforts to protect his team, the elimination of the flower coordinator seemed to push him over the edge. Or maybe he was already there. Whatever the case, soon I heard that A.C. was frustrated by the disruption caused by the acquisition and had turned in his resignation. David Lannon, head of operations at Bread & Circus, had quit as well. I was frustrated to be losing talent. But I'd gone through enough acquisitions by this point to accept that it was part of the process. People have a right to make changes when change happens to them.

A few months later, I was visiting one of our stores in Newton, Massachusetts, when I recognized the man wheeling a shopping cart through our produce department and carefully selecting apples. "A.C.!" I greeted him warmly, and we struck up a conversation. After some pleasantries, I got right to the point. "A.C., if you ever want to come back to work at Whole Foods, we'd love to have you. Just give me a call and let me know." A.C. seemed a bit surprised but not displeased by my offer. *At least I planted a seed,* I thought.

By the summer of 1993, the Bread & Circus integration finally seemed to be getting on track. But Chris Hitt, who was up in Boston overseeing it all, called me with some concerning news.

"Anthony's working on that store he insisted on putting in the contract. You're not going to like it."

"What do you mean? He was only supposed to do one store, 10 miles from our stores. Is he breaking those terms?"

"No, not exactly," Chris said. "It's just that—well, his one store is not small. It's going to be a 100,000-square-foot store based on the Harry's Farmers Market concept."

Damn! I knew I should never have agreed to Anthony's "just one store to play around with." Harry's was a very popular concept based in Atlanta, and if that was what Anthony had in mind, 10 miles was not going to be enough of a buffer zone. And that wasn't all. Chris added that he'd heard A.C. and David Lannon were planning to join the new store.

"You want to talk to Anthony?" Chris asked.

"Do I want to? No, I don't want to. We had an agreement. But yes, I will, of course."

The next day I called Anthony and asked him directly about the plans for a new store. He told me the basics, and I reminded him of his promise.

"Don't worry, John. It's only one store," he assured me.

"But it's not a small store to play around with!" I replied with some frustration in my voice. "It's more square footage than all six of your old stores combined. You didn't say anything about a massive superstore."

"John, if I would've told you all of those details, you wouldn't have agreed to that stipulation."

"I know. That's my point. You should have been honest with me about what you were planning. I trusted you to act with transparency and integrity, not to try to put one over on me!"

I hung up in frustration, feeling like I'd been tricked by my old friend. But a funny thing happened on the way to Anthony's superstore. His wife divorced him, and he lost about half of his money in the settlement, and more to capital gains taxes after the Bread & Circus sale. He also began to embrace the realization that even after these losses he was now wealthy, and he didn't need to work again or have the pressure of a large new business weighing on him. Finally, and perhaps most relevant, he realized that superstores are super expensive. Harry's Farmers Market, Anthony's model, did an IPO and their numbers became public. They were losing money. I suspect that was a bracing wake-up call to Anthony.

In the end, he scaled down his ambitions, and before the year was out he had opened Harnett's Homeopathy & Body Care shop in Cambridge, a much more modest store. A.C. joined his team, but I don't think it was what he had in mind when he jumped ship. I knew that he was loyal to Anthony, and they went back a long way, but when I imagined A.C. stacking soap bars instead of apples, I found it sad to think of the Northeast's prince of perishables toiling away so far from his province. Finally, A.C. called. He was ready to take me up on my offer and come back to work for Whole Foods. He later told me that, like Anthony before him, he'd visited Mill Valley and been very impressed with Walter Robb and the excellence of the store, which had helped him to realize that he might just fit in at Whole Foods Market after all.

I was thrilled and promised I would talk to Chris about finding a good position for him. We soon conjured up an idea. We had already been studying how Bread & Circus managed their perishables. We wanted to take this very successful model and implement it in all our stores. Would A.C. be interested in becoming our Vice President of Perishables? He was delighted with the idea and immediately accepted the job. Sometimes, amid the twists and turns of a life, a business, and a career, people do end up exactly where they are supposed to be.

We were still in the throes of the Bread & Circus integration when another incredible opportunity showed up—one that I knew we couldn't afford to miss. Mrs. Gooch's, Southern California's natural foods superstar, was ready to sell. And they were giving us an opportunity to buy.

"This is our moment!" I exclaimed, when the Board met to discuss the opportunity. "If we don't take it now, we'll lose it forever."

"John, this is ridiculous," my father shouted before I'd even finished my pitch. "You're being reckless. It's too much, too soon. We're growing too fast. We're diluting our stock. We still need to integrate Bread & Circus into the company. You won't be able to manage a company of this size."

"But Dad, this isn't just any acquisition. This is Mrs. Gooch's! Just think—Whole Foods, Bread & Circus, Mrs. Gooch's, all as one company. We'll be unbeatable! We HAVE to do it." I jumped to my feet in frustration. "I know the timing isn't perfect. We're not ready to buy them. But they're ready to sell. And they have plenty of other interested buyers. The opportunity is there right now and it won't come around again. We need to seize it before someone else does."

I sat down abruptly, a little embarrassed at this emotional exchange in the middle of a Board meeting. The other Board members were quiet. They knew better than to try to intervene in one of these father-son blowouts. And this was the worst one yet. The thought flashed across my mind: What if our investors could see this? What if the press got hold of it? We were a public company now. It wouldn't look good. Why was Dad so determined to oppose me every step of the way? And why was he so worked up about it all? I knew I wasn't going to easily convince him, but we needed to do this deal. I was the cofounder and the CEO of the company—not him.

To get the Mrs. Gooch's deal done, we planned a Board meeting in Los Angeles, so that the Board could approve the deal as soon as negotiations were complete. We decamped to a hotel in Marina Del Rey, along with our bankers. It was a beautiful, still-warm fall day, and hordes of sun-kissed, carefree locals were out enjoying the oceanfront, while we were stuck in an air-conditioned conference room full of bankers and lawyers. The Gooch people set up in a conference room down the hall, with their bankers and lawyers. And the dealmaking began.

By this point, my father had accepted that the acquisition was happening and had gotten on board. He loved dealmaking, and I enjoyed seeing him in his element as we debated the finer details and tried to hammer out an agreement, going back and forth between our respective conference rooms. We'd almost come to terms when I noticed something odd. Sandy

Gooch and John Moorman owned the buildings that housed three of the stores and rented them to the company—at a very reasonable rate. They would continue to do so when the company merged with Whole Foods Market. But in the deal memo I was looking at, the rent appeared to have gone up. A lot.

"Wait a minute!" I strode down the hallway and demanded to know why the rent had changed. They countered that it was a fair market rate.

"That's not the point," I protested. "Changing the rent changes the whole economics of the stores, and we came to an agreement based on the number you were paying."

Back and forth we went, but they wouldn't budge. I was furious. I felt like I was back in the church with that Catholic priest, calmly telling me that I couldn't get married unless I signed over the souls of my future children to his church. The marriage of Mrs. Gooch's and Whole Foods Market may not have had hundreds of guests waiting to witness it, but a lot had gone into getting us to this day, and I didn't want it to all fall through at the last minute. The Gooch people, of course, knew that too, which was why they thought they could get away with it.

I was almost ready to walk out, to leave them at the altar, but I reminded myself how important this deal was to our future. By buying Mrs. Gooch's, Whole Foods would gain the jewel of the West Coast to match the jewel of the East Coast we'd just bought. We'd have the best talent in the business and be well positioned to grow Whole Foods Market into a truly national company. In the big picture, paying a bit more in rent wouldn't stop our stores being profitable. We needed to get it done.

And so, I told the Board I thought we should accept their terms. "We'll make up for that increased rent—and more—when we cut out the bloat in their overhead," I reasoned. I could see my father fuming—he hated to lose, especially when he thought the other party had pulled a fast one on him—but he nodded. Jim and Craig were also in agreement, and the rest of the Board signed off.

The next morning, we headed to LAX with a signed deal memo in hand. As the plane slowly ascended over the Pacific and banked to head east over the golden hills, encrusted with mansions and jewel-like swimming pools, I looked down and imagined all those health-conscious Southern Californians soon shopping at a Whole Foods Market down the street. Flying over the country that day, I felt like I could almost see the web we were weaving from coast to coast—from Los Angeles to Boston, from the Bay Area to North Carolina to New Orleans, and at the heart of it, our Texas stores, where it all began.

Chapter 22

Growing Company, Growing Leader

"John, please don't do this."

My father looked suddenly frail, sitting across the desk from me at his home in Houston. His customary air of authority and confidence had drained from his face as I'd uttered the words, "Dad, I'd like you to resign from the Board."

My father had never begged me for anything in my life, but now he was begging me to change my mind. I was 40 years old; he was 72. He'd been my mentor, adviser, investor, and ally for every step of the journey since Safer Way—16 years now. He'd put his trust in his college-dropout hippie son and helped me grow into a more mature leader of a $200 million public company. And yet, in recent years, he'd also, increasingly, been my adversary. Again and again, he'd tried to put the brakes on when we needed to seize opportunities to move forward. Our blowup over the Mrs. Gooch's acquisition a few months earlier had been the final straw. It was past time we made this change. But as I saw the hurt in his eyes, my resolve wavered for a moment.

"Please," he repeated. "This is the last thing I'm doing in my life that's actually relevant."

I got up and came around the desk to sit beside him. "Look, Dad," I said, "you're always going to be my most trusted adviser. I'm still going to talk to you about everything. That won't change. But we're fighting all the time. You're increasingly risk averse, and I want to grow the company. It's ruining our relationship. Plus, Whole Foods is a public company. If we're yelling at each other in a Board meeting, that's unseemly. Sooner or later, that'll get out in the media."

"I know, I know," he replied, "but we can change that!"

"I don't know that we can," I said gently. "We've tried to stop, but we can't, because of who we are. And that's a good thing. We're both passionate guys—I got that from you. We both have strong points of view. And if there's one thing you've taught me, it's never to let someone else win! I'm the Chairman of the Board and the CEO, but everybody trusts you on the Board, so we get into these titanic fights. If you stay, I worry it's going to ruin our relationship."

He was silent, ruminating over what I'd said, so I pressed on. "Dad, ask yourself this: What's more important, our relationship or your Board seat?" He nodded slowly, and I knew he was accepting the inevitable. I went on to propose that he should sell half of his stock—that way, he'd worry less about the financial risks of my decisions. But he should also keep half—just in case I turned out to be right. And, I assured him, I would turn out to be right.

"Ten years from now, that half that you don't sell is going to be worth a lot more money, I promise you. But in the meantime, I don't want you to worry."

When the conversation ended, I felt deflated and more than a little sad. It wasn't the first time I'd had a table-turning moment with my father, but earlier ones had come in the competitive spirit that had always defined our relationship. This was different. This wasn't beating him at Ping-Pong or outreasoning him in a friendly debate. Asking him to resign from our Board was absolutely the most difficult thing I'd ever had to do as a leader. I knew it was the right thing—for me, for him, and for Whole Foods Market. But that didn't make it feel any better.

Although asking my father to leave the Board was difficult, it was an important step in my personal growth. I was coming into my own as a leader and as a man. Much of this, I felt, was due to my marriage. Deborah's calm, loving energy gave me a new foundation. For the first time since the start of the company, I was going home to someone who was not part of that "work" world—someone who grounded me in the spiritual dimension of life. I felt a greater sense of ease and trust that allowed me to focus more fully on Whole Foods and gave me confidence to ride the wave of growth we were experiencing.

We'd also begun to put down roots in a place that revitalized me. With some of the money from the IPO, Deborah and I had purchased some land in the hill country west of the city, a place to spend our weekends and holidays and escape the urban bustle. We call it the "ranch," but there was no longer any ranching going on out there. We'd applied for and received a wildlife exemption, which removed the need for us to lease the land for cow grazing in order to keep the agriculture tax exemption. Now it was just a large tract of relatively untamed country and two houses, one older mobile home at the entrance to the property and one fifties-era single-story home situated above a bend in a beautiful limestone creek bed that the Texas rains turned into a tumbling cascade during the wetter seasons of the year.

Most Friday evenings, we would make the hour or so drive out to the ranch, and it became our refuge to rest, renew, and nurture our marriage. I would pull up to the main house, get out of the car, gaze up at the incredible night sky, seeing the Milky Way in its full glory away from the city lights. Every weekend at the ranch, I'd enter another milieu—one of hiking, swimming, reading, sitting down in the creek bed listening to the water, and otherwise enjoying a respite from the demands and urgencies of the business world.

Those moments of peace were much needed, as the growth of the business continued unabated. In the couple of years since the IPO, not only had we made two major acquisitions, we'd also opened several new stores of our own. It was always a challenge going into a new market. Even though our brand was becoming more established, it still took time to really get going and have our sales grow. It was an act of courage and faith—to go somewhere that no one knew us and to hang in there until word got around and the store grew and became profitable.

Our Lincoln Park store, in Chicago, had gotten off to a rocky start when it opened in 1993, but the tide turned when none other than Oprah Winfrey was revealed to be a customer, and she filmed several episodes of the show right there in our store. Soon, it became one of our highest volume stores. That same year, we'd opened the Fresh Pond store in Cambridge, Massachusetts, which would go on to hold our highest weekly sales record for over five years. And in 1994 we expanded into Ann Arbor, Michigan.

We also made another acquisition: Terry Dalton's Unicorn Village in Miami. I knew Terry as one of the founding members of the Natural Foods Network. His waterfront store and adjacent vegetarian restaurant was a favorite destination for our members' gatherings. I remember being particularly struck by how well he did prepared foods, long before Whole Foods Market had cracked that code. His café, deli, and juice bar were impressive—he was the best operator in our industry when it came to food service. He catered to the wealthy yacht owners who moored just outside his store, as well as several local celebrities. He was proud of telling us that the stars of *Miami Vice*, the popular eighties TV show, frequented his restaurant. Unicorn Village married natural foods with a hip, sophisticated vibe.

Terry called me up right after it was announced that Whole Foods Market had bought Mrs. Gooch's.

"I see what's happening!" he said. "You're buying up all the Network stores. Why don't you buy mine too?" We did a deal and took over the store. A couple of years later, we would cement our presence in the state by acquiring another South Florida chain, Bread of Life, with two small stores.

The following year, we reached another milestone, and one that was especially meaningful to me. Our stock doubled from just a year earlier, and I was able to say to my father, "Aren't you glad you kept half of your shares?" He graciously said yes.

Also in 1995, we finally made it to San Francisco. Under Walter's leadership, our other Bay Area stores were thriving. We found a perfect location—an old car dealership at the intersection of Franklin and California Streets. Walter is a very good negotiator, but his approach can at times be perceived as aggressive. He doesn't like to leave anything on the table, as I remembered well from our very first negotiation, buying his Mill Valley store. Sometimes that strategy works great, but sometimes it can turn against you. In this case, the site's owner, Mrs. Brooks, felt like she was being nickel-and-dimed. "I'm done!" she declared to Walter. He called me that night and told me we'd lost the site. "I pushed too hard," he admitted.

I wasn't ready to let it go. I called Mrs. Brooks and introduced myself as Whole Foods' CEO. "I'm sorry we haven't managed to make a deal that works for you," I said. "But I'm confident we can get there. I'm flying in tomorrow and I'd like to meet with you, if you'd be willing." She agreed. It turned out she just needed a different approach. An older lady, she didn't have a background in business, but she was shrewd and didn't take kindly to what she perceived as bullying. I agreed to compromise on a few things that mattered to her but really weren't so important to us, and we got the deal done.

I was visiting Houston as I often could in those days. I enjoyed spending time with Dorothy and Jean-Claude, who was now heading up real estate for Whole Foods, finding sites and negotiating leases—a job at which he excelled. He'd stroll into meetings full of lawyers in fancy suits, throwing them off guard with his Whole Foods T-shirt, sneakers, and French accent, and then outfox them all with his brilliant negotiating skills. Their two boys, Andy and Will, were now 15 and 8, and I loved being an uncle. Dorothy is one of the very best mothers I have ever known and she raised two amazing sons. I would also visit my father and his new wife, Barbara. They'd married not long after my mother passed, and they seemed genuinely happy. I was glad that my father had a second chance to enjoy love and companionship at this stage of his life—especially following all his hard years of caretaking.

As I'd hoped, our relationship had improved since he left the Board. I tried hard to keep him in the loop, discussing strategy with him and sharing our financial statements. He'd write up financial analyses of our situation and we'd go over them together. Now that he wasn't formally weighing in on decisions, we no longer had blowout fights, but I made sure to ask his advice as I considered new growth opportunities. Being engaged with the business clearly still energized him, and I could tell he looked forward to our conversations.

On one visit in the summer of 1996, however, his usually upbeat face looked weary. I sat down in the living room next to him, and we talked for a few minutes about the latest developments at Whole Foods. But soon his tone turned more sober.

"John, I have something I need to tell you. Barbara insisted I see a doctor last week. She'd noticed that I was forgetting things more often. They did some tests, and the results just came back. I have Alzheimer's."

The news was concerning but, to be honest, I didn't fully understand the repercussions of what he was telling me. I knew that Alzheimer's disease affected the brain and memory, but it would take me a few days, and some research, before I began to appreciate the severity of the diagnosis. Still, my face must have shown concern because he quickly tried to set a more positive tone.

"Look, I feel good. I feel normal. They're giving me some drugs that should slow the decline. Everything's fine right now. I don't want you to worry any time soon."

Of course, I did worry. It was a shock to think that my always mentally sharp and physically robust father might drift into forgetfulness and confusion. And yet, as I learned more about Alzheimer's, it quickly became clear to me that this diagnosis should not have been a surprise to me. In fact, it explained much of my father's erratic behavior and the emotionally charged outbursts that had led to me asking him to leave the Board.

Over the weeks and months that followed, each time I visited, I noticed that he was indeed losing some of his mental acuity. Still, Bill Mackey wasn't one to go gently into that good night. On one visit, the two of us were engaged in a particularly intense discussion. I don't even remember what it was about, but it was one of our typical fun father-son debates. My perspective clearly won the day. After Dad ran out of ways to challenge me, he exclaimed, "Good argument, son, but I would have wiped the floor with you if it wasn't for this goddamn Alzheimer's!"

We both laughed. Sometimes the only honest response to the relentless march of mortality is to find and share moments of humor. But most of the time, there was little to laugh about. It was hard to see my father slowly but surely lose access to the sharpness of mind that he so valued and that I had always relied upon. Yes, I'd been ready for him to leave the Board and make space for me to grow more fully as a leader. But I wasn't ready to lose him.

Chapter 23

A Fight on Two Fronts

I've always enjoyed competition in many forms, but the truth is that in the arena of business, I hadn't really faced direct competitors in Whole Foods Market's first decade of existence. The first-generation natural foods supermarkets all started out as kings in their own territories. And then, one by one, Whole Foods started buying our friends' businesses and proving we were superior operators as we absorbed those companies and made them far more profitable than they had been. But that began to change in the late eighties and early nineties, as a new breed of business entered the natural foods market. These were no bootstrapped hippie labors of love; from day one they were venture-backed, growth-oriented, and targeted at an upscale clientele. While most of the first-generation founders were idealists, looking to change the ways Americans thought about food, the second-generation founders were opportunists, looking to capitalize on the changes that the pioneers had wrought.

Among these new entrants, two significant competitors had emerged by the mid-nineties, Wild Oats in the west, and Fresh Fields in the east. With the Bread & Circus and Mrs. Gooch's acquisitions done, Whole Foods Market faced a fight on two fronts.

I'd first heard the name Wild Oats spoken with great disdain in the late eighties by Hass Hassan, who was furious that this new company had encroached on Alfalfa's territory in Boulder, Colorado, and was undercutting them on price. I soon met Wild Oats cofounder Mike Gilliland. He was a good decade or so younger than me—youthful, energetic, and charming. He struck me as more of a capitalist than my Network buddies—something I really respected him for. Natural and organic food wasn't so much a passion for him; it was more of a good business opportunity.

For me, it was both. While I shared my old Network friends' high ideals and values, and had enormous appreciation for their pioneering stores, I'd often felt that we differed when it came to our business sensibilities. Most of them had not embraced capitalism in the same way I had. They were sometimes conflicted about playing and winning over the long term in the marketplace, and you could see it in their financial statements. Honestly, I think that's why Whole Foods Market emerged out of that first generation as the only dominant national company, buying up all those other brands. It wasn't always because we had the best stores; it was because we were more ambitious and thought strategically about the long term. We ran our business frugally and our stores to be highly profitable, and we weren't ambivalent about either money or growth. And yet we retained our high standards and ideals as well—something that the second generation of stores too often lacked.

Indeed, while I liked Mike as a fellow entrepreneur, I wasn't impressed with Wild Oats' stores. They were so focused on growth that their real estate strategy suffered, leaving them with many subpar locations that we'd never have considered for Whole Foods. One notable exception to this was a site in Santa Fe, New Mexico, which we passed up (to Jean-Claude's frustration), that turned out to be a great location and a top-grossing store that put Wild Oats on the map. On the whole, however, they weren't great operators, as Hass Hassan always complained, and didn't have the expertise in perishables or the quality standards we had. But they had the capital to compete on price and undercut much better operators like Alfalfa's.

Knowing Whole Foods' ability to improve poor operations, we were very interested in buying Wild Oats. Mike and I had numerous friendly conversations over the years about merging our companies, but we never could sync up on price. He was always willing to sell but always wanted much more than we were willing to pay. We also tried to buy Alfalfa's after cofounder Mark Retzloff left the company in 1990. Hass was struggling with the sudden competition from Wild Oats and we saw an opportunity for a win-win. Whole Foods could get a foothold in Boulder and be much better positioned to compete with the upstarts. Hass and I came to an agreement on price fairly quickly. Both Boards approved the deal. Then it went to the Alfalfa's shareholders for a vote. Unfortunately, Mark Retzloff still owned a lot of shares and wielded influence with many of the small shareholders, and he sabotaged the deal. I don't know to what extent this was directed at Hass and to what extent it was directed at me, but it left both of us frustrated.

That same year, 1991, our other new competitor, Fresh Fields, had opened its first store in Rockville, Maryland. Cofounder Leo Kahn was an older entrepreneur of my father's generation who had founded the conventional supermarket chain Purity Supreme and cofounded office supplies store Staples. While living in Boston, he had fallen in love with Bread & Circus, seduced, like me, by the quality of their perishables. He'd been inspired to create his own stores in a similar mold and had teamed up with Mark Ordan—a much younger Harvard MBA with a passion for retail who'd been working at Goldman Sachs.

Leveraging Mark's prestigious Harvard Business School and Goldman Sachs networks, the Fresh Fields founders had raised $7 million from Goldman and others, and Kahn put up $7 million of his own considerable fortune—an unheard-of war chest for a startup in our industry. They also assembled a star-studded Board, with members including Starbucks' CEO Howard Schultz. After quickly opening several successful stores in the Washington, DC, market, which lacked a natural foods supermarket in those days, they established a presence in Philadelphia, the New York metro area, and Chicago as well. They made no secret of the fact that they wanted to surpass Whole Foods Market and become the preeminent natural foods supermarket company in the country.

I had no idea how they were doing, financially speaking, but their rapid growth caught everyone's attention, as did their prices, which often undercut Whole Foods'. Were they making money? Or were they just burning through their capital? I had no way to know. So when I got an unexpected call from Fresh Fields CEO Mark Ordan one day in 1996 asking if we could meet in private, over a weekend, my curiosity was piqued.

"Sure," I told him. "Why don't you fly out to Austin—we can meet in my office. There won't be anyone around on a Sunday."

Mark arrived for the meeting looking much more like an investment banker than a natural foods retailer in his suit and wire-framed glasses. He cut to the chase: "Why don't we merge our companies?" At this point, Fresh Fields had 22 stores, while Whole Foods had 47 units in 12 states.

"Well," I said, "we'd certainly be interested in acquiring you."

"No, no," he replied. "I'm not talking about an acquisition. We'd be equal partners. We have Goldman behind us, so we have access to massive pools of capital."

I reminded Mark that we were a public company and had our own access to capital. And then I asked the question that really mattered in any "merger of equals"—who's going to be in charge?

"Well . . ." Mark hesitated. "We'll work that out later."

I laughed. "That sounds like you being in charge. And I'm afraid we're not interested in that. But if you ever decide you want us to buy you out, let me know."

After Mark left, we adopted an "if you can't join 'em, beat 'em" strategy. There were rumors that the money guys weren't happy with Fresh Fields' performance. There were rumors that Mark was becoming increasingly dictatorial in his leadership style. There were rumors of an impending IPO. We decided to put pressure on them right where they'd feel it the most: on their home turf in DC.

We found two great sites in Glover Park in DC and in Arlington, Virginia, where we decided to open stores under the Bread & Circus brand, which we had not yet renamed to Whole Foods Market. They were expensive investments, but I felt sure it would be worth it if Fresh Fields took a hit and they were more motivated to sell. In retaliation, Fresh Fields started scouting locations in Austin and Dallas. The battle was on!

A couple of months passed, and then I got another unexpected phone call, this time from Fresh Fields cofounder Leo Kahn, who had left the company a year earlier, selling his shares to the Carlyle Group for $40 million and starting a rival chain, Nature's Heartland, in Boston in 1996.

"John, would you be interested in acquiring Fresh Fields?"

I laughed. "Sure, I'm interested. In fact, just a month or so ago I had a conversation with Mark Ordan about it. But he only seemed to be interested in acquiring Whole Foods."

"That sounds like Ordan," Leo said, a note of bitterness in his voice. "Why would you want to do that deal?"

"I didn't want to do it," I told him.

"Well, I think you can buy Fresh Fields if you want it," Leo said. "You need to talk to David Dupree at Carlyle. They're not happy with Mark. The company's losing tens of millions of dollars."

I was encouraged and asked Leo if he could broker a meeting, which he agreed to do. Privately, I wondered if this was his way of retaliating against his former partner for pushing him out of the company.

When I showed up for the meeting at the Carlyle offices in DC, I was surprised to see Mark Ordan sitting beside David Dupree, looking distinctly uncomfortable. I went ahead with my pitch, proposing that we buy Fresh Fields with Whole Foods stock and do a secondary public offering right after the deal closed to give the Goldman and Carlyle guys the option to cash out if they wanted.

Ordan sat there silently, just nodding occasionally. David too was impassive. *That was a waste of time,* I thought as I left. I called Leo that night to tell him as much.

"Be patient," he said, "the company isn't doing well. They may not quite be ready to take your deal, but trust me, they're getting there."

A few more months passed. And then one day I got a call from David Dupree. "John, we'd like to talk further."

I wasn't going to get on a plane again unless two things were clear. One, this was an acquisition, not a merger of equals. And two, Ordan needed to be on board. They assured me that this was the case, and negotiations began.

Once the NDAs were signed, we finally got a look at Fresh Fields' financial statements. As Leo had hinted, they weren't pretty. In their five years as an independent company, they had lost about $35 million. They'd built a massive bureaucracy, way ahead of their growth. Their sales were good—not as good as Bread & Circus, Mrs. Gooch's, or Whole Foods Market, but good. But their cash burn rate was high. For us, this was all good news. By this point, we were experts at cutting back bureaucracy and tightening up operations.

It was the largest deal we had ever done—around $140 million for their 22 stores, of which we would need to close down about a third due to poor performance or close proximity to our existing stores. We were now, without question, the preeminent natural foods retailer in the country, with more than 60 stores in 13 states. But one significant natural foods supermarket competitor remained: Wild Oats. And the war in the west was heating up: Wild Oats was trying to buy Alfalfa's.

When Hass told me about our rival's bid, Whole Foods scrambled to put together our own. But Wild Oats prevailed and acquired the 11 Alfalfa's stores in the US and Canada to add to its own 21. Later that year, Wild Oats did an IPO, raising $42 million. Suddenly, our western competitor loomed much larger.

By 1997, we felt like old hands at the acquisition game. Again and again, we'd proven that we could take a struggling or moderately successful company; add our signature mix of culture, values, and operational excellence; and turn their stores into thriving Whole Foods Markets. I was so confident in our ability to assimilate and transform other companies that I started to wonder if it would work with businesses that weren't natural foods stores. Could Whole Foods Market expand into adjacent business lines in the same way we'd expanded into new states: by buying up existing companies and making them profitable? That year we set our sights on three promising avenues for this kind of growth: wine, coffee, and vitamins. All of these were products we already sold in our stores. But merging with a specialty company would allow us to expand our offerings and deepen our expertise in each area.

From a business perspective, this strategy seemed to make good sense. From a personal perspective, it also satisfied my own need for both growth and novelty. I've never been someone who can just keep doing the same thing over and over. It's both a strength and a weakness, as I'd learned by this point in my life. It had been a major driver for the company's growth, I knew. It was also an ongoing source of frustration for some of my partners. They struggled with the fact that I wasn't the kind of leader who just shows up at the office every day to do the day-to-day tasks. I relished the changing demands of the growing business—creating partnerships, raising money, scouting locations, developing new ideas, doing deals. I wanted new challenges—and I saw new opportunities.

Merchant of Vino was a Detroit-area company founded in 1974, with six stores and an excellent reputation. Buying them would give us first-rate expertise and connections in wine retail, which we lacked. And while wine was their central offering, over the years they'd added various gourmet foods and natural foods, as well as body-care and nutrition products. Detroit was the only top-ten major US city where Whole Foods Market did not yet have a presence. Plus, we'd heard that Wild Oats was thinking of buying Merchant of Vino. We got into a bit of a bidding war with our rival, and I confess that in our determination to win we probably overpaid. Soon after the deal was done, their president Marc Jonna, son of founder John Jonna, joined us as our national wine buyer.

Boulder-based Allegro Coffee was a company we knew well, since they'd supplied our stores with their specialty coffees and teas for many years. I had met the founders, Jeff and Roger Cohn, and had visited their popular Brewing Market coffeehouse in Boulder, Colorado, where they had two retail stores and a wholesale business. When the idea of an acquisition was raised, we didn't think twice.

When it came to vitamins, we set our sights on another Boulder-based company, Amrion. It too was a family business, founded by a father-and-son team a decade earlier. It was also a company we knew something about—Amrion had worked with Whole Foods to develop a private-label line of vitamins and supplements. Now, cofounder Mark Crossen was ready to retire and wanted to sell the profitable mail-order business. They'd done about $80 million in sales the previous year, and it seemed like a great company. We'd never done mail order, but I knew it was a chance to reach a demographic that might not come into our stores—older folks who took lots of supplements. I was also starting to think seriously about another channel of business: the exciting and still-new world of e-commerce. Just two years earlier, in 1995, Amazon had launched its online bookstore. Was this the future of mail order? Was it going to transition to the internet? It was hard to say for sure back then, but buying Amrion might give us a leg up as we began to think seriously about Whole Foods Market's web presence. We paid $140 million to acquire the company in September 1997.

We weren't just buying up Boulder companies. In 1998, Whole Foods opened its first store in a prime location on Boulder's Pearl Street. These encroachments into their territory didn't escape the notice of Wild Oats. In fact, I heard from a friend that Jim Lee, Wild Oats' COO at that time, had said, "Damn, have they acquired the Boulder courthouse yet?" I was glad they were feeling the pressure. In fact, in acknowledgment that we'd escalated the somewhat friendly competition between us, I sent CEO Mike Gilliland a gift: the board game Risk. The accompanying note read: "Mike, we're playing Risk now. Forewarned is forearmed. Good luck!"

Mike, who had a playful sense of humor, sent a gift in return: a Twister set. His note read: "You may be playing Risk, but I'm playing Twister."

Well played, I thought, laughing out loud. And it was true. Wild Oats was engaged in trying to contort itself around the larger and more established Whole Foods Market. They knew it, we knew it, and I respected Mike for being able to make a joke about it. Sooner or later, I hoped we would be able to buy them, but in the meantime, I was happy to watch them stretch and strain to compete with us on their home territory.

The truth was, however, that at that moment, my focus wasn't really on Boulder—or any other city for that matter. I was much more excited about the new territory that was opening up in the virtual world.

Chapter 24

A Hundred-Million-Dollar Mistake

Our forays into Colorado consumed much of my attention during 1998, but as the year came to a close, I became uncomfortably aware that there was trouble brewing closer to home. I'd faced challenges to my leadership before, from Mark Skiles and the venture capitalists. I knew that any time we acquired a company we got an influx of talent, but I also knew that anyone who has run their own company finds it hard to let go of the CEO role. Some former CEOs chose to cash out and retire; others came over to Whole Foods and carved out powerful niches for themselves—like Peter Roy, Lex Alexander, and Walter Robb. I always tried to honor these folks with significant roles within the company, but I felt some friction nonetheless as they chafed against no longer being top dog.

Such was the case with Peter. I'd made him President, and he had made great contributions to the company over the years, but recently, we'd been clashing more. He seemed unhappy with his role. *Does he want to leave?* I wondered. *Or does he simply want to be in charge?* Whatever the reason, his respect for me as CEO was visibly and publicly diminishing. Once again, I could feel the company dividing, with Peter and John camps forming. Peter and I went into counseling together to try to work out our differences and create a win-win relationship, but that didn't go very well. After a few months of unsuccessful attempts at reconciliation, the writing was on the wall. One day in the fall of 1998, I scheduled an early-morning meeting together.

"John, before you say anything—" Peter began speaking the moment he entered, having studied my face and correctly guessed what was going to happen. "I want you to know that I'm going to resign. It's time for me to move on. I have other things I want to do, and I don't want to be the richest man in the cemetery."

Peter always did have a way with words, and in this moment, I was content to let him have the last one. He left at the end of that year and went on to work at a venture capital firm in the natural foods industry, a perfect match for his unique skill set. Chris Hitt was promoted to President after Peter left, a role he eagerly stepped into.

There was a new term being thrown around in retail in the late nineties: "LOHAS," which stood for Lifestyles of Health and Sustainability. The *New York Times* summed it up neatly in a headline a few years later: "they care about the world and they shop, too." This was definitely our market. I thought of the category in simpler terms—middle-aged baby boomer hippies. Whole Foods Market saw itself as the premier food retail company catering to this demographic—and we'd been doing so long before it had an acronym. We were experts at selling them natural foods; why not other products as well? That was my reasoning in 1999 as I envisioned our foray into the brave new world of e-commerce. We saw our online store as a place where you would be able to buy health supplements, eco-friendly products, health products, clothing, yoga gear, books, travel packages, and more—a one-stop shop for the conscious consumer.

The first version of WholeFoods.com had already launched in 1998, but it was little more than an online brochure for our physical stores with a very limited product mix. I approached the Board with an ambitious proposal: Let's combine the new website division with Amrion and lease a large distribution center where we could also do Amrion production. Soon, we'd come up with a new brand that captured the breadth of our vision: WholePeople.com.

It was a giddy time. There was so much possibility in the air—and a sense of urgency that comes with knowing you still have a chance to be the first to do something. We could own this space in the same way that we'd come to own the natural foods retail space. But we needed to be fast and decisive.

We also needed cash—a lot of it. Creating an online store in those days meant a large and complex software development operation. There were no e-commerce apps you could just plug into your site nor had software as a service (SaaS) been developed yet. Instead, we had to build everything from scratch, and very few people had done it before. To fund this development, and the enormous distribution center, we went out and raised venture capital money once again.

Just over a decade earlier, the $4.5 million we'd raised for Whole Foods Market had seemed like an enormous sum. Now, we raised more than six times that amount: $30 million. And it was much easier to do so, despite the enormous risk. We kept the new subsidiary legally separate from Whole Foods Market so the parent company would not be liable if it failed. These were the heady days when people were throwing money at unproven internet ventures, desperate to plant their stake in the online future.

As the scope—and the stakes—of the endeavor grew, it was consuming more and more of my time and attention. The operations center for the new company, as well as the relocated Allegro and Amrion, was in Colorado, at a location in Thornton, outside Denver. I decided that I needed to be there, at least until the new business got off the ground. My entrepreneurial spirit was lit up by this new adventure, and my natural idealism was running high. I couldn't do it from afar; I needed to be right at the center of it. Consequently, in 1999, Deborah and I rented a house in Boulder and moved out there.

I was ready to make the move—perhaps permanently. I'd already been spending a lot of time in Boulder, between the acquisitions and the new store, which had quickly become one of our highest sales locations in the company. I felt at home there. The tree-lined streets of stately old Victorian homes reminded me of my favorite Austin neighborhoods, but the fresh mountain air was a welcome change from the Texas heat and humidity. And of course, it was a mecca for the counterculture—those LOHAS types, or, to use another popular term of the day, "cultural creatives."

Like many others, I'd read the recently published book *The Cultural Creatives: How 50 Million People Are Changing the World* by sociologist Paul Ray and psychologist Sherry Ruth Anderson. Based on extensive studies and surveys, the book proposed that a certain segment of the population, mostly in the boomer generation, had achieved a new level of growth, represented by a new set of values and a distinct lifestyle. These cultural creatives held emerging values like concern for the environment, a commitment to equality between the sexes, and a greater focus on global issues. Authenticity, self-actualization, and self-expression were paramount. They were less concerned about traditional measures of success and achievement, disenchanted with materialism, and more spiritual than religious. The book distinguished this sociological cohort from more secular "moderns" focused on material success and conservative "traditionals" with their religious bent. He suggested that 50 million Americans may fit this designation, and millions more globally.

Always seeking to understand the culture, or counterculture, that had defined my life, I found the book interesting, and I identified strongly with several aspects of Ray's designation, though not all. I had the opportunity to speak to him about it, as we briefly shared a position on the Board of Directors at the Boulder-based yoga lifestyle company Gaiam, whose CEO Jirka Rysavy served on the Whole Foods Board at the same time. I explained to Paul that I would call myself a cultural creative, except that I had a very different political orientation, and some of his categories didn't seem to fit.

"That's because you're a modern," he responded.

"But I fit so many of your cultural creative categories, I don't see how that makes sense."

I appreciated talking it through with Paul, but he never could provide a satisfying answer to my confusion. Just because I was a free-market-oriented businessman and appreciated capitalism—that disqualified me from being a cultural creative? I concluded there must be something missing from his categorizations. It would be several years before I understood exactly what that was.

These musings on cultural types and stereotypes were not just theoretical—they gave shape to the strange experiences I often had living and working in Boulder, and indeed, in the broader field of the natural foods industry. In so many ways, I fit right in. And yet, there would be moments when I was reminded, abruptly, that I didn't.

My move to Boulder was not entirely popular among my fellow Whole Foods executives, but I was determined to make it work without giving up my CEO title in the process. At least, not yet. In the back of my mind, I thought that if WholePeople really took off, maybe I'd let Chris eventually take over my role at Whole Foods Market while I ran the new online business. But we weren't there yet, and I wasn't about to give up my leadership of the company. However, I acknowledged that it was going to be hard for me to act as CEO from afar, especially in that pre-videoconferencing era, so I asked Chris to step up temporarily in my absence.

WholePeople quickly ran into trouble. Remember, these were early days as far as the internet was concerned. Forget Wi-Fi; we were still on dial-up modems. We'd sit and listen to that strange chirping refrain as our computers struggled to connect. We had little tech expertise, and we couldn't find many people in Boulder who did. All the internet tech folks were out in the Bay Area, so we realized we were going to have to set up an office out there. This made it easier to attract talent but harder to run the company. There was endless squabbling between the Colorado team and the California team. After only a few months, I realized it just wasn't working. I flew down to California and told the team that we'd be shutting down the office.

"We'll pay for you to relocate to Boulder," I told them all. "We want you to still be part of the team. But we need our team in one place." They did not react with the enthusiasm I had hoped for. It was such a boom time for the California tech scene, people just didn't want to leave. They all had dreams of being part of the next big internet success story, and they felt like they needed to stay close to the epicenter. In the end, we only persuaded four or five to make the move. The rest left the company, embittered.

One of the guys who did come over to Boulder was a smart young man by the name of Huy Lam. He seemed happier than most about the move, and when we were chatting, he told me that one of his favorite philosophers—Ken Wilber—lived in the area, and he was excited to get connected to the community around him. Anyone who had a favorite philosopher got my attention right away, and soon we were deep in conversation about Eastern mysticism, psychology, and philosophy. He gave me a book by Wilber. I had actually read a few of Wilber's earlier books, but I hadn't kept up with his subsequent books for probably a decade. The cover proclaimed the nothing-if-not-grandiose title *A Theory of Everything: An Integral Vision for Business, Politics, Science, and Spirituality*. I wasn't at all sure such a thing was possible—could one philosophy really make sense of such diverse domains? In my own life experience, these often felt like very different tracks, though I tried my best to apply the values I'd learned in my spiritual journey to my business and my politics.

Reading Wilber was a revelation to me. The title of his book actually delivered! His frameworks connected Eastern mysticism with Western philosophy and psychology and even business and politics in ways I'd never considered before. Soon, I was devouring every piece of his writing I could get my hands on and discussing it all in great detail with Huy and other friends who were interested in integral thinking.

It felt like we were hemorrhaging money just trying to get the website up at WholePeople.com. It was a strange experience to spend so much on something I couldn't even see. When you pour capital into a new store, at least you get to see the walls going up, the lights turning on, the fresh new paint, the gleaming appliances. This was just code. Finally, the site went live in November 1999. But there was no flurry of orders. There were almost no sales at all. Amrion kept getting mail-order business through the catalog, but the online store was eerily quiet. Amrion's mail-order customers were mostly my father's generation, and they were not early adopters of the internet!

The turn of the millennium came and went, with its breathless fears of Y2K digital meltdowns, which predictably never occurred. We were too consumed with our own struggling business to pay much attention to the prophets of doom or to the parties. It wasn't just the sluggish sales from the online store that were concerning. Whole Foods' stock price was declining as well. Part of the problem was that our investors didn't understand the notion of an "omni-channel" business back then. The market preferred "pure plays"; it didn't like hybrids. Were we a grocery store or an internet company? Investors had put their money behind the former and were decidedly suspicious of the latter, especially given that it was losing money. Even Amrion's mail-order business was declining—it was a dying business model—and the folks running it only had one answer: give us more money for direct-mail marketing. This didn't fix the problem, and no one on my team had any expertise in that world. We just didn't know how to revive it. For all these reasons, I was under increasing pressure from the Board. It began to look like we might be forced to spin off WholePeople quickly in order to protect Whole Foods Market from the fallout, a move to which I was strongly opposed.

In the spring of 2000, Deborah and I purchased a home on a beautiful, quiet street in downtown Boulder, but I was already wondering how long we'd really be able to live there. By early summer, it had become clear that WholePeople was going nowhere and the entire internet bubble had become the dot-com bust. There was nothing to do but sell off the assets. We sold the WholePeople.com subsidiary to Gaiam.com. In return, we got Gaiam.com stock, which turned out to be worth nothing. We remained part owners, at least for now, but the site was shut down and merged with Gaiam's site. In the end, we sold Amrion too, but we only received $40 million for it—a $100 million loss on what we'd paid. We were also forced to lay off 177 team members between the two brands. It was a very rude awakening from my dreams of online triumph.

What was starting to become clear to me in the wake of our failure was that the LOHAS ideal was more of a marketer's fantasy than an actual reality—at least for now. Just because someone bought organic food and vitamins at Whole Foods Market didn't mean they also wanted to buy books, yoga gear, or a walking tour in France from some page on the internet.

That summer, a year after we'd left, Deborah and I returned to live in Austin. I wasn't welcomed with open arms. I still had many supporters on the leadership team, but the simmering disapproval had also increased. Not only had I been absent from the headquarters for the past year; my new ventures had been unequivocal failures. The Amrion acquisition and the WholePeople launch were very costly mistakes. By any standard, $100 million is a lot of money, and at the time it was a huge hit for the company. And yet that monetary loss, for all its impact, might not have been the greatest price I paid for our ill-fated foray into online retailing. I almost lost something much more precious—the Board's confidence in my leadership of the company.

Chapter 25

The Coup

August in Austin is brutally hot, and I found myself missing Boulder, where I could escape even the warmest days for a hike on the high mountain trails. Back in Austin, the only refuges were air-conditioned buildings or a refreshing swim in Barton Springs. And the atmosphere inside Whole Foods Market HQ in the summer of 2000 was as oppressive as the heat outdoors.

Despite the WholePeople.com and Amrion failures, Whole Foods Market was doing well, with our sales increasing and our national footprint continuing to grow. We'd opened our 100th store just before the turn of the millennium, and in early 2000 we'd expanded our presence in Northern California to 12 stores with the acquisition of three Food for Thought stores in Sonoma County. But the failures hung heavily over the E-Team. I knew that some folks in the company blamed me for the loss, since I'd been the new venture's biggest cheerleader. Glenda was as warm and supportive as ever; and Jim Sud, now COO, was philosophical about it all. But Chris Hitt had an air of smug superiority, and I sensed some irritation when we spoke.

Chris and I had once been good friends, connecting not only in our vision for the business but our mutual spiritual interests. I knew he had resented and complained about my absence in Boulder; now he seemed to resent my return. Clearly, he'd thrived being in charge—and by all accounts had done a good job, though I got the sense he brought a more directive style to the role than I had done. Chris was brilliant, but also intense and domineering when he thought he knew better—which was most of the time. I also suspected he was talking to others at the company about his problems with me.

Another heavy weight on my mind that summer and fall was a fast-unfolding family tragedy. My dear brother-in-law, Jean-Claude, had been diagnosed with stage 4 lung cancer. The prognosis was grim. Jean-Claude and Dorothy and my younger nephew, Will, were living in Houston, while Andy was now at Stanford. On recent visits, I'd been shocked by how quickly the disease had taken a toll on this once vital, larger-than-life man.

Jean-Claude's cancer progressed rapidly, and he passed away in December 2000. His death hit me hard. He'd been family, he'd been a friend, and he'd also been another mentor—an older man with a seasoned outlook on the world who I'd often called up for advice.

As I mourned his death, I felt a curious sense of aloneness that went beyond this particular loss. I keenly felt the absence of the older, wiser figures I'd always turned to. Of course, I still had allies and close companions, both at Whole Foods and in my personal life. But in just a couple of years, I'd lost several mentors—my father, though still alive, to the fog of Alzheimer's; and now Jean-Claude to cancer. And Craig Weller had recently departed my close circle as well. About a year earlier, he'd finally reached that stop he'd told me would one day come and stepped off the Whole Foods elevator. I missed his steady presence in the company, even though it had been many years since we'd actually worked side by side. In a sense, Craig had always been the grown-up in the room—the calm, exemplary servant leader and quintessential grocer, whistling while he swept the floors. With him filling that role so beautifully, I'd felt more freedom to be playful, creative, even boyish. Now, at 47, there was no longer any doubt: I was the grown-up in the room.

And it was a room that was feeling less and less friendly. Our Board, in those days, consisted of David Dupree, who'd joined with the Fresh Fields acquisition; Avram Goldberg, former CEO of Stop & Shop supermarkets; Jirka Rysavy, CEO of Gaiam; Bud Sorenson, former dean of the Colorado University business school; Fred "Chico" Lager, former CEO of

Ben & Jerry's; and John Elstrott, a professor of entrepreneurship at Tulane. There were certainly friendly colleagues among that group, Elstrott and Sorenson in particular, but it was not the "friends and family" Board of earlier Whole Foods Market eras.

The ongoing success of our core business was real and undeniable, but our recent missteps were a black mark against me, and I knew that I had some credibility to regain in the eyes of the Board and Whole Foods' regional leadership. After all, I'd not been captaining the ship day-to-day over the past year, and it was natural for there to be some concern about who was really in charge and in what direction we were heading. Fundamentally, though, I still considered the Board supportive of my leadership. I had no notion of how quickly that conviction would be tested.

I eased off my ski boots and enjoyed the feeling of being able to move my toes again after a long day on the slopes. My nose and cheeks and fingertips tingled as they warmed up. Beside me, my teenage nephew Will wrestled with his own boots. I'd brought him to Colorado for a week together in December 2000 to take his mind off the loss of his father. I loved both boys deeply, and it hurt to see them burdened by a grief like this at such a young age. In a sense, I understood how they were feeling. I was already grieving my own father, as the cruel disease took him away from me little by little. But Will was still only a boy himself. We picked up our gear, threw our skis on our shoulders, and headed for our room, and I told him I just needed a few minutes to check my messages before dinner.

"Sounds good, Uncle John," he replied.

I hit "play" on my voicemails as I got changed, half listening to the day's updates from the team and half preoccupied with my earlier musings about fathers and sons and loss. Then my assistant's voice cut through my thoughts:

"John Elstrott is trying to reach you. He says it's urgent."

That got my attention. What could be urgent? It must be something Board related, which didn't make me any less concerned.

"Is everything okay?" Will asked.

"I don't know yet. It's something about Whole Foods. The message wasn't specific."

I called Elstrott back, and soon a picture began to take shape. It wasn't a pretty one. There seemed to be a move against me among the Board, a desire to remove me as CEO. Elstrott couldn't say much more than that, but he wanted me to be prepared. Had I unknowingly paved the way for this when I temporarily departed for Boulder and entrusted Chris with my role? Was Chris part of this plan? Was he conspiring to take my job? Or was it being entirely driven by disgruntled Board members? And were enough of them feeling that way to actually oust me? Despite recent events, I still was surprised that they would want me gone. Whole Foods was my baby—I was the only one of the four founders still with the company.

Unfortunately, my position wasn't exactly rock solid. I didn't have a huge ownership share at this point; all I had was my track record. But that was pretty darn good! Whatever missteps we had made in the past year, the heart of the business was thriving and growing. I was Chairman of the Board, CEO, and had been the one constant in the company for over two decades. And yet, the fact remained: one simple vote could change all of that.

Next, I called Jim Sud, who was also on a ski trip at the time, in Park City, Utah. He didn't know much, not being on the Board anymore, but he knew the players. As always, he was steady and clearheaded, and I wished he was still a director. I could have used that kind of support. As we discussed what we could piece together, I started to suspect that Fred "Chico" Lager might be key to the impending coup attempt. Chico was a successful operator who had been largely responsible for building up Ben & Jerry's in its early days. He had seemed a natural fit for our Board, as a former CEO of a wildly successful, mission-driven company. The only problem was that I had gotten the sense that he didn't particularly like me.

"Here's what I think about Chico," I told Jim. "I mean, he largely built Ben & Jerry's, operationally. But who remembers him? He's not Ben and he's not Jerry. I sometimes wonder if he's a bit frustrated that, as the operator who essentially built the company, he gets so little credit. Does he see me as being a head-in-the-clouds founder like the guys with their names on the ice cream cartons? And does he see Chris as being more like him, a responsible leader who can build the company?"

I paused for a moment, thinking through the implications. "Still, even if that's true, he's just one Board member. Does he really have the support of the Board? Do they really think Chris is going to do a better job than me?"

"You may be right, John," Jim said, "but we just don't know. All we can do is present our case. We can tell the truth about your leadership, and I think at least some of the Board will believe in you. Obviously, WholePeople and Amrion were missteps, but a lot of businesses have stumbled in the last year. The whole economy is suffering. Whole Foods is hardly alone in trying to take advantage of the internet and biting off more than we can chew."

Jim was right. Over the last year, the dot-com boom had turned into the dot-com bust. Nevertheless, I understood that I wasn't facing this challenge at a moment of my greatest personal strength. I was vulnerable.

That night, I tried to bring my attention back to my uncle-nephew trip, but it was difficult to stop ruminating on all the unanswered questions. Plus, Will had fallen sick, which further ruined the mood.

"I'm sorry we didn't get to enjoy more of a break," I told him as we packed up and headed for the airport. I promised we'd do it again soon.

After dropping Will off in Houston and paying a short visit to my father, who was too confused to really give me any helpful advice on the predicament I was facing, I drove back to Austin. As the familiar miles ticked by, I thought about this latest challenge to my leadership, and the many that had come before. Indeed, I was beginning to learn that in business, no matter how successful you are and how much you have accomplished, there are always people who are highly confident that they could do a much better job if given a chance. I had dealt with this throughout my career, and it only seemed to be exacerbated by the fact that I wasn't a "professional" CEO. I didn't have an MBA from Wharton or Harvard or a résumé filled with blue-chip consulting firms. I had been schooled on the job.

I thought about Mark Skiles and his conviction that he could run Whole Foods better than Wacky Mackey. I thought about the VC hitch-hikers and their intended replacement manager who died the day he was supposed to start work. Peter Roy never directly challenged me for my job, but it was pretty clear that he thought he could do a better job running the company. And now Chris, who had helped give voice to the company's values, seemed, intentionally or not, to be the face of yet one more attempt to dislodge me from leading the company I had worked so hard to build.

I called Chris, who was now back in Boston.

"Are you trying to push me out?" I asked, seeing no reason to beat about the bush. Chris was cryptic in his reply. He said he'd been contacted by some of the directors (he wouldn't say who) who were concerned about my job performance and the future of the CEO role.

"And what did you tell them?" I demanded.

"I didn't deny I was concerned as well, and that I think it may be time for a leadership change."

Well, I guessed that was the closest I was going to get to an admis-sion. And whether he had instigated the coup attempt or it had begun on the Board, it was clear that he was no longer supportive of my leadership.

"Would you stand down if I asked you to? Would you turn down the CEO role if the Board offered it to you?" I asked, hoping that our history as good friends might prevail upon him to act honorably.

"No, I would not," he replied. "This isn't about you and me, John. It's about Whole Foods."

Not about him and me? *Leave it to Chris to make a power grab sound high-minded*, I thought.

Following this conversation, over the holiday period, Chris and I exchanged a series of emails in which we aired the issues that had come between us and tried, unsuccessfully, to resolve them. In his missives, Chris expressed his frustrations and reiterated his conviction that I was not the right person to lead Whole Foods forward. He pushed me to consider an alternative role within the company. While stopping short of expressly coveting the CEO role for himself, he was full of conviction that I needed to vacate it. The breakdown of this once-close relationship, along with the anxiety that I might lose control of the company, made for an extremely stressful few weeks. And looming over it all was an ominous deadline: The Board had called for a January meeting at our Florida offices in Miami and asked both Chris and me to be there, as well as Jim and Glenda. We'd each be invited to address the Board, and then there would be a vote to resolve the leadership challenge.

Most people who go to Miami in January are looking forward to lazy days on sun-drenched beaches; playing some golf, tennis, or water sports; and hitting the restaurants and clubs after sunset. I felt profoundly out of place among the vacationing throngs as Glenda, Jim, and I waited for our bags at the airport. It was an incongruous spot for an epic battle, which was what the upcoming Board meeting felt like to me. Weren't such events supposed to take place in gilded throne rooms or on ramparted towers overlooking the disputed kingdom? Scenes from my favorite fantasy novels filled my mind, especially my old favorite, *The Lord of the Rings*. So many people wanted the Ring of Power. So many people were convinced that they were the best one to carry it. While I had no illusions of myself being a pure-hearted, near-incorruptible little hobbit like Frodo, I did see myself as a servant leader—and my position at the head of the company as a higher calling. I wasn't in it for the power or prestige. I'm not saying that those who coveted my job were merely self-serving; I'm sure many of them genuinely believed they would be better stewards of the company than I was. And I'm sure they were correct about some of my failings. But I still truly loved Whole Foods Market and believed that I had the company's best interests at heart. I honestly felt that it was in the company's best interests for me to continue to carry the Ring of Power—at least for now.

It was hard for me to accept the possibility that I might be about to lose the role that gave me such a sense of purpose. By the end of tomorrow afternoon, the Board meeting would be over. I'd done everything I could to prepare for this fateful meeting. The three of us had already talked it through from every possible angle. How was I to fill my time and keep my mind from uselessly ruminating on possible outcomes? Well, I was still CEO of Whole Foods Market, and as such, I always visited our stores whenever I traveled. So I'd scheduled a tour for the following morning at the Ft. Lauderdale store.

We'd been in the Sunshine State since 1994 when we acquired Terry Dalton's Unicorn Village, to which we added the two Bread of Life stores in 1997, establishing a real presence in the region. More than once we'd considered just getting the hell out of Florida, and I'd wondered if the average resident was just too old or too set in their ways to be interested in natural and organic foods. But once we moved to larger locations and began to gain respect as a true alternative to the traditional supermarkets, business improved significantly. Since 1998, the region had been flourishing under the excellent leadership of Juan Núñez, who'd come into Whole Foods with the Mrs. Gooch's merger.

The next morning, I stepped out into the bright Florida sunshine and headed over to meet Juan at the store. I had left a message for Chris to see if he would be willing to meet me there for one last attempt at a reconciliation, but he hadn't responded. Stepping inside, I was hit with a blast of cold air and an equally powerful blast of uplifting energy. Our stores always made me feel that way, and today it was even more true. After weeks of feeling worried and hurt and betrayed and angry, it was as if the clouds had parted.

I walked through the aisles, admiring the beautiful produce and immaculate displays. Team members who recognized me stopped to introduce themselves and show me their favorite local products, and their enthusiasm lifted my spirits even further. I looked at the faces of customers, smiling as they chatted with our bakery team about the various fresh breads or serious and focused as they tested the firmness of an avocado. The spirit of Whole Foods Market—the love that had built and infused this company from day one—came alive for me as I stood there in midst of our bustling store. And I realized that it had been absent from my awareness for too long.

Sure, I'd been thinking about the business—consumed with the fortunes and misfortunes of our online venture, and more recently, the drama of our boardroom battles—but that wasn't what Whole Foods was all about. Whole Foods wasn't about power and intrigue and taking sides. *This* was what Whole Foods was all about: selling fresh, wholesome, natural foods to people who appreciated them, in beautiful stores staffed by team members who truly cared about our mission. It was simple, but it was everything. It was my passion and my purpose. It was love!

I felt a wave of gratitude surge through me for everything Whole Foods had brought into my life. It reminded me of my experiences taking MDMA—everything was infused with love. Anxiety and fear seemed unable to touch me anymore. And in place of all the resolve and defensiveness I'd been feeling about my role at Whole Foods, I just felt a pure glow of longing. A hope. I deeply, fervently hoped I would be given the opportunity to continue to steward this amazing company into its future. I had so much more I still wanted to do—so much more energy and creativity to give.

In the midst of my reverie, I looked up and there was the man himself. Chris was walking toward me down the produce aisle and stopped abruptly when he saw me. Still caught up in the feeling of love and gratitude, I walked right up to him without a moment's hesitation and put my hand on his shoulder.

"Hey," I said. "Thank you so much for coming. Let's go into the Store

Team Leader's office and talk for a few minutes. Would you be willing to do that?" I could tell that Chris was not enthusiastic about the prospect of a conversation, but he agreed.

I closed the door to the office and it was just him and me, finally face-to-face. "Chris, it's still not too late," I said. "We've had a great partnership together and this doesn't have to be the end of it. We can have a wonderful future continuing to build this amazing company together. We've been friends and colleagues now for 16 years. Don't throw that away. All I need you to do is support my leadership."

For a moment, I thought I glimpsed our old friendship in his face, but then a hardness set over his features.

"John," he said, "here's how it is. It's time for you to go. Either you can go quietly and peacefully with honor and accept a different role more suited to your talents. Or you're going to get thrown out on your ass. That's your choice."

"It doesn't have to be this way," I insisted. "We can stop this now and go back to the way things were. But once we walk into that Board meeting, there will be no going back."

He shook his head. "Your time has come, John."

"But you don't have the votes," I told him.

"I guess we'll find out," he said, walking past me and out of the store to attend his meeting with the Board.

Even this blunt conversation could not shake the sense of joy and peace I felt as I left the store a little later that afternoon and headed over for my meeting with the Board. The outcome of it all was beyond my control. I could accept that now, because I was in touch with my purpose, and I knew I'd done everything I could do.

When it was my turn to speak to the Board, I still was very much in an altered state of consciousness. John Elstrott gave me an encouraging nod as I began the presentation I'd prepared. The words were the same ones I'd crafted and pored over for the past few weeks, but now they were infused with the love and purpose that had reawakened in me. Afterward, when the Board began asking me questions, I simply answered from my heart. I had nothing to prove—just an overwhelming love for the company and a desire to lead it forward into the new century.

That next morning, I flew back to Austin. I was still waiting on the Board's decision. But inwardly, I didn't feel like I was waiting for anything. In the wake of my store-tour revelation, so much was becoming clear. Whether I continued as CEO or not, I saw that I needed to become a different kind of leader—and a different kind of man. I was no longer preoccupied with feeling angry or betrayed. I recognized that whatever others had done to precipitate this crisis, I'd played a role in it too. And at this moment, all I could do was take responsibility for my part and change the things about myself that had led to this moment.

Bottom line, I needed to step up—to be more fully present and wholehearted in my leadership. My absence, I realized, had not just been my physical move to Boulder or even my preoccupation with WholePeople. There was a deeper way in which I'd not been showing up as the leader Whole Foods needed at this stage in its development. Yes, I loved the company, but I'd been too ready to let others step in and fill the void from day to day—people who had the drive and ability to run things but not always the best motivations. I was the only one of the founding team still here, and that made me spiritually responsible for the company. But I'd been distracting myself with novelty rather than doing the inner work to grow into a more conscious and skilled steward.

That disconcerting feeling I'd had since my father's decline, Jean-Claude's death, and Craig's retirement now came into focus: I needed to fully mature. I needed to lead not just with passion and inspiration but by example. In this regard, I thought particularly about Craig. He'd always been such a wonderful example to me—and to the whole company. Perhaps this was his parting gift as he stepped off the elevator: to create a space—indeed, an imperative—for me to truly lead by example. I needed to internalize Craig Weller into my soul.

I wasn't a boy anymore, and Whole Foods wasn't just a store, or even a few stores. We were a $1.5 billion company with 117 stores in 22 states plus the District of Columbia. My natural strengths and entrepreneurial passion had taken me a long way, but this moment called for a more deliberate approach to developing my leadership. I knew that my ability to delegate and, even more importantly, to empower my team members, was a critical strength—and one not necessarily shared by those who sought to oust me from my job. But a mature company needs a mature CEO who deeply embraces the full responsibility of leadership, as well as a healthy, productive executive team that can complement the leader's strengths rather than just picking up the slack.

These reflections accompanied me on my morning run the next day, as my feet pounded the trails alongside Town Lake. They continued to unfold as I went about my work at the office, and I explored them further with my closest confidantes, particularly Jim and Glenda, and Deborah when I got home. Would it be too late for me to bring a higher level of conscious leadership to Whole Foods? Maybe. But it wasn't too late for me to become the man I sensed I could be, regardless of how things worked out.

Finally, John Elstrott called. The Board had decided to keep me as CEO. Of course, I felt tremendous relief. He added that the Board had specified a number of changes they wanted to make—in the E-Team, the Board of Directors, and the organizational structure. I was ready—indeed, I was happy—to hear that.

Over the next several years, in many one-on-one dinners with various Board members, aided by a lot of good red wine, I gradually learned more about what had gone down that day in Florida. I never knew for sure how the whole thing got started and who was the instigator of the attempted coup. But I did learn that my heartfelt presentation—with its clear focus on where we'd come from, the mistakes that had been made, where I saw the company going, how I needed to change, and how the company needed to change in order to get there—had been very well received. Chris, on the other hand, had come to the Board full of anger toward me and went on a passionate rant about everything that was wrong with my leadership. A few years later, one of the directors told me that afterward, the Board weren't sure they wanted me to stay on as CEO, but they sure as hell weren't going to turn the company over to Chris. He was just too damn angry to be an effective leader.

I also eventually learned that only Chico voted against me, and the rest of the Board backed me as CEO. Initially, the Board asked Chris to take a temporary leave of absence from his role as President, but it quickly became clear that he was unable to make peace with my continuing to lead the company, and eventually we mutually agreed that he should resign. Chris had contributed an enormous amount to the development of Whole Foods Market, and we were happy to give him a generous send-off. But there was no way he could stay. Chico also left the Board, and John Elstrott took over as the Lead Director. And we made some much-needed changes on the E-Team. The most important of these was the promotion of A.C. Gallo and Walter Robb from Regional Presidents to Co-Chief Operating Officers, to which was later added the title of Co-Presidents. They brought an ethic of operational excellence to the company as a whole that we'd never had before at the executive level. Jim Sud became our Executive Vice President of Business Development and Real Estate.

At the end of that long week, still raw from the intense emotions, I couldn't wait to get out to the ranch. Deborah and I packed up the car and made the drive early Saturday morning, arriving with the dew still heavy on the grass and the creek running high. It was chilly out, but I pulled on a jacket, grabbed a chair and a couple of books, and went down to the water's edge.

Spring comes early in Texas Hill Country. In February, you can feel it just beginning to stir. Settled in my favorite spot, I closed my eyes and listened to the sounds of the land waking up. The first robins had arrived—their companionable *tuk tuk* calls a welcome signal of the new season. The morning sun caressed the limestone along the creek bed, and when I reached out and laid my hand on the familiar stone, it was warm to the touch. The water danced and gurgled as it passed. I breathed in the energy of nature's annual rebirth and thought about how I was undergoing a rebirth of my own.

I had survived a betrayal from someone I considered one of my closest friends and a near-death experience as the CEO of the company I had co-founded 22 years earlier. In the process, I'd found a renewed connection to the higher purpose of Whole Foods and to the importance of love in both life and leadership. I could still feel it sparkling in my heart and warming me like the spring sunshine. I felt relieved to have come through this crisis without losing the trust of the Board and the job I loved. But I was not jubilant. I'd come too close to disaster, and I was estranged from a friend who'd meant a lot to me. I was no longer the same person I had been.

Sitting by the creek that spring morning, I felt the two major streams of my life coming together and comingling: my business journey and my personal and spiritual development. Conscious leadership required both. It called me to be more present and accountable in my stewardship of Whole Foods, and to do so, it also demanded that I grow spiritually—becoming a more awake, humble, loving, and self-aware human being.

My mentors were all gone now, but they had all taught me well. My father, Craig, and Jean-Claude had all given me so much wisdom. Even those who had challenged me—Mark, Peter, and Chris—had called forth new strength and conviction in me. I was grateful to all of them for what they had taught me. I was ready to embrace it all and step into the next phase of my life. And so was Whole Foods Market. The company was poised to launch its greatest growth spurt as we entered the new millennium, and I was ready to lead our expanding team with all the love and wisdom I could muster. I was 47 years old, and it had taken me a really long time to grow up.

PART III

WHOLE LIFE

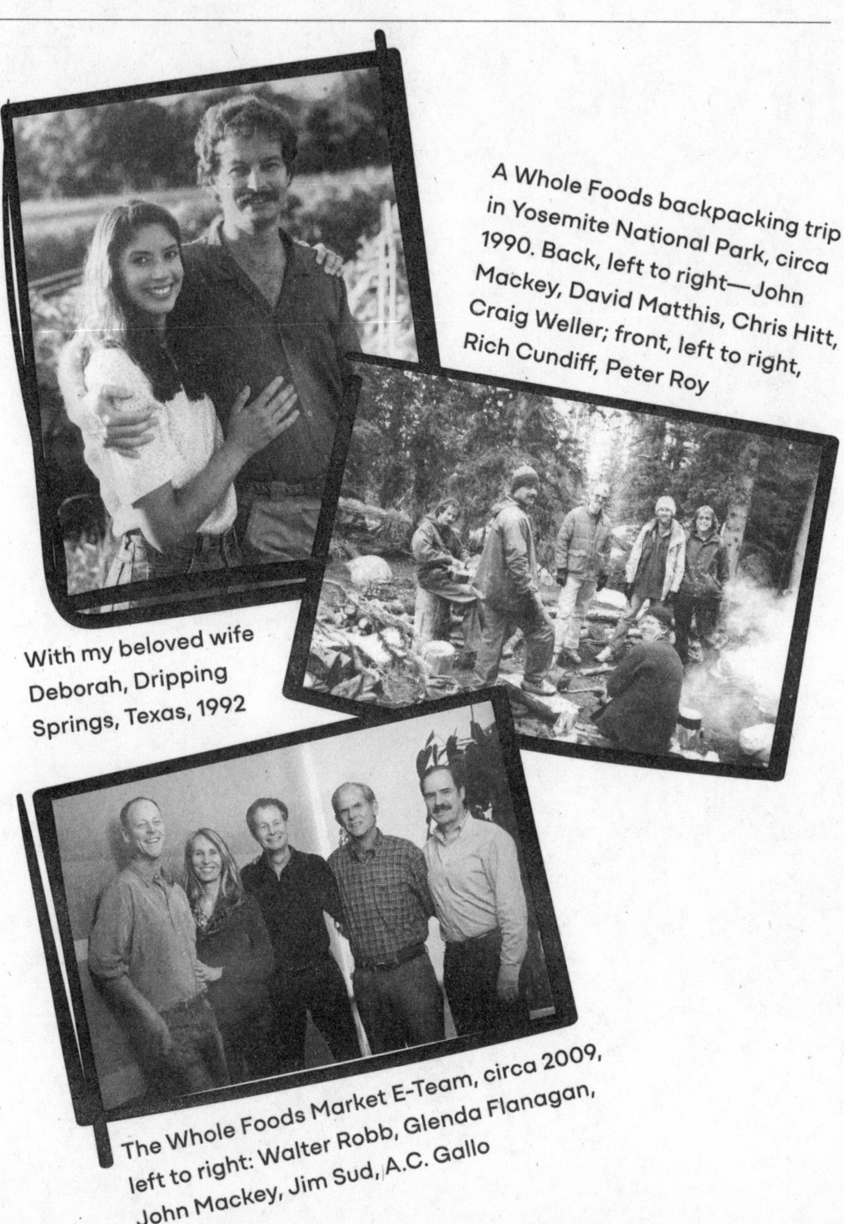

A Whole Foods backpacking trip in Yosemite National Park, circa 1990. Back, left to right—John Mackey, David Matthis, Chris Hitt, Craig Weller; front, left to right, Rich Cundiff, Peter Roy

With my beloved wife Deborah, Dripping Springs, Texas, 1992

The Whole Foods Market E-Team, circa 2009, left to right: Walter Robb, Glenda Flanagan, John Mackey, Jim Sud, A.C. Gallo

Chapter 26

Strider

One foot, then the other. The soft crunch of my shoes on the narrow dirt path was like a mantra, drawing me into a meditative state. Among the branches that arched overhead, a bird was singing. A soft breeze rustled the leaves. High above, an eagle soared in slow, graceful circles. My attention lightly scanned the trail ahead for roots and rocks, keeping me alert and present. I felt more at peace than at any time I could remember.

It was June 2002, and for the past two months I'd been hiking the Appalachian Trail. Beginning in Georgia, my companions and I had covered more than 1,300 miles on foot, and we still had about 900 miles ahead of us before we reached the end of the trail in Maine.

The pack on my shoulders, which had felt awkward when I first set out, now seemed almost like a part of me. I barely noticed its weight. I had just about worn out my third pair of trail running shoes and would wear out another two pairs before I summited Mount Katahdin. My trekking poles, lightly grasped in each hand, moved at an easy counterpoint to my footfalls. My body felt strong, lean, and comfortable with this natural motion. Indeed, it felt like this was what it had been made to do. I imagined myself as a nomadic hunter-gatherer, living off the land, moving with the seasons. The pace of my life had slowed to match the rhythm of the trail. And I liked it that way.

One foot, then the other. Always moving forward but never in a hurry, like the sun moving steadily across the sky. In contrast, I realized how frenetic my regular life had become in recent years—the amped-up pace of city living, the increasing media attention that came with success, the adrenaline rush of dealmaking, the boardroom negotiations. These days, weeks, and months on the trail had brought me home into my body, making me aware of how much I'd been living in my head. I also realized how much of my attention was typically tied up in the future—in dreams and strategies and targets and growth. There was nothing wrong with all that; indeed, it energized me and pulled me forward, giving purpose to my life. But as I walked, I landed softly in the present moment with each footfall and appreciated just flowing along.

As I often did, I hiked in silence, at my own pace, enjoying the feeling of solitude while knowing my companions weren't far ahead or behind. The trail began to wind uphill, skirting boulders and trees until the canopy thinned and the "green tunnel," as the A.T. is sometimes called, opened up to the sky. I stepped out of the forest onto a large slab of granite at the crown of the hill and stopped to catch my breath, taking in the sudden vastness of the landscape when seen from above. Looking south, the mountains faded into the blue horizon—hundreds of miles that we'd covered by foot. It was hard to believe we'd come so far. Looking north, I imagined the miles that lay ahead between us and the summit of Mount Katahdin in Maine where the trail would end.

There are certain places on the A.T. where you get a sudden perspective like that. Much of the time, you are simply following a narrow path through the trees. That's part of its charm—the way you can lose yourself in the moment-to-moment experience of the trail and forget about the larger world for a while. But every now and then, on a ridgeline or mountaintop or through a break in the trees, the scale of the surrounding wilderness catches you by surprise all over again, as it did for me that day somewhere just north of the New Jersey/New York border.

A flag fluttered in the summer breeze, its pole anchored deep in the rock. I unclipped the belt of my pack and eased its weight off my shoulders, stretching out my arms and back. The temperature had mercifully dropped, after a week of punishing heat and humidity. To the east, the forest rolled down to a long, narrow lake and then rose again on the other side. On the far horizon, I could just make out the Hudson River and the Manhattan skyline. And even from this distance, I could see the gaping hole in that concrete forest where the Twin Towers had stood—as starkly empty as the rocky hilltop from which I observed it. My mind was pulled back to that day nine months earlier that had shocked the world. In a strange way, it was the events of September 11, 2001, that had set me on the path that would eventually lead to this now-beloved trail.

I'd woken up early, that fateful September morning, in a Manhattan hotel room. I dressed in a suit and tie and met Glenda and Cindy McCann, our VP of investor relations, for a quick breakfast downstairs. We were headed downtown for a day of meetings with the bond-rating agencies S&P and Moody's. It was a beautiful morning, and as our driver inched through traffic, I looked out the window at the crush of people on their way to the office, soaking in the unmistakable energy and chaos of that great city. Taxi horns blared, competing with the pop music playing on the car radio. I closed my eyes for a moment and slowed my breathing, trying to tune out the noise and center myself for the meetings ahead. And then, without warning, the music stopped, and a voice cut into the broadcast. *Breaking news . . . a plane has struck the World Trade Center . . .*

Glenda, Cindy, and I looked at each other in shock and alarm. Our driver, an older man who'd lived in the city all his life, seemed remarkably calm.

"Y'know, it's not the first time that's happened," he declared. "You're all too young to remember, but after the Second World War we had a plane fly into the Empire State Building. Mind you, it was just a small plane and didn't do too much damage."

I'd never heard this story, but it eased my mind a little. *I guess these things happen,* I thought. We continued downtown, getting close to Wall Street, when suddenly, we heard a tremendous explosion! The driver hit the brakes and we sat there, stunned, as people poured out of buildings on all sides. Ash and debris hit the car. Everyone was looking up and pointing at the sky. I jumped out and then I saw it too: both towers consumed by flames, black smoke billowing across the blue sky. In an instant, I knew this was no coincidence. One plane could have been an accident. Two were definitely some sort of an attack.

My survival instincts kicked in, focusing my mind. Turns out I'm a quick thinker in a crisis.

"We need to get out of here," I told Glenda and Cindy as I got back in the car. "The city is under attack. We don't know what's coming next. The first thing they're going to do is shut down the airports, so we can't get out that way. We should cancel our meetings and go straight to the train station." Glenda and I were scheduled to take a train to Philadelphia later that day for a Board meeting anyway, but my gut told me not to wait, to get out of New York ASAP.

Glenda just nodded, at a loss for words. Cindy, however, didn't seem to get it. "I'm not going to leave," she said. "I have plans in the city this weekend." Plans? Didn't she realize what was happening? Did she think people would just keep shopping and dining out and going to Broadway shows in the middle of a terrorist attack? But she was not to be persuaded otherwise.

"Well, we're going straight to Penn Station," I told her. "I guess you can take a taxi back to the hotel if that's what you want." She got out of the car. Our driver, stunned into silence, drove us slowly through the panic-stricken crowd and headed north.

At Penn Station, we purchased tickets to Philadelphia from an oddly nonchalant salesclerk and headed straight to the platform. No one else seemed to be in a hurry, and when we boarded the train, the whole atmosphere seemed weirdly normal. People were reading newspapers, talking to their companions, settling into their seats.

I turned to Glenda. "They don't know what's happening!" News traveled slower in those days, when mobile phones were still not too common, there was no such thing as a smartphone, and Twitter/X was just science fiction. As the train pulled out, I found myself holding court, informing a train car full of disbelieving commuters that the city was under attack and the Twin Towers were on fire. Once the train emerged on the other side of the Hudson, I didn't need to convince anyone. The car fell silent as we all looked back at the horrifying sight of both towers burning. I believe that the train we caught was the last one to leave the city that day. We made it to Philadelphia right before train stations across the nation were shut down, along with all the airports.

A.C. was already in Philly, having flown in from Boston that morning, right over New York as the first plane hit. We met at the hotel, and he told us that both towers had fallen, a plane had hit the Pentagon, and one had been downed in rural Pennsylvania. News channels showed the horrific images on repeat, commentators barely able to contain the panic in their voices. Many of our Board members called in to say that their flights had been canceled. Walter was stuck in Chicago; Jim in Atlanta. The Board meeting turned into an emergency travel meeting. How on earth were we going to get home? The three of us wandered the streets of Philly for a day, feeling shell-shocked. Everyone seemed to be trying to figure out how to function in this altered reality. A couple of times we saw crowds of office workers spilling onto the sidewalk because of bomb threats. Eventually, after calling around, we managed to rent cars. A.C. set out for Boston, and Glenda and I hit the road to Austin. Walter had the longest drive, from Chicago to Northern California.

It was only once we got out on the open road that I let myself contemplate how close we'd come to the awful events of that day. True, our meetings that morning hadn't been in either of the towers, but we'd been a dozen times before. We might have sat in those very offices that we'd seen consumed by flames. It wasn't that much of a stretch to think that in some parallel universe it could have been us jumping from those windows. It felt like we'd dodged death.

We drove across the country in that state of giddy adrenaline-charged relief that comes with a near miss. The shock and horror of what we'd witnessed hovered just outside the boundaries of our consciousness, but our rental car felt like a little bubble in which we could escape the drama unfolding behind us and maybe escape reality altogether, at least for a while. I felt proud that my quick thinking had gotten us out of the city so fast. Later we learned that it took Cindy almost a week to escape from New York. I remember buying a bunch of CDs at a gas station somewhere along the road, so we'd have music for the trip, and playing golden oldies, which Glenda and I both love, as we took turns behind the wheel. We talked to A.C. and Walter on our cell phones as one drove north and the other drove west. "How's Iowa?" I asked Walter on one such call. "Did you spot any good locations for a Whole Foods Market?"

"It's gonna be a while before Whole Foods comes to Iowa, John," he replied. "It's just cornfields as far as the eye can see."

"What about Des Moines?" I pressed. "It's a college town." But Walter remained unconvinced.

Our own drive took us southwest through the Appalachian mountains of Virginia and Tennessee. There weren't many likely sites for a natural foods supermarket in those rolling, densely forested hills. But I felt drawn to the area nonetheless. I remembered being just 10 or maybe 12 years old and driving through these same hills on a family road trip. A couple of guys carrying giant backpacks had stepped out of the trees and waved as we passed. Their hair and beards were long, and their skin was tanned a deep brown.

"Who are they?" I had asked Dad. "What are they doing out here?"

"They're backpackers, hiking the Appalachian Trail," he replied, and went on to tell me how the trail stretched more than 2,000 miles from Georgia to Maine. People walked the whole length of it, he explained.

Two thousand miles? I'd never heard of a trail like that. I wasn't sure I could carry one of those packs, but it sounded like a grand adventure—the kind of thing people did in my favorite books. I never forgot about that trail, and many years later, when I was hitchhiking to New York with a college buddy, I got a chance to hike a short section—about 18 miles in the Great Smoky Mountains National Park. Our packs were way too heavy. We got blisters. We worried about bears. But I loved it out there. *Someday,* I thought, *I'd like to hike that whole trail.* I'd almost forgotten about it in the intervening years, consumed by the adventure of building Whole Foods. But now, as we drove through those tree-blanketed slopes, I began to imagine once again what it would be like to walk all the way from Georgia to Maine.

In some places, the interstates were busy and frenetic, as if everyone had decided they needed to get out of wherever they'd been. In others, the roads were eerily quiet, as if everyone was hunkered down, afraid to leave their homes. We left the mountains and drove through Nashville and Memphis, blue-green horizons slowly giving way to dusty plains and sprawling cities.

By our third day on the road, the adrenaline of our near escape from danger receded. My thoughts turned more serious. Life felt fragile and precious. I was 48 years old. What if I had died that morning? What would my time on this earth have amounted to? Sure, I was proud of what I'd accomplished with Whole Foods—of that I had no doubt. But had I lived the whole life I wanted to live?

When I looked back at the past 23 years since starting Safer Way, I saw all the things I loved about what we'd created. But I also saw relentless focus on the business. In fact, it became clear to me that I'd allowed Whole Foods to all but consume my energy and attention for half of my lifetime. When my time came—and it really could come at any moment—did I want to look back and say, "I built a great business"? Yes—but not only that. I wanted to live a whole life, not only an entrepreneurial life. I was also aware that my health had suffered, especially in the last couple of stressful years. I'd gained weight, and my digestion and sleep were poor. As the miles sped by, a resolve began to strengthen in my heart. It was time for a change of pace, an expansion of my existence. I didn't know how much time I had left, but I was going to use my time more wisely, more fully.

And that was how, in the spring of 2002, I came to be starting my own journey on the Appalachian Trail, following in the footsteps of many thousands of other pilgrims and adventurers.

Once I decided to undertake the journey, I read every book I could get my hands on about the Appalachian Trail and about long-distance hiking in general. I read about bears and snakes and bugs; bogs and thunderstorms and fires that wouldn't light; small towns and the Smoky Mountains and never-ending miles of dense forest. I enjoyed Bill Bryson's classic, *A Walk in the Woods*, though I was disappointed to realize that he hadn't actually hiked the entire trail. To be honest, I wasn't sure I could hike it all either. My occasional experiences of backpacking, as a young man, had involved an enormous pack laden with camping gear. I would schlep that 50-plus-pound pack, loaded with everything I thought I needed, for five miles into a national park and set up camp. From there, I would take 10-mile day hikes with a very light pack and enjoy the beauty of the park relatively unencumbered. I couldn't imagine carrying 50 pounds of pack weight for almost 2,200 miles. Then I found another book: *Beyond Backpacking* by Ray Jardine. Ray was a former aerospace engineer who had thru-hiked the Pacific Crest Trail, the A.T., and the Continental Divide Trail multiple times carrying as little weight as possible—he used the term "ultralight" to describe his approach. Suddenly my A.T. dreams seemed more possible. I could do it with a light pack—just like I did when I day-hiked.

I became obsessed with the weight of various items, joining backpacking forums online and comparing gear. Eventually I got my base weight down to 10 or 12 pounds (excluding food, water, and fuel), which was quite an achievement back then (today, thanks to advances in lightweight materials, my base weight has fallen to only 6.5 pounds). I studied the trail. I read every hiker account that was available.

It wasn't just the technicalities of gear that appealed to me in Ray's writings. I also loved the philosophy that he described as being the underpinning of his lightweight approach. "I feel that our wilderness outings should be more than just physical walks along trails, and our camping experiences more than pitching a tent and zipping ourselves inside," he wrote. "More important is our presence in the wilds: how we carry ourselves, how softly we move upon the landscape, how aware we are of the patterns of life around us and how we interact with them." He used the term "the Connection" to describe the bridge between humans and nature, "a bringing together for a greater awareness and deeper understanding—of the natural world around us in all its glory, of our relationship with that world, and of our own inner nature." I felt called to explore this connection myself—to walk lightly and purposefully on the trail, in harmony with nature, and discover new parts of myself as well as new places.

It was around this time that one of my all-time favorite books made it to the big screen: J.R.R. Tolkien's *The Lord of the Rings.* The first installment of Peter Jackson's epic trilogy, *The Fellowship of the Ring,* was released in November 2001, and I invited my stepdaughter Evening, then in her mid-twenties, to go with me. I hadn't seen too much of Evening in the 10 years or so since Mary Kay and I had broken up. I'd stayed closer to her younger sister, Allie, but at some point Evening had joined us for dinner, and I'd been happy to get to know the amazing young woman she'd become. I remembered how much she'd loved Tolkien's books as a child, and we had a great time at the movie and at dinner afterward.

"You know, I'm going on my own epic adventure next year," I told her. "I'm going to hike the Appalachian Trail!"

Her face lit up. "Wow, that's amazing."

"You should come with me!" I said, and to my delight, she said yes. Not long after this, we enlisted a third companion: a friend named Grant Sible, whom I'd met on a dive trip in the Galapagos—an adventurer, mountain climber, world traveler, and former cowboy-hippie. I hired someone to drive a support car, which would meet us at certain road crossings to either resupply us or to take us off the trail and into a town for a night of restaurant food, hot showers, and comfortable beds. Most thru-hikers are in their very early twenties and can't afford to have a car support them. The fact that we had one was beneficial to many of them as we could share meals and drinks and do some trail magic and take many of them off the trail for one night along the way. A few other friends, including Deborah, agreed to join us for certain sections. I cleared my desk and my inbox—an epic feat in itself. It was really happening!

I enjoyed the logistics of preparing my gear and studying the trail conditions and weather forecasts. Grant and I would geek out on calculating our pace and mileage for the days ahead, estimating how long it would take to reach our destination. According to my reading, 90% of people who set out to thru-hike the A.T. don't complete it, but I was determined we'd be among the exceptions. One day, I asked Evening what her plan was. She smiled wisely and said, "I'm just going to keep putting one foot in front of the other and trust that eventually I will be standing on the top of Katahdin."

We flew into Atlanta and began our hike on April 6, 2002. It was still chilly in the mountains, especially at night. I'll never forget the experience of hiking down a mountainside and watching the seasons change before my eyes, winter turning into spring as we reached lower elevations. Flowers were suddenly blooming around our feet, and the air came alive with insects. And then we'd start climbing again, and winter would return. Day after day, mountain after mountain, we'd ascend into winter and descend into spring. And then, I began to notice that spring was creeping higher and higher up the slopes, until suddenly it was all around, all the time.

People often ask how you train for a long-distance hike like that. The honest answer is, you don't. Sure, you can go hiking and that can help a little bit. But the only way to really prepare for walking 12 hours a day is to . . . well . . . walk 12 hours a day. And it's not just the mileage—the A.T. includes 250 mountains that must be climbed. So our first few days and weeks were tough. We had to build our fitness and stamina on the trail and harden ourselves to the sore muscles and blisters that go with the territory. But the beauty of a long hike like the A.T. is that once you get your trail legs, your fitness just keeps improving. You're able to hike more miles in less time, you recover quicker, and you are able to hike even farther the next week. In all those months, I never felt like I hit a final plateau—I just kept getting fitter and fitter and fitter all the way to the end of the trail. The vitality I experienced was like nothing else. Every day I felt more intensely alive.

"Hey, Strider! Is it time for lunch yet?"

Grant emerged out of the trees onto the granite hilltop, and I grinned, as I always did, to hear him using my "trail name." One of the things I'd learned before we set out, along with how to assemble a very light pack, was that serious hikers have special nicknames by which they're known on the trail. If you don't already have one, you'll be given one by other hikers—and it might not be very flattering. I decided to break the unspoken rule of long-distance hiking and gave myself a trail name. Strider was the pseudonym used by Tolkien's exiled king Aragorn when he was passing anonymously through Middle Earth. I too was anonymous on the trail—and glad to be so. No one knew that I was the CEO of Whole Foods Market. No one wanted to do a deal with me or find out when Whole Foods was coming to their city or tell me their favorite meal from the hot bar. I was just another long-haired and long-legged hiker striding through the woods. I was Strider.

"Okay, Gorilla, I guess we can stop and eat." Grant got his trail name on account of being tall and powerfully built—at six foot four, he towered over Evening. She often joked about having to take two steps for every one that Strider and Gorilla would take, but in fact she was usually out in front of us, the strongest hiker in the group. She might have appeared petite or even fragile to someone who didn't know her, but she could keep going all day. During our first week on the trail, Grant and our friend Bruce Epstein, who'd joined us for that segment, kept coming up with trail names that she rejected as being too girly or cute—things like Evening Star or other such plays on her name. Finally, I told them, "Y'all don't know Evening at all. She's the toughest one of us." It became kind of a joke that she wasn't what she appeared, and so we called her The Princess, always with a tone of sarcasm. I soon shortened it to P, a nickname and term of endearment I still use with her to this day.

P soon emerged out of the trees, gazing around at the expansive view, and we all agreed this was a perfect spot to eat our lunch. We pulled the day's rations out of our packs. This was no Whole Foods Market feast, but our simple meal of dried fruit, nuts, nutrition bars, and crackers with peanut butter tasted like gourmet cuisine after a long morning on the trail. After we were done eating, we spent a few more minutes enjoying the view and the warmth of the sunbaked rocks before locating the trail and beginning our descent. I picked up my pace, and soon my companions were out of earshot.

That's another thing I love about the A.T.: It's almost impossible to be lost. You can let your companions drift ahead or behind because there's little chance they'll take a wrong turn, and you'll all end up in the same place eventually. Grant, Evening, and I had an easy rapport and each of us enjoyed spending much of our time walking quietly, alone with our thoughts. We encountered plenty of nonhuman fellow travelers as well—snakes, bears and bear cubs, beavers, foxes, porcupines, deer, squirrels, chipmunks, and an endless variety of colorful birds.

For several sections, we were joined by a much more talkative companion, Mo Siegel, founder of the herbal tea company Celestial Seasonings. Grant soon gave him the trail name "Verbal Tea," which he absolutely hated, although we all thought it was both a great trail name and quite accurate! Despite his propensity for chattiness, he was a very strong and tireless hiker, so I gave him a name he was proud to accept, Rocket Man—because of the way he could blast up the hills faster than anyone else.

Hiking the A.T. was an immersion in nature, but it was also an unusual immersion in a side of American culture I didn't know well. The trail passes through numerous small towns as it winds its way north—the kinds of towns that people don't tend to go to unless they happen to be hiking through. Some of those towns were struggling, left behind by the modern world and deserted by young people who couldn't wait to get out. Others were thriving little communities with a rich sense of history and connection to the land. In most of them, we were welcomed and offered hospitality. I learned a lot about America on that trip.

Along the way, we also enjoyed meeting other hikers who'd come from all over the US and from many dozens of countries around the world to walk this iconic trail. Early on, someone dubbed us "the Lightfoot Crew" on account of our preference for trail runners over boots and our ultralight packs. The name stuck. A hiker named Space Monkey passed us one day, with a lightweight pack like ours. Comparing notes, I learned we had the same base weight, 12 pounds, and my playful, competitive spirit immediately designated him as the person I wanted to beat to the end of the trail. Surely, we could catch him soon. We rarely talked about who we were or what we did in the "real" world. I relished the anonymity of the trail—this parallel universe that was just a few feet wide and over 2,000 miles long. When one guy heard me talking about natural foods, he started raving about this store in Boulder named Whole Foods. I just smiled and told him I'd been there too—and loved it. The A.T. tribe bonded over the challenges and joys of this strange and delightful trail world we all inhabited, with its own set of rules and rituals.

One of my favorite A.T. traditions were the trail journals. These journals were placed in the many three-sided shelters that were usually located every 8 to 10 miles along the trail. Hikers would write about what they were doing or where they hoped to meet up with other hikers who were behind them. I began writing a serialized fantasy novel in the trail journals. Its heroes—Strider, Gorilla, and The Princess—were visiting Earth from another dimension. They were hiking the A.T. as a way to escape from the evil denizens of their own dimension, who were trying to take over the planet. Their mission was to get The Princess safely to Mount Katahdin, where she could use her powers to save Earth and the human race. I even wrote storylines featuring others we'd met on the trail. Space Monkey, whose advantage over us I tracked carefully through the journals, was actually a secret agent. I had a great deal of fun writing these installments, and I liked to think that perhaps others who came after us were reading them, eagerly anticipating each new chapter at the end of their daily hikes.

During those weeks and months on the A.T., I found that for the first time in more than 24 years, I could go days at a time without thinking much about the business. It helped that often there was no cell signal, so I was protected from incoming demands. At night, we'd either camp or meet our support car and sleep in a motel or a bed-and-breakfast in a nearby town, where I could catch up with the E-Team when needed.

But for most of the time, day after day, my mind was quietly observing nature, thinking about the mysteries of life, or coming up with fun plot twists for my trail journal novel. I felt playful and boyish again, my imagination set free to roam. Other times, I'd choose to turn my thoughts to Whole Foods, feeling enormous gratitude for how it had brought me to this point. I loved the company, but I wasn't anxious to return too quickly. I relished this time away from it all.

Unfortunately, you can only live in a parallel universe for so long. The real world still continues alongside, and I still had things I cared about and responsibilities in that world. Indeed, as we left that granite hilltop where I'd contemplated the Manhattan skyline, my idyllic adventure was about to be rudely interrupted.

Chapter 27

Culture Shock

"Why did I ever leave the trail?"

That was all I could think as the door slid open and I entered the noisy, frenetic chaos of the Newark airport. I checked in and joined the security line. My feet itched to stride out freely, but all I could do was shuffle forward at a painfully slow pace until my turn came to begin the laborious process of the new post-9/11 protocols. Less than a year after the attacks, everyone was still adjusting to the heightened intensity and additional rules. I felt like an alien just dropped in from another planet—a planet of calm, leafy trails, full of birdsong and sunlight. My weeks on the A.T. seemed to have restructured my mind, decelerated my consciousness. I had trouble keeping up with the rapid-fire instructions of the TSA agents and the impatient comments of the people behind me, who felt it necessary to remind everyone that they had a flight to catch. As if no one else had a flight to catch.

I had grown accustomed to nature's rhythm and the pace of my own two feet. I'd surrendered to a different sense of time, and the long to-do lists inside my CEO brain had faded into a quieter background. I'd enjoyed being no one in particular and not really being required to do anything but put one foot in front of the other until we reached the day's destination. Now, suddenly, I was someone and I had to be somewhere and do something—right away. The transition wasn't proving easy. The bright lights, the glaring screens, the jarring announcements, the harsh air-conditioning, the processed food—none of it felt right to me. People rushed by, their attention focused elsewhere. I noticed that they looked anxious, angry, or unhappy. Many also looked unhealthy.

I took a deep breath and tried to pull my mind into the present moment. The TSA agent was asking me a question.

"Sir, would you please remove your shoes and send them through the scanner?"

Shoes? Oh yes. Since last December, when the so-called "shoe bomber" had failed to blow up a flight to Miami, the TSA had been requesting that travelers take off their shoes. I looked down at my trail runners—faded, frayed, and dusty from hundreds of miles of hiking. Unlacing them, I placed them in the gray plastic tray, where they looked as out of place as I felt. I watched them glide into the scanner and then disappear, feeling strangely bereft without those trusty companions that had carried me so far. I strode through the metal detector, imagining for a moment that it was simply an arch of tree limbs enclosing the trail. But amid the bumping and jostling of people trying to retrieve their belongings and tie their shoes and repack their bags, the illusion quickly vanished. There was no getting around it—Strider was back in "civilization."

It was, of course, business that had called me back. While I had found some freedom from the day-to-day requirements of my position, that temporary respite only went so far. A crisis had arisen that couldn't be delayed or delegated. Our Madison, Wisconsin, store had encountered a situation that had potential implications for the entire company: union activism.

Not again, I'd thought, when I first heard the news, one night when I'd checked in with the team after a long day of hiking.

"Can't we just ignore it and wait for them to go away?" I'd asked. That's what we'd done in the past. Over the years, we had been the target of several "informational pickets" like the one in Berkeley. Usually, it would have little impact on our team members, who were happy with their work and liked our company culture, and sooner or later, the union would give up the effort, once it became obvious that it was a waste of their resources. But not this time. This time it wasn't just happening in our parking lot; it was inside the store and inside the company.

In fact, the Madison group had used a different and more effective tactic. A local professor at the University of Wisconsin with a reputation for his socialist beliefs had made it a class project to get a union into Whole Foods. Some of his students had been hired into the store and then started agitating for a union from the inside. The campaign had started in May. They had presented the company with their demand that we recognize a union, and when we refused, they had filed a petition with the National Labor Relations Board (NLRB), setting the stage for a vote to be held on July 12. But before that vote, I would have a chance to speak to the team members at the store.

The letter of complaint to the NLRB came with a public letter from the organizers. It declared that our store had a "high turnover rate, wages that are lower than the industry standard, pervasive lack of respect" as well as "constant understaffing" and "widespread low morale." I thought those claims must be overstated for effect. If anything, our stores were broadly praised for having a worker-friendly company culture. But I needed to see for myself—and hear from our team members directly. Why were they unhappy enough to vote for a union for the first time in Whole Foods' 24-year history?

As I pulled up to the store that evening and was briefed by Walter and the Store Team Leader, I tried to understand: How had the situation devolved to this point? Why hadn't we caught it and defused the tensions sooner? One thing that quickly became clear was that the Madison store, which was just a few years old at this point, was unusually isolated within our company ecosystem. Technically, it was part of the Midwest region, but it was very far from any other store. Chicago was the regional center, and Madison was 150 miles away. And our decentralized approach to management had left them largely to their own devices.

Decentralization was, in many ways, a strength of our company. We had always believed that those on the ground in a particular city or region knew their own team members and customers better than anyone, so we empowered Store Team Leaders to bring their own creativity to their offerings and their culture. In most places, the Regional Leadership Teams naturally kept an eye on what was going on at the store level. But occasionally, there was a downside to decentralization, and the head didn't know enough about what the hand was doing. This was what happened in Madison. While Whole Foods leadership was looking the other way, those enterprising students infiltrated the Madison store and took advantage of festering discontent that we'd been oblivious to.

What became clear to me after talking to some team members was that the union complaints, while overstated, contained a kernel of truth. The store was, in fact, poorly led. Indeed, I began to see that our company culture, usually a point of pride, had not really taken root in this store. There was a general frustration with store leadership and several issues that had not been adequately addressed. Regardless of the outcome of this vote, I knew the store leader in Madison needed to go or be reassigned—and the Midwest Regional President based in Chicago as well. Both had made inexcusable mistakes. But in the end, this situation was much more than a failure of one or two people.

"They're not entirely wrong in their complaints," I reported back to my team. "But we can fix it. We can change the culture for the better and make Madison a great place to work." To my frustration, however, I wasn't allowed to say this to our Madison team members. That's not the way union organizing campaigns work. The union—in this case the United Food and Commercial Workers—was allowed to say whatever they wanted to our team members, promising them all kinds of changes under union management. Pay raises, new freedoms, more permissive dress codes, better benefits, choice of music—all of these utopian dreams would come to pass if the union was voted in, they whispered in our team members' ears. Meanwhile, the NLRB forbade management from promising anything. I could only listen to our team members and ask them to give us another chance.

I understood these rules all too well by this point, but I didn't like them. They weren't fair to both sides. Since the Berkeley picket, I'd spent a great deal of time reading about the history of unions and the impact they'd had on American business over the years. And that extensive research didn't make me any more inclined to welcome unionization than I had been back in the days when I was arguing with the Berkeley mayor.

Bottom line, I didn't want that us vs. them relationship to infect our company culture. Of course, I understood that the needs of various stakeholders in a business are never exactly aligned. Inevitably there will be conflicts for resources between them. But conflicts can be negotiated and resolved in a win-win context, in a manner that moves the business forward and helps it grow and thrive. The union mindset pits stakeholders against each other, creating mistrust, envy, and resentment, as if their fortunes weren't irrevocably interdependent.

Another reason I chafed against unionization was that I was aware that a good deal of the agitation was coming from those who simply disliked capitalism as a system. They felt that all large corporations—and Whole Foods had now become a large corporation—were essentially greedy and exploitative and must be resisted and limited in every way possible. And by extension, corporate leaders like me were Machiavellian figures, unconcerned about the well-being of people who work in our companies. There seemed to be no reasoning with people like this; it was a matter of ideology and deeply held beliefs.

On the evening of July 11, the night before the union vote, I met with 100 or so team members at the store. I did my best to follow the rules of not making any pay or benefits promises, while still stating my intention clearly. I started with an apology, and it was sincere. I felt like we had failed our people in Madison, and I told them as much.

"I want to ask you to give us another chance. I realize that we have allowed store leadership to lose touch with some of your concerns. We have work to do to change that, and I promise you we will change it." That was as much as I could promise, but I hoped that they knew I meant it.

The truth was, I really did. It was clear to me now that this might not be an isolated problem. Yes, Madison might have been poorly operated and the culture had suffered as a result. But the fact that we had not caught it sooner was a broader issue. As the company had grown, and grown fast, we had allowed ourselves to lose touch with many of our store team members and their needs. Whole Foods now had 134 stores, with tens of thousands of team members across the nation. As I looked around the room that night in Madison, I was reminded that these individuals and thousands like them around the country were the foundation of the company. And we, as leaders, needed to find new ways to reaffirm the company's connection with every single person who was on our payroll.

Connection. I'd been on a journey seeking connection over the past months on the trail—the deeper connection to nature and to myself that Ray Jardine had described. But I felt another kind of connection calling me as I gave my short talk, pausing to look around the room at our team members. I needed to connect—and reconnect—with the people who made up our company.

"Don't believe it! He's just another rich, lying capitalist. He doesn't care about you. He only cares about profit!"

This outburst was echoed by another voice in the crowd. "He's just trying to protect the millions he makes off your hard work!"

This kind of interruption had already happened a couple of times during my talk, and as frustrating as it was, I tried not to take the bait. I described the company's long-term plans, its higher purpose, its commitment to natural foods and sustainable agriculture. I reminded all our team members of the core values that had inspired them and all of us. But the interruptions continued until finally, the most vocal of my detractors shouted, "This is such bullshit!" and proceeded to get up and walk out of the room, followed by the other student activists.

After this exodus, the atmosphere improved significantly. I finally felt like people were really listening to me, and I was better able to communicate my perspective on the imminent vote. Bottom line, I cautioned our team members that this was an activist campaign, and it was questionable how much the union really cared about the individual workers. I felt our team members were being misled by a vocal minority who disliked capitalism and were using Whole Foods' progressive reputation as an outlet to make their point that even "good" corporations were actually evil. Despite our failures, Whole Foods Market had built a great culture over the past two and a half decades. And given the opportunity, we could and would make things right.

I walked out of that meeting more hopeful than I had been in days. Perhaps by the next night it would all be over, the union question would be resolved in our favor, and I could return to the trail. I missed it, emotionally and physically. My body felt tired and lazy from not walking. My mind felt small and contracted with the anxiety of the past few days. I felt strangely like I was missing out on something—as if Strider, Gorilla, and The Princess were continuing their journey without me. Of course, this wasn't true. Gorilla was undergoing some unpleasant dental work, and The Princess was visiting family and hanging out by the pool. As for Strider—well, he seemed to have temporarily deserted me, but I knew I'd find him again once I had dirt beneath my feet. It couldn't come soon enough. I wondered if, somewhere on the A.T., hikers were opening trail journals, disappointed not to find a new installment of the epic fantasy adventure they'd been following for weeks. And I was pretty sure I was never going to catch Space Monkey now.

In the end, my entreaties were not enough. We lost the vote, 65–54. I was deeply disappointed and concerned about what this might mean for our other stores. The local president of the union called it a "sweet victory." I'm sure he imagined the other 133 stores falling like dominos to local union activism. Privately, I vowed we wouldn't let this happen again. I was determined to reaffirm the company's commitment to making our team members' experience of working at Whole Foods second to none, and in doing so, make union activism irrelevant to our people.

The next day, I wrote a letter to our entire company, expressing my regret and disappointment with the decision. "Madison made a mistake in their choice," I wrote. "It may take time for them to realize it, but I believe that they eventually will. We all make many mistakes in life. It is all part of our growth process because that is how we learn, that is how we grow. When confronted by great stress in life, we have only two choices: 1. Contract into fear. 2. Expand into love."

This last point was true for me as well. This was not the time for me to contract into fear. I'd faced an important truth in Madison, and love was at the heart of it. As I'd told Mark Skiles all those years ago, I wanted Whole Foods Market to be a company built on love. The kind of love I'd been overwhelmed by when I'd taken my mind-altering psychedelic journeys. The love I'd recognized as the true nature of everything. The love that inspired me to create a company that sold nourishing food and gave people a joyful, meaningful place to work. The love I'd reconnected with when I'd almost lost my leadership role. If people were no longer experiencing Whole Foods that way—and clearly some were not—I needed to know why. And I needed to figure out, with an expansive, open heart, how we could do better.

But first, I had about 900 more miles to walk.

I quickly found my hiking rhythm again, and my body readjusted. The short break had done me good, and I felt energized. It took a little longer for my mind to reestablish its equanimity, for the thoughts and stresses of the past week to fade into the background. The exertion helped, and at the end of each day, I relished the deep sleep that only comes when your body has been pushed hard. But as much as I loved the peaceful atmosphere of the trail, the company was never far from my heart or mind. As we made our way northward, I thought long and hard about what I'd learned, and my plan began to take shape.

Whole Foods had become a large public company, growing its store count more than tenfold in a decade. We'd acquired Harry's Farmers Markets in Atlanta, dramatically expanding our footprint in the South, with Ken Meyer becoming President of the newly formed region. We'd recently opened our first store outside the US, in Toronto, making us an international company. But from a cultural perspective, we were still operating as if we were in a smaller business environment of 10 or 20 stores in a couple of regions. I'd taken our culture for granted. I thought back to the early days, when I'd travel between our handful of stores, talking to everyone regularly and seeing for myself how things were working. That simply wasn't possible anymore.

On the phone one night with Walter, A.C., Jim, and Glenda, I told them my plan.

"As soon as I get back from the trail, I'm going to begin touring the entire company."

"Every store?"

"Yes, every single store! We need to reconnect with our on-the-ground team members. I want to hear from them directly about how to make Whole Foods the best company to work for in America."

"John, I think that's a great idea." Walter was immediately supportive. The others affirmed the plan as well, and they promised to start setting things up while I finished my hike.

As I clicked off the phone, I felt my heart doing exactly what I'd asked of our team members: expanding into love. I truly loved the E-Team! For perhaps the first time in my history as CEO, or at least since the early days, there was no jockeying at the executive level for power and prestige and influence. They understood me and respected my strengths, while also stepping up to balance out my weaknesses. They appreciated the company's needs and didn't just protect their own territory. They exemplified our core values. I felt their support of my leadership, but more than that, I felt their talent, commitment, and genuine willingness to work as a high-functioning team. I had been lucky to work with many intelligent, creative leaders at Whole Foods; but never had I felt such a tight sense of comradery in the group. We had a lot to learn about being a growing public company, but the team was rising to the challenge.

On a personal level, I appreciated their support for me finishing what I'd started. Even with the company facing serious challenges, they understood how important it was for me to complete the trail. I kept walking, through New York, Massachusetts, Vermont, and New Hampshire as the summer heat set in and we donned netted hats to protect our faces from the ever-present hungry swarms of mosquitoes, deer flies, and gnats. Finally, we entered Maine, joyfully struggling through the hardest mile on the entire trail, the Mahoosuc Notch. Two hundred miles later, we began our traverse of the Hundred-Mile Wilderness, generally considered the wildest and most challenging section of the trail. Perhaps, I thought to myself, the events in Madison had been a blessing.

Sometimes the difficulties we encounter, in business and in life, are our most fertile opportunities for growth. Had it not been for the union drive, we might have remained blind to the issues with our company culture, opening a door for unions to steal away the hearts and minds of our entire workforce. And once trust in the company and faith in our leadership were lost, it would be hard to regain. I didn't want to just resist the unions; I wanted us to excel in creating cultures that made them irrelevant. And we still had a chance to do so. In that sense, the union was forcing us to evolve.

On August 31, Strider, Gorilla, and The Princess shouldered their packs and stepped onto the trail for the final day. We were joined by other hikers we had met on the trail, including Irish and Cowboy, with whom I would form a lasting friendship, still hiking with them every year to this day. Deborah—who'd been given the fitting trail name Cloud Nine—also flew up to join us and to celebrate with us. Under the blazing sun of high summer, we made our way up Maine's Mount Katahdin. Ordinarily, this is not an easy hike—it's steep and can be dangerously slippery if it rains. But by this time we were so incredibly fit and pumped full of adrenaline that we just cruised up the mountain.

As we came to the summit, Gorilla, The Princess, and Strider all held hands together and simultaneously touched the A.T.'s northern terminus, just as we'd touched the southern terminus on Springer Mountain. We began the trail together and we finished the trail together. I could hardly believe we'd finally made it: 2,168 miles. It was one of the proudest moments of my life!

I wasn't the same person who'd set out from Georgia four months earlier. I felt more at home in my body, more confident, more centered—the fittest I ever had been. Strider would come with me, I knew, when I returned to my other life. All the same, there was a bittersweet edge to the celebration on the mountaintop that day. I'd miss waking up every morning with nothing to do but walk and ending each day with nothing to do but fall into a deep sleep and replenish in order to walk again the next morning.

Fast-forward a few weeks, and I was once again sitting in a store, surrounded by almost 100 team members. A.C. sat beside me, as well as the Regional President and the Store Team Leader.

"I'm here in Miami to hear from all of you. I want you to tell me what we need to do to make Whole Foods Market the best place to work in America."

Thankfully, this was a much warmer environment than Madison, and the spirit among the team members was less confrontational. But still, they had concerns, needs, opinions, and frustrations to share. The number one request, not surprisingly, was better pay. Everyone wants better pay. I couldn't promise to do everything they asked, but we could listen and assure them that their voices would be heard not only by me but by the entire E-Team.

Over the next several months, I visited each city where Whole Foods had stores. It was a different kind of pilgrimage than my A.T. hike, but it truly was a journey of spiritual reckoning for me and for the company—a quest for connection. One foot, then the other. One store, then the next. At each stop, I paid close attention to the quality of the store and the level of local leadership. Of course, I was aware that team members dressed up their stores for my visits, so I wasn't getting an unfiltered perception of its day-to-day functioning. But I've been visiting our stores for so long that despite the extra effort, I can usually tell within just 10 minutes how well a store is being operated and whether the team members are happy or not. And more often than I would have liked, I found that we were falling short. Over and over, I reminded myself: *Expand into love, don't contract into fear.* Love was at the heart of Whole Foods Market. We can improve. We can evolve. And we did.

We made significant changes as a direct result of these company-wide meetings. Again and again, I noticed a concern that showed up somewhere after "better pay" but very close in importance. Healthcare. Team members consistently told me that our benefits package wasn't good enough. We had not kept up with the needs of our workforce and the evolution of the company. In the last 24 years, the company had grown older, and so had our team members. The young hippies had become middle-aged, and they now had families and children and more significant healthcare needs. This concern became more obvious with every store I toured, and soon we began the process of revamping our benefits.

I was grateful that this crisis had brought to the surface such a critical need. We soon upgraded the benefits package for all team members across the country. All team members, that is, except those in Madison. In Wisconsin, we were prevented from giving our team members the same escalation of benefits that nonunionized team members received. The union wanted to negotiate their own contract and refused to accept this new package. That didn't go over very well with our team members in Madison, but our hands were tied. The requirement on our side was simply that we negotiate in good faith with the union on a contract, which we continued to do without resolution.

Fortunately, my tour also gave me confidence that unionization was not inevitable. I felt the overall positivity of our team members and a renewed possibility of a win-win relationship with our ever-growing team. We had lost the union battle in Madison, but we could still win it everywhere else. And if the Madison store didn't eventually reconsider, I was ready to hit the jettison button. Quietly, I reached out to John Moorman, the former Mrs. Gooch's CEO. He was willing to buy the store; I was willing to sell—but only if circumstances proved untenable, meaning if the union proved intractable. I hoped it was an option that I wouldn't need to execute.

In the end, the tempest never escaped the teapot. A year after the union vote—a year that saw all the original organizers of the union leave the company—the store held a second vote. Our team members voted overwhelmingly to decertify the union. Immediately after the NLRB recognized the decertification vote, the team members received the upgraded package of benefits, and with new and better leadership, the store was moving on to happier days. And so was the entire company.

Chapter 28

A Crisis of Conscience

"Murderer!"

"Animals have rights!"

"Animals want to live!"

"Foie gras is torture!"

The voices shouting at me were angry and intense. Ducking my head, I made my way into the Santa Monica, California, hotel past the protesters on the street. I was headed into our annual shareholders' meeting, on March 31, 2003, but first, I had to run the gauntlet of animal rights activists.

"Look at this, Mr. Mackey!" Placards were thrust in my face that declared "Whole Foods Supports Animal Cruelty!" alongside gruesome images of suffering birds. One particularly intense individual stepped out in front of me, blocking my way and yelling with such ferocity that I stopped dead, surprised by the personal hatred coming my way.

I shouldn't have been. Over the last decades, with Whole Foods becoming a larger and more prominent company, I had come to grudgingly accept our role as a punching bag for various forms of anti-corporate activism. I was still getting used to the fact that the idealism and higher values that had informed Whole Foods since the founding of the company only made us *more* of a target for activism of all sorts, not less. It puzzled and frustrated me. Why didn't they go after the much more egregious offenders, like the stores that actually sold foie gras? We did not, for ethical reasons. And those same ethics had driven Whole Foods to make countless other decisions to fight the industrialization of the food supply and to promote humanely raised animal foods. For the past couple of years, our meat coordinators had been engaged in meetings with producers to articulate a set of standards for the humane treatment of animals. And yet it only seemed to draw more protests from the activists. I consoled myself with the idea that this attention, while negative, was a natural and probably inevitable result of our ongoing growth and success.

The first years of the new millennium had largely been positive for Whole Foods. As the clock hit midnight in our 135 stores at the end of 2002, the future seemed as bright as ever. However, with larger size comes more attention, and we were quickly learning that not all of it would be positive, or even fair. We wore our ethics and our values on our sleeves. And that put a target on our back. At the shareholder meeting in Los Angeles, I found it particularly difficult because the organizations targeting us represented a stakeholder group that was very close to my own heart: animals.

I'd always been an animal lover—Deborah and I were devoted to our dogs—and I'd been essentially a vegetarian (though occasionally eating fish) since moving into Prana House some 25 years earlier. When Safer Way became Whole Foods Market, I'd come to terms with the fact that our stores would sell foods I did not personally eat—we'd never have been a viable business if we'd refused to carry animal foods. But we made an effort to source animal foods from producers that had a reputation for better animal welfare, and to work with our producers to raise their standards.

Inside the hotel ballroom, our Board of Directors, as well as most members of the E-Team, were gathered. But along with the usual attendees—our Store Team Leaders from around the country and their spouses, as well as various representatives of our stakeholder ecosystem—two groups of protesters had shown up, determined to disrupt the proceedings. One group was from PETA (People for the Ethical Treatment of Animals) and another from a lesser-known animal-rights organization known as Viva! USA.

The issue they were protesting had to do with a particular supplier of duck, Grimaud Farms. The activists claimed that this supplier was involved with Sonoma Foie Gras, selling them hatchling ducks and distributing their products. We didn't sell foie gras because of its inhumane and unethical origins, which involves a quite horrendous method of force-feeding. But according to the protesters, we were guilty by association. The animal rights organizations had been running a campaign to get us to drop Grimaud but had felt like they were stonewalled by the team responsible for these issues at Whole Foods. Hence, their presence at our shareholders' meeting, to escalate the issue and get our attention.

When it was my turn to speak, I stepped up to the podium, said a few words, and began to take questions. That prompted another round of chanting and yelling and general disruption from the protesters. This went on for some time, the occasional questions from shareholders being drowned out or interrupted by activists with their rants and complaints. I tried to be respectful and patient. My goal was just to get through this event with some relative dignity. But it wasn't easy. And the time dragged on. Finally, one of the activists asked a question, which turned into another lengthy diatribe against Whole Foods. She talked and talked, and I got more and more uncomfortable—not just because of the content of her remarks, or the circus our shareholder meeting had become, but because I really needed to use the men's room. And yet, there was no end in sight.

Finally, I just had to go. I asked Margaret Wittenberg, our Vice President of Quality Standards and our expert on animal welfare, to field the questions, while I stepped away from the podium to relieve myself. When I left the men's room, I was surprised to see that my entire E-Team had also exited, which had caused a bit of a stir in the room. I would find out later that they had thought I was staging a walkout and felt like they should express their solidarity by following me out of the ballroom. I'd had no such intentions. Later, my Board of Directors would reprimand me for leading a walkout in the shareholders' meeting. I struggled to explain that I really didn't intend to make a statement; I just had to take a leak.

When the meeting finally came to an end, I knew I needed to do something to move this stalemate toward a more productive conversation. I sought out the executive director of Viva! USA, a petite, passionate Latina woman named Lauren Ornelas.

After briefly introducing myself, I asked her again why she and her colleagues were targeting us, given that our standards were much higher than other players in the industry. Her response was a question:

"Have you been to Grimaud Farms?"

"No, I haven't visited them personally. But our team has. They say they're the best in the industry. That's why we use them."

Lauren was dismissive. "Look, this campaign didn't start out being about Whole Foods. It's about the ducks! But we couldn't get an adequate response from your people, and it's clear that you don't care enough about the abhorrent practices of your suppliers. That's not good!"

While my knowledge of animal agriculture practices had its limits, I certainly knew, as did many people, about the suffering of ducks that was deemed necessary to create foie gras. I reminded Lauren that Whole Foods did not sell this "delicacy."

"Yes, but you're still working with the people who are involved in those practices."

"I hear that Grimaud Farms have been responsive to our requests for more humane practices. I'm sure they're not perfect, but they seem better than most. They've improved their standards." I continued to defend our commitment to humane sourcing, before ending with a more personal admission. "Honestly, Lauren, this is an issue I do care about."

She shook her head and paused for a moment, then looked at me and sighed. Maybe she was just exhausted from the day's activities, but her voice softened and I felt like she let her guard down a bit.

"Mr. Mackey, I can see that you are a very idealistic person who does care about animals. I know you care about the environment, and about selling healthy food. But when it comes to farm animal welfare, quite frankly, you don't know what you're talking about. You believe what your team is telling you, but you've never looked closely at these issues or been to these places yourself. Have you personally visited a slaughterhouse? You should get more involved. Don't delegate it to others. Don't be ignorant. You owe it to your company. And above all, you owe it to the animals to become better informed."

Her words quieted me for a moment. By this time, many of the attendees and activists had left the ballroom, and there were just a few stragglers milling about. I reached into my pocket, pulled out a business card, and asked her to keep in touch.

"Maybe we can continue this conversation?"

She just nodded, took the card, and walked out of the room.

When I got home to the ranch the next night, the creek was high with spring rainwater as I drove across the ford. I stepped out of the car, breathed in the cool night air, and listened to the chirping of the crickets and frogs. I felt something brush my leg and bent down to pet a friendly cat that arched into my hand. Across the yard, the chickens were roosting in their coop and the horses and donkey were safe and warm in their stalls. The deer roamed freely across our acreage without fear of being hunted. I loved each of these fellow creatures. But now I was troubled. Was I doing enough for the animals who did not live under my protection? Was I kidding myself that I was doing all I could? Was there a lack of integrity in my position? Was Lauren right?

That weekend, I made a resolution. I would become better informed. Lauren was right about at least one thing: I should know more. And I wanted to. I had depended on others to inform me on these matters, and while I trusted these individuals, I nevertheless resolved to personally dive deeper into this topic. And the way I dive deep into any topic I care about is to read every book I can get my hands on. I began by rereading one of the classics of the genre, philosopher Peter Singer's *Animal Liberation.* His elegantly rational prose struck me deeply. He spoke equally to my animal-loving heart and to the dinner-table-honed debating skills my father had instilled in me.

> To protest about bullfighting in Spain, the eating of dogs in South Korea, or the slaughter of baby seals in Canada while continuing to eat

> eggs from hens who have spent their lives crammed into cages, or veal from calves who have been deprived of their mothers, their proper diet, and the freedom to lie down with their legs extended, is like denouncing apartheid in South Africa while asking your neighbors not to sell their houses to blacks.

Alongside my reading, my conversation with Lauren continued, virtually. She emailed me soon after our meeting, addressing the issues we had discussed in Santa Monica and reiterating her concerns. I responded by defending Whole Foods. I also pointed out that she was part of an advocacy organization and could therefore pursue a certain type of idealism unimpeded by other concerns, which was simply not possible for a public company. However, I added, we cared about animals, and if she could find us a better producer than Grimaud, we would certainly use them.

As April went on, and the ranch blossomed in its spring glory, I continued this correspondence with Lauren every weekend. Long emails would be sent, and equally long missives would be returned. Over and over, I defended our policies and protested that we were by far the best in the industry, even as I acknowledged the real suffering involved in animal agriculture. I reminded her that I personally chose not to eat animals, but it wasn't our place as a business to insist that all of our customers be vegan or vegetarian. She complained that I wasn't honestly dealing with the reality of the situation at Grimaud or elsewhere.

It was a civil engagement, but it didn't seem like we were moving closer to common ground. She felt it was unacceptable that I could claim to appreciate a book like *Animal Liberation* but not be willing to go further in extracting promises from our suppliers or refusing to work with them altogether. I felt she, like so many activists, was falling into the trap of making the perfect the enemy of the good by refusing to accept pragmatic improvements. There was no doubt that we both cared about the plight of animals in our food systems, but we were approaching it from very different perspectives. There was little agreement to be reached.

Finally, one evening, I responded to her most recent email with a long series of point-by-point rebuttals and declared that this would be my final communication with her on the matter. I simply couldn't keep repeating myself. I did, however, keep reading.

Next up was another book that made a deep impression on me: *Dominion: The Power of Man, the Suffering of Animals, and the Call to Mercy* by Matthew Scully. Scully, a speechwriter who worked for President George W. Bush and several other prominent Republicans, is a passionate advocate for animals. His writing is searing and beautiful.

"Animals are more than ever a test of our character," Scully writes, "of mankind's capacity for empathy and for decent, honorable conduct and faithful stewardship. We are called to treat them with kindness, not because they have rights or power or some claim to equality, but in a sense because they don't; because they all stand unequal and powerless before us. Animals are so easily overlooked, their interests so easily brushed aside."

Perhaps it was because I was in a different, happier, more mature phase of my life; perhaps it was because of the deeper connection I'd made with nature on the Appalachian Trail; or perhaps it was simply that I let myself confront, more directly, the harsh reality of animal agriculture that I had, like so many people, turned away from. Whatever the reasons, something in me began to buckle under the weight of the words I was reading. I felt my own conscience speaking to me, whispering, nudging—that maybe I really could do more. Maybe it was time for a change.

That summer, I was determined to continue my long-distance hiking, and I'd settled on a route that, while challenging, wouldn't take a huge amount of time: the Colorado Trail. This 486-mile trail, created and developed in the seventies and eighties, starts in Waterton Canyon, just south of Denver, runs up through Summit County, and ends in Durango in the southwest part of the state. With most of the trail above 10,000 feet and a high point of 13,271 feet, it presented a very different challenge than the A.T. Along with Irish and Cowboy, whom I'd met hiking the A.T. the previous year, I started the monthlong adventure in the middle of July. The trail was beautiful, and despite a bout with giardia (thankfully mild for Cowboy and me, though worse for Irish), I made it the entire length of the trail, finishing in the middle of August.

There is nothing like long-distance hiking to encourage deep reflections, and as the day-to-day worries and concerns about Whole Foods faded into the background, I continued my musing on the role of animals in my life and in our food systems. I considered the things I had learned from Lauren, as well as from Peter Singer, Matthew Scully, and many other authors I had read in the preceding weeks and months. I thought about factory farms and the extraordinary pain and suffering that these fellow sentient beings were subjected to, just to ultimately give their lives for the sake of our palates.

I reflected that while it's true that no culture in history has ever been vegan (vegetarianism has a rich history in some cultures), it's also true that no culture in history has institutionalized the horror show that makes up animal agriculture today. And no individuals have ever had the options that we currently possess to largely opt out of that ethical nightmare.

For better or worse, we can't always live in perfect alignment with our ethics in a world in which we remain interdependent with and embedded in so many larger cultural and economic systems that are beyond our influence or control. But when it comes to what we eat, we *do* have a choice. We have sovereignty over the types of food that we do or do not put into our bodies. The more I reflected, the clearer the choice became—at least on a personal level. My casual vegetarianism was not a clear enough ethical stance. By continuing to eat dairy products and eggs, I was still complicit in the suffering of animals. It was time to make a change. One day, when we left the trail and hitchhiked into town for a restaurant meal, I enjoyed my final chocolate milkshake. When I completed the Colorado Trail on a hot day in mid-August, I did so as a newly committed, ethical vegan.

I had no doubt that this was the right decision for me. But that was only one part of my contemplation—and in a sense, it was the easier part.

The other, more complex question was also urgent: What was the right thing for Whole Foods? As I'd often had to remind people through the years, I was not a dictator of the company. My word was not law, and my values were not necessarily its values. Many founders have trouble making a distinction between their entrepreneurial creations and themselves. As cofounder and CEO, I certainly had great influence, but I had come to accept that Whole Foods, as an independent entity, had priorities, concerns, and stakeholders that went beyond its founders' personal values or dietary choices.

This was one of the points I still felt that Lauren didn't fully appreciate. She'd never had to deal with the constraints and realities within which any business such as ours operated. But as I allowed my conscience to guide me onto a better path personally, I also began to admit to myself that perhaps she also had a point where Whole Foods was concerned. No, I couldn't force our entire company to go vegan. But perhaps I could make a difference in the lives of the animals that were raised to become products that were sold in our stores.

Now that I'd learned more about the practices of animal agriculture, I was truly appalled. At the very least, these animals should be allowed to live out their fundamental animal nature. Ducks should be allowed to swim. Cows should eat grass. Chickens should scratch in the dirt. Maybe it was time for Whole Foods to overhaul its animal welfare standards. Instead of simply hoping for better suppliers and working for small improvements, maybe Whole Foods could be a leader in this arena. We were now a big company; maybe we could throw our weight around. This idea was growing on me. It no longer felt like a frustrating no-win situation but was starting to look like an opportunity. Perhaps a creative win-win solution would appear once I allowed my mind to start looking for one.

A few days after I returned to the office, I sat down and wrote a long email to Lauren. I expressed my contrition about my earlier defensiveness and told her that she was right. I had been poorly informed. I thanked her for helping me to see this truth and pushing me to educate myself. I told her about my reflections, my readings, and my decision to become an ethical vegan. And I made a proposal: that we work together to upgrade animal welfare standards for Whole Foods Market. I invited her to visit Whole Foods to meet with our team and discuss how to go forward.

As I pushed "send" on my email, I imagined her receiving it. She would surely be happily surprised! It wasn't every day that an activist receives an email like this from a CEO they have been heckling. I looked forward to her response. It hadn't been easy to hear her accusations, but I genuinely appreciated her courage, and I respected that she'd stood her ground.

Very soon, I received an email from her. Now it was my turn to be surprised. Her tone was angry, outraged, expressing frustration at my inaction. After my initial shock, it dawned on me: she hadn't read my message yet!

I quickly replied, "Lauren, please read my earlier email." Soon, I received a very different response. She was surprised and thrilled and made plans to come to visit us in Austin. And so a unique partnership was born.

"Dammit! Who is going to pay for this? We're not running a charity!"

The tension in the room was palpable. I was seated around the table with a group of stakeholders that Whole Foods had assembled to discuss animal welfare standards. Since it had all started with ducks, we began the process with duck producers, along with animal scientists and veterinarians, members of the activist community, and Whole Foods team members. The conversation had gotten off to a rocky start, with a representative from the duck producer Grimaud facing off with Lauren. We were focused on improving conditions for their ducks, including giving the birds a place to swim.

The Grimaud representative repeated his point with increasing emotion: "You just don't understand our economics. I care about the animals too, but what you're suggesting would almost double our costs. I'll ask again; who's going to pay for that?"

"What's right isn't always what's cheap," Lauren responded. "Are we going to have standards or not? Does the suffering of animals actually matter? Or is that all secondary to your profits?"

A silence hung in the air. Things had escalated very quickly between the industry representatives and the activists. At times, the gap between the parties seemed almost unbridgeable. I had to remind myself, again and again, that this was positive. This conversation was exactly what needed to happen—even if it got heated and uncomfortable. The producers needed to reflect on their acceptance of inhumane industry practices, and the activists needed to deal with a world that wasn't going to immediately bend to their most idealistic and emotional appeals. Both sides needed to find some willingness to compromise. But to do so, they had to be in the same room, and that meant we all had to endure some fireworks.

In my deep dive into the current state of animal welfare certification standards in the food industry, I had come across what I considered to be a problem. At that time there were no legal animal welfare standards at all when it came to animal agriculture. The animals that were raised for food were exempted from the laws that protect cats, dogs, horses, and other domesticated animals. Other certification standards such as Organic or Fair Trade were binary. People would do the minimum to meet the standard but had no incentive to improve beyond that. I wanted to incentivize the animal producers to continue to improve animal welfare and reward them with higher ratings and prices for doing so.

As the Whole Foods team and I worked on the problem, we envisioned an escalating series of animal welfare levels. This would encourage both producers and customers to aim higher and move up, tier by tier, a ladder of better treatment and higher standards. I referred to it as the gamification of animal welfare. We'd inspire a kind of virtuous competition. It was a win-win-win: better for the animals, better for the conscience of the customer, and better for the revenue of the producer. And at Whole Foods, we had the advantage of customers who were not only focused on price. They would often pay more in exchange for the confidence that the products they were purchasing were of a higher grade. But I hadn't even had a chance to suggest this approach before the duck guy started yelling at the activists.

"Can I ask you something?" I turned to the producer. "What if you accepted what the animal rights organizations are saying and instituted this new set of practices and standards? What if that almost doubled the cost of the meat you sell? Could you do it if Whole Foods would agree to guarantee you a market—if we would make an agreement to order a certain number of ducks raised with those standards per year?"

"Whole Foods could do that? At double the price?"

"We'd have to work out the details, but yes, for the highest level of welfare, we could probably go that far." I briefly explained the idea of an escalating set of standards.

A tall, dark-haired man across from me was listening intently and nodding as I spoke. Wayne Pacelle was CEO of the Humane Society of the United States, the largest animal protection organization in the world. I'd met him earlier that year after Lauren introduced me to Matthew Scully, and Matthew brought Wayne along to the meeting too. I had been very happy when he volunteered to participate with us in creating new standards.

"We could provide some help," he said. "The Humane Society could help bolster the legitimacy of the program if we could agree on proper inspection and certification processes." I appreciated his ready support. I liked Wayne a lot—he proved to be an invaluable ally in the process, and we'd soon become good friends. Another supportive voice came from Bruce Friedrich, representing PETA. A quiet and extremely intelligent man, Bruce was a great debater, and his calm, logical approach helped temper the high emotions of other participants. I was encouraged. These folks didn't just want to fight.

Agreeing on what exactly would constitute the new set of welfare standards for duck producers would be hard work, taking many months and multiple meetings. In 2006, Whole Foods Market made it a policy to no longer work with any duck producer connected to the foie gras industry, and in response, Grimaud stopped doing business with Sonoma Foie Gras.

The folks at Sonoma Foie Gras were furious, and sued us for "intentional interference with contract." Grimaud had made their own decision, and I didn't see how we could be at fault, but we were not eager to be dragged into a lengthy public trial, so the case was settled out of court.

In the end, we decided to stop working with Grimaud anyway, frustrated that they were dragging their feet in implementing the standards we'd worked so hard to set. So they sued us too, angry that we'd withdrawn our business. This time, we eventually went to trial, but the case was heard in Stockton, California, an agribusiness hot spot and home to the headquarters of both Grimaud Farms and Sonoma Foie Gras. It quickly became clear that this was a case of "home cooking," with a plaintiff-friendly judge and jury, and we didn't have a chance of winning. When I took the stand, I felt like I was back in that shareholder meeting being heckled—only this time, the heckler was the attorney for the plaintiff, who raised an objection pretty much every time I opened my mouth, all of which were sustained by the judge. The whole proceeding attracted a lot of negative publicity, with the terms "Whole Foods" and "animal cruelty" being thrown together again and again. No one seemed to care that we were actually fighting for the right to disassociate ourselves from such practices. Eventually, we lost the suit. Should we appeal the decision in a higher court in a more neutral venue? The competitive part of me wanted to. But we'd wasted so much time already, and by prolonging the case we'd likely invite more bad press. We decided to settle on damages, eager to be done with this circus and move on to more important things.

Our multi-stakeholder animal welfare initiative didn't stop with ducks. We took on beef cattle, pigs, sheep, turkeys, broiler chickens, laying hens, and dairy cattle. We hosted the meetings, listened to complaints, mediated between activists and producers, encouraged the animal scientists to share research with the group, and worked hard on developing and refining standards. Rolling out the full set of standards across our animal product lines and implementing them in our stores would end up taking many years, but even in those early days, I felt like I was engaged in some of the most satisfying and potentially meaningful work of my life.

Eventually, we would develop standards for 10 different animal species, in collaboration with animal scientists, producers, activists, and retailers. In 2005, we created a private foundation, the Animal Compassion Foundation, to help producers learn how to implement the standards, which in 2008 became an independent international foundation, the Global Animal Partnership (GAP), to encourage other retailers to adopt these standards and engage in the process of creating them. Don't get me wrong: GAP is far from perfect and its impact is limited. Animals still suffer every day in our food system, sometimes in unspeakable ways. I took up Lauren's challenge and personally visited many slaughterhouses and farms during the years we were overhauling our standards, and the horrors I witnessed ensured that I will never choose to partake in that food system with my own dietary choices again in this lifetime. But I'm also a realist when it comes to creating change on a societal level—and when it comes to doing business. I know that the work we did in creating these standards has improved the lives of billions of our fellow sentient beings on this planet, mitigated their suffering, and given consumers a pathway to better ethical choices.

Through working on the animal welfare standards, I gained tremendous respect for Lauren Ornelas. She was critical to the process. But when it comes to the killing and eating of animals, the desire for complete abolition can be strong. I understand; I hear that call too. My personal path was not the path of Whole Foods, nor could it be. I accepted that and was able to reconcile it with my own conscience. Lauren could not. Eventually, she would sour on our project and what she saw as our overly pragmatic approach, which felt too far from her idealistic vegan heart. I respect her choice and remain grateful for the role she played in my life and in the evolution of Whole Foods Market into a more responsible and ethical company.

Later, other advocacy organizations like PETA, who had initially been supportive of our work, would come to criticize us for what they saw as putting a sunny face on a fundamentally immoral system. In fact, they accused us of doing more harm than good—arguing that introducing higher degrees of animal welfare would simply make people feel better about what was still an inhumane choice. In this way, they felt that our efforts might even be counterproductive and prolong a flawed system that needed to be overthrown entirely.

Alas, the world is complicated, and certainly not ready to become vegan en masse. Nonprofits arguing for idealistic outcomes have an advantage—they have no customers to satisfy. They are free to advocate for the world as they imagine it in their most elevated visions. That is a beautiful thing—and can inspire and challenge us all to do better, as it did for me. But it comes at a cost. In engaging the world as it *could* be, it is easy to lose touch with the world as it is and therefore fail to actually improve it.

Businesses are structured in such a way as to avoid this pitfall. A business must satisfy customers and sell products and services if it is to survive. Some will interpret that statement cynically, as meaning that businesses must make a profit and therefore their idealism is tempered and constrained by greed. But I see it quite differently.

Businesses cannot reasonably ignore public taste and consumer preferences. They must be in dialogue with their customers. They can lead the way, nudge, educate, and inform, but they cannot dictate or control customer behavior. They must stay in touch with the needs and preferences of those who are buying their products. Yes, perhaps that chains them closer to the stony ground. But it also keeps them from building castles in the air.

My point is that both activist nonprofits and businesses have a role to play in creating a better world. Both have strengths and weaknesses, but they can temper each other's weaknesses and benefit from each other's strengths. I like to think that the development of our animal welfare standards was a time in which each of those strengths was brought to the table to create something truly valuable. To do it, we needed the activists asking hard questions and pushing visionary futures, as well as the pragmatic businesspeople engaging in dialogue with real consumers and measuring real outcomes. For a time, those two stakeholders found a common language and had conversations approaching mutual respect. I trust that it's been the animals who have ultimately benefited from this delicate and unstable alliance, but I appreciate that such conclusions depend on your point of view.

Ever since the summer of 2003, I have continued to struggle with these issues—in public and in private. I don't eat animals and will not do so again in my lifetime. I welcome anyone to join me in that commitment. But those numbers, at least at this moment in history, will inevitably be small. And I guess the question for me has always been, and continues to be—what can we do, and what will we do for our fellow creatures in the meantime?

Chapter 29

Coming into Our Own

When it comes to retail, the most consequential decision you can make is real estate. And when it comes to real estate, as the old saying goes, it's all about "location, location, location." Our original Whole Foods Market on Lamar Boulevard in Austin had a great location in a neighborhood with high population density and a good number of college graduates with high incomes. Plus, it was on a busy street, with fantastic visibility, and lots of cars going by all day long.

As the company grew I stuck to those basic principles. We'd choose densely populated areas where higher income college graduates lived, and then seek sites on busy roads, with plenty of parking that could be easily accessed and good street visibility. Our real estate philosophy was built around population density and education, car traffic, foot traffic, parking, and visibility. Over our two decades of success, these time-tested criteria had not changed significantly. So I think I can be forgiven for the fact that I expressed grave doubts when a senior executive proposed investing in a costly 59,000-square-foot store that was entirely belowground, with zero visibility from the street and no dedicated parking whatsoever. My reservations were shared by the real estate committee. The only reason we didn't end the discussion right then and there was that the proposed store was situated in the heart of Manhattan—the most densely populated and highly educated city in America.

The initial proposal was made around the turn of the millennium. All new real estate leases needed to go through the real estate committee, which consisted primarily of the E-Team and the Regional Presidents.

Our Northeast Regional President, David Lannon, walked us through the slides of his presentation. It was a great opportunity, he insisted, and an amazing location, but it would also require unprecedented investment. The proposed site sat on the west side of Columbus Circle, at the southwest corner of Central Park. A new Time Warner headquarters building was going up with a shopping center on the lower floors. We were being offered the basement. Customers would have to take escalators down from the street.

The site's best feature, besides the neighborhood's incredible density of highly educated people, was that it was a heavily trafficked area and sat at the convergence of eight subway lines. According to David, the foot traffic alone could more than support the store. But would they even know we were there? Despite its unconventional features, David was very enthusiastic about the site, even suggesting that the store had potential to be one of the most successful in the entire company.

The real estate committee balked. Just to break even on this store, we'd have to come out of the gates doing at least a million dollars a week. Only one or two stores were doing that kind of sales volume back then. It would need to open very strong and grow fast. And again—what if no one realized it was there? And did I mention there was no parking? We were still getting our feet wet in New York, learning the market. Our first store in the city, in Chelsea, was doing well under David's capable leadership, but was this the right next step? We listened; we debated. Finally, the committee voted. I voted no and Glenda shared my reservations. Two negative votes were enough to block a real estate decision from going through.

David was frustrated. He thought he had found the perfect spot for our flagship New York store. Luckily, good executives don't always take the first no for a final answer. He and A.C. kept the flame alive for Columbus Circle. And a few weeks later, at a follow-up meeting, they presented the site again.

Again, the debate was intense. We went back and forth; it was a big decision. But I could feel the team was leaning toward giving it a green light. Admittedly, I was excited about the prospect of a beautiful flagship store right in the middle of Manhattan, but I was acutely aware of the enormous risk. At some point during the meeting, I was persuaded that it was a risk worth taking. But I wanted to inject a sense of accountability into the decision.

"If this doesn't work out, someone is going to have to take responsibility for it! And I want to know who that person is going to be. Is anyone here sure enough about this location that they would be willing to bet their job on it?"

There was a moment of silence. Everyone stopped talking and stared at me.

Then David's voice came over the speakerphone, quiet and steady. "John, I think that would be me."

Of course, I had no intention of actually holding David to that bet. He was an outstanding executive, and I'd already lost him once before. In the aftermath of the Bread & Circus acquisition back in 1992, David had been one of their talented team members who had walked out the door. He simply didn't see a future with these long-haired Texans who had just taken over their beautiful, classy New England stores. "We've been acquired by the Allman Brothers," was his half-joking assessment of the situation, he admitted to me later. Luckily, like A.C. Gallo, David would find his way back to Whole Foods, after briefly working with Anthony Harnett on his next big thing that never happened.

David's journey back to Whole Foods began in Mill Valley, where Walter quickly recognized his talents and took him under his wing. He rose rapidly under Walter's tutelage, soon becoming Store Team Leader in Palo Alto, then working with Walter to design and build the Franklin store in San Francisco, which quickly became our first $1 million-a-week store. He was an effective leader and executive, and as we expanded, we desperately needed as many of those as we could possibly get. Eventually,

A.C. poached David back to his East Coast roots and put him in charge of the New York area, where he spearheaded the opening of the Chelsea store in 2001.

As a company, we had once been intimidated by the prospect of opening stores in New York, particularly in Manhattan. It's a unique market, with lots of small neighborhood grocery stores. No major company was dominant. Real estate is extremely expensive, the unions are powerful, and construction is complicated, not to mention the parking difficulties. But our Chelsea store had managed to transcend New York's best attempts to dissuade us, and it became an immediate success. Emboldened, I'd asked David to look for a new location. And that's how he came to propose Columbus Circle.

The Columbus Circle store opened in February 2004, the largest grocery store in Manhattan at the time. It was quite an event—this was not just the opening of Whole Foods Market, but of the entire building, with all its shops and amenities. Jon Stewart hosted. It was a New York media and celebrity blowout. The next morning, I joined a crowd of commuters and dog walkers and crossed the busy traffic circle, dodging taxis, bicycles, and the occasional horse carriage taking tourists into Central Park. I admired the shiny new building towering above the bustle, but I still couldn't help but notice that nowhere was there a large, green Whole Foods Market sign. As I made my way down the escalators and into the new store, however, the lack of visibility was quickly forgotten.

I was simply amazed at what our team had accomplished! Below the streets of New York City was an enormous Whole Foods Market, bursting with magnificent produce, freshly baked goods, tantalizing prepared foods, and an abundance of natural food choices. The store included a large wine store, the biggest selection of natural and organic body care products we'd ever carried, and a café area that could seat almost 250 people. To me, every new store seems like the most beautiful yet, but this one truly had something about it that stopped me in my tracks the moment I stepped off the escalator. It seemed like all our learnings from 26 years of experience had come together to create this remarkable food fantasia in the heart of the urban world.

All I could think, as I stepped aside to make way for a flood of customers coming down behind me, was that Whole Foods Market had come into its own. It hadn't happened overnight of course—we'd been growing and evolving and maturing as a company in the 12 years since our IPO. But this was like one of those moments on the trail when I stepped out above the trees and was able to appreciate how far we'd come. How ironic, I thought, that this glimpse of perspective happened below street level.

I looked for David, wanting to acknowledge him and his team for this tremendous success. He smiled, looking around at the teeming crowd and the customers still pouring in. "I don't think anyone's too worried about parking, John."

My favorite vignette from that day was quintessential New York. The store filled up, but the crowds just kept coming. Eventually, lines formed out onto the street, and we had to limit the flow of customers into the store. That meant letting people down the escalator in groups only as the same number exited and went up.

With every other team member occupied, David grabbed a walkie-talkie and manned the tops of the escalators, like a cop directing traffic. After one group was directed forward, he put his hand up to halt the line. The guy at the very front stopped and looked at David with a sense of anticipation.

"Hey, buddy, what's down there anyway?"

I guess he had just got caught up in the excitement. If New Yorkers are actually standing in line, there must be something special happening.

"It's a supermarket," David replied.

"Get the fuck outta here! This is a line for a supermarket?" He looked taken aback, and disappointed.

David just looked him straight in the eye and smiled. "It's a really nice supermarket."

Indeed, it was. A few weeks later, as sales continued to outperform, I sat down at my computer and composed a brief message to David, acknowledging that he'd been 100% right and thanking him for sticking to his guns.

People tell me I can be blunt and highly opinionated, maybe to a fault. And it's true that I've never been afraid to be honest and express my views—a habit I no doubt picked up from my father. Whole Foods executive team meetings in those days could be tough. We argued; we debated; we expressed ourselves with conviction. It wasn't personal; it was never callous. But we cared about the company and our occasional passionate disagreements reflected it. Some were intimidated by that culture. I came to believe that it was a feature, not a bug. When you have an uncensored debate, you know there's nothing unsaid and as a result you can make better-informed decisions. People feel heard, reservations are taken into account, and the group can collectively get behind the outcome.

But I also think being a conscious leader means being honest not just with our perceptions and opinions, but with ourselves. In this case, I was mistaken. And to David's credit, he didn't back down. Columbus Circle, as he had predicted, became our highest sales volume store, far exceeding expectations from day one. And as I sat there in Austin and considered Whole Foods' incredibly bright future in the Big Apple, I was so very happy to be wrong.

I wasn't the only one who suddenly noticed how far Whole Foods Market had come. After our triumph in Manhattan, the national media, which had largely ignored our rise, seemed to wake up to our presence en masse. "Whole Foods Takes Manhattan!" shouted the headlines. People sometimes talk about an East Coast media bias, and I can honestly say that from the moment we started selling lots of natural and organic foods in the New York area, the national media started to take notice of our success. That attention would turn out to be both a blessing and a curse.

Initially, it was almost all positive and helped spur the growth of the business. Over time, it would become a more complicated burden. And the media weren't the only ones suddenly taking notice. Although it would be many years before we saw the impact, I believe it was our Columbus Circle store that caught the attention of the conventional grocery stores and made them start to take us seriously as a competitor.

As summer became fall, and the company went from strength to strength, I went through another significant transition in my personal life. My father, who had lived with Alzheimer's for years and was now barely recognizable as the wise mentor I so greatly loved and had depended on so much in our early days, died in November 2004. It had been more than a decade since his wisdom had graced our Board meetings, and many years since I'd been able to call him for advice about strategy. Sadly, his personality had long since succumbed to this horrible disease. But still, while he lived I'd felt some connection to the continuum of generational wisdom he represented. Now that link was permanently severed.

I was 51 years old, and both my parents were now gone. I was an orphan. Like all parents, mine were far from perfect, but they had loved me, and raised me, and championed my success. No one ever loves you quite like your parents do. And my father had been an essential part of shaping not only who I was as a man but also who I was as a business leader and entrepreneur.

I gave one of the eulogies at his service. Tears came to my eyes as I looked around the church and I entered into what I can only describe as an altered state of consciousness. Stepping away from the pulpit and listening as others gave their own eulogies and shared remembrances of my father, it suddenly seemed as if it was not my father's memorial service I was attending but my own. All around me, people seemed to be talking about me. They were remembering me. I was at my own memorial service listening to the words that others would use about my life and my time on Earth.

It was a disconcerting experience that plunged me into deeper reflections on my own life and mortality. I had the strange sense that a mirror was being held up that reflected my own time on this earth. Who was I and what was the truth about my own life? Was it good? Was it beautiful? Was it enough? Was *I* enough?

The memorial service ended and the altered state slowly wore off, but its resonance stayed with me through the evening. And as my tired head hit the pillow, I found myself swept into a highly lucid dream that I remember vividly to this day.

I'm at a party in a large, crowded warehouse. Music is pounding through the cavernous space, and people are dancing. Suddenly, several men in dark suits enter the building. They look serious and intent on a mission, unlike the carefree revelers all around. As they begin moving through the crowd, it dawns on me: They're looking for me. And they are armed with automatic weapons. I try to hide, but they find me and open fire. Riddled with bullets, I collapse and die. As I slowly float upward, looking down at my bleeding, broken body, I think, "Shit, that doesn't look good. I must be dead." But I feel curiously detached. I watch as the gangsters slap each other on the back in celebration—"We got Mackey!"—and then leave the scene through the crowd of panicked guests. It's clear to me that this attack was about me, and no one else at the party was hurt.

I become aware of a light above me. Even in the dream state, I recognize that this is like the classic scenes we hear about from near-death experiences. The light above me is intensely bright, and I'm ascending farther and farther away from my dead body toward this shining brightness. And then I suddenly have a thought: "What if I'm not worthy to go into the light?"

Immediately, with that thought, I stop ascending and begin to slowly descend. "Uh-oh, I shouldn't have thought that about not being worthy!" I scold myself. But then I remember that life is really all about love, so I begin to focus on loving thoughts and feelings. The moment I center that truth in my heart, I stop falling and the scene immediately shifts, and I pop into what seems like a different universe. I can sense that I am now in a universe that is far more evolved and filled with love and light than the one we usually occupy. Everything I can see is incredibly beautiful—more beautiful than anything I have ever seen before.

As things come into focus, I realize that I am once again a little boy, perhaps four or five years old, sitting in the waiting room in what I interpret as perhaps a doctor's office. As I look around at the other children in the waiting room, something immediately strikes me. They are all so very beautiful! I've never seen such extraordinary, radiant, and loving people. They are literally glowing with love.

A nurse of some sort opens the door and comes into the room. She is also beautiful and glowing. She looks at me and says, "John, it's your turn now."

"It can't be my turn," I tell myself.

But as if she'd read my mind, the nurse smiles and says, "Yes, it's your turn now."

I look at the boy sitting next to me. I think it's my brother, Jim, and he is emanating beauty and love. "It must be a mistake," I tell him. "It must be your turn. You should go next. You're so beautiful. You should go."

Jim looks into my eyes, his gaze full of compassion.

"Have you seen yourself?" he asks. "You are beautiful too. It's your time. Go."

And the nurse reaches out and takes my hand, and as I walk through the door, I wake up.

In the weeks and months that followed, I often thought back to that dream. I came to see it as my father's final gift to me. Reflecting on its message—*you are beautiful too, John*—helped to crystallize a shift that had been slowly occurring in my inner life over the past decade. As a child, I'd been plagued by a sense of inferiority, no doubt intensified by my mother's anxious personality and my father's overbearing, critical presence. For all my successes, some insecurities had lingered into adulthood. For years, I'd still felt like an upstart among the older, more worldly members of the Natural Foods Network. I'd struggled with social awkwardness, especially around women. I'd been challenged, again and again, by people who thought they were smarter and more capable than me of doing my job. And on some subconscious level, I'd harbored a sense that I didn't fully deserve the success, love, and beauty that filled my life. Few were more surprised than me when, at the end of 2003, I was selected as Ernst & Young's national overall winner of Entrepreneur of the Year.

Now, in the wake of my father's passing, I realized those insecurities had largely fallen away. For the first time in my life, I began to feel like I might actually be worthy of all the good things I'd worked so hard for. I was no longer afraid. I was no longer really that concerned about what others thought of me. I too was coming into my own. Like the success of Whole Foods Market, it hadn't happened overnight, but somewhere along the way I'd reached a tipping point. The dream opened up a moment of perspective on my own journey too, and I became newly conscious that my own sense of self had evolved and was continuing to evolve.

Some of this I attributed to simply maturing and gaining confidence through the trials, triumphs, and ongoing success story of the business. Much of it I attributed to the deep, unconditional love and support I'd found in my marriage to Deborah, as well as in my meditation practices and continuing studies of *A Course in Miracles.* I was able to be more fully in the present moment, unafraid. Even when I didn't know exactly how things were going to work out, I knew I'd be fine. And I no longer felt intimidated by other successful people, even those whose educational qualifications or achievements exceeded mine. I knew in my heart that we were equals. I was finally beginning to accept that I was beautiful too.

Chapter 30

Conscious Capitalism

When I meet other entrepreneurs, there's always a spark—an instantaneous recognition that we're wired the same way. We might not agree on politics or religion or what to eat for lunch, but we view the world through a lens of possibility, and that creates an immediate bond. Entrepreneurs look around and see opportunity. We're oriented toward the future. We're creative problem solvers. We're optimistic. I can sit down with a young entrepreneur who's just launched their first startup or an older one with a series of successful exits, a fellow grocery store founder or the creator of a tech company, and I just know we're going to find acres of common ground.

Never was this so apparent to me as when I sat down on a rickety chair under a thatched roof with a circle of about 10 women in a small village in the high country of Guatemala. They wore brightly colored, traditional clothes. Some were older, matriarchal figures; some were young mothers whose children played around our feet on the handwoven rugs that covered the dirt floor. Outside, the sounds of village life—car horns, chickens, music from an old crackly radio—drifted through the hot, humid afternoon. Inside, there was a focused, positive energy, punctuated by a lot of laughter. Someone passed around glasses of fresh, cold *limonada*, and the conversation began.

On the surface, the life these women lived was a world away from my day-to-day existence as CEO of a large North American company. Their businesses were mostly small retail ventures, selling handmade crafts or foods or clothing. And yet we had so much in common. Their favorite topic of conversation? What they were going to do with their next infusion of capital—the plans they had to grow their businesses. I could relate. There was nothing I loved to talk about more than our plans for growing Whole Foods Market. And it was thanks to the growth of Whole Foods Market that I sat here today, on a fall afternoon in 2005. We were here to meet recipients of microcredit loans that had been made through our recently launched Whole Planet Foundation.

I'd learned about the concept of microcredit a couple of years earlier, through reading Muhammad Yunus's book *Banker to the Poor*. His stories and his worldview captivated me. It felt like he'd cracked an important code when it came to the entrenched global issue of poverty. Of course, it's a vast and complex problem, and no one program can fix it. And it's even more difficult in countries where the rule of law isn't well established with firm property rights, and people don't necessarily have the freedom and the access to capital that are required to kick-start entrepreneurial dreams. Yunus solved for this with the microcredit programs he offered through Grameen Bank in his home country of Bangladesh.

The genius of his model was that it focused primarily on women and it didn't require collateral. Instead, it used peer pressure to ensure a phenomenally high repayment rate, putting the women in groups and stipulating that no one could get a new loan until everyone had paid back the previous one. This had the added benefit of creating supportive communities for the entrepreneurs. And as their businesses grew, they employed more people. *What a brilliant solution*, I thought when I first read the book. Yunus didn't view the poor as exploited victims; he viewed them as potential entrepreneurs who just needed to be given the freedom and the funding to get started. How much more effective—and dignifying—to give people, as the saying goes, a hand up rather than just a handout.

Meeting Yunus in person only deepened my respect. I gave him a tour of our P Street store in DC, and he struck me as a genuinely humble, smart, and compassionate man.

"I really admire the work you're doing," I told him, "and I'd like to do something similar. Whole Foods is doing business all over the world.

Maybe we could help set up little Grameen banks in all the villages where we're buying coffee and produce and other things we sell in our stores?" He was very enthusiastic.

Next, I needed someone to help me get this thing going. And I knew just the guy. I called up my old friend Philip Sansone, companion on so many of my spiritual and psychedelic adventures. Philip had spent eight years in the Peace Corps, working in Paraguay and Honduras. Later, he did volunteer relief work in places like Afghanistan that were suffering from the ravages of war. He was no longer running BookPeople and had recently suffered a horrible personal loss when his only daughter was murdered by her husband. I sensed that he needed something new to give his life direction, and I couldn't imagine anyone better suited to running the program I was envisioning. I outlined the idea—and also extended an invitation.

"Why don't you come with me on this trip that Deborah and I are taking to Bodh Gaya, India, and we can discuss it more. I promise you'll like it."

Now, for most people, the notion of traveling halfway around the world to the dust and dirt of rural India might not be the most attractive vacation plan. But I knew Philip, and I knew his spiritual soul wouldn't be able to resist visiting the legendary site of the Buddha's enlightenment.

Deborah, by this point, was studying with a Sufi master and had been a committed meditator for a couple of decades. She liked to travel to pilgrimage sites around the world, and I was more than happy to go with her on some of these trips. We'd been to India a couple of times before, visiting holy sites in the Himalayan foothills, but this was quite a different experience. Bodh Gaya is in Bihar, in eastern India, one of the subcontinent's most densely populated and impoverished states. The small town has benefited from its status as an international spiritual and religious destination, but still, there is no getting around the harsh reality of life in rural Bihar, which confronted us every day as we walked the hot, rutted dirt streets from our hotel to the ancient Bodhi tree where the Buddha is said to have attained enlightenment.

Cows wandered freely; traffic fumes mingled with the smell of open sewers in the dusty air; and everywhere people begged for food and money. Most disturbing were the children who had been deliberately mutilated and disabled by ruthless beggar pimps to prey on the sympathies of pilgrims. The sight of these poor children, missing arms and legs and often disfigured through burning and knife cuts, would bring me to tears every day as we had to pass through their gauntlet.

Yet, the spiritual fragrance of the temple complex in this Buddhist holy site was undeniable. The quality of devotion seemed to waft up from the procession of monks, lamas, and pilgrims of all types who visited from dawn to dusk. Tibetans, in particular, made up a large percentage of the assembled visitors. They would come down from their mountain homes in the winter and spend time on the warmer plains, a mixture of seasonal escape and religious pilgrimage. We sat and meditated while pilgrims performed prostrations in the vicinity of the large tree that adorned the temple (not the original Bodhi tree, of course, though some like to defy science and claim it is the very one beneath which the Buddha sat). I felt the concentrated spiritual power of thousands of years of human prayer and practice.

After making our own short pilgrimage each day, we'd walk back to the hotel, or pay some rupees to a local rickshaw driver, and I'd talk with Philip about my plans for the microfinance organization. There was something about being in that place that brought the idea alive: seeing the need of people living below subsistence level, and yet the resilience of the human character, as people went about their lives working to move forward in the world. I've no doubt the spiritual inspiration also lifted our hearts and gave us hope that this idea could actually make a difference.

By the time the trip was over, Philip was committed. Back in the US, we proposed our plan to the Whole Foods Board, and they were supportive. We reached out to Yunus to create an initial partnership, and the Whole Planet Foundation was born. Eventually, we'd expand to partner with multiple local microfinance organizations that replicated the Grameen Bank model, allowing us to operate in the various parts of the world where Whole Foods sourced its products—including that Guatemalan village where I spent such an energizing afternoon talking with fellow entrepreneurs.

"What do your husbands think about all this business stuff?" I asked the group of Guatemalan entrepreneurs. The translator relayed the question, and the women fell apart laughing.

One of them replied in rapid Spanish, and the ensuing hilarity was so loud I could barely hear the translation: "We know how to keep our husbands in line!"

I laughed too. Their humor and enthusiasm were infectious. So too was their pride in their growing businesses, and the seriousness with which they deployed the capital we loaned them—often just a few dollars at a time. I also noted the spirit of camaraderie among them. These women may have been living in conditions that by most standards would be called poverty. But they were rapidly changing that story for themselves, for each other, and for their families. They had hope. They saw a better future, for themselves and for their children and grandchildren. As I listened to one after another sharing the successes of their ventures, I felt an upwelling of gratitude and appreciation for the incredible system that had made all this possible: capitalism.

By this point in my life, I embraced the label "capitalist" wholeheartedly. I had no patience for those who sanctimoniously criticized business as greedy and exploitative, even as they benefited from the countless blessings that capitalism has brought to society as a whole and to most of us as individuals. Indeed, it astounded me how many people seemed to be ignorant or in outright denial of what capitalism has done for humanity. My reading had convinced me beyond a doubt that economic freedom, combined with free markets, property rights, the rule of law, and entrepreneurship (or the "ability to have a go," as economic historian Deirdre McCloskey likes to say), is the greatest thing we as a species have ever created. The practice of these ideas has lifted billions and billions of people out of poverty in the past 250 years; created a large, sustained global middle class for the first time in history; forged a platform for ongoing technological innovation and economic growth; and helped establish levels of wealth and wellness unthinkable just a few generations ago. Simply put, it made the modern world possible. And all of it is built on the simple, beautiful principle of voluntary exchange for mutual benefit. The very essence of capitalism is a win-win-win philosophy. I add that third "win" because it's not just two parties in an exchange who benefit, but all the major stakeholders as well—customers, employees, suppliers, investors, and the communities that business is a part of.

Of course, we can look back in disgust and regret at some of what has historically happened in the name of capitalism. No economic system has the power to change human nature and its tendencies toward short-term self-interest, greed, or worse. But when we consider the overall journey, it's extraordinary how far we have come. The last 250 years have unleashed human potential and transformed our world for the better. And that journey is still continuing.

This brings me to another idea that captivated me during the early 2000s: the idea that cultures are *evolving*. It sounds simple, but when you talk to people, it quickly becomes clear that many don't really believe in the notion of progress. They don't believe things are getting better. In fact, they romanticize the past and demonize the modern world. To me, the understanding that we—as a human race, as cultures, and as individuals—are part of a larger evolutionary process made powerful, intuitive sense. Reading the philosopher Ken Wilber and other thinkers who espoused this view helped me find words to explain my conviction that little by little, the world was getting better and better.

I'm not just talking about the economic sphere. These thinkers pointed out that humans are actually evolving in our consciousness. Our values and ethics are evolving. Our ways of making meaning are evolving. Does that mean the future is predetermined, or that there is no chance of a significant setback? Of course not. We have much further to go, and the beautiful breakthroughs of the modern world also come with their own set of problems and challenges. Evolution is never a simple or straight ascent. Sometimes we must reconnect with the wisdom of the past to move forward into the future. Moreover, building a brighter future will depend on conscious human choice and wise action. But if you compare the world of today to the world of 10,000 years ago, 1,000 years ago, or even 100 years ago, there's simply no question that extraordinary progress has occurred. And as we evolve in our consciousness and values, the potential impact of the win-win-wins we can create only grows.

It never ceases to amaze me how many people will deny the obvious truth of progress. One good way to challenge such denialism is to ask: At what other time in history would you rather have been born? Most people can't answer that question—and for good reason: There has never been a better time to be alive than right now.

I believe we'll look back on the 20th century as a great struggle between capitalism and socialism. Capitalism won this battle—and did so decisively—but it failed to capture the minds of the intellectual class, and it often failed to win the hearts of the people it lifted up. That unfortunate truth is why so many of its beneficiaries perpetuate the all-too-common narrative that capitalism, and the corporations that practice it, are nothing more than greedy, exploitative, selfish, and untrustworthy—despite the utterly compelling evidence of the past few centuries. It is perhaps a sign of the remarkable success of capitalism that so many, now well established in the escape from millennia of grinding poverty, can believe that the very ladder that elevated them is a vehicle of human suffering rather than human liberation. Only by rejecting the profit motive, they claim, blind to the irony of their own position, can we truly be altruistic and loving.

I reject this dichotomy. It is possible to love oneself *and* love others; to take care of one's own needs while making the world a better place; to be profitable *and* generous.

As my own thinking around these issues took shape, I adopted the term "Conscious Capitalism," coined by Muhammad Yunus. Those were carefully chosen words. I didn't mean it to imply that this was "good" capitalism and other forms were "bad." Rather, I believed that capitalism by its nature had several important virtues, and by making those more conscious—explicitly stating the positive impacts of capitalism as part of its philosophy rather than simply by-products—we might reframe the notion and help it shed some of the negative associations.

Many of these ideas were refined as I worked to create the Whole Planet Foundation, but they'd initially been incubated in the context of a nonprofit I launched in 2005, together with a libertarian friend, Michael Strong. We called it FLOW (an acronym of Freedom Lights Our World). Our mission was "liberating the entrepreneurial spirit for good"—bringing together an appreciation for economic freedom, voluntary exchange, and individual initiative with social and environmental consciousness. In addition to Conscious Capitalism, our programs focused on Peace Through Commerce and Accelerating Women Entrepreneurs.

Another outlet for my commitment to using business to make meaningful change was the creation of the Whole Trade program at Whole Foods Market, inspired by the Fair Trade movement. I'll admit, I was initially suspicious of Fair Trade, which I perceived as projecting a "holier than thou" image and asserting, by implication, that other kinds of trade were unfair. I didn't see it that way. Trade meant voluntary exchange. We shouldn't be coercing people into buying one kind of thing over another. That smacked of anti-capitalism to me.

It was my friend Peter Singer, the animal rights pioneer who had helped me rethink my ethical relationship to food, who also challenged me to rethink my attitude toward Fair Trade.

"I don't understand your problem, John. No one's being coerced into buying Fair Trade products. People are just being given information to help them make a better choice about where their purchases come from. What's wrong with that?"

I was stunned. Peter had once again presented such a coherent argument that I had no choice but to shift my beliefs. He'd shown me that there was no contradiction between initiatives like Fair Trade and my vision of capitalism. Not long after this, I met the guy behind Fair Trade

USA, Paul Rice, and the shift in my attitude was complete. Paul was charming, smart, playful, charismatic, and idealistic. I knew immediately that this guy was someone I could be very good friends with. And I told him so—at that first meeting. We did go on to become close friends, and Whole Foods launched the Whole Trade program, brainchild of the brilliant Whole Foods executive Michael Besancon, which worked with Fair Trade and other certifiers to give our customers the information they wanted about where their coffee, rice, chocolate, and all kinds of other products came from.

"Do you know how much more the average US CEO makes than the average worker?" I asked Glenda.

It was 2006, and we were filling our plates from the expansive salad bar at our beautiful flagship store in Austin, located on Lamar Boulevard and 6th Street. The 80,000-square-foot store was our biggest in the US—almost one and a half football fields—and it had been opened to mark our 25th anniversary as Whole Foods Market a year earlier. Walter had spearheaded the project; I'd stayed away until it was completely done, because, as I explained it to him, "I don't like to unwrap my presents before Christmas." The day I first walked into that store was one of the best instances of delayed gratification I can remember. Walter had truly created a retail masterpiece, and it became our second store to hit $2 million in weekly sales.

Glenda and I made our way over to the checkout line, busy with local office workers picking up lunch, and I answered my own rhetorical question.

"In 2004, the average CEO made $431 for every $1 the average worker earned. That's much higher than I thought. It's statistics like this that feed the negative narrative the anti-capitalist intellectuals use to attack business."

At Whole Foods, we'd put a cap on executive pay, stipulating that the highest-paid team members could never make more than a certain multiple of what the average team member earned. We started at 10X; over time we had to raise it to 19X, just to keep executive salaries competitive and avoid losing our best people to higher paying jobs. Great disparities in compensation can sometimes be detrimental for team-member morale. If the average person working in our stores knew that management was making hundreds of times their salary, would they still feel good about working there?

We also made sure to distribute our stock options widely. I'd learned that the average corporation in the US distributed 75% of its total stock options to its top five executives. Our top 16 executives received only 7% of options granted, with 93% being distributed throughout the entire company. Again, this was something I was proud of. But personally, I wanted to go further.

"I want to stop taking a salary," I told Glenda. "Starting next year, I'm going to set my salary at $1."

She looked taken aback, but I loved the idea, explaining that I wouldn't be the first to take such a salary. In fact, the first "dollar-a-year men" were prominent businesspeople who essentially donated their time and expertise to their country after the Second World War, taking the nominal salary to circumvent a prohibition on volunteerism in government. They were capitalists, like me, who also felt a strong sense of civic duty. A more recent example—and one that spoke strongly to me—was Steve Jobs, who returned to Apple in 1999 at a salary of $1.

To be clear, I had more money than I needed for my personal security, comfort, and happiness. I had nothing against personal wealth and wasn't advocating for others to copy me or make personal sacrifices. But this felt like the appropriate thing for me, to take servant leadership to a new level and simply work for the joy it gave me. And so, starting in January 2007, my compensation was set at $1. I still owned some stock in the company, but from that date onward, I donated 100% of my stock options to the Whole Planet Foundation to help poor entrepreneurs around the world.

We were by no means the only company experimenting with forms of

Conscious Capitalism in the early 2000s. In 2007, Raj Sisodia, a professor at Babson College, along with David Wolfe and Jag Sheth, gathered the stories of many such companies, including Whole Foods, in his cleverly titled *Firms of Endearment.* I read the book eagerly, encouraged to learn that so many other entrepreneurs and business leaders were thinking in similar ways. Soon afterward, I reached out to David and Raj and suggested we partner in hosting a Conscious Capitalism conclave. This collaboration took over the nonprofit Conscious Capitalism, which we spun off from FLOW, and would eventually lead to a book coauthored by Raj and myself.

I look back on those early years of the 21st century as some of the best in Whole Foods Market's history. By the end of 2007, we operated 276 stores with locations in 37 US states and the District of Columbia, Canada, and even the UK. The steps we'd taken toward becoming a more conscious, sustainable, and ethical company uplifted all of us on the leadership team—and many more of our team members as well. It was energizing to know that as well as raising standards for animal welfare and striving to create an equitable and healthy culture in our stores, we were now promoting entrepreneurship and sustainability in the communities where we sourced our products. As of this writing, the Whole Planet Foundation has disbursed more than $124 million in approximately 7.5 million loans, creating almost 38 million opportunities for entrepreneurs and their families in 79 countries around the world.

The beauty of a win-win-win is that it keeps fueling itself—everyone benefits and is in turn inspired to give more. We attracted great people to work in our offices, facilities, and stores. We inspired loyalty among those who'd been with us for a long time. Our customers loved learning about the foundations and felt aligned with the company's purpose. They donated generously to our work as well as continuing to shop in our stores. Even the media seemed to love us. And Whole Foods just continued to grow and grow and grow.

Chapter 31

It's All Fun and Games Until the Bureaucrats Get Involved

I quickened my pace, determined not to let my friend Will Paradise get too far ahead of me on the rocky trail. Immediately, I noticed my elevated heart rate and the sweat already breaking out on my brow. *You're not in Texas anymore, John,* I reminded myself. The first few days after arriving in Colorado were always a bit of a shock to the system as my body adjusted to the altitude. Will had the advantage of living here year-round, while I returned only for a few months to escape the worst of Austin's summer. Still, I hated to let him beat me to the top, so I jogged to catch up.

Deborah and I had kept the lovely house we'd purchased in Boulder's historic district when I'd moved there to run WholePeople.com. I felt immense gratitude for having these beautiful trails just a few blocks from my front door every summer—and for having friends like Will who shared two of my great loves: physical activity and competition. Will had been one of the folks who'd joined our team with the Bread & Circus merger, and he'd become one of my closest friends. Which meant we competed pretty much anytime we got the opportunity: at tennis, Ping-Pong, basketball, rock throwing, running, and hiking up mountains like this one.

As Will slowed to navigate a particularly steep section of trail, I pushed myself to surge past him and cover the last few hundred yards to the top of Boulder's Mount Sanitas. Unfortunately, Will saw me make my move, and he began running too. He beat me to the top by a few yards and raised his arms above his head, declaring victory. Breathless and laughing, we sat down to take in the view, when a couple of twentysomething trail runners came cruising up the trail, keeping up an animated conversation while they ran and barely breaking a sweat. *It's all relative,* I thought, smiling.

If it wasn't clear by now, I'm a highly competitive guy. Among my friends and partners, I've gained a reputation for approaching any kind of sport or game with a kind of intensity that most would reserve for high-stakes dealmaking. To be clear, my intensity isn't just about winning. I can handle being beaten fairly by another individual or other team. In fact, I don't mind losing if the game has been fun and I know I've given it my all. I love games and competition for their own sake, not just for the satisfaction of victory.

If I treat games like serious business, it's equally true that I treat business like a serious game. Indeed, one of the reasons I love business is because it activates my competitive drive, my strategic capacities, my playful energy, and my desire to outwit my competitors. Like any good game, business has rules that make it fair and equitable, and it rewards rational thinking, practice, and a commitment to excellence. It also involves intense rivalries, like the game of Risk I'd played for several years in the late nineties with Wild Oats CEO Mike Gilliland.

Unfortunately, that particular rivalry had gotten less friendly of late. Our competitor had continued growing rapidly, briefly surpassing Whole Foods in store count in 1999 with 110 stores, but never coming close to surpassing our total sales numbers. Mike Gilliland had left the company in 2001 and went on to launch a new company, Sunflower Farmers Market. I met his successor, Perry Odak, former CEO of Ben & Jerry's, after he showed up at one of our investor conferences and joined the Whole Foods breakout session after I had finished speaking (with his name tag turned backward to hide his identity). These sessions are not designed for competitors, so when he introduced himself afterward, I reminded him that he shouldn't really have been there. He was unrepentant, declaring that it's a free country. This irritated me, and I told him in no uncertain terms that Whole Foods intended to outcompete Wild Oats. And we did just that. When Odak resigned, in October 2006, I saw that we might now have a chance to finally buy Wild Oats. I reached out to interim CEO Greg Mays and Chairman of the Board Bob Miller, and they were immediately interested. By February 2007, we had the outline of a deal in place. That might have been the end of the story—game, set, and match—were it not for several factors that conspired to almost cheat me of that long-awaited victory.

By way of context, let me introduce another of my favorite outlets for my competitive spirit: investing. I enjoy investing in the stock market because it brings together my love of games with my love of business. Jeremy Siegel's incredible book *Stocks for the Long Run* convinced me beyond a doubt that, over the long term, investing in stocks outperforms all other asset classes including real estate, gold, bonds, and cash. Most of my investments were for the long term and went into low-cost Vanguard index funds, but starting in the early nineties after the IPO, I also dabbled in some stock picking myself. It was fun!

I'd pay close attention to the economic climate, trying to predict which companies were going up and which might be headed for a fall. It was a thrill to get it right—to feel like I'd scored a win in this stock market game. And when I lost, it just spurred me to learn more and get better. Don't get me wrong—when I refer to investing as a game, I don't mean to imply that I approached it frivolously, treating the stock market like a casino. Remember, I take my games seriously. But I also enjoyed making carefully timed, strategic speculative bets. And to get good at doing so, I read dozens of books about investing and economics, schooling myself in market dynamics and trading strategies.

Of course, I couldn't speculate on Whole Foods stock—that would have been insider trading. I could, however, use what I knew about our industry, coupled with my ever-sharpening business skills, to make speculative bets for or against other public companies. Sometimes, when we'd had a bad quarter and were about to report earnings, I'd think: *If we're doing poorly, and I know we're a good operator, it's highly likely that certain competitors, like Wild Oats, who are not nearly such good operators as we are, might be doing worse.* So I'd short their stock (make a bet that their stock would fall). I never made a lot of money that way, but I made enough to take a little of the sting out of Whole Foods' down quarters.

The advent of the internet made it easy to keep track of various stocks and play the game of investing. One of my favorite pastimes since 1999 had been reading and posting on the Yahoo Finance message boards related to particular stocks. This was an era before social media had really caught on, so it was something of a novelty to have a real-time online conversation with dozens of strangers about the merits of this company or that stock.

The debates on the Whole Foods Market message board were lively, fierce, and often extremely well informed. I had no idea who most of those fellow posters were. We all used screen names—mine was Rahodeb, an anagram of my wife's name. And I was pretty certain that the guy I spent a lot of time arguing with was not actually William Tell. Occasionally people tried to guess my identity, and I had some fun with that, since the consensus opinion seemed to be that I was a woman. Sometimes we argued hard numbers; other times we digressed into sharing our favorite things to buy at Whole Foods. I was known on the Yahoo Whole Foods board as a shameless cheerleader for the company and an advocate for long-term value investing. Once, I even defended John Mackey's haircut against a guy who was making comments about the photo in the annual report, but that was just an inside joke that my friends had a good laugh over (my curly hair never looks very good). Mostly, what I posted were my own views, but occasionally, just as I would in real-life debates, I'd play devil's advocate and throw out an opinion I didn't agree with at all, just to see what response it would get.

The anonymity was part of the fun in that early internet era. A classic

New Yorker cartoon from 1993 by Peter Steiner showed two dogs at a computer, with the caption "On the internet, no one knows you're a dog." On the internet, no one knows you're a CEO either. It reminded me of my time on the Appalachian Trail, where I could simply be Strider and nobody cared what I did for a living. I enjoyed being able to express my thoughts and opinions freely without worrying that it would affect the company. I also loved being able to dodge the stereotypes that people tended to apply in the real world. I could be a smart-ass, a passionate libertarian, an unabashed capitalist, a philosopher, and a provocateur.

Another of the people I argued with regularly went by the name Hubris12000. Seemed like an accurate name to me—he was a short seller who was always arrogantly claiming that Whole Foods was overvalued and advising people to bet on the stock going down. I spent many satisfying late-night interludes arguing for the long-term health of our business. These online conversations were another type of game that I enjoy: debating. All those family-dinner-table-honed debating skills came in very handy as I defended Whole Foods from its critics—and occasionally poked holes in some of our competitors when it suited me to do so.

It was an engaging outlet, and I learned a lot, even—perhaps especially—from folks I disagreed with. I think best when I'm thinking dialectically and found it energizing to clarify my own thoughts as I made my arguments. All good things must come to an end, however, and my time on the Yahoo message boards was cut short after almost eight years by a lost bet. Hubris12000, tired of our ongoing arguments, bet me that Whole Foods' stock price would fall below $50. If he was right, I'd have to quit the forum. I took the bet, confident that our stock price would continue to rise. But on August 8, 2006, after we'd released a disappointing quarterly sales report, our stock hit $48.90. I accepted defeat graciously, never again posted on Yahoo, and barely gave it another thought until a year later, when I was embroiled in trying to salvage the Wild Oats deal. The FTC had declared Whole Foods Market a monopoly and sued to block it.

I was sitting in my office that July morning in 2007 when Jim Sud came in with a concerned expression on his usually calm face and shut the door.

"John, I've got bad news." He placed a copy of the day's *Wall Street Journal* on my desk. There, on the front page, was the headline:

"Whole Foods Is Hot, Wild Oats a Dud—So Said 'Rahodeb'"

The article, which read like an exposé, described my online activity on the Yahoo message boards, which it reported had "come to light" as part of the FTC's antitrust suit. It insinuated that I'd essentially gone incognito in order to drive down the share price of Wild Oats ahead of our attempted acquisition.

This was a ludicrous idea for a couple of reasons. First, I'd stopped posting on the message boards a good six months before we made the offer for Wild Oats. And second, the very fact that I used a pseudonym—which the article seemed to consider proof of my ill intent—meant that my views had no more weight than any other random person (or dog, for that matter). Why would the posts of someone named Rahodeb have any meaningful influence on a company's stock price? But the media, which jumped on the story, seemed to want to have it both ways—to criticize me for being anonymous even as they also acted as if I'd been posting as myself when it came to the impact of those posts.

I hate bullies! And this felt like a classic bullying tactic. Images of junior high school came back to me. I'd been younger and smaller than most of my classmates, and I had a smart mouth on me that sometimes got the wrong kind of attention. There were a couple of big guys who'd corner me at lunch and declare, "John, it's time to go talk to the toilet."

Talking to the toilet meant getting my head dunked, repeatedly. The smell of industrial disinfectant and urine comes back to me even today. Every time, I'd try to joke my way out of it: "I really don't think the toilet has much to say today. We had a long talk just a couple of days ago." But they were twice my size and there was little I could do.

I was a big boy now, and I'd be damned if I was going to let the FTC make me talk to the toilet! I said as much, at great length, in a 14,000-word post on my CEO blog. First, I channeled all my debating skills into arguing point by point why the FTC was wrong about the merger being a monopoly and exposing what I saw as a misuse of taxpayer money by the government agency in mounting this clearly biased campaign against us. I pointed out that we now competed not just with other natural foods supermarkets but with mainstream grocers like Walmart, Kroger, Safeway, H-E-B, Albertsons, and many, many other chains, which made the monopoly claim absurd. Of course, if you reduce the playing field to be essentially the niche we created—"premium natural organic supermarkets," or PNOS as they put it (an acronym that sparked a lot of joking in our offices)—there isn't much competition. But even then, I argued, there was no barrier to entry for new businesses. The FTC was essentially trying to rewrite the rules and invent new categories to support its argument.

Then, I addressed the Rahodeb posts. I was adamant that I'd done nothing wrong. I'd never disclosed inside information. I explained that I'd posted for fun, that I'd never intended the views to be associated with me as CEO, and that as far as I could see, the FTC was simply using this as a way to attack and discredit me and embarrass the company.

Behind the scenes, some of my team and Board defended me, while others were sharply critical. But the six-month gap between my final post and the Wild Oats deal pretty clearly refuted what the media was claiming about my comments having any impact on the merger.

I hoped the matter would just fade away, but it quickly took a turn for the worse. The SEC announced that it was launching its own investigation: this one accusing me of insider trading. They claimed that my trades related to Wild Oats showed a pattern that indicated I'd had inside information about the company.

Again, the claim was ludicrous. For starters, I didn't possess any inside information about Wild Oats, because I didn't work for Wild Oats and had no access to any of their operational or financial information. While I had a fiduciary duty to Whole Foods shareholders as the CEO, I had no similar duties to Wild Oats' shareholders. The only information I had was my understanding of how the overall market was doing, based on what was happening at Whole Foods. There was nothing illegal about that.

But the bullying had gotten personal now. Clearly, some of these governmental bureaucrats had decided that publicly shaming and unseating the idealistic, outspoken CEO of a large public company would be a feather in their caps and might earn them a raise and a promotion.

Who was behind all this? I'll probably never know. But several people with reasons to resent me had known I was active on the Yahoo boards, and some of those people had been interviewed by the FTC as part of their antitrust suit.

The SEC told the Whole Foods Board they should fire me for "conduct unbecoming to a CEO." Under pressure from my Board, I issued a public apology, and the Board announced that they would launch an internal investigation.

Of course, I fully cooperated with both the SEC's and our Board's investigations. I did ask the Board to please read all my posts—not just the cherry-picked ones the media quoted to try to make me look bad. We printed out all 1,400 of Rahodeb's posts from the past eight years and put them in large binders for the Board. They weren't going to find anything in there except my love and passion for the company (and a few jokes about haircuts and recommendations for salad dressings). That kind of conviction is exactly what a company needs from its CEO. Only about 10 or so posts ever mentioned Wild Oats.

Honestly, I wasn't ashamed of my postings. I was proud of them because I thought I did an excellent job of making the case for how good a company Whole Foods is. Of course, I had learned an incredibly valuable lesson about being more careful on the internet—I'd had no idea my personal activity would put the company at risk, or that something that was just a game for me had been turned into something so nefarious. To their credit, the Board did not allow themselves to be bullied, and after reading all of the Yahoo posts, they decided to back me.

Meanwhile, at the end of August, we went to trial in the FTC antitrust case and won. The federal court agreed with our assessment that the market in which we were competing included larger supermarket chains.

We'd spent $30 million and an incalculable amount of our executives' time and energy defending the case, but we'd won. At least, for now.

The SEC insider trading investigation dragged on through the fall and into the spring, with numerous requests for my trading records and other related documents, with which we complied. Eventually, a hearing was held at the SEC offices in Dallas, Texas. There was an air of anticipation among the assembled governmental bureaucrats, several of whom had traveled down from DC just to watch me get my head handed to me.

Instead, the SEC's central claim quickly fell apart. Essentially, they were saying to me, "Mr. Mackey, there's a pattern to your trading. You always short Wild Oats just before Whole Foods Market announces its quarterly results."

My reply? "No, I don't."

They immediately claimed to have the records right in front of them. But what they had were only the records they'd asked for, which were the ones showing my Wild Oats trades on the eve of Whole Foods earnings announcements. What I was able to show them were numerous other times when I had not in fact shorted Wild Oats before our quarterly earnings announcement, and plenty of Wild Oats trades that happened at other times. As a result, over the next couple of weeks the case collapsed and I was never indicted.

That should have been the end of the story on both fronts. I should have been free to proceed with my life and my job, and Whole Foods should have been free to move ahead with the acquisition of Wild Oats. But no. The FTC announced that they were planning to appeal the antitrust verdict into their own "administrative court"—essentially a kangaroo court, from what I could see, because the FTC would be passing judgment on us in its own court! And they'd already decided we were monopolists! *The bullying continues,* I thought, infuriated.

I sat down with our lawyers to strategize. The conversation went something like this:

"What happens now?"

"Well, we go through another trial."

"And how much will that cost?"

"Another $30 million."

"And if we lose?"

"Win or lose, we end up going back to the federal court at a higher level. Oh, and that will cost another $30 million."

"And if we win in the federal court?"

"The FTC can go to the Supreme Court. And that will cost"—you guessed it—"another $30 million."

Four rounds: $120 million in total. Countless hours of my time and my team's time going down the proverbial toilet. And for what? So that we could buy a company with several bad locations we'd probably have to shut down anyway. Some of our Board members and E-Team thought we should just walk away. But still—I wanted to do the deal. Buying Wild Oats would increase our intellectual capital, bring in more talent, and shore up our competitive positioning with the big supermarket chains, which—as I'd argued to the FTC—were finally starting to catch on to the consumer desire for natural and organic foods.

Predictably, our lawyers, who were all former DOJ and FTC guys, counseled us to fight.

"That's easy for them to say!" I fumed. "They'll potentially get paid another $90 million!"

My libertarian friends, infuriated, also tried to convince me to fight. "Take these bogus claims all the way to the Supreme Court!" they said. "Then you can win and establish a new precedent that will greatly curb the power of these overregulating federal agencies."

"That's easy for you to say!" I told them. "It's not going to cost you $120 million and two years of your life." But I was sympathetic to their cause. I hated being railroaded into any kind of compromise when we hadn't done anything wrong in the first place.

A couple of days later, I was on a plane and began talking to the guy in the seat next to me. It turned out he was a lawyer. He'd heard all about the antitrust lawsuit and was a sympathetic audience, so I shared the story and my frustration. And he offered some sage advice: You're fighting this the wrong way. He said he'd introduce me to a friend of his, Lanny Davis, a well-known DC lawyer who was tight with the Clintons and had a reputation for being something of a maverick.

When I called Lanny, I liked him immediately. He was a character—no more fitting the stereotype of a lawyer than I fit the stereotype of a CEO. Politically, we didn't see eye to eye at all, but we had a similar love of friendly debate and enjoyed our good-natured sparring. He encouraged us to reach out to certain senators who oversee the FTC, pointing out how the FTC was abusing its regulatory power, and highlighting the unfairness of the FTC having its own administrative court. *I guess this is how the game is played in Washington,* I thought. Sure enough, when I met with several senators, all of whom had been unaware of this situation, they were angry to learn that we were being unfairly targeted in this way. They sent letters to the FTC that threatened to open up an investigation of the way the FTC was "weaponizing" its administrative court. And shortly thereafter, the FTC reached out to us with an olive branch of sorts, inviting us to meet and try to reach a mutually beneficial settlement.

The whole experience reinforced my libertarian values and my distrust of governmental overreach. But in the end, this particular saga worked out okay. We had to agree to put up for sale the Wild Oats brand and 32 of the Wild Oats stores, and the media trumpeted the FTC's victory in "forcing us to divest" so many assets. In reality, the majority of those stores were poor locations we didn't want anyway. The biggest loss was the old Alfalfa's store in Boulder. Once again, Whole Foods lost out on the chance to hang our name on Mark Retzloff and Hass Hassan's lovely downtown store. Ironically, Mark was able to buy the store back for only a few dollars because he was the only one who bid on the location. But we accepted the settlement, glad that our lives could return to normal.

You win some; you lose some. It's all part of the game. I don't like to lose, but losing is one of the best teachers we have in business and in life. I've learned many lessons over the years about how to play smarter and more skillfully. I've certainly learned how to be more judicious in my online postings (always under my real name and always with the assumption that they could end up on the front page of the *New York Times*). But I'm still highly competitive, and that's something I'll never apologize for. I still want to try to beat Will Paradise to the top of the mountain or in a pickleball match, even as we both get older and slower. I still love to play cards, to play board games of all kinds, to play sports, to debate, to trade stocks, and to compete passionately in business. All of it is fun, and all of it is very serious. That's just how I play the game of life.

Chapter 32

Rising Waters

I stepped up to the podium and looked out at the sea of capped-and-gowned students. It was a warm spring day in May 2008, and I was about to finally make my mother proud. Two decades after her death, I was doing what I'd told her I'd one day do—receiving an honorary PhD degree from Bentley University in Waltham, Massachusetts. I wondered if, in some other dimension, she was looking down and smiling.

I opened my commencement speech by telling the assembled graduates the story of my mother's deathbed request. "It has taken me 37 years, but, Mom and Dad—I finally have that college degree that you wanted me to get so badly!" I thanked the college for fulfilling my mother's last wish for me and then addressed the young people in the audience:

> Honor and appreciate your parents. No one will ever love you quite like your parents do, and although they have no doubt made plenty of mistakes in helping you to grow up, they've also done the very best job that they knew how to do. They've made far more sacrifices on your behalf than you will ever really know. Please forgive them for their mistakes and imperfections and fully love them and honor them while you can, because the simple truth is that you won't always have them with you as you move further along your life journey.

I felt those words deeply in my heart that day, as I wished my own parents could have been sitting there in the audience.

I went on to speak about the ideas that were dearest to my heart at that time—Conscious Capitalism. I challenged my audience to be part of this vision. "Who will create the conscious businesses of the 21st century—businesses that have deeper purpose and are managed consciously to create value on behalf of all their stakeholders? . . . Why not you?" I ended with a challenge: "What is your own heart calling you to do? Whatever it is, have the courage to follow it. The grand adventure of your own life now lies open before you. Seize the day!"

Rarely had I spoken so passionately and unselfconsciously as I did that summer afternoon. As I stepped away from the podium, to thunderous applause and the tossing of caps in the air, the minister who had given the prayer invocation came up to shake my hand.

"I think you should have gone into my line of work," she whispered, laughing.

I smiled, and simply said, "I think I already have."

This moment came back to me, a few months later, as I stared out at another audience—one that couldn't have looked more different. This was no happy crowd of cap-tossing graduates, but a sea of dark-suited, grim-faced investors. I was different too. In fact, the whole world had changed by late 2008. The days of spring sunshine and preaching the gospel of Conscious Capitalism had given way to a harsh winter of desperately trying to reassure frightened investors that we weren't all going down with the seemingly sinking economic ship. Lehman had failed, the banking system was on the brink. And Whole Foods had just had a very bad quarter.

I was under no illusion that the investors in the audience that day had any emotional attachment to our company. They cared about their own returns. And on this particular day, those returns were not looking very good at all—hence the expressions of doom and gloom on their faces. Their fear was palpable—you could hear it in people's voices and feel it in the air.

Virtually no business was spared from the ravages of the unfolding crisis. Like that hundred-year flood that had hit our store in its very first year, this was the kind of event you couldn't really be prepared for. Some companies were getting bailouts; others were being left to sink. It seemed like basically the government was trying to run the business world, which it really didn't understand very well. I found this frustrating and disturbing, and as a classical liberal who believes in free minds and free markets, I worried that little good would ultimately come from all this meddling.

When the economic flood hit, Whole Foods was in a better position than many—like that original store standing on its extra two-foot slab of concrete. Our same-store sales numbers, a key metric in retail, were still growing, though they'd fallen into single digits after a long run of double-digit growth. Our gross profit margins remained strong. However, our stock price took a serious hit. As the year went on, we watched it steadily fall, like a tire leaking air, until it was essentially flat. By the time I was talking to those investors, we were down a dizzying 90% from our 2007 peak!

This left us deeply vulnerable to shareholder activists—opportunistic investors who might buy up a large swath of the company and then impose their own agendas on us to make a quick profit. And the fact that our core business was still very profitable despite the crisis just made us more of a target. We needed to take action, fast. But how?

The answer came to me thanks to an old friend with whom I'd recently reconnected. Kip Tindell and I had been housemates at the University of Texas, sharing a house near campus with three other guys. Like me, he'd been on the very slow train through college, and like me, he never graduated. Kip was also the best damn poker player I'd ever met! He beat me consistently, and I never could quite figure out how he did it. I reluctantly had to conclude that he was just a better player than me.

After we both dropped out, we lost touch, but our lives continued on parallel paths. While Renee and I were launching Safer Way with just $45,000 from friends and family, Kip and his buddy Garrett Boone scraped together $35,000 to start their own retail business. Their original idea was to sell handmade furniture, but it evolved into a store selling storage and organization solutions. For every time we got asked the question "So you're selling hippie food?" they got asked, "So you're selling empty boxes?" But it turned out that a lot of people wanted those empty boxes, and The Container Store, like Whole Foods Market, became a market-leading business.

The parallels didn't stop there. Like me, Kip was passionate about his company's core values, about serving all stakeholders, and about the power of Conscious Capitalism. In fact, both of our companies had been featured in the 2007 book *Firms of Endearment*. It was that book, and the subsequent Conscious Capitalism gatherings that Raj Sisodia and I hosted, that reconnected me with Kip. I'd enjoyed getting to know him again, and in 2008, our Board invited him to become a Director for Whole Foods Market.

During one of our conversations that year, I shared our precarious position. "Our stock is trading so low that someone could literally buy the company with our own cash flow and fully pay for it in only three years." The Container Store was still private, so Kip was protected from the activist threat, but he told me he'd faced his own crisis a year earlier. He'd run into irreconcilable conflicts with his cofounder and needed someone to buy Boone out and take a majority stake in the company.

"You know, John," he said, "I went looking for a buyer who thought like I did. I didn't know if I'd find one that was culturally compatible, but I did! They give us total operational control and have been really supportive of our core values."

I was intrigued, though cautiously so, remembering my experience with the VC hitchhikers. I could see that Kip was enjoying his newfound wealth, freedom, and sole leadership, and he was hopeful—trusting that this partnership really could be everything it promised.

"It must be nice to be left alone to build value without the pressure of quarterly earnings announcements hanging over you," I acknowledged. "But how long will that last? Surely, sooner or later they'll want a return on their investment. What happens then? You might be forced to sell, or to IPO, or be forced out if you don't agree."

"Sure," Kip said. "But so far they've been great to work with. Honestly, John, I think you should talk to them. Maybe you can take on some friendly private equity money to shore up your balance sheet."

The private equity firm Kip was talking up was Leonard Green, a company that specialized in retail investing. They did indeed seem to be an unusual firm, and they were very interested in Whole Foods Market. Perhaps, I thought, these guys could be the equivalent of Mark Monroe, the friendly Austin banker who bailed us out after the flood. Maybe they really did recognize that we were a good business, with integrity, and worthy of a helping hand at a moment of need. We had a few conversations, and in November 2008, they invested $425 million in Whole Foods Market, in return for a 17% stake in the company. As part of the deal, they agreed to always vote with management for the first 18 months, essentially assuring us control of the company, at least for a time. Two of their partners, Jonathan Sokoloff and Jonathan Seiffer, joined our Board in December, along with Kip and Stephanie Kugelman, who had been a senior executive at a major advertising company.

We had barely announced their investment when the very thing we'd been afraid of came about. A shareholder activist, Ron Burkle, bought 15% of the company. But thanks to that quick deal with Leonard Green, Burkle was not well positioned to take over Whole Foods Market. Our stock started trading up, the company's prospects improved, and the economy began to slowly strengthen. The fears of the economy going into a depression began to subside.

That deal would turn out to be the best one Leonard Green ever did. By the time they sold their shares in 2011, just three years after investing, our stock had regained all of its previous value and much more, and they made about $4 billion. Ron Burkle also sold his entire position in less than a year with a very nice profit. If they had had faith in the company and stayed with us for a little longer, their profit would have been much greater, as Whole Foods continued its rise. In fact, I told the folks at Leonard Green as much. I'd noticed, looking back over the history of the company, that every six or seven years, Whole Foods seemed to go through a terrible crisis and then recover and go on to new heights. "You guys should stick with us for six years, and then sell," I joked with them. But what did I know?

As the slow-leaking tire of our stock price reinflated, Glenda, Walter, A.C., Jim, and I all breathed a sigh of relief. We'd made it through the worst economic crisis since the Great Depression without losing the company. We'd all added to our gray hairs, but we'd proven ourselves resilient and were well positioned for the decade ahead. Our new Board members were welcome additions to the team. The Leonard Green guys seemed to be what Kip had promised: smart, supportive, long-term thinkers who seemed sympathetic to our values.

In the executive suite, I made another important decision. In the years since I had promoted A.C. Gallo and Walter Robb, first as co-Chief Operating Officers and then as co-Presidents, Whole Foods had experienced its greatest success, and it was in no small part a result of the efforts of those two leaders. A.C. continued to shine at driving excellence in perishables—perhaps the single most important area of Whole Foods' consistent industry outperformance. Walter was a master of operations, especially when it came to store innovation and design, and simply the best retailer I have ever known. Both men presided over a remarkable era of business expansion at Whole Foods, and I was thrilled with their contributions.

At the same time, I knew that Walter was hungry for more. He was extremely hardworking, with a drive for excellence. He was also ambitious and restless. That's just the way he was wired. He certainly had the capacity to take on more responsibility—a fact that did not escape the notice of executive search firms and other companies, including Apple, who recognized and coveted his considerable talents, trying to hire him for their Apple Stores. Walter was good at the public side of leadership. He developed relationships with other business leaders. He seemed to be able to speak the language investors on Wall Street really liked. I was often surprised by his impressive connections in the political world. I had no doubt that sooner or later, someone would make him an offer to be CEO that would be difficult for him to turn down. As much as he loved Whole Foods, it would be easy for the grass to seem greener in another executive suite. I didn't want to lose Walter, but I worried it was only a matter of time.

The best way—perhaps the only way—to keep him, I thought, was to promote him and pay him more. There was just one problem with that strategy: There was only one job above his, and that was mine. I wasn't ready to give up being CEO just yet. But was I willing to share it? I began to consider offering Walter the position of co-CEO.

Before broaching the idea with the Board, I spoke to A.C. He and Walter had been such a good team, as co-Presidents, and now I was considering promoting one above the other. I wanted A.C. to understand my reasons for doing so and know that it wasn't a negative review of his performance; it was just the only way I could see of keeping Walter. A.C. would be sole President after the change. I'm sure he wasn't entirely happy with the decision, but A.C. is a true servant leader. After I finished explaining my rationale, he simply said, "John, if you think that's what's best for the company, then that's what we should do." I would hear later that Walter also consulted A.C. about taking on the new role, and the two longtime partners agreed that such an arrangement could still work for both of them and for the company.

Soon after that, with the consent of the board, we named Walter co-CEO. For the first time in the company's history, I was not its sole CEO.

Chapter 33

The Best of Both Worldviews

"The problem with socialism is that eventually you run out of other people's money."

I typed this favorite quote from former British Prime Minister Margaret Thatcher at the top of the page and smiled. *Perfect.* A quick check told me that the op-ed I was writing for the *Wall Street Journal* was within the word count, so after a final read through I clicked save, attached it to an email, and sent it off to the editor. I'd argued a persuasive and tightly reasoned case for something I cared deeply about: an alternative approach to the bureaucratically overreaching, enormously costly, socialistic mess that the government was currently proposing in the name of healthcare.

Now it just needed a title. I couldn't come up with anything clever, so I simply called it "Healthcare Reform." I was happy with my work. And what made me even happier was the fact that it was finished. It was almost midnight, and this was the final task on my list before I could unplug, both literally and metaphorically, for a couple of weeks of hiking on my favorite trail. John Mackey had signed his name on the op-ed and closed the laptop; Strider would wake up in the morning and shoulder his pack.

Starting in 2009, I planned to hike the Appalachian Trail again, in stretches lasting two or three weeks each time (a practice known among long-distance hikers as "section hiking" as opposed to "thru-hiking"). After the intensity of the past few years—the battles with the FTC and the SEC and the stresses of the financial crisis—I desperately needed the reprieves that each hike provided, even if they were relatively short. The section that awaited me in early August 2009 was a favorite: Maine's Hundred-Mile Wilderness. I'd started on the summit of Mount Katahdin, reversing the route that I'd hiked with Gorilla and The Princess seven years earlier to conclude our thru-hike. That night, in the hotel, I finished the last essential tasks, including my op-ed, knowing that I'd be completely without cell signal for the six days it would take me to traverse this remote and beautiful part of the trail. Such uninterrupted solitude was a luxury that was becoming increasingly rare in my busy, demanding schedule. I looked forward to having no public events, no flood of emails to deal with each morning, no analysts to answer to, no calls or meetings to attend, no op-eds to write. Just my two feet, the trail, a good audiobook, my hiking companions, and a few million bugs for company.

The week was everything I'd hoped for—physically challenging, mentally rejuvenating, emotionally and spiritually uplifting. It had been an unusually wet spring and summer, with 24 inches of rain in July alone, so the trail had knee-deep water and mud in many spots, making what is already a tough hike feel near impossible at times. Last time, we'd cruised through, fit and vital from months on the trail. Now, every step was soggy, slippery, and treacherous. And I wasn't in my best hiking shape. But it felt great to worry about how to keep my feet under me and how not to lose a shoe in the mud rather than quarterly income statements and investors' demands. As we approached the end of the Hundred-Mile Wilderness, I wished I could just keep hiking all the way to Georgia. Up ahead, signs on the trail indicated that we'd reached the road near Monson, which is considered to be the southern terminus of the Hundred-Mile Wilderness, our destination for the first week. As I stepped onto the road, it occurred to me that we were back in civilization, and I should probably turn on my phone.

Ping! Ping! Ping! I'd expected a flood of messages, but nothing could have prepared me for the firestorm that erupted on the small screen in my hand. "CALL WALTER IMMEDIATELY," was the first thing I saw.

While I'd been hiking in blissful disconnection from the outside world, the *Wall Street Journal* had published my op-ed under a new clickbait headline: "The Whole Foods Alternative to ObamaCare: Eight things we can do to improve health care without adding to the deficit." And it seemed like just about every journalist, analyst, investor, and customer had collectively freaked out. People were boycotting our stores. I was labeled extremist, elitist, ill informed, out of touch. My E-Team had been dealing with the fallout for several days at this point, with me unavailable for comment.

Once I'd gotten off the trail, opened my laptop, and held an emergency meeting with the E-Team, I sat down to reread the offending article. There was no question that the headline made the piece more inflammatory, immediately taking a political side that I hadn't intended to take quite so blatantly. That frustrated me. And opening with the Thatcher quote might have been unnecessarily provocative. But I stood by the points I'd made.

I'd never expected it to be so controversial for me to suggest that healthcare was not an intrinsic human right. I didn't mean that some people were more deserving of healthcare than others. I was simply arguing that it is better seen as a fundamental human need, similar to food and shelter. These are things we can't live without, but in our society we provide for these needs through voluntary and mutually beneficial market exchanges. I believe that's a better way to look at healthcare too. For some people, calling healthcare a "right" is an attempt to make an end run around the troublesome set of costs, considerations, complicated trade-offs, and concerns that we all must engage in around this issue, and already do. Ignoring those issues doesn't change them or magically generate new resources. It only makes us less able to consciously create and generate the best overall set of solutions.

Of course, we can acknowledge that the marketplace hasn't been working very well for many people due to all kinds of unhelpful regulation, lack of cost transparency, and special interests. A large part of my op-ed had been devoted to laying out ways in which we could help the market work better. But when we declare something a "right," we stop seeing it as primarily an individual responsibility and start expecting someone else, usually the government, to give it to us, free of charge. The truth is we're just paying in a different way. That approach, from my perspective, is problematic.

It's also problematic that our public discourse denies the shocking fact that so many of our healthcare problems are self-inflicted, largely through poor diet and lifestyle choices. I'd stated this clearly and given many examples of what we'd done and were doing at Whole Foods Market to incentivize team members to improve their health and to give them options about the healthcare benefits they received. I was passionate about these programs, which had been inspired by the changes I'd made in my own diet over the past few years as I learned more about the extraordinary power of a whole foods, plant-based diet to prevent and even reverse chronic disease.

As I read the outraged responses to my op-ed, I realized that what was happening here was about much more than healthcare and policy differences. It had triggered something deeper, something that didn't answer to rational debate. The right to healthcare was an article of faith for most progressive Americans. Questioning it was akin to blasphemy. These people—many of whom were our customers—felt a sense of personal and ideological betrayal as they read my words. They'd read between the lines of my op-ed and taken it as an attack on the entire progressive worldview—a worldview that many of them held dear and that they might have assumed that I shared. Indeed, so many things about Whole Foods tended to sync up well with the values of our customers that we were often seen as synonymous with—even a symbol of—progressive politics. But it was more complex than that. And I was certainly more complex than that.

For a while now, I'd been aware that it was hard for people to fit me into their narrow political and ideological boxes. I sold natural foods, practiced meditation, espoused veganism, and wore hiking shorts to work. I believed business should be informed by love, serve a higher purpose, and benefit all stakeholders. And yet, I pushed back against compulsive unionization. I defended capitalism and free markets. I argued for freedom of thought and personal responsibility. And, as I'd made clear in this recent op-ed, I resisted anything that resulted in more governmental controls and subsidies and moved us away from the natural discipline and innovation of free markets toward the stultifying inefficiencies of socialism.

In my heart and mind, these values and positions weren't contradictory. They came together in Conscious Capitalism, the philosophy that guided my life and work. But sometimes I wondered if the more progressive folks among our customers and the general public only heard the "conscious" part of that term and conveniently missed the "capitalism." They wanted to see Whole Foods Market as another of the trendy social enterprises of the day, businesses that put purpose and public good above profits. That wasn't who we were. Yes, we had a higher purpose, and at the same time, we saw capitalism—including profit—as the engine that fueled our ability to fulfill that purpose. Competing and winning in the marketplace wasn't just a necessary evil; it was part of what we were here to do. And as a committed capitalist myself, I abhorred government attempts to overly control and manipulate that marketplace: a position that put me in direct opposition with the views of many of Whole Foods' customers. This had been true for a long time, but it seemed like a lot of people only realized it when they read that 2009 op-ed.

I'd never made a secret of who I was and what I believed. And yet now I—and Whole Foods Market by association—was being publicly tarred and feathered for not toeing a party line I'd never espoused in the first place. And my positions, which grew out of my deep care for the health of my fellow Americans, were being interpreted as callous and offensive. It's one thing to have people disagree with you—I'm quite comfortable with that. But it's another thing altogether to have people misunderstand and misinterpret your motives simply because you see the world differently than they do. That hurts. No matter what I said, people believed what they wanted to believe. In the aftermath of the op-ed, I felt mired in public hatred that was as thick and treacherous as the mud I'd left behind on the trail. People had thought I was in one tribal box; now they were determined to put me in a different one, which I also didn't fit into. Feeling those narrow sidewalls press against my consciousness only made me want to escape such rigid ideological boxes altogether!

The Board received thousands of letters, emails, and texts demanding that I be fired. The boycotts spread around the country, with boycott groups on social media attracting tens of thousands of members. At the same time, "buycotts" by people who supported my values also happened throughout the US. I posted a response to the controversy on my CEO Blog, which attracted thousands of comments—both positive and negative. Some praised me as a true patriot and suggested I run for President. Others declared me a traitor to the people who'd made Whole Foods successful. The Board told me in no uncertain terms that I needed to stop writing op-eds unless they were Board-approved. I hated this! Of course, the last thing I wanted to do was hurt Whole Foods by expressing my personal views, but it felt unfair that I had no platform to explain my thinking more fully.

Thankfully, while the media furor over the boycotts was frustrating, it didn't materially hurt the company. Sales actually increased. The controversy slowly faded. Over the next few years, Whole Foods Market went from strength to strength. I continued to marvel at how we were welcomed even in communities that I once would have thought to be unsuited to our business. I remembered Walter, during our post-9/11 road trip, laughing at the notion of a Whole Foods in Iowa. Well, a little more than a decade later, we'd just opened our first store in Des Moines. During our IPO back in 1992, I'd confidently told investors that I believed someday Whole Foods would have 100 stores and that would pretty much saturate the entire United States market. As our store count approached four times that in 2014, serving seven million customers per week, I looked back on that prediction and laughed. Sometimes it's great to be wrong.

Our new locations weren't just enclaves of the wealthy, progressive elite. In fact, in 2009 we'd made a decision, championed by Walter, to begin the process of creating a store in Detroit, a city plagued by poverty, crime, and urban blight, and teetering on the edge of bankruptcy. It didn't check any of the boxes the Real Estate Committee typically looked to check. It was a place we'd never have even considered just a few years earlier. Walter pushed for it, over the objections of some of the E-Team. I backed him, partially because I could see how excited he was about the opportunity. For one, it went against criticisms that had dogged us in recent years—accusations of elitism. Walter saw the store as a means to bridge the gap between the rich and poor when it came to food access. It was also, to my mind, an opportunity to prove what I'd claimed in that op-ed: that health outcomes could be improved through access to and education about healthier food choices.

We took care to work closely with city leaders and local community organizations and churches as we designed and built the store. We added an entire educational element to our presence in the community—classes on how to shop and cook healthy foods—that helped build a positive relationship with locals. When the store opened, on June 5, 2012, exceeding all expectations, other similarly troubled cities quickly took note. Rahm Emanuel, then mayor of Chicago, and Cory Booker, then mayor of Newark, personally asked Whole Foods to consider expanding to their municipalities as well, and we began to make plans to do so (with mixed results over the years ahead, including a failed store in Chicago's Englewood neighborhood). It felt like the whole country had opened up to us. We could grow beyond anything we'd considered possible and make a real impact in cities where change was desperately needed. We set ourselves an ambitious goal: to grow from 400 to 1,200 stores in the years ahead.

This positive momentum continued to boost the company's fortunes. Our total stock market capitalization had grown from $1.3 billion in November 2008 to $24 billion in October 2013—an 18X increase in only five years! Our stock price hit an all-time split-adjusted high of $65 as 2013 came to an end, and *Fortune* published a cover story a few months later with the headline: "How Whole Foods Is Taking Over America." Coverage of the Detroit store was largely positive. The progressive media loved Whole Foods again, even if they didn't love its CEO. In retrospect, this cover story was probably a classic contrarian indicator for the business.

At the same time, I was enjoying a different kind of coverage myself for once. In January 2013 I'd published my first book, coauthored with my good friend, Babson professor Raj Sisodia. Entitled *Conscious Capitalism: Liberating the Heroic Spirit of Business,* it crystallized and expanded upon the philosophy I'd been slowly developing ever since I became an entrepreneur. I truly hoped that when people read the book, they'd understand what made me tick. They might not agree with it, but my intent was that the logic of our argument would be undeniable. When the book launched and sold out within a few days, requiring a new print run, I was thrilled. Maybe the tide was turning. Maybe there was room in American culture for an independent thinker who hated to be put in an ideological box and didn't subscribe to progressive articles of faith. Or maybe not. Maybe people were once again reading the "conscious" and skipping the "capitalism."

My own thinking about the relationship between "conscious" and "capitalism" was helped along by my continued reading in the field of Integral Philosophy. Philosopher Ken Wilber's evolutionary approach to history and psychology (and plenty of other fields) was still a source of inspiration. I also learned a great deal from the work of mid-20th-century social psychologist Clare Graves, whose work was later adapted into color-coded cultural stages of Spiral Dynamics. Books like *Integral Consciousness and the Future of Evolution* by philosopher Steve McIntosh and *Evolutionaries* by journalist Carter Phipps added to my conviction that it's not just the outer world that is evolving but the inner universe of consciousness and culture as well. These thinkers pointed out that this inner domain is structured by foundational worldviews that, in turn, influence the values and ideals we express in our own lives. They suggested that it was possible to inhabit a new type of integrative or "integral" perspective, one that embraces the healthy, underlying truths inherent in other worldviews, without falling prey to narrow ideology or fundamentalism.

For example, the word "conscious" was very much associated with a progressive worldview, held by Paul Ray's "cultural creatives," steeped in the countercultural values incubated in the 1960s. The word "capitalism," however, was associated with a worldview often referred to as "modernism"—the rational values of liberalism, science, and secularism that were incubated in the Enlightenment and Industrial Revolution. My problem was that I loved, and lived, elements of both these worldviews. I had close friends who identified with each. Paul Ray had been right—I wasn't exactly a cultural creative. But I wasn't exactly a modernist either! Integral Philosophy showed me that I need not be defined or constrained by only one of these sets of values. In this way, Conscious Capitalism was an "integral" statement, intended to synthesize the best of both worldviews.

As a result of this exploration, I felt like I had finally found an intellectual home. In its spacious halls, I could be a rationalist *and* a mystic. I could champion free markets *and* meditation. My veganism could live alongside my critique of big government. It was big enough to contain all of me. *Conscious Capitalism* became an important artifact to express that new understanding—not just of business but of myself.

If imitation is the sincerest form of flattery, Whole Foods had a lot of admirers in the 2010s. Over the past few years, our tremendous growth, as well as our penetration into new markets, had alerted conventional grocers to the opportunity represented by the cultural shift toward healthier eating. It had taken years, even decades, for them to start catching up with our market innovations, but now that significant gap was finally beginning to shrink. This was observable in several key changes you could see if you walked into any conventional grocery store in that era. Indeed, when I visited a new Kroger, Albertsons, or H-E-B, I was quite taken aback at what I found.

First, you could see it in the quality of the stores and the range of products they offered. No longer were natural and organic products consigned to only a shelf or two. Suddenly they were everywhere. Since the turn of the millennium, Walmart and then Costco had become major players in groceries, including organics, gobbling up market share and heavily impacting the conventional stores. In response, other supermarket competitors like Kroger, Albertsons, Wegmans, and H-E-B had started to compete by upgrading their offerings and adding more organics (including private-label organic brands, inspired by Trader Joe's). They also took cues from Whole Foods when it came to improving the look and feel of their stores and invested considerably more in store design than they'd ever done before. Hand-lettered signage and abundant, beautifully displayed, unwrapped produce became increasingly common. I would still take the Whole Foods Market experience above Kroger any day, but even I could see that the chasm of difference between us was no longer so wide. In investment terms, the "moat" that separated us from our competitors was being filled in.

The second dynamic in the shifting competitive landscape had to do with price. Other supermarket chains had discovered that it was easier to focus on the higher-quality end of the market and try to appeal to Whole Foods customers while undercutting our prices than it was to focus on the lower-quality end and try to compete with Walmart and Costco on price alone. This further encouraged them to encroach on our market share. What I'd known to be true for many years—that we were competing not just with other natural foods stores but with conventional grocery stores—was now clearly evident. We hadn't really been alone in our niche; we'd just been ahead of the cultural curve. Now, we had company—a lot of company, in fact!

I had very mixed feelings about this shift in the competitive landscape. On the one hand, Whole Foods Market's higher purpose was "to nourish people and the planet." If we were doing that by inspiring the whole market to change, we were fulfilling our higher purpose! As I look back at our legacy, I'm as proud of the shift that took place in the entire market as I am of the achievements in our particular corner of that market.

But of course, on the other hand, increased competition from conventional grocers wasn't great for our business. We were at risk, in a very real sense, of becoming victims of our own success. As Walmart, Kroger, Wegmans, and H-E-B began to encroach on our market share, I thought back wryly to the FTC's claims just a few years earlier when they'd been trying to block the Wild Oats deal. *How's that monopoly looking now?*

Chapter 34

Narrative Fallacies

Absentee . . . Petulant . . . Disruptive . . . Undermining . . . Disconnected from reality . . . A problem for the company and the leadership team.

I finished the email and stared at the screen in disbelief, each of those words and phrases reverberating in my mind. The person referred to was me. The company mentioned was Whole Foods. And according to the author of this email, Whole Foods was in "disarray" as a result of this litany of personal failings on the part of its leader.

My leadership has been criticized plenty of times in my life, but rarely so stridently by someone I barely knew and who had no direct involvement or significant investment in the company. In fact, I had met the author of this email just once, and very briefly. It would have been easy to dismiss the criticisms as uninformed and illegitimate, except that they came from the highly respected leader of one of America's most prominent companies. Howard Schultz, CEO of Starbucks, had sent me this unprompted personal performance review.

In addition to berating me for the troubles in our business, Schultz made clear his true intention: He believed it was time for me to step down and make Walter the sole CEO. He claimed that I was incapable of leading the company in its current phase. Never mind the 36 years of growth and success that had unfolded under my leadership. Once again, someone was claiming I was too absent and too distracted to lead the company. I had a moment of déjà vu. Was this 1984? Or 1998? Or 2001? No, it was May 14, 2014. Same song, new decade.

The timing was no accident—just a few days after our second quarter earnings call. Admittedly, it had been a difficult one. The company had been going from success to more success for many, many years. Yes, there had been challenging periods, like the financial crisis. But generally, the steady expansion of Whole Foods across the country, with enviable profits and fantastic sales per square foot—the best of all public food retailers—was ongoing. However, the market winds that had been at our back for years had finally shifted, largely as a consequence of our success.

To put things in perspective, it's not like we were losing money or our business was declining. We still had fantastic growth, good margins, market-leading sales per square foot, and we were highly profitable. We were still an excellent growth story by most metrics. But our "comps" or "same store sales" (a key retail metric showing how much a particular store has grown its sales in comparison to the previous year) were no longer as impressive. This wasn't too surprising. Comps look impressive when you start with fairly low sales and then grow rapidly for several consecutive years. As our company became better known, our new stores would open with much higher sales, so the year-over-year comparative growth wasn't as dramatic. And once existing stores reached a certain level, their growth rate slowed.

Wall Street is a "what have you done for me lately" kind of place. When you've been overperforming for years, even a mild wobble seems like a crisis—at least to folks like the analysts on our recent quarterly earnings call. They wanted to put us on notice that we needed to step up—and their message was reinforced by the stock price, which tumbled 14% that day. As one analyst put it: "Does Whole Foods management appreciate that the world has changed?"

Now, on top of the doom-and-gloom narratives, I had Howard Schultz's perplexing email to deal with as well. How exactly should I respond to this unsolicited and inappropriate message? Putting aside whether his claims were remotely accurate, why did Howard think he knew enough about what went on at Whole Foods to even have an opinion on such matters, and what right did he have to communicate it in such forceful terms? I noted that while the email was addressed to me, Howard also copied Board member Jon Sokoloff, one of the Leonard Green partners, on the email. When the private equity firm had cashed out, the two Jonathans—Sokoloff and Seiffer—had stayed on our Board. In general, I'd valued their contributions and Sokoloff and I got along fine, or so it seemed to me. But seeing his name in the cc field sparked concerns. Was he somehow involved with Howard?

Howard explicitly stated in the email that Walter had no idea he was writing the email and wouldn't approve if he did. However, the only connection I had to Schultz was through Walter. They had been close friends for several years. In fact, the only time I'd met Howard had been at Walter's 60th birthday party, along with a host of celebrities, politicians, and other movers and shakers. In my brief conversation with Howard at the party, I told him how much I respected his business acumen and his extraordinary leadership run at Starbucks. In light of this email, perhaps I needed to reconsider my opinion of the man! I just hoped I didn't need to reconsider my opinion of my co-CEO as well. Had Walter had conversations with Howard about my leadership? Were the accusations in the email reflective of those conversations? And what did this mean about my relationship with Walter going forward?

It wasn't surprising to me to think that Walter might have frustrations, and that he occasionally needed to vent to someone outside the company. Being co-CEOs isn't easy, and we'd had our share of differences. But I'd believed these to be primarily about strategy and leadership style. We had different approaches to Wall Street: Walter was inclined to be very optimistic about the future, which would raise the projections of the analysts covering our company's earnings, and then he would pressure our operations management to meet those projections. In contrast, I preferred to underpromise about the future and work to overdeliver. We also thought differently about our future growth: I wanted to grow only as fast as we could find outstanding locations, while Walter was always pushing for faster growth. There were numerous other issues we didn't agree about as well. I knew Walter was ambitious and saw himself as my eventual successor when I decided to retire. But none of this had prepared me for another outright challenge to my leadership. Was that what this email represented? Or had Walter just spoken a little too freely to his friend Howard, prompting Howard to take steps Walter had never intended?

I decided to forward the message to the entire E-Team, including Walter. Openness with my team is my policy in moments like this. I prefaced the message with a brief note:

"FYI—I'm in total shock about this email! I've met and talked to Howard Schultz exactly one time in my life—at Walter's 60th birthday party last fall... I'm at a loss for words and definitely not sure what to do."

I then picked up the phone and called Walter directly. He was just pulling out of the Lamar store parking lot in Austin. I asked if he had seen the email, and he responded that he had not. I quickly explained what Howard had written, and he took a moment to look it over on his phone. When he finished, he sounded a bit shocked.

"John, I want you to know that I had no idea that Howard was going to write this. And I don't agree with him. He was out of line."

"Okay, Walter." I wanted to believe him, but I still had questions. "If that is true, then why did he write me the email? How would he know anything that is going on at Whole Foods? He isn't on our Board. He doesn't work for the company. He is not a major investor. Where did it come from?"

"John, I really don't know," he protested. "But it didn't come from me. It isn't accurate and I'm almost as upset about it as you are."

"Okay, if you say so, I believe you." I took a deep breath and tried to calm myself. "Look, Walter, I know we've had our differences, and we should sit down and talk about those at an appropriate time, if we need to. And I understand that we all occasionally need a sympathetic ear. We need to blow off steam and voice our frustrations. I get it. But for god's sake, please, be careful who you choose to vent to!"

"I hear you, John, and I'm sorry. But again, I want you to know I had nothing to do with the email." And then he paused and added, "If you think I'm working behind your back, you can ask me to resign, and I will do that. I know it's important that there is trust between us."

Next, I called Jon Sokoloff. He told me that he didn't know Howard particularly well and that he had no idea why he had been copied on the email. He also condemned the letter and said it never should have been sent. Nevertheless, the question remained—why did Howard copy him?

After talking to Sokoloff, I took the next logical step and called Howard Schultz directly. It wasn't a conversation I was looking forward to, but it had to happen, nonetheless. I didn't have the energy for many pleasantries, so I got right to the point.

"Howard, we need to talk about this letter. You speak about Whole Foods as if you have inside knowledge of the workings of the company. But you're not on our Board. You're not a major shareholder. You haven't worked at the company. You're close friends with Walter. What am I supposed to believe here? The logical conclusion is that this must have come from Walter, at least to some degree. How am I supposed to relate to that knowledge? What were you thinking? By writing this letter, you have done incalculable damage to my relationship with Walter by undermining trust between us."

"No, John," Howard insisted, "this wasn't Walter. He had nothing to do with this. He would be mad at me if he knew."

"Well, first, he does know. I sent your letter to our entire E-Team! But if Walter's not behind this, how could you possibly have such confidence about what you believe is going on at Whole Foods?"

Howard was cagey. "I just know. People tell me things. I have connections."

"*People?* I mean, if those people aren't involved in the company, it's just gossip and hearsay. But if they are involved in the company, that's problematic. Again, *who* are we talking about?"

"I'm sorry, I can't tell you."

I tried another tack. "Why did you copy Jon Sokoloff on the email and no one else?"

Howard continued to dodge. "I know Jon is on the Board and I don't know any of the other directors. I thought he should know how I feel."

The rest of the conversation continued in the same vein. Finally, I told him as politely as I could what I thought about the whole thing.

"Look, Howard, you really don't know what you are talking about concerning Whole Foods. You don't know me at all, and your opinions about me aren't based on any direct experience with me—just hearsay from other people. Let's make a deal going forward. I'll stay out of Starbucks' business. And you stay out of Whole Foods' business."

I got off the phone frustrated. The most charitable explanation I could come up with was that Walter had just been venting—too much and too often—to his friend Howard, and he had inadvertently inspired Howard to write that letter. It was an egregious mistake, yes, but still an honest one. I decided to adopt this narrative until another one became more likely. At least it was preferable to the idea that there was anything more nefarious going on.

Next time I was in Los Angeles, I made sure to connect with Sokoloff. I spoke briefly about the letter and about the conversations between Walter and me. I wanted to make sure he knew that we were still a united leadership team. He listened but didn't say much, and soon the conversation turned to our broader competitive position. He had another suggestion to make.

"You know, John, we could consider going private. The public markets are not the easiest place to execute a turnaround. Whole Foods has a balance sheet that would easily support it. I promise we could work out the financing."

I knew what that meant. Lots and lots of debt. A "going private" deal would mean that a financial entity (like Leonard Green) would put up some of the capital, maybe a billion dollars or so. Then they would borrow the remaining amount from investment banks, such as Goldman Sachs, Morgan Stanley, and Chase. This would function as a bridge loan. Once the transaction was completed and they officially owned the company, they would borrow billions in long-term debt using Whole Foods' balance sheet to guarantee the loan. They would then pay back the bridge loan and use the cash flow of Whole Foods to service the debt. Because Whole Foods had very little debt on its balance sheet and very strong cash flow, such a transaction had even more appeal. Then, of course, a few years later when the time was ripe, they would seek to take the company public again at a higher valuation, profiting off the resulting gain in valuation.

There was significant risk involved in such a strategy. If Whole Foods had a couple of bad years and was unable to service the massive debt it had taken on, then we would be risking bankruptcy. That risk had to be weighed against the potential billions that the private equity firms could make if the company was able to significantly increase its valuation. CEOs who led such private companies were often lavishly rewarded, with generous pay and stock options, but this wasn't a factor for me, given my commitment to my $1 salary and not taking stock options. There were other enticing aspects to going private as well—one temporarily escapes the constant pressure to report rising quarterly earnings and the ever-intrusive nature of market expectations.

The idea of having more time to execute a long-term strategy, refashion and restructure the company out of the public limelight, was appealing. Walter and I had discussed the pros and cons of this idea before, and in those conversations, he'd agreed with me that it was not a good option. I worried that putting that much debt on our books would endanger the company. Not to mention that the private equity firms would control the company, and their purposes would not be well aligned with ours. I remembered how eager I was to get the venture capitalist hitchhikers out of the Whole Foods car before they took our company over. I was not eager to invite new private-equity hitchhikers back into the car, especially since this time they would have control of the car. My ability to protect Whole Foods at that point would be reduced significantly.

"That's an interesting idea," I told Sokoloff. "But I don't think it's right for Whole Foods Market right now. Putting that much debt on our books is something I'm very hesitant to do. For now, I think we're okay as a public company."

Sokoloff nodded and didn't push it.

I put Schultz's letter and my nagging questions about who was behind it out of my mind for the moment. There was plenty else to worry about. Top of my mind was a growing conviction that we as a company had allowed ourselves to become complacent over the years when our stock price was flying high, and as a result, we had made a significant strategic error—one that was now difficult to reverse.

We were still fighting the public perception that our prices were too high, reflected in the frustrating label "Whole Paycheck," which we just couldn't seem to shake. We'd always prided ourselves on our high standards and been confident that our core customer base was willing to pay a little more for the assurance that their purchases were organic, sustainable, humane, and better quality. They were also willing to pay a little more for the uplifting experience of shopping in our beautiful stores and being served by enthusiastic, happy team members. This had been one of the keys to our success—upending the traditional price-dominated approach to competing in the low-margin grocery business. Our customers allowed us more price leeway and higher margins to invest in all the things that they loved about our stores.

However, there were plenty of people who resented our higher prices. It seemed like every other day someone would tell me the "Whole Paycheck" joke as if I'd never heard it before. I'd roll my eyes and launch into my well-practiced refutations, explaining all the benefits our customers were getting when they paid our prices. But when the financial crisis hit in 2008, even our core customers began to feel the pinch and cut back. In response, we began to offer more discounts, add more value-focused brands, and highlight these items in our advertising. But looking back, it was increasingly clear to me that we didn't do enough.

As the conventional grocery stores began to offer similar products at lower prices, the perception of Whole Foods as overpriced only intensified. In 2014, we desperately needed to lower our prices to remain competitive, but to do that would significantly impact our short-term profitability, which would further depress our stock price. It was now clear that we had missed a wonderful opportunity to lower prices—right after the financial crisis back in 2008 began to improve. We could easily have done so, at the end of that economic downturn, without triggering massive reactions on Wall Street. Our margins would have compressed, yes, but few would have noticed—or cared. Lowering prices would have slowed the meteoric rise in our stock price coming out of the recession, but it would have positioned the company for greater success over the long term.

The problem with high profit margins is that everyone gets hooked on them. Each business unit wants to keep its profits up. Store Team Leaders don't want to take the sales hit. Senior executives don't want to compromise overall profitability, which would lower their annual bonuses and the value of their stock options. I pushed the pricing issue in E-Team meetings, but it seemed to only go so far. I could never build a consensus within the leadership team to do it over a sustained period.

Our struggles with pricing over the preceding several years reflected the challenge any public company faces when it comes to balancing the short-term interests of Wall Street with the long-term interests of the business and its customers. For a public company, every quarter looms large. When you make your numbers, the bar is now set higher for the next, like an ever-increasing high jump you must keep clearing. When outperformance becomes expected, anything less is particularly painful. Narratives in the media can change overnight. Suddenly, "brilliant" and "effective" executives are "out of touch" and "incapable." Pressure builds from investors, board members, and analysts.

After decades of experiencing these highs and lows for myself, I understood why Ben Graham and Warren Buffett loved the parable of "Mr. Market," a kind of manic-depressive business partner who comes running in with a new price for the company every day. For many years, Mr. Market loved us and would buy our stock at virtually any price; now he seemed to think we were heading toward disaster and would sell our stock at virtually any price. One day he saw me as a visionary, giving me credit for brilliant foresight when it came to the natural and organic foods trend. The next day he saw me as the village idiot, ranting about vegan diets and Conscious Capitalism. I'd taken Buffett's advice to heart over the years and done my best not to give too much credence or emotional weight to the ramblings of Mr. Market.

By 2014, however, I had to concede that it was more than just ramblings. There was no getting around the fact that "the world had changed" as that analyst bluntly, but truthfully, stated in our earnings call. In the midst of all this, the idea of lowering prices significantly, and reducing our enviable margins, became an even tougher proposition. But our failure to do so was about to set us up for a plot twist that none of us anticipated.

It began with the kind of bureaucratic shakedown that is all too common in heavily regulated states—in this case, California. California has made a fine art of extracting money from businesses through its regulatory functions, as I learned the hard way in 2014, when I was informed that we needed to pay $800,000 to settle the charge that we were failing to accurately charge customers for our weighed and measured prepared food.

Weights and measures are routinely inspected in grocery stores to ensure that customers are being fairly charged for the items they buy that have been weighed, packaged, and priced by team members. Take, for example, a container of precut fruit or a wedge of cheese, individually labeled and priced according to weight. Some occasional small degree of inaccuracy is unavoidable, usually due to packaging tare weight calculations, but Whole Foods Market had always taken great care to be as accurate as possible. This accusation from the state of California came as a shock. I tried to get more clarity from the E-Team.

"Are they saying we intentionally overcharged people?"

"Not exactly," Walter said. "An inspector found what they call 'widespread pricing violations' in their investigation. We aren't the only supermarket they fined. And of course, the media has already jumped on it."

"Okay, but you could find that at any grocery store!" I protested. "Everyone makes mistakes—and we're talking pennies, right?" They nodded. "The systems just aren't designed to be perfectly accurate every time, and it is just as likely that a customer is slightly undercharged as she is overcharged."

"Actually, there were more undercharges than overcharges," Walter replied. "Overall, our customers were gaining, not losing. For some reason, that doesn't feature in their press release."

I considered this basically governmental extortion, but I eventually accepted our fate. We had little option but to pay the fine and move forward. We agreed to conduct random audits of our stores and take steps to ensure better accuracy—something I supported. Still, it felt performative. We could have fought the charges, but that would have cost the company in other ways, prolonging the entire saga and inviting more negative media coverage. I consoled myself that this was simply the cost of doing business in California. But I chafed against the further hit to our reputation.

The problem with narratives is that they're self-reinforcing. "As if Whole Foods wasn't expensive enough . . ." began one typical story at the time. The problem with shakedowns is that they rarely end with one payment. In 2015, it happened again, this time in New York City. And while there was no proof that one led to the other, it wasn't hard to imagine that some ambitious bureaucrat in the Big Apple took notice of the $800,000 fine we'd paid and wondered if they could get a similar result.

In June 2015, the New York City Commissioner on Consumer Affairs announced the results of an investigation uncovering what it called "systematic overcharging for pre-packaged foods." She added, "Our inspectors tell me this is the worst case of mislabeling they have seen in their careers." Note the term "mislabeling," not "overpricing." As with California, we believed that more of the mislabeling benefited customers, which clearly undercut the claim that it was systematic. But no one really cared about that. The media loved it. Headlines proliferated.

Whole Foods Accused of Massive Overcharging . . . Whole Foods Resurrects the Thumb on the Scale Trick . . . Whole Foods Under Fire for Overcharging Customers . . . Whole Foods Caught Systematically Overcharging Customers . . .

Sales immediately dived, and not just in New York City. The negative press about this went national. Walter and I made a joint public statement, trying to address the fallout as best we could, but it only served to extend the news cycle. The whole idea was ludicrous—that we sat around in the executive offices at Whole Foods Market and worked out ways to pocket a few extra cents per transaction by defrauding our customers through a nefarious weights-and-measures scheme. But to a media and a public already sold on the narrative that we were greedy and overpriced, it didn't seem like such a leap.

As 2015 drew to a close, I felt tangled in a web of other people's stories—about me, about the company, about our future, our value, our integrity, and our intentions. None of these narratives reflected the person I knew myself to be or the company I led. Schultz's misplaced accusations mingled with the media's gleeful headlines as I lay awake at night. The bureaucrats' carefully worded reports echoed in my head, punctuated by exhortations to go private and Wall Street's pessimistic future projections. None of these stories had a happy ending. None of them accounted for the resilience, commitment, and creativity of our company and our team. None of them took into consideration how many times we'd faced challenges and emerged stronger and better positioned to serve our stakeholders. And yet these were the stories people were listening to. And as they listened, they imagined a troubled future for my entrepreneurial offspring.

These narratives mattered. They would help determine the options we would have to reinvent our future on our own terms. I could feel those windows of possibility narrowing. Could we take back control of the narrative before it was too late?

Chapter 35

A Man of His Word

"A *what?*" I asked.

"A produce butcher."

I'm sure the expression on my face was as bemused as our first landlord's had been when I told him I was creating a natural foods supermarket.

I glanced at Walter, who was sitting beside me and nodding enthusiastically. It was spring 2016, and we were being briefed on plans for one of our most ambitious stores yet, at a prime location opposite New York City's Bryant Park, due to open early the following year. In addition to all our usual departments, this store would have multiple prepared food outlets and a sit-down seafood-focused bar with menu items by renowned chef Daniel Boulud, as well as a couple of dozen beers on tap, wine, and cocktails. The team had formed partnerships with numerous artisanal food producers, and customers would be able to watch their own tahini being milled, choose from eight varieties of halva, or enjoy a selection of premium avocado toasts. And, as I had just been informed, the store would feature a produce butcher, who, as the team now hastened to explain, would take any produce item a customer chose and cut it to their desired specifications—sliced, diced, julienned, chopped, or grated—for a small additional fee per pound.

I laughed out loud, impressed and still more than a little bemused by this exuberant vision. I'd thought we hit "peak foodie" with the chocolate-enrobing station we'd featured at the Lamar flagship store, where customers could have anything dipped in chocolate. Strawberries? Of course. But also, any other item from our produce section or beyond. Once, according to company legend, a customer enrobed a piece of salmon. It certainly wasn't what I'd have dreamed up for a new store, but I appreciated the creativity and passion of the team, including Walter, whose retail genius I'd always trusted implicitly.

There was no question that the folks working on Bryant Park represented the "foodie" side of our company culture. They wanted to surprise and delight customers with high-quality, carefully curated gourmet foods from around the world. They saw Whole Foods as a kind of European market, bursting with epicurean delicacies. And we were that—to a point. But there was always a tension within the company between the foodie cohort and the health-conscious cohort, who focused on quality and simplicity, catering to all the specialty diets that our customers followed, whether they be vegan, paleo, gluten free, coconut everything, or whatever the latest diet bestseller was recommending. While I raised my eyebrows at fad diets, I leaned heavily toward a health-conscious approach to food.

This internal divide went back to the very early days of the company. Safer Way had been firmly on the health side, as had Clarksville, but the foodies joined Whole Foods with some of our earliest acquisitions, including Lex Alexander and Peter Roy. Chris Hitt was also in this camp. In the nineties, their love of fine food and wine brought a much-needed refinement to our company sensibility, helping Whole Foods reach a more sophisticated customer. We became a go-to source for gourmet and specialty foods, and as American palates evolved and expanded, we benefited enormously. Lex developed our Whole Foods Market private-label premium brand as a way to highlight some of his carefully sourced suite of high-quality global products.

There was also a third customer need that loomed large and sometimes created tension with both these cohorts. We needed to be value focused as well. In response to that, we had developed our more affordable "365" private-label brand and eventually expanded it to include an entire suite of organic products. Yes, you could come into Whole Foods and spend lavishly on a cart filled with delicious specialty products, both local and global. But you could also spend frugally and live healthily by focusing on our 365 selection. The success and expansion of the 365 brand proved too much for the foodie sensibilities of Lex, who preferred to keep the private-label territory for his higher-end specialty foods. It was part of the reason he had left the company back in 1998, soon after his close friend Peter did.

Part of my job, as I saw it, was to make sure none of these biases within the company ever achieved a decisive victory over the others. We needed to serve foodies around the country, to attract affluent customers with a taste for quality. We also need to serve the health-conscious consumer. And we needed to have value offerings that were competitive in price.

On this last front, things were looking up. Another new store was just about to open, and I was much more excited about this one than the foodie mecca at Bryant Park. It was the first in a new line of budget-friendly spin-off stores under the brand "365 by Whole Foods Market." Designed to target the price-conscious consumer, these smaller stores would primarily feature the 365 brand and be packed with technologically savvy features to appeal to a new generation. Affordability and convenience—that was our mantra. Instacart agreed to an extensive delivery relationship. I was excited about this new brand, which would allow us to compete more directly on price with stores like Trader Joe's and more recent market entrant Sprouts. I was even more enthused when the first 365 store in Silver Lake, Los Angeles, opened like gangbusters in May 2016. This could solve several problems at once, allowing us to compete in multiple market segments simultaneously—to undermine the "Whole Paycheck" narrative while still maintaining and growing the larger Whole Foods Market locations.

As Deborah and I decamped to Boulder for six weeks in the summer, I was feeling a bit more hopeful. It had been a tough couple of years since Schultz had sent his "step aside" email, but we had made lots of upgrades. We'd invested more in technology across our fleet of stores; we were planning a new loyalty program (our first); we had lowered prices (though not as much as we needed to); we were implementing various operational efficiencies, had invested more in marketing, and had begun to remodel and improve stores that were getting old. All of it was needed; all of it was positive; all of it was making the business better.

The stock price received a boost from the first 365 store opening. Soon we would lap the anniversary of the "weights and measures" scandal and begin enjoying a period of easier comps. But then July came around, and my brief bout of optimism faded. We reported a disappointing quarter with minimal overall sales growth and falling comps, causing the stock price to take yet another hit, and Wall Street to lament the time it was taking for the company to turn around. We were still very profitable and growing, and we still possessed enviable profit margins and per-square-foot sales, as I had to occasionally remind myself. But no one seemed to care much about any of that.

An unexpected weekend phone call from the Chairman of the Board is a rare event. So when I glanced at my phone one Saturday in September 2016 and noticed a missed call from John Elstrott, my heart sank. John was an excellent Chairman and a good and trusted friend, but the nature of that era meant that our conversations rarely focused on positive topics. What new piece of bad news was he calling to report today?

I stepped outside the hotel to return his call, looking up at the large, garish, neon flamingo that adorned the building. I was spending that weekend in Santa Rosa, California, at a resort named after that pink bird, where a conference was being held on diet and health, organized by Dr. John McDougall, a pioneer in the healthy plant-based eating movement. McDougall had been influential on my healthy-eating journey, and I'd attended several of his weekend events, often bringing friends. Now, I was working on a book about the topic. I'd hoped that for at least a couple of days, I could put aside the ongoing worries of the company and focus on the higher purpose behind it all—nourishing people and the planet. But Elstrott's call signaled that this was not to be.

His warm New Orleans accent was as reassuring as always, but I could tell by the tone of his voice that this wasn't good news. "Sorry to bother you on a Saturday, but I knew you would want to hear this as soon as possible. Gaby got a call from Sokoloff." Gabrielle Sulzberger was a long-time independent director who'd been on the Board since 2003. "It seems like there is a move afoot to replace you. There is some discontent on the Board. He was trying to enroll her."

Another coup attempt! I cursed under my breath.

"Sokoloff wants to kick me out? Why now? And who does he want to replace me with?"

"We all know the business is struggling," Elstrott replied. "Comps are down. Walter is a better operations guy, and the feeling is that's what Whole Foods needs today—tighter operations. I imagine that Sokoloff feels Walter is better suited to lead that charge. He wants you to step aside and become Executive Chairman. And he appears to have support, I'm sorry to say."

None of it was surprising. And none of it was good news for me. Walter and I had worked very well together for 25 years, but the Schultz email had shaken the trust between us. He was still a close friend and colleague, however, and his sweat, vision, and hard work were deeply interwoven in the success of Whole Foods. I understood that he really wanted to be sole CEO someday. I also knew that for all his ambition, he prided himself on his integrity. I found it hard to imagine that he could be the primary source of this effort to remove me. But maybe I was being naïve. Had his strong desire to be the sole CEO, to ascend to the next rung on the power ladder, gotten the better of him? I hoped it wasn't true. More likely, this was coming from a faction of the Board, with Sokoloff as the clear ringleader. Of course, Walter was also much closer to Sokoloff than I was.

I thanked John for his call—I was glad to be aware of all this, given the upcoming Board meeting. I wasn't quite ready to plunge back into the conference, so I sat down on a bench in the sun, taking in my surroundings. Apparently, the Flamingo had been the height of luxury back in the fifties, a glamorous gateway to Northern California. The glamour was long gone, but it was still elegant—obviously someone had invested money in a significant facelift. It was now "family friendly" and considered a historical landmark. But what was left of its beauty seemed to highlight its age rather than restore its youth. Could the same be said of me? Or Whole Foods Market?

I wrested my thoughts away from such melancholy and considered the crisis at hand. I was sure there were at least a few on our 11-person Board who shared Sokoloff's conviction that it was time for me to step aside. I didn't blame them for that. Evaluating the performance of the CEO was part of their job. They had every right to have an opinion about what was best for Whole Foods, even if that opinion was that it was my time to hit the highway. But I also had every right to resist that conclusion!

Indeed, I wasn't ready to step aside. At least not until we were able to right the company ship. Whole Foods was still very much my entrepreneurial child, and no cofounder wants to abandon their child amid stormy seas. We needed to steer the company onto a better long-term trajectory, and then, yes, I would step aside, and Walter could take over. But I wasn't going to do so prematurely because a Board member who'd already made a fortune off his investment in the company under my leadership had no patience for a transition that would naturally take some time.

I flew directly from Santa Rosa to New York for the Board meeting later that week, held at a hotel in Brooklyn. Elstrott had spoken to Walter after me, and the two of us had connected over the weekend and worked on our presentation for the Board about moving the company forward. But there were no shortcuts to appease the Board. This turnaround was going to have to be done the old-fashioned way, with careful blocking and tackling, not quick strike scoring. Moreover, the second 365 store had had a disappointing opening in Oregon, and it now appeared that the spectacular success of the Silver Lake store might have been unique to that location. This news cast a pall over the already tense meeting. At the very least, it was going to take some time to perfect this new store format, which cast doubt on the one ace we'd hoped to have in our hand.

Sokoloff wasn't one for pleasantries. He launched right in.

"John, I speak for many on this Board when I say that we're concerned about the leadership of the company. Would you be willing to step aside and take an Executive Chairman position?"

Without hesitation, I replied, "Not at this time. The company needs leadership and continuity right now, and I want to help lead the turnaround. Once we feel good about where things are at, maybe in a year or two, I'd be happy to consider moving into the Executive Chairman role and turning over the CEO position to Walter, or whoever the Board chooses to replace me. Walter and I have had those conversations."

"I agree with John." Walter was sitting to my left and looked as surprised by Sokoloff's bluntness as anyone. "We've had conversations about succession in the future, but I don't support an immediate CEO change."

"No! That's not good enough." Sokoloff's voice rose, sounding a note of frustration hardly ever heard in these generally staid and professional meetings. "That's too long to wait. You need to step away sooner. This company needs change. We want you to step down in the next few months."

I thought I caught a couple of nods of agreement around the room, but most Board members looked exceedingly uncomfortable with the open confrontation that was unfolding.

"Jon, I'm not going to resign," I stated flatly. "I agree that we're struggling, but you're not going to fix Whole Foods by kicking me out against my wishes. That would be highly destructive to the morale of the company. Whole Foods needs me right now to work together with Walter and the rest of the E-Team to get us on track for long-term success."

I looked around at the Board, defiant, but for the first time in many years, I wondered if I really had enough support to survive. Even when Chris had challenged my leadership, I'd been fairly confident I had the votes. But was that still true?

The meeting continued within the same highly charged atmosphere. Emotions ran high and everyone was on edge. I was reminded of those Board meetings with my father back in the nineties, when we were practically shouting at each other over our acquisition strategy. This was equally unpleasant, and it ended with no resolution.

On the way back to the Brooklyn hotel, Walter and I discussed the meeting, both of us reeling. I still found it hard to believe that Walter was as disconnected from these backchannel discussions as he claimed, and said as much. Did he really not know that these Board machinations had progressed so far? He insisted on his genuine surprise at this turn of events, and once again, as he had done with Howard's letter a couple of years before, offered to resign if I had truly lost faith in his loyalty to my leadership.

I flew back to Boulder the next day, brooding and troubled. Walter headed to Chicago for the grand opening of our Englewood store. My options were narrowing. I wanted and needed to spend more time thinking about the company's future, but here I was, consumed by power struggles. I spent time talking it all through with Glenda, Jim, and Deborah, and consulted with a few Board members, but there was no easy answer. Sooner or later, my fate was going to come down to a vote. Win or lose, I knew this could turn out very harmful to the company.

I estimated that Sokoloff probably had four clear votes for his agenda. With nine on the Board besides Walter and me, he needed only five for a majority. I was pretty sure I could count on Elstrott, Gaby, longtime director Bud Sorenson, and possibly my old friend Hass Hassan, although he was also close with Walter. I would have said the same about Mo Siegel, founder of Celestial Seasonings and my longtime friend and hiking buddy, but he'd surprised me recently by raising the idea of me becoming Executive Chairman and trying to convince me to do so. Would Mo be the swing vote? Had Sokoloff already persuaded him?

What I couldn't understand was why Sokoloff was so determined to move me out as the CEO and so quickly. We'd always had a pretty good relationship, and his company, Leonard Green, had made about $4 billion profit on its $425 million investment in less than three years under my leadership. I couldn't help wondering, might my opposition to taking Whole Foods private be a factor?

Over the next few days, I tried hard to get a bigger perspective on it all and transcend the knot of frustration and fear that would occasionally form in my stomach. In the mornings, after a good hike, I'd make my smoothie and relax in my favorite chair in the front window, or perhaps immerse myself in a good book to escape my mental fog.

The book that captured my attention in those days was a good one—*Team of Rivals* by Doris Kearns Goodwin. It's the enthralling historical account of how Lincoln managed to lead a team of strong, diverse, and often competing personalities through an era of national crisis and division. As fall slowly crept over the mountainsides, and the aspens turned from green to gold, I thought about my own "team of rivals." Most of all, I considered my relationship with Walter. We had worked together for so long, through so many difficult trials and incredible successes, we were like brothers. But I had reached some sort of limit of frustration with our interpersonal challenges. While I had no reason or desire to conclude that he was intentionally orchestrating the events that had recently unfolded, it did seem like his friends were determined to push me out and install him in the CEO role. First Howard Schultz and now Jon Sokoloff.

It was tempting to see him as just another challenger for my role. But Walter wasn't Chris Hitt, who had refused to back down and present a united front with me to the Board. He certainly wasn't Mark Skiles, who had insisted that he was unable to even work with me after his challenge to my leadership failed. And he wasn't even Peter Roy, who, while he never directly challenged me for my role, had too much independent ambition to stay with the company over the long term. I believed in Walter's integrity and saw our values as being aligned. Nevertheless, as I thought through the situation, it became clear that the deep trust between Walter and me had been compromised. The co-CEO setup had become untenable. We were now rivals, in a sense, even if neither of us intended it to be this way.

What would Lincoln do? I casually wondered, my recent readings coming to mind.

Boom! Suddenly, it hit me. I knew the answer. With crystal clarity, I saw the path forward.

I would ask Walter to resign—as he had already offered to do, on at least two occasions. And he would agree to it.

I thought about Salmon Chase, Lincoln's ambitious rival for the presidency in 1864 and Secretary of the Treasury, who had offered his resignation many times until one day Lincoln surprised him and accepted. It was time for me to accept Walter's offer. And I had confidence that my partner would follow through and be a man of his word.

I spoke to Walter in exactly those terms, and reluctantly, he accepted my request. He wasn't happy, and it was not his preferred resolution to the impasse we had reached. Nor was it mine. But circumstances had outrun us both.

On November 3, we announced our quarterly earnings, with sales continuing to grow but comps falling yet again. But the big news of the day wasn't in the numbers; it was in the announcement of Walter's resignation. Thankfully, he agreed to remain on the Board, where he could still be involved in shaping the company he loved. His retirement package was appropriately generous. In the same press release, we announced that Glenda also would retire at the end of fiscal year 2017. She had been at the company for almost three decades and was ready for a change of pace.

Losing Walter and Glenda was like losing my right and left hands. It was hard to envision an E-Team without either of them. They had each put their unique stamp on the evolution of the company. I relied on each of them, in different ways, and now the burden of this corporate turnaround fell even more heavily on my shoulders. But that was as it should be.

The Board was still divided and restless, and to say that Sokoloff was not happy with this turn of events would be an understatement. Upon hearing the news of Walter's resignation, he phoned Elstrott to express his extreme displeasure. As Elstrott later told it to me, he had only just settled down in his living room chair with a glass of wine on a Sunday evening when the phone rang. Rousing himself from his repose, he answered, only to be bombarded by Sokoloff's frustrations about how the Board needed to stop this madness immediately.

After listening patiently to the long diatribe, Elstrott quietly replied,

"I'm sorry, Jon, it's done. It's finalized. The decision has been made." And then in an uncharacteristically unguarded moment, he added, "You lost."

The explosion of obscenities on the other end of the line was loud and lasted for a long time. Elstrott held the phone at arm's length until, abruptly, it stopped.

Chapter 36

Evolve or Die

Did you know that every single one of the world's longest-lived populations eats a diet that is primarily plant based?

Heart disease doesn't have to be a death sentence. It's preventable—and even reversible!—through eating a whole foods, plant-based diet.

As the plane began its descent into New York City, I was running through my talking points in my head. I felt energized, my inner evangelist getting ready to deliver a sermon of hope and redemption. It was April 10, 2017, a day I'd been anticipating for months. My new book was finally launching, and I was looking forward to telling the world about it. *The Whole Foods Diet,* coauthored with doctors Matt Lederman and Alona Pulde, brought together everything I'd learned about food and health in the past decade or so. I'd interviewed all my heroes in the field—pioneering doctors, dedicated researchers, visionary chefs—as well as ordinary people, many of them Whole Foods team members, who'd undergone dramatic shifts in their own health through changing their diet.

Getting this book out into the world had become something of a bucket list goal for me. Over the past few years, I'd seen such measurable changes in my own health from cutting out not only animal foods but highly processed foods as well. And I'd heard so many incredible stories of lives changed and even saved that I felt compelled to share what I knew.

I wasn't making an ethical argument for veganism. In fact, the book acknowledged that while the longest-lived people in the world ate a largely whole foods, plant-based diet, very few got 100% of their calories from plants. We concluded that an optimal diet was 90-plus-% plant based but left room for up to 10% animal foods. This was important to me. While I was still deeply committed to my own vegan diet, I wanted to separate my ethical stance from what the science revealed when it came to health. I'd seen too many people conflate the two and use the science to promote their ethical agenda. This was counterproductive, I felt, and likely to scare away many of those who most needed to make a change. Some of my vegan friends criticized me for this stance, but I was very proud of the book we'd written and had high hopes for its impact.

In the days ahead, I was scheduled to speak about *The Whole Foods Diet* on several national TV shows, starting tomorrow with *CBS This Morning*. It was a relief to temporarily shift my focus away from the issues that continued to dog Whole Foods Market over the months since Walter's resignation—the stock price, the headlines, and the tensions on the Board. My mood was as bright as the spring sunshine streaming in through the plane's windows—until we touched down, I turned on my phone, and a flood of notifications appeared on my screen—texts, emails, and voicemails from the E-Team, several Board members, and my book publicist. In every message, I registered only two words: "shareholder activists."

Just like that, my hopeful mood was snuffed out. Like most public company CEOs, I feared few things more than shareholder activists—calculating speculators who buy up shares in a company with the sole intention of engineering short-term increases in the stock price so they can cash out at a quick profit. As a purpose-driven leader with a long-term vision, I felt threatened at an existential level by the notion that some person who might never have set foot in a Whole Foods could just show up, buy a bunch of stock, and then start dictating strategies with little regard for the long-term cost to the company. My friend Ron Shaich, founder of Panera Bread, compares shareholder activists to predatory sharks—attuned to vulnerability in a company like the smell of blood in the water. And on that spring day in 2017, I learned that the sharks had their teeth in Whole Foods.

Jana Partners, a New York hedge fund, had just announced its purchase of 8.8% of our stock. They'd given us no warning, and I had no doubt their intentions were not going to be in the long-term interests of the company.

I'd known for a while that Whole Foods was vulnerable to exactly this kind of attack, just as we had been in 2008. In fact, we'd already acquired one shareholder activist in 2016, Neuberger Berman, whose representatives weren't shy about letting us know that they were not pleased with Whole Foods' financial performance and wanted us to improve quickly.

In 2017, we had nearly 500 stores and were on track to gross $16 billion in sales that year. For more than 30 years, we'd delivered an average of 8% same-store sales growth—one of the best track records in the history of the US food retail industry. We had the highest EBITDA (earnings before interest, tax, depreciation, and amortization) percentage among all public food retailers. Our sales per square foot were twice the industry average. But all this wasn't enough to keep the sharks at bay. The shifts in the competitive landscape, our consequent slowdown in sales growth, the weights-and-measures scandal, and our flagging stock price all made us a target.

From the outset, Jana Partners took a much more aggressive stance than Neuberger Berman. They clearly weren't going to be patient and allow our long-term strategies to play out. The messages on my phone were filled with alarm, calling emergency E-Team and Board meetings. And one thing was crystal clear: There was no way our PR people were going to let me appear on national television the next morning to promote *The Whole Foods Diet*.

I understood why, but it was frustrating nonetheless. This book was important! But I couldn't kid myself that anyone was going to be interested in asking me about the dangers of processed foods, the relative merits of paleo diets, and whether or not carbs are the root of all evil when a juicy story about an activist attack had just broken. If I went on television, I would make myself a target for a barrage of questions I wasn't yet prepared to answer.

Privately, I mused that the timing of this attack was surely no accident. The headlines would write themselves—"Out-of-Touch CEO

Promotes Book While Company Struggles"—which would serve Jana's agenda perfectly, making the company look inept and undermining my leadership. I called my coauthors to let them know what was happening, and then I called my book publicist and canceled most of the book tour. Instead of spending my next few weeks preaching the gospel of plants, I would be spending them in conference rooms making battle plans.

Before I could do either an E-Team or Board call, however, there was one book event that I thought I shouldn't skip. I'd been invited to be a guest in a Goldman Sachs speaker series, "Talks at GS," hosted by Kathy Elsesser, global co-head of consumer retail at the investment banking firm. The invitation had taken me a little by surprise—investment bankers were not who I pictured when I thought about our intended readership—but I was happy to share my message with anyone who was interested. As I was waiting to go onstage, trying to reconnect with the enthusiasm and passion I'd been feeling just a few hours earlier, a bald-headed gentleman approached me and introduced himself: David Solomon, the soon-to-be CEO of the firm. After a few pleasantries, he got right to the point.

"John, I know you must be in shock right now," he said sympathetically. "But I want you to know that we can help. We can defend Whole Foods and we can support you in finding a good solution. We have a lot of experience with situations like this. Just say the word, and we'll mobilize."

Obviously, the Jana story was quickly making the rounds.

"Thank you," I replied. "I need to meet with my team and choose our next course of action. I appreciate your support." I shook Solomon's hand and stepped out onto the stage as the audience applauded. Despite my state of significant distraction, I thoroughly enjoyed the dialogue with Elsesser and hoped I made a convincing case for the power of a whole foods, plant-based diet.

At the time, I didn't think much of my brief interaction with Solomon. After all, this kind of situation was Goldman Sachs's sweet spot. Of course they wanted to represent us! If a merger or a buyout was the result of Jana's activism, they would love to help us with that deal—and enjoy the subsequent large payday. In the end, we chose a different company to defend us, Evercore. They had fewer conflicts of interest, since they only focus on defending companies against shareholder activists and don't play all sides as so many investment banks do. As time passed, however, and I reflected on the circumstances of that day, I began to wonder: Was the invitation to speak at Goldman Sachs on the very day of the Jana announcement and the subsequent meeting with Solomon as coincidental as it first seemed?

It was only later that I discovered that Goldman had been the investment banker in the Safeway/Albertsons merger a few years earlier. Safeway too had struggled with shareholder activists—none other than Jana Partners—a crisis that had ended with Goldman Sachs helping to facilitate a lucrative sale to Cerberus Capital Management, owner of Albertsons. I could only imagine that shepherding Whole Foods into the arms of Albertsons might seem a natural move, pulled from the same playbook, an easy and sensible merger for a struggling but pioneering retail company, all nudged along by a "fortuitous" meeting at Goldman Sachs on the afternoon of April 10.

And then I learned of another interesting coincidence. Leonard Green (Jon Sokoloff's firm) had been one of the bidders in the 2014 sale of Safeway. Was Sokoloff working from that same playbook? Was he somehow coordinating with the guys at Jana Partners? Was it possible that this was his next move, after Walter's resignation foiled the last one? And did Goldman get a tip about the activist battles to come at Whole Foods before they invited me to speak? Were investment bankers really that interested in plant-based eating? The questions multiplied in my mind. Of course, I have no idea what conversations happened when, about what, or with whom. But sometimes Wall Street is a very small world indeed!

A few days after Jana made the investment, they sent a message demanding that we come to their offices for a meeting. *No way,* I thought. *I'm not doing this on their turf.* We countered with a firm invitation to meet at our Austin headquarters.

From the moment they sat down with us in Austin it was clear that Jana wasn't interested in any kind of collaboration to make Whole Foods a better company. They launched right into a PowerPoint presentation that told a damning (and often inaccurate) tale of the company's fortunes over the past few years—selectively focusing on our all-time highest stock price in 2013 and then framing everything since then as a precipitous decline. Apparently, they'd been going around town telling this story to some of our larger investors. And when I asked for a copy of the presentation so I could address their concerns, they refused. They weren't interested in having us address the issues. They weren't interested in working with us. Essentially, their message was this: "We're going to take over Whole Foods Market, we're going to take control of your Board, we're going to replace management, and then we're going to sell this company to the highest bidder. Resistance is futile. There's not a damn thing you can do about it." And before we could protest, they added that most of our existing major investors already agreed with their plan.

It was a bullying tactic, plain and simple. And as such, it was guaranteed to fully awaken my competitive drive. I was determined to fight Jana with everything we had. We weren't going to just roll over and watch Whole Foods be sold off to Albertsons or another grocery company that would eliminate our headquarters, radically change our stores, destroy our culture, and lose sight of our mission. But I knew there was no way through this crisis without significant changes. We met immediately with Evercore, our new advisory bankers, to strategize.

First up, the Board. Evercore advised us that it was time for a "Board refreshment," which meant replacing several longtime directors with new independent directors. Jana had proposed its own new slate of directors in an attempt to take control. We'd tried to broker a peace deal of sorts, offering to accept two of their picks if they agreed to back off and stop publicly agitating for changes over the next 18 months, but they were uninterested. With Evercore's help, we replaced directors who had served for more than 15 years or who had potential conflicts of interest. The good news was that we got to say goodbye to Sokoloff, whose partnership in Leonard Green fell under potential conflicts. The bad news was that we had to say goodbye to several dear and loyal friends as well—John Elstrott, Mo Siegel, and Bud Sorenson, all of whom were deemed to have been around too long. Kip Tindell was also asked to step down due to his connection to Leonard Green, who owned The Container Store. Gaby Sulzberger became chair, and we welcomed five new directors: Ron Shaich, founder, chairman, and CEO of Panera Bread; Joe Mansueto, founder and executive chairman of Morningstar; Ken Hicks, chairman, president, and CEO of Foot Locker; Sharon McCollam, former EVP and CFO of Best Buy; and Scott Powers from State Street.

The boardroom wasn't the only place I saw new faces. The E-Team had undergone radical changes as well. Jim and A.C. were still with me, but now a day had come that I'd been dreading for months—Glenda's retirement. After more than 28 years working together, I couldn't quite imagine what it would be like to not have her just down the hall whenever I needed to talk something through. In her place, we'd hired Keith Manbeck, formerly of Kohl's and Nike, who turned out to be an excellent CFO. When it came to talking things through, I found myself turning most often to Jason Buechel, our CTO, a young man of keen intelligence and high integrity who'd been with the company since 2013 and had become a trusted adviser. The E-Team was filled out by Sonya Gafsi Oblisk, who'd joined the company as EVP of Marketing the previous year, and Ken Meyer and David Lannon, our EVPs of Operations.

Together, we created a plan to cut costs and improve operations, which we announced on May 10 along with the changes on the Board. I wasn't entirely happy about the plan, since it partly relied on a shift to greater centralization, something we'd always resisted as a company, despite some efficiency gains. I loved the many distinctive innovations that regional leaders brought to their stores, and so did our customers, even if they resented the higher prices that allowed for it. Now that trade-off was going to reverse itself. By centralizing more of our ordering, we increased our leverage to get better pricing and we hoped the gain there would offset the costs.

The changes we'd made, along with a healthy rebound in our stock price, backed off Jana temporarily. But I knew it wasn't enough. Around this time, Jim suggested I speak with an Austin investor we both knew, Michael Shearn, who had a stake in the company, had been inspired by *Conscious Capitalism*, and was familiar with the world of private equity and activist investing. He pointed out that Jana Partners had won the vast majority of their activist battles by quickly and easily taking control of the Board. As a founder and iconoclast, I was simply an obstacle to be removed. "I know you think your new Board is a friendly one," he explained. "But I suspect they're still going to vote you out, and quickly. The lure of those longer-term relationships with private equity players, the promise of future Board positions—they can be powerful motivators. They'll apologize, say something about 'fiduciary responsibility' and 'professional management,' and cast their vote against you."

His warning added to my concerns. The ongoing drama made it near impossible to focus on making Whole Foods competitive for the long term. I felt like the activists were looking over my shoulder constantly, seeking signs of weakness. It kept me on edge, and I had to work hard not to let my competitive instincts take over. Yes, we needed to fight and win—but coming from a reactive and defensive mindset wouldn't serve the company. This moment needed more from me.

Don't contract into fear, I reminded myself a dozen times a day. *Expand into love. Respond only from your higher self.* But it was hard. I doubled down on my meditation practice, retreating every day into my book-lined "man cave" at home to sit quietly and center myself. I reread my favorite spiritual texts. I also relied even more than usual on the calming effect of my early morning walks along Shoal Creek Trail or Lady Bird Lake.

In my more enlightened moments, I recognized that what was happening was a kind of evolutionary test for Whole Foods Market. We needed to evolve—that was true regardless of shareholder activist demands or pessimistic analyst projections. Striding along the familiar trails, I marveled at how, even in the center of the city, an exuberant Texas spring was bursting forth—wildflowers feeding bees and butterflies, birds nesting in the rich green canopy of the trees, rivers and creeks teeming with life. Our company was an ecosystem of sorts, just like this park, which had found a way to flourish despite the pressure of encroaching roads and homes and high-rises. That's nature's way. Evolution occurs when systems come under pressure from external conditions in their environment, and this forces them to innovate and find new solutions or risk extinction. *Evolve or die.*

Whole Foods was under extreme evolutionary pressure from several sides. If we didn't find a way to become a new and better version of ourselves, we might go extinct. But if we could imitate nature's resilience and creativity, everyone would benefit. The most loving, openhearted perspective I could find on our current situation was to see it as an amazing opportunity to find an even greater win-win-win. Yes, it was a challenging moment, but one always feels that way in the middle of evolutionary emergence when the outcome is not yet clear.

In my less enlightened moments, fear, anger, and frustration took hold. Would Jana give us time to find that next evolutionary step? Or would their impatience cut off our creative options and leave no choice but to sell? The prospect infuriated me. This kind of predatory investor strategy was exactly what gave capitalism a bad name. It was the antithesis of every tenet of the Conscious Capitalism philosophy. It had no concern for any stakeholder other than the shareholders—and even that was a short-term concern focused on quick profit, not long-term value creation. It had no loyalty to our higher purpose, no care for our culture, and no long-term leadership vision. All these activists cared about was making more money as fast as possible. I felt like I was caught in a morality play to see which version of capitalism would prevail: the Conscious Capitalism that had guided us so well up to this point, or the short-term, narrow-minded financial capitalism represented by Jana and others like them.

One day that spring, my frustration got the better of me, and I vented about Jana to a journalist who was interviewing me for a long-form profile in *Texas Monthly.*

"Yes, we need to evolve," I told him. "We need to get better, and we're doing that. But these guys just want to sell us, because they think they can make 40 or 50% in a short period of time. They're greedy bastards, and they're putting a bunch of propaganda out there, trying to destroy my reputation and the reputation of Whole Foods, because it's in their self-interest to do so."

I was on a roll. It felt good to get some of this off my chest. I likened Jana to the Ringwraiths in Tolkien's *The Lord of the Rings,* consumed by the desire for money and power and never satisfied. I pictured them, cloaked and hooded, riding their fearsome skeletal horses through the night in search of the Ring of Power. It was a cathartic rant.

A few hours later, when I started to tell Deborah about the interview, I knew I'd gone too far. She didn't have to say a word, but the expression on her face mirrored back to me that this had not been the voice of my higher self. Yes, I had good reasons to feel that way and Jana deserved those epithets. But telling that to the press probably wasn't going to help our embattled company as we tried to get Jana off our backs.

The E-Team was sympathetic, but like me, they were out of solutions. The possibility of going private was back on the table, but we still feared the debt load might sink us. The press kept speculating about a possible sale. *Kroger? Albertsons? Walmart?* I met informally with Cerebus, who owned Albertsons, but didn't leave feeling good about the prospect of entrusting Whole Foods to them. If a sale was inevitable, should we proactively seek a buyer we felt would take better care of the company? At some point, the name Warren Buffett came up in conversation. *Why not?* we thought. He could certainly afford to buy Whole Foods. And perhaps the iconic value investor would recognize the long-term value in our company and be interested in helping to protect it and grow it right. We reached out to him, but he replied that it wasn't a good fit.

Day after day I walked, meditated, and debated. Night after night I tossed and turned, trying to come up with a solution that didn't mean losing the company I loved. And more than that—a solution that would be a positive outcome for everyone involved (perhaps even the activists!). A true evolutionary win-win-win. I knew it had to be out there—a creative, out-of-the-box idea. I just couldn't see it yet. My frustration grew as the days passed. And then one morning, immediately after I woke up, a question popped into my head that changed everything:

What about Amazon?

Chapter 37

The Amazon Solution

Amazon. Once the idea had entered my mind, I couldn't stop thinking about it. Could it possibly work? Would they be interested in buying Whole Foods Market? Could this be the creative solution I'd been looking for?

By chance, I had been on a two-person panel with Jeff Bezos at the Microsoft CEO Summit in 2016. I liked Bezos—he was a brilliant entrepreneur, and he seemed to possess a certain authenticity that resonated with me. He was his own man and didn't care too much what other people thought about him. And of course, I admired what he'd created. There are very few people who have ever achieved that level of success, much less at the speed at which he achieved it. Before the panel, when we met at the CEO mixer, he asked me about Whole Foods, and we discovered a shared passion for scuba diving. I told him about some of the best places in the world to dive.

Now, a year later, I found myself trying to get inside Bezos's head. Would Amazon be interested in purchasing Whole Foods? The company was clearly trying to become a serious player in the grocery business. In fact, for years they had been making overtures to us about forming a strategic partnership. I had always been hesitant. The benefits were many. The risks were alarming. Walter and I had often discussed it, and he rightly pointed out the plethora of advantages in such a deal. But I was acutely aware of Amazon's reputation for entering into a partnership, gaining access to the critical data of the company, and then, well, launching their own version. I didn't want that to happen to Whole Foods—to partner with them for a few years and then watch them open a competitor using the knowledge they had obtained from us. I respected Amazon, but I didn't want us to be taken advantage of. Or, to put it more bluntly, if we were going to get in bed with Amazon, I wanted a prenup and the full benefits of a marriage!

And that's exactly what I now had in mind: a marriage. Would they accept? There was only one way to find out: ask.

It's not like I had Bezos on speed dial, so we reached out to Matt Yale, who worked with Tusk Strategies—a consulting group that was helping us with media strategy. Matt was friends with Jay Carney, Obama's former communications director who now worked for Amazon. An encouraging response came quickly, and within just a few days, we had a meeting scheduled. One thing I appreciate to this day about Amazon's culture is they don't like to waste time.

I flew to Seattle the next day with three executives—David Lannon, Ken Meyer, and Jason Buechel. Jason had an unparalleled knowledge of Whole Foods technology. David and Ken knew our operations through and through. But I planned on taking the lead in the discussion myself. It one of those magical Pacific Northwest days when the rain takes a break and Mount Rainier looms over the city like a storybook mountain. It seemed like a fitting setting for what might be the most unexpected plot twist yet. For almost four decades I had led the company, protecting Whole Foods as best I could. But nothing lasts forever. What was next? Where did this meeting sit in the narrative of my own entrepreneurial quest? Would this be the action that led me to finally surrender the ring? And if I did, would it be a wise move, the kind that Gandalf would counsel me to make?

Unfortunately, I no longer had a Gandalf with me on my journey. My father, Craig, Jean-Claude, Walter, and Glenda were all gone from the company now. I could only hope that I had enough wisdom to make a win-win-win decision for the greater good.

As soon as we landed, we received directions to the meeting place. It was all very cloak-and-dagger. Right away, I could see that Amazon was constantly under an entirely different level of scrutiny than a company like Whole Foods, and Bezos even more so. Before we could enter, we were searched for weapons. Being one of the richest men in the world comes with layers of security far beyond anything I've ever needed. I don't envy Bezos that reality; I've always found that some level of anonymity can be its own blessing.

The top-secret location turned out to be Bezos's boathouse on Lake Union, located right next door to his palatial home. Don't be misled by that term—this was no damp waterside shed but a beautiful building with more than adequate space for the purpose of holding meetings. Several Amazon executives were there when we arrived, introducing themselves as Steve Kessel, Doug Herrington, and Peter Krawiec. A few moments later, Bezos entered and welcomed us warmly. I had brought him a copy of *The Whole Foods Diet* as a gift, which quickly led us into a conversation about books. As fellow bibliophiles, we had a moment of bonding over our mutual appreciation for the joys of reading, especially science fiction and fantasy, before we got down to the business at hand.

The meeting started with a brief presentation from our team. We gave them a primer on the trajectory of Whole Foods, the shifting market, the increased competition, our overall success, our reasons for seeking a buyer. Even given our current challenges, I emphasized, we were an established leader in our market, and perhaps most important, we were making a lot of money. The business was generating significant EBITDA at over $1.3 billion per year, even if it didn't have quite the same profit margins as a few years earlier. I thought this might be relevant to Amazon, a company that had prioritized massive growth but sometimes struggled to show profits, at least in its retail business. Also, I added, Whole Foods was defining its category. We were a trusted leader when it comes to healthy diet and lifestyle, and a pioneer in organics, sustainable agriculture, and animal welfare. As I spoke, and the team filled in the gaps, I paid careful attention to the Amazon group, particularly Bezos. He was attentive and focused. Everyone was.

As the conversation continued, I grew increasingly impressed with the Amazon team. I could see their creative minds working, figuring, probing, analyzing. I began to sense some of the secrets of their company's success. They asked great questions—a reliable sign of high intelligence. Interestingly, they all shopped at local Whole Foods stores (clearly, another reliable sign of intelligence!).

Notably, none of the Amazon executives struck me as what I might call typical corporate types—those whose native soil is navigating organizational bureaucracies, often more oriented toward financial management than entrepreneurial innovation. Of course, those are important skills, but as a self-taught business leader, I had a well-honed suspicion of MBA-carrying business mercenaries who always think they know better. I found the Amazon team's authentic interest, openness, and creativity refreshing in that regard. It struck me that they were all in their late forties and early fifties—in other words, about the same general age as their CEO. This is a trend I've come to notice across the business landscape: the core management teams generally fall within a certain age range, and, as in this case, it will tend to match with the age of the founder or leader. I get it: There's a natural synergy and we all easily trust people who share a similar level of life experience. This had been true of Jim, Glenda, A.C., Walter, and me during Whole Foods Market's heyday. On the other hand, such companies can miss out on the range of perspectives that age diversity can bring to the conversation. I'd experienced both sides of this trade-off myself. These days, I was surrounded by several younger executives, and I appreciated their fresh outlook and different set of cultural biases. But I also missed the days when my core team was made up of my close peers.

By the time an hour had passed, it was clear that the conversation was going well. Both teams were engaged and energized, and the connection between us was palpable. There was much to like about the potential deal. On our side, Whole Foods would immediately get an influx of technological prowess, long a weakness of ours. Amazon's laser focus on the customer and expertise in loyalty programs—something we'd struggled to get off the ground—would make a tangible difference for our customers. But most important for me was the flexibility they might bring to our pricing strategy. The idea of being able to materially decrease prices—a relatively small line item in Amazon's massive income statement—without raising alarms on Wall Street practically gave me goose bumps. Maybe we could shed the "Whole Paycheck" label for good! And of course, Amazon's deep pockets could help fund the next stage of our growth.

Amazon, on the other hand, would be purchasing a tremendous amount of grocery expertise, a skill set they badly needed. The company had wanted to make inroads into the grocery space for years. They even had tried, unsuccessfully, to hire my friend and competitor Doug Rauch, the former President of Trader Joe's, after he stepped down from that company. Their grocery ambitions were as grand as they were troubled. Here was a chance for them to import decades of expertise and wisdom in one fell swoop, not to mention expand their offerings to an affluent customer base that had a lot of overlap with their core "Prime" members. This customer base was one of Whole Foods' most valuable yet underappreciated assets, and I knew that the Amazon team were well aware of the value we brought to the table.

One hour turned into two or three and eventually the conversation came to a natural close. They assured us they would consider everything and be in touch soon. We decamped to a local watering hole overlooking the lake. We sat down, ordered drinks, and looked at each other across the table, all smiles and starry eyes, like giddy teenagers after a first date.

"What'd you think?" I asked.

Jason didn't hesitate. "That was a great conversation."

"Honestly, I think that went about as well as it possibly could," David added, raising his glass.

"Those were some very smart people. How awesome would it be to work with them on a daily basis," Ken exclaimed.

As each of my team voiced their enthusiasm, an unspoken question still hung in the air. I looked earnestly around the table and decided to voice it. "Do you think they liked us too?"

We all let out a laugh—at ourselves, primarily—for the somewhat comical mix of adolescent first-date anxiety and high-stakes corporate mergers and acquisitions that we were engaged in.

Did they like us too? I was hopeful; all the signs pointed in that direction. Could we turn this whirlwind courtship into a lasting union? I had nurtured Whole Foods, my proverbial child, my baby, from her infancy. I'd watched her take her first steps, held her hand as she entered the adult world, and looked on with pride as she slowly grew into this mature, thriving business. Was I now ready to let her go, to marry her off to the richest man in the world?

It took just two days to get Amazon's answer.

PART IV

LOVE LIFE

Back on the Appalachian Trail, 2022

Excited about my new venture, Love.Life, 2023

Chapter 38

Trust the Process

"Trust the process, John. It unfolds a layer at a time. Trust that your soul knows what's best for you."

My spiritual guide's voice was steady and calming. I was in the middle of a five-day guided solo retreat in the mountains, during which I was doing daily sessions of intensive breathwork, as well as three ceremonies involving a combination of MDMA and psilocybin, the active compound found in magic mushrooms. It had been 25 years since I'd taken any significant doses of psychedelics, though I'd continued my other spiritual practices, including meditation, yoga, and my studies of *A Course in Miracles*. I wasn't quite sure what to expect, but I'd come to this retreat with a clear intention: to let go into love and to live more fully in my heart.

Love had been my guiding light for decades, in all its many beautiful forms. There was the cosmic love that I'd recognized in my spiritual and psychedelic experiences as the force that is continually bringing the universe into being out of nothing. There was the unconditional love I'd found in my marriage to Deborah that kept me grounded and connected to my higher self. There was the creative love that motivated me as an entrepreneur—the deep care I felt for Whole Foods, the fellowship I felt with our team, the passion that inspired my higher purpose. There was the human love and appreciation I'd felt immersed in for the last several months as I toured our stores around the country, saying goodbye and thank you to thousands of team members. It was the summer of 2022, and I was getting ready to make the biggest transition of my life—leaving Whole Foods Market after 44 years as its leader. I hoped that over this time, I had become better at listening to love's guidance, at forgiving people, at staying in my heart. But now, as I prepared for the next phase of my personal journey, I wanted to take it to the next level. It felt like a deep yearning to let go.

A couple of days into the retreat, however, it wasn't unfolding in the way I'd expected. I'd had powerful experiences and insights, but it felt like something was blocking me, preventing me from fully letting go into love. My guide, who was very intuitive, had quickly sensed that I'm a doer, and I'd approached the initial breathwork sessions quite forcefully, like a mountain I needed to hike up. She'd encouraged me to take a different approach—softer and more receptive—which created more openness and receptivity in my heart. Rather than focusing on exhaling intensely, as I'd learned in Holotropic Breathwork, she encouraged me to focus on inhaling deeply. Then, she encouraged me to breathe as naturally and effortlessly as possible, thinking of my breath as a smooth circle, in and out. Doing this practice, I glimpsed two insights that felt deeply true, although I struggled to accept them: I *am* love, and when I am in my heart, I am perfect as I am.

Yet the sense of being blocked remained. On the second day, I did my first ceremony, which involved taking MDMA. Remembering the ecstatic love I'd felt when taking the substance at those gatherings back in the eighties, I looked forward to the experience. The setting was quite different. Instead of journeying with a group of friends, I was alone, except for my guide and her two wise cats. We began with prayer and intention setting, and then I took the medicine and closed my eyes. Within 45 minutes or so, as the waves of energy and euphoria began to embrace me, I noticed that it felt softer and calmer than I remembered. (I would later learn that Ecstasy, in the eighties, was often cut with amphetamines, whereas the version I took on my retreat was pure MDMA.) I felt deeply relaxed and blissful, and in this safe cradle of love I was able to probe the shadows that seemed to linger between me and my heart.

Several things became clear. There were certain individuals I recognized I needed to make amends with—a colleague I'd spoken harshly to, and a beloved family member I'd hurt with some unfiltered and careless criticism. I sent them messages and received quick responses of forgiveness. I felt some of the shadows lift. Another shadow was a fear of death—not my own death but the possibility of losing the person I loved the most, Deborah. I breathed through that fear, reminding myself to expand into love. And then there were two emotions I hesitated to touch: anger and guilt.

Trust the process, John. In order to go where I needed to go, to reach that more loving state I yearned for, these negative emotions had to be faced. I was angry. And I felt guilty. Somewhere on the other side of those pent-up feelings was the deeper love in which I longed to reside.

The anger was closer to the surface. It was not hard to access, even in this peaceful mountain hideaway, with two cats purring by my side, the medicine guiding me into deeper states, and no one demanding anything from me. I didn't want to feel anger in this place, but I trusted that as my guide had told me, my soul knew what was best. This layer needed to be experienced—the ways in which I'd felt disrespected and disempowered since the sale of Whole Foods to Amazon five years earlier. It surprised me in its intensity. And beneath the anger was a more subtle and corrosive emotion: guilt. *Had I done the right thing in selling to Amazon? Should I have fought harder to keep Whole Foods independent?* There wasn't an easy answer to those questions. But they needed to be asked. Inhaling deeply, as my guide had shown me, I allowed it all to wash over me, trusting that love would guide me.

Ever since that fateful day in the summer of 2017 when I signed the merger agreement, the first question everyone asks me is: Do you regret selling to Amazon? The most honest answer I can give is that I regret the circumstances that made it the best option. I still believe it was the best strategic choice available at that time, and while not every hope and dream I had for this marriage of companies has come true, there were several wonderful positives that came out of it. At the same time, there were a few disappointments and frustrations.

On the positive side, Amazon is one of the greatest corporations in the entire world and one that truly cares about making long-term investments and being patient to let them fully develop. They also have a super smart and capable management team. Our initial impressions of these essential attributes proved to be accurate. Freed from the demands of the public markets, Whole Foods was able to operate with a different set of financial metrics and operational targets. Soon after the sale was completed, we raised team member pay and significantly lowered prices for our customers, even while continuing to rapidly expand our total store count.

And we kept lowering prices—four times in the first two years. Finally, we were able to take that desperately needed step, making our stores accessible to more customers. We reduced our prices enough that our smaller, budget-focused 365 stores became redundant, so we decided to convert them to Whole Foods Market–branded stores. I'm very proud of these changes we made during those initial years under Amazon. They helped partially change the "Whole Paycheck" narrative and brought the company into greater alignment with our higher purpose. Amazon is a highly customer-centric company, and these price reductions were just one of several ways in which they helped us to give more attention to that key stakeholder. We were also able to quickly roll out a loyalty program that was directly connected with their Prime membership program.

Amazon helped us a great deal with technology too. In many ways, expertise in technology is their greatest strength, and they helped us make massive upgrades in an area that had generally taken a back seat to the more tangible demands of everyday brick-and-mortar retailing. We centralized more of our operations and significantly invested in our data systems, online ordering, and food delivery, integrating those functions with Amazon's ubiquitous online presence and delivery network. It was a huge undertaking, which became even more important when the Covid-19 pandemic hit only a couple of years after the acquisition was completed. We were able to serve millions of customers in their homes during those immensely challenging initial months of lockdown. And the investments we made in technology have helped to ensure that Whole Foods will thrive in the increasing virtual retail world for decades into the future.

For all of these changes and more, I'm deeply grateful to Amazon. I honestly don't know how we'd ever have been able to make such price investments under the tyranny of quarterly earnings pressure. With Wall Street clamoring for short-term profits and rising comp store sales, it's hard to see how Whole Foods could have grown into the company it is today without Amazon's help.

Yet there were, unquestionably, a few downsides to the sale, which began to reveal themselves as time passed. While Amazon no doubt helped improve our operational efficiency to a certain extent, we lost much of the decentralization that had proven to be such an engine of innovation within Whole Foods. Our stores began to look and feel more similar, their product mixes containing less local color and flavor.

Part of this centralization transformation was due to encouragement from Amazon, but I think perhaps even more of it came from the corporate professionals who were increasingly gaining important positions of leadership at Whole Foods. Almost all of these professionals were external hires who did not align well with our mission or culture. They were much more interested in professional advancement, enlarging their teams, and increasing their compensation. They continually pushed for greater centralization in purchasing, marketing, operations, and HR. Their arguments were the same ones I had been hearing for decades: greater efficiencies, lower costs, more control. However, this turned out to be no more true for Whole Foods than it had been true for Bread & Circus, Mrs. Gooch's, Fresh Fields, or any of the centralized companies that we had acquired back in the 1990s.

Our G&A costs were no longer operating at the low 2% of total sales at which we had operated throughout most of our history, despite our much greater size and scale. The so-called "greater efficiencies" did not seem to show up on our bottom line, while the increased internal bureaucracy and control definitely resulted in fewer innovations in store design, product diversity, and store operations. The drive to centralization really accelerated during the Covid-19 pandemic crisis, and I regret that I didn't fight harder to slow it down.

I think this is a problem most successful companies eventually face, as the leaders who created and built the organization grow older and retire. They are gradually replaced by "business professionals," who are very smart and capable but ultimately more loyal to their own careers than they are to the company. The entrepreneurial spirit is slowly extinguished, and a lack of meaningful innovation ultimately slows growth and leads to stasis. Capitalism solves for this problem through innovative entrepreneurs birthing new businesses that successfully outcompete the older, much larger, but far less creative businesses—a process Austrian economist Joseph Schumpeter called "creative destruction."

Soon after the merger, I'd been very hopeful that not only would Whole Foods benefit from Amazon's expertise and deep pockets, but Amazon might benefit from Whole Foods as well. For all our difference in size, we'd done something they had not: built a successful brick-and-mortar retailing operation. I thought this experience would prove valuable to them, and when they began including me in the strategic group working on their physical stores soon after the acquisition was completed, I told them honestly what I thought: they were being too aggressive in the rollout of Amazon Fresh and other physical stores without first establishing a successful store business model to grow with.

However, my thoughts and strategic suggestions about Amazon Fresh and other physical stores were probably seen as too negative and were not welcomed by the leaders in charge. After only a few months of trying to help Amazon's larger grocery strategy, I was simply cut from the team with no further explanation. I was no longer invited to any of these meetings, and my voice and vision were no longer heard.

This disrespect hurt. Some of the leaders responsible for Amazon Fresh just didn't seem to see the most valuable things about the company they'd bought. Instead of working closely with us to better understand how to successfully operate physical grocery, the leadership at Amazon Fresh pretty much ignored us and disregarded our advice. Rather than seeing us as an ally who could help them, Amazon Fresh chose to see us as a rival, and Whole Foods' unique retail expertise went largely underappreciated.

A few months before I retired from Whole Foods Market, Amazon hired a grocery executive from the UK grocery company Tesco named Tony Hoggett. I only met with Tony a few times, but I was impressed with his grocery knowledge, and he seemed to value Whole Foods Market much more than his predecessors had. My successor as CEO, Jason Buechel, reports to Tony, and I retired from the company more hopeful about Whole Foods' future than I had been the last few years.

I also had some small hope that our culture of higher purpose, empathy, empowerment, independent initiative, and team member appreciation—the culture that inspired so much success and fierce internal loyalty—might have some influence on the innovative but more transactional business culture of Amazon. After all, Whole Foods had been named by *Fortune* magazine as one of the "100 Best Companies to Work For" for 20 consecutive years before the merger. Might Amazon perhaps study our culture and experiment with adopting some of our best practices? This hope was somewhat bolstered by a positive response to a letter I sent Jeff Bezos and his successor, Andy Jassy, suggesting that they establish a new Amazon Leadership Principle focused on the company's employees and workplace culture. Eventually, Amazon's leadership added two: "Strive to Be the Earth's Best Employer" and "Success and Scale Bring Broad Responsibility." I had a chance to give input on those principles and was encouraged by their creation. Perhaps over time, their impact will grow in significance.

In my time at the company, however, my aspiration for Whole Foods having greater cultural influence at Amazon was largely unrealized. It is not unusual for an acquiring company to assume they don't have much to learn from the company they buy. A few of the most senior leaders may be interested in learning, but the management below them almost never are. Surely, the thinking goes, their culture must be superior or the acquisition would have been the other way around—as in Whole Foods acquiring

Amazon. We had ourselves struggled with the same type of "superiority trap" in the many acquisitions that we had done over the years. It requires truly excellent leadership to escape this trap, and I was naïve in thinking Amazon was such an incredible company with such amazing senior leadership that they would be different. The Amazon professionals just didn't think they had much to learn from this somewhat unconventional contributor to their retail team. And eventually, not only did they largely ignore our culture, but they unconsciously began to make a few decisions that damaged it. In some respects, it was this issue of culture that brought my time at Whole Foods Market to an end.

The tipping point occurred in a videoconference meeting I had in February 2021 with Dave Clark, Amazon's CEO of Consumer Business, and my direct supervisor. I was sitting at my desk in Austin, in an office that was eerily quiet and empty. And that was the topic of our conversation that day: the thorny issue of bringing our corporate team members back to the office after almost a year of remote work.

"Dave, we need to do this," I insisted. "It's time. We need to get our people back in the office."

I really liked and respected Dave and his leadership talents. In one of the largest companies in the world, filled with a great deal of bureaucratic inertia, he was one of the best decision-makers I had ever worked with. Meaning, firstly, he was decisive! And, secondly, I thought most of his decisions were excellent. That counted for a lot in my book, as did his formidable intelligence. He was independent minded and didn't seem to care too much about following the internal political tides. One of Amazon's principles of leadership is "leaders are right, a lot." This was certainly true of Dave. However, that didn't mean he was right all the time. On this particular occasion, I was convinced that he was not only wrong but dangerously shortsighted.

Patiently, I explained my reasoning again. It was hurting our culture to have all our store team members working in person while only the corporate teams worked remotely. It created a weird divide and was fostering some internal resentment and no doubt undermining our work ethic. Our inclusive and egalitarian culture was central to our success, and this was damaging its delicate fabric. Now that vaccinations were available and the initial strict lockdowns had lifted, I felt that on balance it was the right decision for Whole Foods to begin in-person work again in our offices.

"Look, John, I've told you this before." Dave sounded irritated now. "It's too soon. We're not ready to sign off on this. Amazon's not doing this yet."

"Dave, I can't speak for Amazon. But I do know Whole Foods. I know what makes our culture work. And I know when something's not healthy for the company. I'm your general in the field here, and I believe this is one of those times when you need to trust your general in the field. Remote work is not good for Whole Foods Market when it creates a two-tiered system within our team."

I must have touched a nerve, or maybe I just pushed it too far. Dave's voice went from mildly irritated to very angry.

"Damn it, John, I told you, we're not doing it! What do you not understand about that statement? You always want to argue about every fucking thing! Sometimes you need to just be a team player and do what you are told to do!" His outburst was so loud I had to turn down the volume on my computer.

As I said, Dave was a decisive person. He was fine about hearing alternative opinions during the decision-making process, but once he decided, he didn't like to be questioned. And I had clearly crossed that invisible line. I was no longer raising a potentially relevant view; I was being insubordinate and challenging his authority.

This wasn't the first time I'd crossed such a line with an important Amazon leader. I hate feeling that poor decisions are being made and feel obligated to speak up when I see this happening, even if I'm in a minority. Plus, my default mode is to treat everyone like an equal wherever they stand in the hierarchy. That's just my style. It's how the E-Team at Whole Foods Market always related to each other: respectful, but not deferential. At Amazon, a more hierarchical company where the top executives were used to being treated with more deference, my egalitarian style may sometimes have been interpreted as disrespect—not knowing my place in the pecking order. And sometimes, as in that conversation with Dave, it triggered unexpected pushback and even anger.

I tried to put things in perspective. "Dave, I don't think that's accurate. I don't argue about everything. Can you give me another example of when I've argued with you?"

"John, I don't have to give you a fucking example. I work with you. I know it's true. And it's not just me. *Everyone* at Amazon knows it too." And then he said the words that really hit hard. "If you didn't want to give up control of Whole Foods, then you shouldn't have sold the company to Amazon."

It was a moment of anger, but also a moment of unfiltered honesty. His last statement stayed with me, even as we concluded our conversation. Sitting at my desk in that empty office building, Dave's angry voice still echoing in my head, a thought arose: *Why am I still here?*

It was a question to which I didn't have a good answer. After the sale, I'd agreed to stay at least four or five years, but that deadline was coming up soon. Dave's harsh words had made explicit something I'd suspected for a while: At least some of the Amazon leadership no longer wanted me here. They had come to the conclusion that John Mackey was a maverick and an argumentative troublemaker. They'd prefer it if I was gone. And Dave was right. I had given up control when the company was sold to Amazon. I no longer had the power to protect Whole Foods. Also—and I don't mean this lightly—I was no longer having much fun or expressing my creativity. As I finished up work for that day, closed my computer, and walked past empty desk after empty desk on my way to the elevator, I knew it was time for me to go.

I didn't announce it to the world right away. I think that when any really important decision needs to be made, it's best not to take it lightly or finalize it quickly. It is better to sit with it for a while and let the residue of an emotionally charged encounter pass. It's also important to seek counsel with the people you most love and trust. I wanted to talk this through with Deborah, Glenda, Jim, A.C., and Jason. Would I still feel the same in a few days, a few weeks? And would Dave respond in some way following his outburst? Would he apologize for losing his temper? If he did, would that change how I felt about our future? But my feelings didn't change. And Dave canceled our next two scheduled meetings without explanation. When we finally spoke again, three months later, he didn't even mention our last conversation.

Whatever doubts I might still have had about my decision, that helped seal the deal. In June I told Dave that I wanted to retire soon after the fifth anniversary of the acquisition, and he readily accepted my decision. In September 2021, I publicly announced my intention to retire the following year. I made sure Whole Foods would be in good hands when I was gone, naming COO Jason Buechel, by then my most trusted colleague, as my successor—something that Dave had preapproved. I planned a farewell tour in which I'd visit every one of our 10 regions. And I scheduled my solo retreat for the summer of 2022, knowing that I'd need all the help I could get, in every dimension, as I made this major life transition.

Trust the process. As the effects of the MDMA I'd taken in the first ceremony of my retreat began to wear off, I felt physically drained but emotionally less burdened. It had surprised me a little how much anger I felt about the disrespect Amazon had shown toward me. And how much guilt I'd harbored over the decision to sell. One of the great gifts of MDMA—and a reason for its amazing effectiveness when used to heal trauma such as PTSD—is that it allows you to look at difficult aspects of your life without being overwhelmed by pain. That's what happened for me. I felt a new sense of closure with my decision to leave Whole Foods Market—and with everything that had happened in the last five years. I let go of my hurt and anger toward Amazon as unnecessary, and my feelings of guilt were brought out into the light of compassion and forgiveness. Had I done everything perfectly? No. But I'd done the best I could, motivated by my love for Whole Foods and my desire to protect its higher purpose.

And I trusted that all of this was part of the process of my own spiritual evolution.

Over the next couple of days, my breathwork sessions were powerful. Among many insights, I gently confronted a deeply held fear that I am not truly worthy of love due to my many faults and my lack of perfection. I remembered that dream after my father's death—*you are beautiful too, John.* For all the growth, increasing maturity, and self-confidence I'd developed over years, it was still hard for me to accept that truth—to love myself unconditionally and to truly receive love from others.

When the time came for the final ceremony of the retreat—a smaller dose of MDMA combined with a much larger dose of psilocybin—I was excited but a little nervous. Would this be the day when I voluntarily let go fully into love, as I'd set out to do? When I discussed this intention with my guide before the ceremony, she gently cautioned me.

"Trust the process," she repeated once again. "If you go into this work with expectations, then you may be disappointed. You must be willing to accept what's shown to you and not be too attached to a particular outcome. Your soul is very wise and will guide you if you let it."

The experience of the combined medicines was intense. I've never felt more vibrantly energized and present. It reminded me of a slogan some friends had shared with me: "Holy shit, I'm alive!" Waves of bliss flooded my body and were released. It felt incredibly joyful to be here, in human flesh, breathing, moving, living, and loving! What a gift! I was overwhelmed with gratitude. At one point, my guide suggested that I look at myself in the mirror. When I did so, it was as if I met myself, face-to-face, for the first time. And without thinking, I told myself not to be so hard on myself, to lighten up, to forgive myself, and to love myself.

After the ceremony ended, I felt complete. I hadn't quite had the experience I'd planned—the sense of merging fully into love. But I'd seen and understood so many powerful things. The process had led me where I needed to go, and I was thankful for all of it. In fact, I couldn't wait to share it with Deborah. Suddenly, I missed her intensely and wanted to drive home right away. I was supposed to stay a final night and do my last breathwork session in the morning. But I was done. I thanked my guide and told her I wanted to leave early in the morning and skip the final breathwork session.

She shook her head. "John, you're not done yet. Trust the process. Stay for the final session."

I assented. After all, I'd committed to being here for the full five days, and if she wanted me to make good on that commitment, I was willing. But I had no expectations. After the intensity of the previous day, I was pretty sure this particular spiritual journey was complete.

I couldn't have been more wrong. As I lay down on the breathwork mattress and began the gentle circular breathing technique she had taught me, it seemed as if all the previous days of spiritual work came together. Perhaps it was my lack of expectations that opened the door to the most powerful journey of all. The message that came to me quickly was: "I am perfect—always." Immediately, I rejected the statement as preposterous. I knew I was very far from perfect! But there it was anyway, accompanied by powerful energetic releases. I saw that there was nothing that I need to do, nothing that I need to strive for—I just need to be in my heart. The perfection, I realized, is in my heart, in my core being. For the first time in my life, I felt unconditional love for myself, for all of life, and for God, all wrapped into one. I cried for a very long time. A tremendous weight lifted off my soul.

Chapter 39

Playing the Infinite Game

Half veggies (kale, spinach, chard, broccoli, bok choy, and radishes) and half fruit (berries, a banana, a few seasonal fruits, and dates). Three heaping tablespoons of freshly ground flax and chia seeds. That's the recipe for my perfect smoothie. I add water, hit the button on my Vitamix blender, and take a minute or so to clean up the kitchen while it does its work. I've just finished a brisk five-mile hike along Austin's Shoal Creek Trail. It felt good to move my body, and I'm looking forward to much longer and more challenging hikes in just a couple of weeks when I fly to Europe to complete a journey I began last year: hiking the 750-kilometer Alpe Adria Trail from Austria through Slovenia to Italy. I pour my delicious breakfast into a tall glass and raise a silent toast, as I do each morning, to my continuing health and vitality. I know it's not something I can ever afford to take for granted. I just turned 70, and I'm immensely grateful to still be able to live the life I love and do the things that matter to me.

Checking the app on my Apple Watch, I'm pleased to see that I got a good night's sleep, including plenty of restorative deep sleep. The importance of sleep has been a recent, technology-aided revelation for me, and I've become fiercely protective of those critical hours when my body recovers and renews itself. In fact, about two years ago, I made the choice to remove alcohol from my life after I observed the effect of even a single glass of wine on my precious sleep. I'm still learning so much about what promotes health and longevity, and as I learn new things, I tweak my carefully created habits. As I enter my eighth decade, I'm more committed than ever to doing everything I can to ensure that not just my life span but my health span is as long as possible. After all, what does a long life mean if a healthy mind and body aren't along for the ride?

I finish my smoothie, grab my laptop, and head for the garage. No time to linger this morning catching up with Deborah or reading a book—I've got a busy day full of meetings ahead. But that's okay with me. In fact, it's great! As I start the car and pull out, I become aware of a familiar feeling—like an old friend, but one that has been too often absent in recent years. I'm really excited to get to work!

It reminds me of the feeling I used to get as a kid when I waited impatiently on the sidelines for a game of pickup basketball to begin. The eager anticipation of play. *Play.* That's what this is to me. A phrase springs to mind that came to me in a recent breathwork session: *I am a god of play.*

The memory makes me smile. I certainly don't mean to deify myself, but it has a powerful resonance for me in the sense that my greatest creative powers are found when I'm playing. And what is God if not creativity? My joy is found when I am creative, and I'm most effective—in business, in life, in relationships—when I'm playing and having fun. Play, or *lila* as the ancient Hindus called it, is a deep and fundamental energy of existence. For whatever reason, my personality connects with that archetypal activity—deeply, primally, passionately. That's how I express my higher purpose—through creativity and play. And the primary field on which I love to play, be creative, and improvise is in business.

I have a lot of fun living my life. It's truly a wonderful adventure. Whether I'm working, hiking, diving, traveling, doing yoga or Pilates, playing pickleball, exploring inner and outer worlds, or spending time in the company of the people I care about, I love life, and I like to imagine the feeling is mutual. But I don't believe life is simply about our happiness or pleasure. It's also about discovering and following our higher purpose and contributing our unique gifts and talents in the brief time that we have on this planet as a human being. The beauty of a whole life is that those things can all go together.

When I first came up with the idea for Safer Way, and Renee said,

"Let's do it, Macko Man!" we thought it would be fun. That was the initial impulse. We also needed to make a living. And we wanted to do so in a way that benefited other people in the process. If you'd told us then that the little venture we'd started in a Victorian house would, by the time I retired, grow to be a company with 540 stores, 105,000 team members, and $22 billion in annual sales that changed the way America eats, we'd have fallen over laughing. But then we'd have gotten right back to work building the company we loved. And it was because we loved and enjoyed it so much that it became all those things we could never have imagined. That's why I love playing the game of life—and of business. I love that it keeps surprising all of us.

Whole Foods was and is a magnificent expression of my own higher purpose. I'm endlessly proud of it. But what I understand now is that my higher purpose did not begin or end with Whole Foods Market. That's another reason I love business: at its best it's a wonderful, creative, ever-evolving game. It's a complex game—the best kind of game, as far as I'm concerned, because the deeper you get into it, the more you must learn in order to keep playing at a high level. And the most important aspect of the game is that it keeps moving and changing and developing, even as we play it—in fact, *because* we play it!

Business is what has been called an "infinite game," a term coined by theologian James Carse and notably applied to business by Simon Sinek. Finite games have fixed rules and clear endings. Infinite games are open-ended. They are played for the purpose of continuing the game itself. In this sense, life itself is an infinite game. Indeed, evolution is an infinite game. How else could hydrogen gas eventually have evolved into this marvelous, complex universe and a beautiful planet like ours teeming with intelligent life? It's because evolution is playing an infinite game. To me, that's also true of business and capitalism at its very best—always developing, always morphing into something new, always inviting new players into the mix, inventing new solutions and creating new opportunities. The point is not to win and finish the game. The point is to continue to play at higher and higher levels, forever creating.

I honor the long-term wisdom of this game of capitalism, how it continues to harness our cooperative and competitive instincts in the service of human advancement and prosperity. And I trust that the more conscious the players, the more evolved will be the game. It's a game that the human species has only been playing in earnest for a few hundred years. Who knows where it can take us in the future? Who knows what wondrous solutions and unexpected opportunities will come our way? Where will the infinite game of Conscious Capitalism lead us all?

My love for Whole Foods runs very deep, which is probably why I stayed longer than any of my former team. It took a lot to dislodge me from my stewardship role. Despite the departure of many close colleagues, the occasional clashes with a few Amazon leaders, and a hundred other small issues, I still might have remained at Whole Foods. It took something else to finally convince me to hang up the metaphorical grocer's apron my mother never wanted me to wear and walk out of those familiar offices once and for all. It took a new entrepreneurial venture. It took a new and challenging game to play.

I park the car and walk across the parking lot with a spring in my step, to a familiar office building. You see, while I call this a new venture, in so many ways it's also old. Our offices are housed in a building that once housed Whole Foods' headquarters 20 years ago. The flagship Lamar store is right next door. My partners include many of the dear friends who built Whole Foods Market with me, including Walter Robb, Glenda Flanagan, A.C. Gallo, Jim Sud, Betsy Foster, Michael Bashaw, and Robin Kelly. And the strands that are woven together in this new startup are like all the loose threads of decades of my entrepreneurial life and my personal journey, finally forming a coherent picture. *Love, community, health, natural foods, personal growth.*

I think back to the promise of Prana House, the co-op where I first found like-minded people building a lifestyle around natural foods. I think of the orphaned wellness center LifeWorks, a vision of combining personal growth and health, which never saw the light of day. I think of all the ways I've tried to promote and share the potential of a whole foods, plant-based diet as a very effective way to prevent and reverse chronic disease. I think of my frustrations with the healthcare system and my often-misunderstood attempts to envision another way to heal America. I think of all the consciousness-expanding practices, novel therapies, and transformational modalities I've personally tried. Little by little, I have pulled together these loose threads of my life and woven a new pattern. All of this, under one roof. Just as Whole Foods Market was a one-stop shop for people looking to eat a diet centered around natural foods, this will be a one-stop shop for wellness, vitality, disease prevention and reversal, longevity, spiritual growth, and like-minded community. I can envision a time in the future when this new business has locations in every major American city. And the name says everything about why I'm doing it: Love.Life.

The creation and growth of Whole Foods was a delight to be part of. Others will continue moving that ball down the field. But I'm not done with business. I'm not done pursuing my own higher purpose. I'm not done with this wondrous infinite game of Conscious Capitalism. I'm on a new adventure now. I love being back in startup mode again, free from the shackles of bureaucracy.

Love.Life called me forward, beckoning me back onto the field with a new opportunity to create, to risk, to play, to learn, to evolve, and to grow. Another chance to choose love over fear, to pursue innovation and contribution rather than settling for stasis and limitation. Will it succeed? I honestly don't know. It might still be ahead of its time. But it's what my heart calls me to do. It's what makes me feel alive, exuberant, and young in spirit. Another wonderful game to play. Another beautiful vision to bring into reality. New worlds to create out of nothing. Let us love. Let us create. And let us play—again and again and again—forever!

Appreciations

Like all life journeys, mine has been blessed with many wonderful fellow travelers, and as I've worked to capture my journey in these pages, I've been enormously grateful for their contributions, both to my life and to this book.

First, I want to thank my book team. Writing a book is a massive amount of work and it takes far longer to complete the entire project than people who have never written a book realize. This one took just over three years from when the day the idea first came to me, during a two-week backpacking trip on the Ouachita Trail in Oklahoma and Arkansas, until the book was published.

Ellen Daly and Carter Phipps were my writing collaborators every step along the way. Besides being personal friends whom I dearly love, they are both amazing and supremely talented professional writers. I am very grateful that they worked with me on this book and they helped make my personal journey, as well as Whole Foods Market's journey, come alive.

Rafe Sagalyn was my literary agent for this book, along with my previous coauthored books, *Conscious Capitalism* and *Conscious Leadership*. I love working with Rafe as he has excellent ideas but doesn't push me too hard.

I've appreciated all the different publishers I've worked with, but Matt Holt and his team at Matt Holt Books/BenBella Books are my personal favorite. They've had many great ideas and been a pleasure to work with. Thanks to Katie Dickman, Jessika Rieck, Mallory Hyde, Morgan Carr,

Brigid Pearson, Ariel Fagiola, Kerri Stebbens, and Lydia Choi. My gratitude also goes to Scott Calamar for his careful and sensitive copyediting.

Robin Kelly once headed up the Public Relations team for Whole Foods and now does so for Love.Life. Her advice and counsel to me have saved me from countless PR mistakes and the ones that occurred anyway were the times when I didn't take her advice. Nina Nocciolini, Barbara Henricks, and the team at Cave Henricks are our book publicists and I appreciate both their professionalism and competence.

Many people graciously gave their time to be interviewed and/or review and correct drafts of this manuscript, including Michael Bashaw, Jason Buechel, Dan Buettner, John Elstrott, Glenda Flanagan, A.C. Gallo, Evening Galvin, Alex Green, Chris Hitt, Robin Kelly, David Lannon, Dorothy Lurie, Steve McIntosh, David Matthis, Matt O'Hayer, David O'Neil, Wayne Pacelle, Doug Rauch, Walter Robb, Peter Roy, Karen Saadeh, Philip Sansone, Michael Shearn, Jim Sud, Glen Van Peski, Craig Weller, Renee Weller, and Margaret Wittenberg.

My deepest appreciation extends to all the people who grew Whole Foods Market with me, including:

My cofounders—Renee Lawson Hardy, Craig Weller, Mark Skiles, and David Matthis. What a wonderful company we created together! Thank you! Mark—wherever you are now—I think about you and I love you.

My teachers and mentors—Bill Mackey, Jean-Claude Lurie, Craig Weller, Bob Solomon, Jim Sud, Glenda Flanagan, A.C. Gallo, Walter Robb, Philip Sansone, Will Paradise, and Deborah Morin. I know I was not always a very good student, but I'm deeply grateful for all that you taught me.

People who believed in me from the beginning—Bill Mackey, Jim Sud, Jay Templeton, Don Schaeffer, Renee Lawson Hardy, Casey Wren, and Mark Monroe. Without your faith in me and our vision, the company would never have existed in the first place or survived for very long.

Our E-Team throughout the 44 years I was CEO—Renee Lawson Hardy, Craig Weller, Mark Skiles, David Matthis, Tom Calzone,

Lex Alexander, Chris Hitt, Peter Roy, Rich Cundiff, Glenda Flanagan, Walter Robb, A.C. Gallo, Jim Sud, Lee Valkenaar, David Lannon, Ken Meyer, Jason Buechel, Keith Manbeck, Sonya Gafsi Oblisk, Christina Minardi, Bill Jordan.

The many fantastic Regional Presidents who innovated and grew their Regions. There are more people in this category than space allows me to call out, and several are already mentioned above, having been promoted from Regional Presidents to the E-Team. A few of the outstanding ones who were never on the E-Team while I was CEO include Michael Bashaw, Michael Besancon, Mary Kay Hagen, Will Paradise, Don Moffitt, Juan Nunez, Patric Bradley, Scott Allshouse, Nicole Wescoe, Mark "Flash" Dixon, Jeff Turnas, Matt Ray, Angela Lorenzen, David Schwartz, Omar Gaye.

Our Board of Directors for the 39 years we were an independent company. I especially want to appreciate Bill Mackey, Jim Sud, John Elstrott, Gaby Sulzberger, Avram Goldberg, Bud Sorenson, Mo Siegel, Hass Hassan, Kip Tindell, Walter Robb, and Ron Shaich.

I also want to appreciate the other early founders of natural foods supermarkets. Each of these people greatly inspired me and I want to thank them: Anthony Harnett, Sandy Gooch, John Moorman, Dan Volland, Bill Frazier, Peter Roy, Hass Hassan, Mark Retzloff, Stan Amy, Lex Alexander, Terry Dalton.

I also want to thank Doug Greene, who created the trade magazine *Natural Foods Merchandiser* and the trade show The Natural Foods Expo. Without Doug, the natural foods supermarket movement would probably have been delayed many years. Thanks for all you did, Doug!

Lastly, I want to appreciate the many, many friends and family who have positively impacted my life. These include:

Deborah Morin, Bill Mackey, Margaret Mackey, Dorothy Lurie, Jim Mackey, Jean-Claude Lurie, Barbara Mackey, Glenda Flanagan, Evening Galvin, Allison Clark, Chica Hulvey, Andy Lurie, Will Lurie, Renee Lawson Hardy, Mary Kay Hagen, Will Paradise, Philip Sansone, Chris Hitt, Peter Roy, Craig Weller, Matt O'Hayer, Dan Buettner, Alex Green,

Lisa Versaci, John Papola, Heath Diekert, David O'Neil, Mo Siegel, Mollie Harter, Paul Rice, Glen Van Peski, Rip Esselstyn, Joel Fuhrman, John McDougall, David Matthis, Carter Phipps, Ellen Daly, A.C. Gallo, Raj Sisodia, Steve McIntosh, Grant Sible, Jason Buechel, Ken Meyer, David Lannon, Anthony Harnett, Rand Stagen, Doug Rauch, Ed Freeman, Michael Strong, Annie Harvilicz, David Harvilicz, Arthur Evans, Betsy Foster, Casey Wren, Danny Lee, David Gardner, Tom Gardner, David Less, George Eckrich, Jacquie Small, Bill Finnerty, Tish Wood, John Blankenship, John Jacobs, John Kepner, Robin Kelly, Kip Tindell, Marc Gafni, Wayne Pacelle, Lisa Fletcher, Bruce Friedrich, Lauren Ornelas, Michael Bashaw, Lucas Siegel, Tonia Pankopf, Vidar Jorgensen, Wayne Silverman, Renee Starnes Bertopro, Gurpreet Gill, Jeff Colley (Cowboy), Taru Soilikki, Craig Rice, Kaye Simmons, Warren Farrell, Suzi Sosa, Timothy Henry, Traci Sanderson, Scott Mushkin, Adam Sud, Jason Weiss, Luke Nosek, Stephen Oskoui, Ray McCrackin, Peter Singer, Juan Nunez, Patric Bradley, Jason Buechel, Michael Shearn, John Elstrott, Bud Sorenson, Mary Saunders, Kimbal Musk, Christiana Musk, Hass Hassan, Jeremiah Cunningham, Lex Alexander, Lee Valkenaar, Khotso Khabele, Kathy Dragon, Karen Dawn, Josh Garrett, Scott and Jenny Jurek, John Brew, Joe Lonsdale, Mark Skousen, Jerry Gallagher, Gary Hoover, Gurubachan Sing Khalsa, James Maxfield, Huy Lam, Hildy Teegan, Brandon Taylor, Jonathan Wilson, Doug Greene, Gary Newton, Gaby Sulzberger, Drake Sadler, Doug Casey, Dean Ornish, Cindy Wigglesworth, Cheryl Rosner, Karen Sammon, Carol Pierce, Alan Lazarus, Bruce Epstein, Brian Johnson, Magatte Wade, Bruce Hallett, Brett Hurt, Bart Beilman.